24th Iberoamerican Conference on Software Engineering (CIbSE 2021)

Held online

San Jose, Costa Rica
30 August – 3 September 2021

ISBN: 978-1-7138-3944-6

Printed from e-media with permission by:

Curran Associates, Inc.
57 Morehouse Lane
Red Hook, NY 12571

Some format issues inherent in the e-media version may also appear in this print version.

CIbSE - IberoAmerican Conference on Software Engineering
c/o Luca Cernuzzi
Universidad Católica "Nuestra Seóra de la Asunción",
Campus Universitario, Asunción
Barrio Santa Ana, C.C.1683, C.P. 1364
Asunción - Paraguay

Phone: +595 21 334650
Fax: +595 21 310587

lcernuzz@uca.edu.py

Additional copies of this publication are available from:

Curran Associates, Inc.
57 Morehouse Lane
Red Hook, NY 12571 USA
Phone: 845-758-0400
Fax: 845-758-2633
Email: curran@proceedings.com
Web: www.proceedings.com

TABLE OF CONTENTS

RET

SET

CIbSE 2021

XXIV Ibero-American Conference on Software Engineering

San Jose, Costa Rica, August 30 - September 3, 2021

Virtual mode

Preface

On behalf of the CIbSE Organizing Committee, we are proud to present the proceedings of the 24th Iberoamerican Conference on Software Engineering (CIbSE 2021) to be held virtually from Costa Rica. The hosting institution is the Universidad de Costa Rica. This year, for the second time, CIBSE will be held virtually, due to the COVID-19 pandemic. In spite of the social distancing, we are certain that this second virtual CIBSE will bring the Software Engineering community together, presenting a high-quality event.

CIbSE is the leading research forum on Software Engineering (SE) in Ibero-America. Its primary objective is to promote high-quality scientific research in Ibero-American countries and, thus, support the researchers in this community in publishing and discussing their work. In addition, the conference fosters collaboration and cross-fertilization among academics, students, and practitioners from industry. CIbSE has distinct characteristics as it welcomes contributions in three languages: Portuguese, Spanish, or English. It is backed by 23 previous conferences held in various countries:

Torres, Brazil (IDEAS'98)
San Jose, Costa Rica (IDEAS'99)
Cancun, Mexico (IDEAS'00)
Heredia, Costa Rica (IDEAS'01)
La Habana, Cuba (IDEAS'02)
Asunción, Paraguay (IDEAS'03)
Arequipa, Peru (IDEAS'04)
Valparaiso, Chile (IDEAS'05)
La Plata, Argentina (IDEAS'06)
Isla Margarita, Venezuela (IDEAS'07)
Recife, Brazil (IDEAS'08)
Medellín, Colombia (CIbSE'09)
Cuenca, Ecuador (CIbSE'10)
Rio de Janeiro, Brazil (CIbSE'11)
Buenos Aires, Argentina (CIbSE'12)
Montevideo, Uruguay (CIbSE'13)
Pucón, Chile (CIbSE'14)
Lima, Peru (CIbSE'15)
Quito, Ecuador (CIbSE'16)
Buenos Aires, Argentina (CIbSE'17)
Bogotá, Colombia (CIbSE'18)
La Habana, Cuba (CIbSE'19)
Curitiba, Brazil (CIbSE'20)

CIbSE is an evolution of the successful (Iberoamerican Workshop on Environments and Software Requirements Engineering (IDEAS), which began in 1998. It was strengthened with the integration of two specialized events: the Workshop on Requirements Engineering (WER) in 2010 and the Experimental Software Engineering Latin American Workshop (ESELAW) in 2011. As a result, nowadays CIbSE consists of three tracks. The issues related to Requirements Engineering are discussed under the RET track, while Experimental Software Engineering topics are handled by ESELAW track. All remaining Software Engineering themes are discussed under the SET Track. In addition, CIbSE hosts a Doctoral Symposium (DS), aiming at bringing together doctoral students working on foundations, techniques, tools, and applications of SE and giving them the opportunity to present and discuss their research in a constructive and international atmosphere.

CIbSE has also hosted the Ibero-American School on Software Engineering (EIbAIS) and the Industry Talks. EIbAIS aims at promoting a forum for discussions regarding SE and its related technologies and theoretical foundations, allowing the participation of practitioners, undergraduate and graduate students, and researchers in the conference's activities. Industry Talks aims at providing the industry and practitioners means to discuss and work together in exploring how SE processes, methods, techniques, and tools can provide the industry with better solutions.

A conference would not be a success without the hard work of the many researchers and practitioners who submitted their papers for review. This year, 65 papers were submitted. Each submission was reviewed by at least three members of the Program Committee, formed by leading experts in the topics of the corresponding tracks. After a careful peer-review process, 19 full Technical Papers were finally selected in all tracks (29% acceptance rate), 3 submissions were accepted as Emerging Ideas papers. The Doctoral Symposium received 5 proposals of which 3 were accepted to be presented in the symposium.

In line with CIbSE's spirit, the authors from the accepted papers come from different countries: Argentina, Brazil, Canada, Chile, Colombia, Costa Rica, Ecuador, Germany, Norway, Spain, and Uruguay. The best papers of each track will be invited to submit an extended version to the Journal of Software Engineering Research and Development (JSERD).

We prepared a high-quality program, with renowned keynote speakers. Laurie Williams (NSCU, USA, Distinguished Professor) addresses how to solve Software Security Challenges with Artificial Intelligence, a relevant aspect in today's society. Leandro Minku (University of Birmingham, UK) presents the latest advancements in dealing with the prediction of defect-inducing software changes in dynamic environments. Alessandro Garcia (PUC-Rio, Brazil) provides an insightful discussion on how stakeholders' intuitions are likely to drive various software design decisions.

In addition, three contemporary tutorials on the subjects of technical debt, power analysis, and foundational ontologies are offered by relevant researchers in the SE community: Carolyn Seaman (University of Maryland Baltimore County, USA), Oscar Dieste (Polytechnic University of Madrid, Spain), Luis Olsina (National University of La Pampa, Argentina), respectively. Finally, we will also have eight selected Industry Talks.

We would like to thank all who contributed to this event. The quality of the technical program is a result of the dedication of the members of the Program Committee together with the additional reviewers. We would also like to thank all authors of submitted manuscripts, presenters, and session chairs for their collaboration in making CIbSE 2021 a success. We express our gratitude to the CIBSE Steering Committee for their great support. Finally, we are thankful for the opportunity of serving as chairs for this conference.

Once again, we welcome you to the CIbSE 2021 and are excited about the wonderful conference program that so many have contributed to in so many ways.

Tayana Conte (UFAM, Brazil)
Martin Solari (Universidad ORT Uruguay, Uruguay)
PC-General Chairs

Alexandra Martinez (Universidad de Costa Rica, Costa Rica)
Marcelo Jenkins (Universidad de Costa Rica, Costa Rica)
Christian Quesada López (Universidad de Costa Rica, Costa Rica)
General Organizing Chairs

Organizing Committee

General Conference Chairs

Marcelo Jenkins (Universidad de Costa Rica, Costa Rica)
Alexandra Martinez (Universidad de Costa Rica, Costa Rica)
Christian Quesada López (Universidad de Costa Rica, Costa Rica)

General Program Co-Chairs

Tayana Conte (Universidade Federal do Amazonas, Brazil)
Martin Solari (Universidad ORT Uruguay, Uruguay)

Software Engineering Track (SET) Chairs

Sheila Reinehr (Pontifícia Universidade Católica do Paraná, Brazil)
Rafael Prikladnicki (Pontifícia Universidade Católica do Rio Grande do Sul, Brazil

Requirements Engineering Track (RET) Chairs

Nelly Condori-Fernández (Universidade da Coruña, Spain)
Vítor E. Silva Souza (Universidade Federal do Espírito Santo, Brazil)

Empirical Software Engineering Track (ESELAW) Chairs

Natasha Valentim (Universidade Federal do Paraná, Brazil)
Silverio Martínez-Fernández (Universitat Politècnica de Catalunya, Spain)

Ibero-American School on Software Engineering (EIbAIS) Chairs

Beatriz Marín (Universidad Politécnica de Valencia, España)
Efraín Rodrigo Fonseca Carrera (Universidad de las Fuerzas Armadas ESPE, Ecuador)l

Doctoral Symposium (DS) Chairs

Marcela Genero (Universidad de Castilla-La Mancha, Spain)
Marcos Kalinowski (Pontifícia Universidade Católica do Rio de Janeiro, Brazil)

Industry Talks Chairs

Marcelo Jenkins (Universidad de Costa Rica, Costa Rica)
Abel Méndez Porras (Tecnológico de Costa Rica, Costa Rica)

Publicity Chairs

Bruno Cartaxo (Pernambuco Federal Institute, Brazil)
Isabel Sousa Brito (Beja Polytechnic Institute, Portugal)
Cynthia López (CPIC, Costa Rica)

Web Chairs

Alexandra Martínez (Universidad de Costa Rica, Costa Rica)
Jose Daniel Sánchez (Universidad de Costa Rica, Costa Rica)

Program Committee - SET Track

SET Program Chairs

Sheila Reinehr (Pontifícia Universidade Católica do Paraná, Brazil)
Rafael Prikladnicki (Pontifícia Universidade Católica do Rio Grande do Sul, Brazil)

SET Program Committee

Hernan Astudillo (Universidad Tecnica Federico Santa María, Chile)
Jean Paul Barddal (PUC-PR, Brazil)
Luciano Baresi (Politecnico di Milano, Italy)
María Cecilia Bastarrica (Universidad de Chile, Chile)
Pablo Becker (Universidad Nacional de La Pampa, Argentina)
Alexandre Bergel (University of Chile, Chile)
Veronica Andrea Bollati (Universidad Tecnológica Nacional, Argentina)
Regina Braga (UFJF, Brazil)
Antonio Brogi (Università di Pisa, Italy)
Juan Pablo Carvallo (Universidad del Azuay, Ecuador)
John W. Castro (Universidad de Atacama, Chile)
Luca Cernuzzi (Universidad Católica Nuestra Señora de la Asunción, Paraguay)
Carlos Cetina (San Jorge University, Spain)
Heitor Costa (Federal University of Lavras, Brazil)
Jácome Cunha (University of Minho, Portugal)
Juan De Lara (Universidad Autonoma de Madrid, Spain)
Kleinner Farias (University of Vale do Rio dos Sinos, Brazil)
Eduardo Figueiredo (Federal University of Minas Gerais, Brazil)
Brenda L. Flores-Rios (UABC, Mexico)
Kelly Garces Pernett (Universidad de los Andes, Colombia)
Alejandra Garrido (LIFIA-Facultad de Informatica-UNLP, Argentina)
Ivan Machado (UFBA - Federal University of Bahia, Brazil)
Beatriz Marín (Universidad Politécnica de Valencia, Spain)
Miguel Monteiro (Universidade NOVA de Lisboa, Portugal)
Miguel Ehécatl Morales Trujillo (University of Canterbury, New Zealand)
Toacy Oliveira (COPPE/UFRJ, Brazil)
Luis Olsina (UNLPam, Argentina)
Ana Paiva (University of Porto, Portugal)
Jose Ignacio Panach Navarrete (Universitat de València, Spain)
Oscar Pastor Lopez (Universidad Politécnica de Valencia, Spain)
Claudia Pons (Universidad Nacional de La Plata, Argentina)
José Raúl Romero (University of Cordoba, Spain)
Gustavo Rossi (LIFIA-F. Informatica. UNLP, Argentina)
Jenny Ruiz de La Peña University of Holguin
Daniela S. Cruzes (NTNU, Norway)
Claudio Sant'Anna (Federal University of Bahia, Brazil)

Victor Santander (Universidad Estadual do Oeste do Paraná, Brazil)
Ronnie Santos (Recife Center for Advanced Studies and Systems – CESAR, Brazil)
Edson E. Scalabrin (Pontifícia Universidade Católica do Paraná – PUCPR, Brazil)
Eugenio Scalise (Universidad Central de Venezuela, Venezuela)
Diego Vallespir (Universidad de la República, Uruguay
Davi Viana (Federal University of Maranhão, Brazil)_
Eduardo Viegas (PUCPR, Brazil)

Program Committee - RET Track

RET Program Chairs

Nelly Condori-Fernández (Universidade da Coruña, Spain)
Vítor E. Silva Souza (Universidade Federal do Espírito Santo, Brazil)

RET Program Committee

Fernanda Alencar (Universidade Federal de Pernambuco, Brazil)
Camilo Almendra (Universidade Federal do Ceará, Brazil)
Wilkerson L.Andrade (Federal University of Campina Grande, Brazil)
Leandro Antonelli (LIFIA, Facultad de Informática, UNLP, Argentina)
Nathalie Aquino (Universidad Católica "Nuestra Señora de la Asunción", Paraguay)
Joao Araujo (Universidade NOVA de Lisboa, Portugal)
Clara Ayora (Tree Technology S.A., Spain)
Jorge Barreiros (ISEC / NOVA-LINCS, Portugal)
Judith Barrios Albornoz (University of Los Andes, Venezuela)
Carlos Cares (CEISUFRO, Universidad de La Frontera, Chile)
Jose Luis de la Vara (University of Castilla-La Mancha, Spain)
Enyo Gonçalves (Universidade Federal do Ceará, Brazil)
Catarina Gralha (Universidade NOVA de Lisboa, Portugal)
Maria Fernanda Granda Juca (Universitad de Cuenca, Ecuador)
Renata Guizzardi (Universidade Federal do Espirito Santo, Brazil)
Graciela Dora Susana Hadad (Universidad Nacional del Oeste, Argentina)
Gladys Kaplan (Universidad Nacional de La Matanza, Argentina)
Raúl Lapeña (SVIT Research Group, Universidad San Jorge, Spain)
Maria Lencastre (Universidade de Pernambuco, Brazil)
Lidia Lopez (Barcelona Supercomputing Center, Spain)
Marcia Lucena (UFRN, Brazil)
Johnny Marques (Instituto Tecnológico de Aeronáutica -ITA, Brazil)
Luiz Eduardo Galvão Martins (UNIFESP, Brazil)
Itzel Morales-Ramirez (Infotec - Centre for Research and Innovation in Information Technology and Communication, Mexico)
Denisse Muñante (SAMOVAR, Télécom SudParis, Institut Polytechnique de Paris, France)
Cristina Palomares (Universitat Politècnica de Catalunya, Spain)
João Pimentel (UFRPE - Universidade Federal Rural de Pernambuco, Brazil)
Maria Pinto-Albuquerque (ISCTE-IUL - Instituto Universitário de Lisboa, Portugal)
Carme Quer (Universitat Politècnica de Catalunya, Spain)
Marcela Ridao (INTIA UNICEN, Argentina)
JuanSanchez (Valencia University of Technology, Spain)
Edgar Sarmiento (PUC-Rio, Brazil

Program Committee - ESELAW Track

ESELAW Program Chairs

Natasha Valentim (Universidade Federal do Paraná, Brazil)
Silverio Martínez-Fernández (Universitat Politècnica de Catalunya, Spain)

ESELAW Program Committee

Raúl Antonio Aguilar Vera (Universidad Autónoma de Yucatán, Mexico)
Nauman Bin Ali Blekinge (Institute of Technology, Sweden)
Domenico Amalfitano (University of Naples Federico II, Italy)
Marco Araujo (IF Sudeste MG, Brazil)
Claudia P. Ayala (Universitat Politècnica de Catalunya, Spain)
Ellen Barbosa (ICMC/USP, Brazil)
Monalessa Barcellos (UFES, Brazil)
Oscar Cabrera (CoDeS, Mexico)
Bruno Cartaxo (IFPE, Brazil)
Jose Antonio Cruz-Lemus (University of Castilla-La Mancha, Spain)
Oscar Dieste (Universidad Politécnica de Madrid, Spain)
Rodrigo Falcão (Fraunhofer IESE, Germany)
Efraín R. Fonseca C. (Universidad de las Fuerzas Armadas ESPE, Ecuador)
Awdren Fontão (Federal University of Mato Grosso do Sul, Brazil)
Oscar Franco-Bedoya (Universidad de Caldas, Colombia)
Breno de França (UNICAMP, Brazil)
César França (Federal Rural University of Pernambuco – UFRPE, Brazil)
Miguel Goulão (Universidade Nova de Lisboa, Portugal)
Luis Iribarne (University of Almería, Spain)
Clemente Izurieta (Montana State University, USA)
Marcos Kalinowski (Pontifical Catholic University of Rio de Janeiro, Brazil)
Adriana Lopes (Universidade Federal do Amazonas, Brazil)
Marcelo Marinho (UFRPE, Brazil)
Anna Beatriz Marques (UFC, Brazil)
Santiago Matalonga (University of the West of Scotlannd, United Kingdom)
Rafael de Mello (CEFET-RJ, Brazil)
Elisa Yumi Nakagawa (University of São Paulo, Brazil)
Vânia Neves (UFF, Brazil)
Rafael Prikladnicki (PUCRS, Brazil)
Sheila Reinehr (PucPR, Brazil)
Luis Jorge Enrique Rivero Cabrejos (UFAM, Brazil)
Rodrigo Santos (UNIRIO, Brazil)
Gleison Santos (UNIRIO, Brazil)
Sergio Soares (Informatics Center – CIn/UFPE, Brazil)
Simone R. S. Souza (ICMC/USP, Brazil)

Guilherme Travassos (COPPE/UFRJ, Brazil)
Juan Pablo Ucán Pech (UADY, Mexico)
George Valença (Universidade Federal de Pernambuco, Brazil)
Diego Vallespir (Universidad de la República, Uruguay)
Jovan Varga (Cargill, Costa Rica)
Davi Viana (Federal University of Maranhão, Brazil)

Additional Reviewers

Amanda Santana
Aurora Ramírez
Cecilia Apa
Euler Marinho
Felipe Beroíza
Fernanda Papa
Fernando Kenji Kamei
Fischer Ferreira
Guido Tebes
Lucrecia Llerena
Rafael Barbudo Lunar
Sebastián Pizard
Vinicius Santos

CIbSE 2021 Keynotes summary

Laurie Williams

Laurie Williams is a Distinguished University Professor in the Computer Science Department of the College of Engineering at North Carolina State University (NCSU). Laurie is a co-director of the NCSU Science of Security Lablet sponsored by the National Security Agency, the NCSU Secure Computing Institute, and is the Principal Cybersecurity Technologist of the SecureAmerica Institute. Laurie's research focuses on software security; agile software development practices and processes, particularly continuous deployment; and software reliability, software testing and analysis. Laurie is an ACM and an IEEE Fellow.

Solving Software Security Challenges with Artificial Intelligence

Software security lies at the intersection of software engineering and cybersecurity – building security into a product. Software security techniques focus on preventing the injection of vulnerabilities and detecting the vulnerabilities that make their way into a product or the deployment pipeline before the product is released. Increasingly, artificial intelligence is being used to power software security techniques to aid organizations in deploying secure products. This talk will present a landscape of research and practice at the intersection of software engineering, cybersecurity, and artificial intelligence to solve cybersecurity challenges. The talk will also present research projects conducted by the speaker's own research group.

Leandro L. Minku

Leandro L. Minku is a Senior Lecturer at the School of Computer Science, University of Birmingham (UK). Dr. Minku's main research interests are machine learning in non-stationary environments / data stream mining, online class imbalance learning, ensembles of learning machines and computational intelligence for software engineering. Among others, Leandro Minku is an Associate Editor-in-Chief of the Neurocomputing journal, Associate Editor of IEEE Transactions on Neural Networks and Learning Systems, Coordinating Editor of Empirical Software Engineering journal and Associate Editor of the Journal of Systems and Software.

Prediction of Defect-Inducing Software Changes in Dynamic Environments

Software systems have become ever larger and more complex. This inevitably leads to software defects, which are costly to debug and fix. To help reducing the number of defects, machine learning approaches have been proposed for predicting defect-inducing changes in software source code at commit time. By inspecting such changes at commit time, developers can reduce the chances of inducing defects that are much more costly to debug and fix at later stages. While results in this field are promising, most existing work assumes that the characteristics of the problem remain the same over time. However, the environment where software projects are conducted is dynamic, being affected by changes in the development team, in the management strategy, in the current stage of the software development, among others. Such dynamism means that the defect generating process can suffer variations over time, impairing the ability of machine learning classifiers to perform well. In this talk, I will discuss the latest advancements in dealing with prediction of defect-inducing software changes in dynamic environments.

Carolyn Seaman

Carolyn Seaman is a Professor of Information Systems at the University of Maryland Baltimore County (UMBC). She is also the Director of the Center for Women in Technology, also at UMBC. Her research consists mainly of empirical studies of software engineering, with particular emphases on maintenance, organizational structure, communication, measurement, and technical debt. She also investigates qualitative research methods in software engineering, as well as computing pedagogy. She holds a PhD in Computer Science from the University of Maryland, College Park, a MS from Georgia Tech, and a BA from the College of Wooster (Ohio).

Decision Making in Software Engineering: The Central Role of Technical Debt

Technical Debt is a metaphor that captures the common tradeoff in software development projects between short-term pressures (e.g. delivery time) and long-term concerns (e.g. maintainability). It refers to the existing liabilities in a software product that were created in response to a short-term pressure but that pose a risk to the ability of the team to maintain the product over time. Common types of technical debt include overly complex code, poorly structured code, undocumented code, degradation of the software architecture, insufficient testing, etc. Decisions about whether to incur debt, or when to pay off debt, or which debt to pay off, perfectly encapsulate the short vs. long term tradeoffs that are typical in software engineering. In fact, it can be argued that nearly all decisions made during a software project are in some way related to Technical Debt. Thus, deeply understanding and improving Technical Debt decision making will have a significant impact on the management of software projects in general. In this keynote, we will review current streams in decision making research, in Technical Debt, in software engineering in general, and in related disciplines.

Alessandro Garcia

Dr. Garcia holds a PhD in Computer Science from the Pontifical Catholic University of Rio de Janeiro (2004). He was an Assistant Professor at Lancaster University (England) from February 2005 to January 2009 and served as a member of the Editorial Board of two major international journals in his area: IEEE Transactions on Software Engineering and Journal of Systems and Software. Professor Garcia has been frequently invited to the Program Committees and/or Organization Committees of the major international Software Engineering conferences and related areas such as ICSE, FSE, ICSME, MODELS, ICPC, ESEM, and several others.

From Intuition to Spirituality: What Are their Roles in Software Design?

Intuition is the ability to understand something “automatically”, without the need for conscious reasoning. The use of intuition along software design may have a major impact on its overall quality. Software design is an activity that requires decisions being made all the time by architects, developers, testers, maintainers, reviewers and others. These stakeholders’ intuitions are likely to drive various design decisions given the need for rapidity and many other software project factors. Despite intuition being widely studied in many disciplines, its role in software design has rarely been investigated in depth. One may suspect that intuition, given the sudden design decisions triggered from it, may do more harm than good in software design. However, this is not necessarily the case. We still have limited knowledge about the influence of intuition in software quality. There are different types of intuition being investigated in other disciplines, including more controversial ones, such as “spiritual intuition”. The purpose of this talk is to make a case on the importance of studying the role of certain intuition types in software design. We will present some possible research directions that are likely to enable us to understand whether and how our methods, tools and IDEs could stimulate “positive” intuition in software design.

Product Quality Evaluation Method and QualityTracker Tool Validation: a Case Study Plan*

Mariana Falco[1] [0000-0002-0959-7435]

LIDTUA/CONICET, Facultad de Ingeniería, Universidad Austral
Mariano Acosta 2050, Pilar, Buenos Aires, Argentina
mfalco@austral.edu.ar

Abstract. Understanding and achieving quality is extremely important in software products, in a context where more and more software products are being delivered regularly. Even though there are different ways of analysing and measuring some aspects of quality such as using SonarQube or Jenkins, there are no fully equipped tools to measure a model of quality characteristics on each iteration. We are currently developing the QualityTracker Tool (QTT) which is the automated version of Product Quality Evaluation Method (PQEM), whose main goal is to perform a thoughtful quality assessment that produces a single value between 0 and 1 as the final outcome of each iteration which represents the product quality level. It is necessary to conduct a proper validation of QTT through a complete case study in order to obtain information on measuring the acceptance, and usefulness of the tool by practitioners and companies.

Keywords: Software Quality Measurement · QualityTracker Tool · Product Quality Evaluation Method

1 Introduction

Measurement is fundamental for the development of effective and efficient software [1]. Iterations are a huge part of developing software products, and project managers and practitioners need a synthetic way to visualize the quality level achieved on each iteration, before proceeding to the next one [4].

Nowadays, there are different ways of analysing and measuring some aspects of quality such as using SonarQube or Jenkins, but there are no fully equipped tools to measure a full set of quality characteristics on each iteration. We are currently developing the QualityTracker Tool (QTT) which is supported by a method previously designed by the author called Product Quality Evaluation Method (PQEM) [2], which is a five-step method (product setup, elicitation, measurement, results synthesis, and assessment), whose main goal is to perform

* This work is supported by a Research Grant from Universidad Austral.

a thoughtful quality assessment of the different iterations within a software product, and that produces a single value between 0 and 1 as the final outcome that represents the product quality level.

The PQEM method is structured around the Goal-Question-Metric approach [18], the set of quality characteristics defined by the standard ISO/IEC 25010: Functional Suitability, Performance Efficiency, Compatibility, Usability, Reliability, Security, Maintainability, and Portability [5], the set of metrics for these quality characteristics defined by the standard ISO/IEC 25023 [11], the extension of coverage testing, and the definition of acceptance criteria related to the expected quality level per each iteration, and the acceptance criteria for each defined question. The main innovation is that PQEM produces an unique value to identify the quality level of each iteration through the aggregation of the coverage values per each analyzed quality characteristic; and so, by analyzing this number and each of the coverage values per characteristic it is possible to obtain and indication of the strength of conformance to the standards on a per-characteristic basis.

QTT supports each step of the PQEM method, letting the stakeholder enter data from the product, indicating amount of expected iterations, quality characteristics (QC), and is able to choose from a set of predefined quality attributes requirements for each QC as well as define new ones with metrics and acceptance criteria. QTT not only saves the data and preferences from each product but also, let the stakeholder to visualize and monitor the progresses from one iteration to the other in terms of quality, not only the final quality value as a whole product.

The main contributions of this research are the following: a) developing a method and a tool that support to help business and industries in the process of measuring software quality; b) allow practitioners, product owners, project leaders, developers, and technical leaders to address a comprehensive understanding of the quality level of each iteration within the software life cycle; c) calculate the quality level as a multidimensional aggregated number, formed by the aggregated coverage values from each quality characteristic; d) define a software tool that will serve as a means of interface with exiting tools such as SonarQube and Jenkins; e) the QualityTracker tool includes a catalog of quality measures applied on an industrial setting. Based on the previous lines, the case study will be conducted within the first semester of 2022 while the PhD dissertation will be within the second semester of 2022.

The following progresses have been made so far: design and definition of the PQEM method [2], as well as it improvement to measure quality on each iteration within the software life cycle. We are currently developing QTT to help businesses and industries in the process of measuring software quality. Consequently, it is necessary to conduct a proper validation of QTT through a complete case study in order to obtain information on measuring the acceptance and usefulness of QTT by practitioners and companies. The present article is structured as follows: Section 2 will describe the related work, while Section 3 will characterize the details of the case study as the research methodology. Finally, Section 4 will address the conclusions and next steps.

2 Related Work

Measurement is a key factor for managing and improving software development, and effective and efficient measurement requires methodological and technological support. In this context, there is a need of a measuring tool to determine whether the product is acceptable [22].

Literature shows some approaches to measure quality, for example, a manual approach was presented by Wingkvist et al. [9], who seek to assess and assure the quality of technical documentation, building on the Goal-Question-Metric paradigm and suggesting a metrics-based quality model. Mostly, automation is easily identifiable in testing as it significantly reduces testing time and avoids repetitive tasks, aiding in improving the quality of the software [10].

In this line, Shchramme et al. [8] have proposed a solution to analyze and measure Usability metrics during the implementation phase, through a framework featuring code annotations that provides a systematic evaluation of the usability throughout the source code. They provided numerical results for Usability metrics as percentage values according to the calculations and optimal values specified in ISO/IEC 25023 [11].

Schrettner et al. [23] presented an approach for modeling, collecting, storing and evaluating such software measurements, which can deal with all types of metrics collected at any stage of the life cycle. They have developed the Unified Quality Monitoring (UQM) application, which integrates the collection of quality data, high level query management and reporting features. Plosch and other [12] built a tool that provides automatic measures for the maintainability related measures of the IT-CISQ standard [13].

Within the context of agile software development, López et al. [14] have integrated a software analytics tool not only to assess software quality but also to support quality requirements management. They have done it with the Softeam Company, and they were able to put together the Quality Feedback Loop process in order to control the full quality requirements life-cycle. They concluded that practitioners can benefit from using this kind of tools as part of their software development life-cycle.

The previous work shows as well as the basis that support PQEM and QTT, that the use and implementation of quality methods and tools can promote quality not only within a company but also improving the decision-making process as well as the communication between teams and other roles.

While automation tools exist, most of them approaches only a subset of quality characteristics, not obtaining a quality value easy to understand. Therefore, the development and validation of QTT will serve as a means of interface with what exists or what will be developed in the future, complemented by the standards, in order to achieve a comprehensive tool that will allow decisions to be made in each iteration of a software product.

3 Research Methodology

Software quality measurement let practitioners, quality managers and project managers to understand how well the software product fulfill its functional and non-functional requirements. We have chosen case study as the suitable research methodology which studies contemporary phenomena in its natural context [15], because measurement quality activities are hard to study in isolation. The following subsections will describe the case study research process.

3.1 Design and Planning

In due consideration that good planning for a case study is crucial for its success, and following Robson [16], the main elements of the plan are as follows:

Objective Our main purpose is explanatory, in order to understand QTT through the own eyes of the people participating in the case study. Likewise, it can be considered as an interpretative study based on the need to understand the tool acceptance and usefulness through the participant's interpretation, which is similar to the exploratory type [17]. It is important to comprehend that by analyzing the acceptance and usefulness of the tool, we are also studying the same for PQEM, due to the fact that QTT is built upon the method.

The case We are studying the use of QTT to measure the quality of a software product, in order to verify if the tool provides the benefits it claims, and to identify opportunities for improvement. We already have a set of candidates products to conduct the case study, where such settings are defined by a context that requires a high level of quality, the size or complexity of the product, the impact of the domain (such as healthcare), and the sensibility related to the quality (all these points form those characteristics that makes a product suitable to be measured with the tool).

Theory The frame of reference is lined up by the PQEM method [2] and its adaptation to each iteration within the software life cycle, which includes the Goal-Question-Metric approach [18], the inclusion of ISO/IEC 25010 [5] to define a set of quality characteristics, the extension of the concept of testing coverage to measure each quality characteristic as well as the quality level, and the representational theory of measurement to define a process to assign numerical values to attributes (in our case, quality attributes requirements) on a way that the relevant qualitative empirical relations among these attributes or characteristics are represented by these numbers [20].

Research questions It is possible to define the following research questions: **RQ1)** The quality level produced by the QTT provides a sound basis for making the decision about rejecting or accepting an iteration of a product?, **RQ2)** Does the automated tool allow the practitioners and project managers achieve the pre-established quality objectives for their company or project?, **RQ3)** Is the calculated quality level similar to the quality level perceived by the experts?, and **RQ4)** Does the improvements of learning PQEM and using QTT justify the costs and time invested? What are the main potential benefits of using QTT?

Methods In order to collect data, it is feasible to consider three categories of methods defined by Lethbridge et al. [19]. We will approach the direct (e.g. interviews), indirect (e.g. tool instrumentation) and independent (e.g. documentation analysis) methods.

Selection strategy In this context, the unit of analysis is represented by each iteration within a product. And consequently, each iteration will be compared to previous measured iterations where the tool wasn't used.

3.2 Ethical considerations

In this case, there are some confidentiality considerations related to private topics embedded on each company where QTT will be applied. And so, a confidentiality agreement will be defined in order to guard the company information.

3.3 Collecting data

Data sources Lethbridge et al. [19] specify three levels of data collection techniques: first degree (direct contact of the researcher with the subjects while collecting data in real time), second degree (the researcher collects raw data without interacting with the subjects), and third degree (independent analysis of work artifacts where data available is used, such as requirements specifications and failure reports from an organization). In this case, we will consider all of the techniques: first (interviews), second (raw data from the tool), and third degree (analyzing data from other iterations from the project).

Interviews Data collection through interviews is important in case studies [15], and are guided by a set of interview questions, which can be divided into unstructured, semi-structured and fully structured interviews [16]. We have decided to conduct semi-structured interviews once the measurement is over, whose main objectives are descriptive and explanatory, and the interview questions are a mix of open and closed questions.

Our main respondents will be product owners or quality leaders, regarding the following topics: what are the improvements experienced with the use of the tool in the software development process?, would you obtain feasible information to make a better decision to move on to the following iteration?, would you recommend the use of this tool to a colleague? And, in which case would you recommend it? (considering the size of the company, the type of project, the costs, time invested, and the level of quality required within the company). Also, we will interview tech leaders, developers and team members, in order to obtain their point of view on time invested while considering the quality requirements per each quality characteristic as well as the usefulness of working with pre-established quality objectives; based on their experience related to whether the calculated quality level matches their intuition of achieved quality within the iteration.

Archival data In our context, and considering our main goals and research questions we will include both qualitative (meeting minutes from interviews, recordings, documents, and charts) and quantitative documentation and archival records (metrics). In this case, the data will come mostly from a) meeting minutes or recordings, b) QTT with respect to quality characteristics defined, amount of iterations per each product, quality attributes requirements (QARs), expected quality level per iteration, measurement of the set of QARs per iteration and quality level; c) preexisting documentation from measurements of previous iterations where PQEM was applied (see [3] for further details); d) time required to use each functionality within the tool, and e) time required to learn and use the QualityTracker tool.

Metrics Based on the previous, the definition of what data to collect will be based on the application of the Goal Question Metric method (GQM) [18] to the quality characteristics per product, because the metrics within PQEM are generated through this approach due to its capability to measure in a purposeful way.

3.4 Data analysis

Quantitative and Qualitative data analysis Descriptive statistics to analysis: the acceptance of the tool from stakeholders (concerning RQ1, RQ2 and RQ3) as well as the improvements in the process of quality measurement of the product, and the man hours invested in the use of QTT (regarding RQ4). We will be measuring developer productivity metrics, agile process metrics, usability and stakeholder/practitioner satisfaction metrics.

Validity In this case study, we will scale up a case study research in order to increase the validity of the method implemented by QTT. Up to this time, only some examples where performed, but we do understand that a case study in an industrial setting is necessary to increase the external validity, and thereby, provide results that are more generalized. With respect to construct validity, the main key here is to choose a proper project with medium-high complexity, in order to measure the potentiality of QTT. Regarding the internal validity, the design of the questions for interviews might not be complete or answered. Also, some aspects might be missing from the measurement.

Likewise, the concern on extending the scope of the case study might impact the validity. We are actually developing the third iteration of this app, and in order to obtain a real perspective of this iteration, we will define a set of questions to be carried out with the developers of this third iteration (which will count as a single sprint). Also, we will use a set of set of applications with a medium level of complexity, developed by a research lab with real stakeholders, including 4 sprints per each app (four apps are being develop, while three are already developed). These apps belong to four different projects, within three different domains: healthcare, fire control and thunder monitoring, real state, and gaming.

We are expecting to interview at least 100 people, looking for the amounts between roles to be similar. Within the context of to what extent the data and the analysis are dependent on the researchers, and so a catalogue of metrics will exist within QTT to allow practitioners select existing metrics instead of eliciting all of the QARs and metrics individually.

3.5 Reporting

In this case, the report will include a synthesis of what was obtained both in the interviews and in the use of the tool, measuring the application time, the different metrics of the application of the PQEM method, along with the identification of the improvements from the application.

4 Conclusions

PQEM [2] is based on the idea that quality plays a vital role in the software life cycle process. The outcome of PQEM is an innovative way of understanding quality, due to the fact that one single multidimensional value can be useful to understand the way the quality level was moving from one iteration to the following. Also, by decomposing this unique value, it is feasible to comprehend the level achieved by each quality characteristic. For now, all of the quality characteristics are treated the same regarding the calculations of quality levels.

With the case study and following the Measurement Theory [20], we will seek to evaluate whether the previous intuitive idea that each stakeholder or practitioner has about the quality of a product is the one they really have, contrasted after the measurement with PQEM and QTT.

The work described earlier will be evaluated as follows: a) continue the development and testing of the QualityTracker tool; b) development of the third iteration of a mobile and web application within the healthcare environment; c) validation of PQEM though illustrative example over two iterations [3], d) measurement of the third iteration of the mobile and web app on the QualityTracker tool; e) analysis and identification of improvement points or functionalities based on the feedback given by project leaders, product owners, technical leaders and developers on the interviews; f) execution of the proposed case study, and g) analysis of the case study results. Likewise, the PQEM method will be updated in order to include weights on quality characteristics, to set a feasible way for stakeholders to specify a hierarchy among them.

References

1. Kan, S.H. Metrics and models in software quality engineering. Addison-Wesley Longman Publishing Co., Inc, 2002.
2. Falco, M., Robiolo, G. A Unique Value that Synthesizes the Quality Level of a Product Architecture: Outcome of a Quality Attributes Requirements Evaluation Method. In: Franch X., Männistö T., Martínez-Fernández S. (eds) Product-Focused Software Process Improvement. PROFES 2019. Lecture Notes in Computer Science, vol 11915. 2019, Springer, Cham.
3. Falco, M., Scott, E., Robiolo, G. Overview of an Automated Framework to Measure and Track the Quality Level of a Product, 2020 IEEE Biennial Congress of Argentina. December 1-4, 2020.
4. H.M. Sneed A. Merey, Automated Software Quality Assurance. IEEE Transactions on Software Engineering, SE-11(9), 1985, pp. 909–916. doi:10.1109/tse.1985.232548
5. ISO 25010, ISO 25000: Software and Data Quality - ISO/IEC 25010, https://iso25000.com/index.php/en/iso-25000-standards/iso-25010
6. Oinas, A. (2000, March). Defining goal-driven fault management metrics in a real world environment: a case-study from Nokia. In Proceedings of the Fourth European Conference on Software Maintenance and Reengineering (pp. 101-107). IEEE.
7. Debnath, N., Salgado, C., Peralta, M., Riesco, D., Roqué, L., Montejano, G., Mazzi, M. (2019, November). A Software Testing Strategy Based on a Software Product Quality Model. In International Conference Europe Middle East North Africa Information Systems and Technologies to Support Learning (pp. 248-259). Springer, Cham.
8. Schramme, M., Macías, J. A. (2019). Analysis and measurement of internal usability metrics through code annotations. Software Quality Journal, 27(4), 1505-1530.
9. Wingkvist, A., Ericsson, M., Lincke, R., Lowe, W. A metrics-based approach to technical documentation quality. In 2010 Seventh International Conference on the Quality of Information and Communications Technology, 2010, pp. 476-481, IEEE
10. Mohammad, D. R., Al-Momani, S., Tashtoush, Y.M., Alsmirat, M. Comparative Analysis of Quality Assurance Automated Testing Tools for Windows Mobile Applications. 2019 IEEE 9th Annual Computing and Communication Workshop and Conference (CCWC), 2019, doi:10.1109/ccwc.2019.8666463
11. ISO 25023, Systems and software engineering — Systems and software Quality Requirements and Evaluation (SQuaRE), ISO/IEC 25023:2016, https://www.iso.org/standard/35747.html
12. Plöesch, R., Schuerz, S., Koerner, C. (2015, July). On the validity of the it-cisq quality model for automatic measurement of maintainability. In 2015 IEEE 39th Annual Computer Software and Applications Conference (Vol. 2, pp. 326-334). IEEE.
13. Consortium for Information and Software Quality (CISQ), Measuring code quality, https://www.it-cisq.org/standards/code-quality-standards/
14. López, L., Bagnato, A., Ahberve, A., Franch, X. (2021, May). QFL: Data-Driven Feedback Loop to Manage Quality in Agile Development. In 2021 IEEE/ACM 43rd International Conference on Software Engineering: Software Engineering in Society (ICSE-SEIS) (pp. 58-66). IEEE.
15. Runeson, P., Höst, M. (2009). Guidelines for conducting and reporting case study research in software engineering. Empirical software engineering, 14(2), 131.
16. Robson, C. (2002) Real World Research. Blackwell, (2nd edition)
17. Klein, H. K., Myers, M.D. (1999) A set of principles for conducting and evaluating interpretative field studies in information systems. MIS Q 23(1):67–88 doi:10.2307/249410

18. Basili, V. R. (1992). Software modeling and measurement: the Goal/Question/Metric paradigm.
19. Lethbridge. T.C., Sim, S.E., Singer, J. (2005) Studying software engineers: data collection techniques for software field studies. Empir Softw Eng 10(3):311–341 see also Chapter 1 in Shull et al. (2008)
20. Fenton, N., Bieman, J. (2014). Software metrics: a rigorous and practical approach. CRC press.
21. Lavazza, L. (2000). Providing automated support for the GQM measurement process. IEEE Software, 17(3), 56-62.
22. Arpaia, P., De Matteis, E., Inglese, V. (2015). Software for measurement automation: A review of the state of the art. Measurement, 66, 10-25. Technical Writer's Handbook. Mill Valley, CA: University Science, 1989.
23. Schrettner, L., Fülöp, L.J., Kiss, A., Gyimóthy, T. Software quality model and framework with applications in industrial context. In 2012 16th European Conference on Software Maintenance and Reengineering, 2012, pp. 453-456, IEEE.

Publicación en Open Science de paquetes de laboratorio experimentales para Ingeniería del Software

Cathy Guevara

Universidad Técnica del Norte, Ecuador
cguevara@utn.edu.ec

Resumen. La replicación de experimentos en Ingeniería del Software va en aumento, sin embargo, no es el caso para el tipo de replicación externa. Para llevar a cabo el proceso de replicación de un experimento o familia de experimentos es necesario conocer a detalle el paquete de laboratorio (PL). El PL contiene artefactos para transferir conocimiento y ayudar a los investigadores a replicar un experimento. Un problema encontrado en la publicación de los PL es su estructura, no existe un estándar formal para desplegar en repositorios digitales. El objetivo de esta investigación es mejorar el proceso de publicación del paquete de laboratorio experimental mediante la evaluación, automatización y publicación en Open Science.

Palabras-clave: Open Science, Paquete de laboratorio, experimentos, Ingeniería del Software.

1 Introducción

La replicación de experimentos en Ingeniería del Software (IS) sigue incrementándose sin embargo se evidencia pocas replicaciones externas[1]. Llevar a cabo replicaciones externas es todo un reto porque su proceso conlleva a que el replicador adquiera de alguna manera los elementos conceptuales y operacionales que fueron aplicados en el experimento original [1], [2]. El conocimiento tácito que tiene el experimentador original posiblemente puede ser adquirido mediante reuniones o consultas personales para preguntar de la fuente original detalles necesarios que clarifiquen la réplica [3]. Además, es necesario obtener los artefactos[2] de replicación los cuales deben estar disponibles, completos y de fácil acceso como hojas de cálculo que contengan datos acerca del análisis estadístico, dataset, guía del proceso de replicación, formularios, herramientas de software, herramientas estadísticas, inclusive videos, fotos, y demás objetos digitales que ayude a bajar la incertidumbre del replicador. La limitación de guías de replicación de experimentos conlleva otro reto por parte de los replicadores [4].

El conjunto de información y artefactos que se necesita para replicar el experimento es conocido por algunos investigadores en IS como Paquete de Laboratorio (PL) [5],

[1] Cuando la replicación es conducida por investigadores independientes [36].

[2] Objeto digital creado por los autores de una investigación para ser utilizado como parte del estudio o generado por el experimento en sí [19].

[6], [7], Paquete experimental [8], [9], Paquetes de Replicación [10], [11]. Para otras disciplinas como Medicina y Biología la replicación experimental se basa en un Protocolo el cual tiene un conjunto de instrumentos y guías basado estrictamente en procedimientos que se siguen para la replicación [5], y también de un PL que contiene elementos (artefactos) para trasmitir la información. El PL es clave para fortalecer y apoyar a la replicación de experimentos pero no garantiza una excelente replicación [12]. Sin embargo, existe limitaciones en la estandarización de la estructura y evaluación de un PL especialmente para Ingeniería del Software, esto hace aún más complejo el proceso de replicación.

El movimiento Open Science [13]es una oportunidad para transparentar y evidenciar el trabajo científico. Permite que la comunidad conozca y haga uso del conocimiento científico de cualquier área sin restricciones. Eso da lugar a mejorar la información que se publica y en este contexto a perfeccionar los paquetes de laboratorio y facilitar la reproducibilidad, replicabilidad de los estudios empíricos [14].

La publicación de los PL es un nuevo reto que los replicadores tienen porque si bien es cierto existe repositorios en la nube que ayudan a la gestión de almacenar y compartir artefactos como el mismo GitHub y herramientas Open Science como Zenodo, OSF, Figshare que son usadas con frecuencia para subir los PL, sin embargo, hace falta una estandarización en la estructura de los LP. El uso de herramientas Open Science ayuda a solventar el fácil acceso de los artefactos y la permanencia de alojamiento, un problema frecuente que presentan algunas investigaciones [15]. IEEE incentiva el movimiento Open Science mediante algunas opciones como Code Ocean [16], IEEE DataPort [17] y TechRxiv [18].

La Association for Computing Machinery (ACM) motiva a los investigadores a evaluar y validar los artefactos de investigación debido a un número importante de fallos como métodos experimentales descuidados, análisis estadísticos defectuosos o enlaces de internet rotos [19]. Es necesario realizar un proceso de arbitraje y auditar formalmente los artefactos para evitar errores en la replicación y reproducción de forma independiente. Algunos congresos como ICSE 2021 ha generado un track AE-Artifact Evaluation para evaluar los artefactos experimentales y asignar insignias (Badges ACM) como reutilizable, disponibles, replicable, reproducible, repetible [20]. Otros organismos como Sandia National Laboratories [21] propone un reporte acerca de una taxonomía de reproducibilidad compatible para las Ciencias de la Computación y la Informática, NISO RP-31-2021 Reproducibility Badging and Definitions [22] propone un reporte para Insignias y Definiciones de reproducibilidad.

2 Preguntas y objetivos de la investigación

Para esta investigación se formula las siguientes preguntas de investigación:

RQ1. ¿Cómo proporcionar a un experimentador la información que necesita para realizar una replicación externa en IS?

RQ2. ¿Cómo evaluar la calidad del paquete de laboratorio en IS?

RQ3. ¿Cómo mejorar la publicación de paquetes de laboratorio experimentales en IS?

El Objetivo de esta investigación es mejorar el proceso de publicación del paquete de laboratorio experimental mediante la evaluación, automatización y publicación en Open Science.

La justificación de contestar a las preguntas de investigación escritas anteriormente se relaciona con la necesidad e importancia de mejorar el proceso de publicación de los paquetes de laboratorio experimentales en IS. Esto ayudará a los replicadores experimentales facilitar el proceso de replicación.

3 Esquema del conocimiento

La presente investigación está fundamentada en varios estudios de investigadores que han profundizado en la necesidad e importancia de crear, mejorar y evaluar paquetes de laboratorio para experimentos en Ingeniería del Software. Como el estudio de Shull et al (2004) [23], Shull et al. (2008) [12]. Vegas et al. (2006) [24] describen los tipos de paquetes de replicación y su contenido. Almqvist (2006) [25] explica la importancia de elaborar paquetes de laboratorio experimentales y el contenido que deben tener. Kitchenham et al. (2006) [26] proponen un checklist definido desde la perspectiva del replicador de experimentos para reportar estudios en IS empírica. Martin Solari et al. (2006) [10] proponen una clasificación y análisis de paquetes de replicación, su contenido y una algunos desafíos a considerar en futuras investigaciones. En este contexto, Martín Solari et al. (2018) [5] definen un template del contenido de un paquete de laboratorio y un checklist de instrucciones para el replicador, los cuales han sido evaluados en siete replicaciones.

4 Esquema de la metodología de investigación

La metodología de investigación se basa en el enfoque Design Science Research (DSR), que ayuda a evaluar los criterios de valor y utilidad del producto de software [27]. La Tabla 1. Indica el diseño de la metodología de investigación.

Table 1. Diseño de la metodología de investigación.

Actividad	Componentes	Objetivo
Diagnóstico del problema.	Problema, preguntas de investigación, objetivo.	Existe evidencia de la necesidad de mejorar los PL. Contestar a RQ1, RQ2 y RQ3.
Diseño del artefacto (modelo, proceso, producto de software).	Diseño de la propuesta.	Diseñar un PL orientado al proceso cumpliendo criterios de calidad.
Implementación de la propuesta.	Desarrollo e implementación de la propuesta.	Comparar las propuestas de PL, identificar diferencias,similitudes.
Evaluación de la propuesta.	Aplicación de un método de evaluación.	Evaluar interna y externamente la propuesta con familias de experimentos.

5 Solución de la propuesta

La solución de la propuesta se enfoca a crear una solución metodológica y tecnológica basada en un proceso de evaluación, automatización y publicación de paquetes de laboratorio en Open Science. Las actividades de la propuesta se definen en tres fases.

5.1 Cronograma para ejecución experimental

El tema del material experimental ha sido profundizado por la comunidad científica, sin embargo, el proceso y cronograma experimental para replicaciones externas es un desafío y se convierte en un nicho de investigación, en especial para los experimentadores noveles. Esto conlleva a desarrollar un cronograma que permita llevar de la mano al experimentador que desea realizar una replicación externa. La idea es favorecer al experimentador ejecutar con claridad desde el inicio el proceso de replicación, es decir, identificar el cuándo, cómo, que tiempo y recursos necesita.

5.2 Heurística para determinar el nivel de calidad de un paquete de laboratorio

Crear una heurística para establecer el nivel de calidad de un paquete de laboratorio mediante una integración de la información publicada en las siguientes propuestas: Artifact Review and Badging de ACM [19], AE-Artifact Evaluation de ICSE 2021 [28], el reporte de Sandia National Laboratories [21], el reporte de NISO [22] y el template propuesto por Martin Solari et al. [5]. Las reglas permitirán evaluar y validar el contenido del paquete y también recomendar una insignia como "Evaluado", "Habilitado", Validado" y dentro de validado esta "Replicado" y Reproducible". A fin de integrar los criterios de calidad seleccionados según las propuestas antes mencionadas para evaluar la calidad de los PL, se empezará por establecer una comparativa entre esas propuestas para identificar diferencias y similitudes, y analizar en qué sentido unas pueden complementar a las otras. Posteriormente, se evaluará las guías de replicación existentes y estudiar en qué medida están alineadas con los criterios de calidad comparados previamente. Por último, se intentará adaptarlas a la experimentación con humanos en IS.

5.3 Solución automatizada

Se determinó dos opciones que den solución tecnológica a la propuesta: 1) Crear una extensión de un navegador web para conectarse a un repositorio digital y subir el PL a una herramienta Open Science. 2) Crear una herramienta que se instale en nuestra máquina que cambie el menú contextual cuando se hace click derecho de una carpeta en el explorador y que permita publicar esa carpeta en un repositorio como Zenodo. La Fig. 1 muestra un diagrama conceptual del proceso de publicación.

Entre los resultados obtenidos esta un Systematic Mapping Study (SMS) acerca de los paquetes de laboratorio, su estructura y publicación en herramientas Open Science.

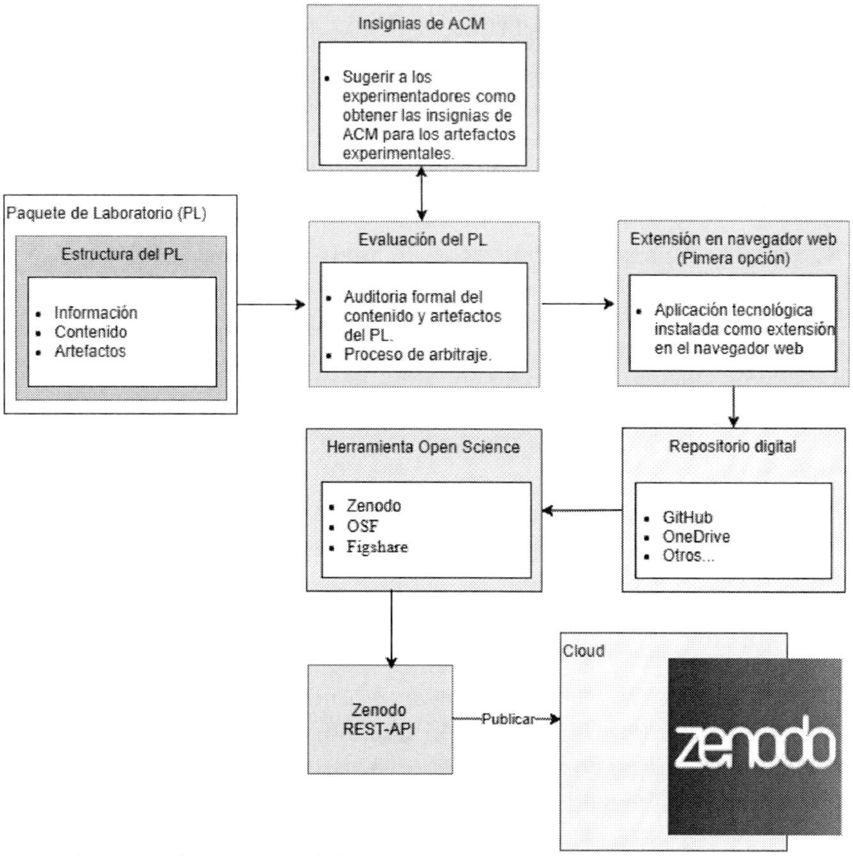

Fig. 1. Diagrama de conceptual del proceso de publicación del paquete de laboratorio experimental en Ingeniería del Software, centrada en la primera opción.

6 Declaración de diferencias o mejoras de la solución sugerida con los enfoques existentes

Para dar respuesta a la cuestión RQ1 relativa a los paquetes de laboratorio, la diferencia de este trabajo con otros es dotar al experimentador de un estudio original un recurso flexible y ágil que ayude a desarrollar un cronograma experimental (guideline step-by-step) [5], para favorecer las replicaciones externas. Dicho de otra forma, realizar un paquete de laboratorio orientado al proceso, en lugar de orientado al producto. Poner a disposición del experimentador externo dicho cronograma puede favorecer que se siente animado a realizar replicaciones externas.

Para dar respuesta a la cuestión RQ2 relativa a las insignias que se pueden otorgar a los paquetes de laboratorio, la solución sugerida en el documento de Submission Instructions and Reviewing de ICSE 2021 [28] para Artifact Evaluation resulta completa y detallada. Sin embargo, revisando los artefactos enviados al ICSE 2021 [29], en algunos casos los autores obvian algunas de las pautas dadas con lo que el paquete resultante no cumple los niveles de calidad exigidos. La propuesta se enfoca en idear mecanismos para asistir al autor del PL, facilitándole conseguir la insignia que desea. Una solución automatizada de dichos mecanismos, implementada con se muestra en la Fig.1, daría respuesta a RQ3. Existen algunas herramientas para paquetes de laboratorio [30],[31] pero pensamos que si la herramienta guía al experimentador, se puede mejorar la calidad del paquete de laboratorio.

En definitiva, la propuesta está enfocada en la evaluación, automatización y publicación de los paquetes de laboratorio experimentales en Ingeniería del Software basándose en el movimiento Open Science. La mejora con los enfoques existentes es el proceso de evaluación de los artefactos y su contenido mediante la automatización que facilitaría la creación y publicación de los PL ayudándoles a los replicadores que disminuyan su tiempo y recursos.

7 Problemas pendientes y próximos pasos

Entre los problemas pendientes esta determinar una taxonomía de los elementos y contenido del paquete de laboratorio para automatizar la evaluación del contenido de los artefactos experimentales. Para esto, integraríamos la información publicada en Artifact Review and Badging de ACM, AE-Artifact Evaluation de ICSE 2021 y el template propuesto por Martin Solari con la finalidad de ayudar y sugerir al replicador que le hace falta para obtener las insignias de ACM. Para llevar a cabo esta tarea, la intención es realizar un estudio de campo en congresos que posean un Track de Artifact Evaluation [32]–[35] para detectar cuáles son las principales dificultades que encuentran los autores al elaborar su PL y poder asistirlos.

Un problema potencial es que dichos PL poseen diferente naturaleza, por ejemplo, para experimentos controlados, para estudios cualitativos, para código fuente, etc. Esta situación puede dificultar la identificación de heurísticas, al ser distintas según la naturaleza del paquete. Una posible vía es centrarnos en PL para experimentos controlados realizados con humanos. Otro problema es la automatización para crear el paquete de laboratorio, crear la extensión en un navegador web para conectarse con un repositorio digital y seguidamente conectarse con Zenodo u otra herramienta de Open Science para la publicación del PL.

Los próximos pasos son crear el diseño de un modelo de evaluación del contenido del PL, el diseño de la arquitectura tecnológica y evaluar la solución propuesta, aplicándola en varios experimentos y luego utilizar los PL para replicar.

8 Referencias

[1] J. Miller, "Triangulation as a basis for knowledge discovery in software engineering," *Empir. Softw. Eng.*, vol. 13, no. 2, pp. 223–228, 2008.

[2] N. Juristo, S. Vegas, M. Solari, S. Abrahão, and I. Ramos, "A process for managing interaction between experimenters to get useful similar replications," *Inf. Softw. Technol.*, vol. 55, no. 2, pp. 215–225, 2013.

[3] J. Krein, "Replication and Knowledge Production in Empirical Software Engineering Research," Brigham Young University, 2014.

[4] A. Santos, S. Vegas, M. Oivo, and N. Juristo, "A Procedure and Guidelines for

Analyzing Groups of Software Engineering Replications," *IEEE Trans. Softw. Eng.*, vol. 5589, no. FEBRUARY, pp. 1–1, 2019.

[5] M. Solari, S. Vegas, and N. Juristo, "Content and structure of laboratory packages for software engineering experiments," *Inf. Softw. Technol.*, vol. 97, no. December 2016, pp. 64–79, 2018.

[6] V. Basili *et al.*, "Packaging Researcher Experience to Assist Replication of Experiments V. Basili, S. Green, O. Laitenberger, F. Lanubile, F. Shull, S. Sorumgard, M. Zelkowitz," in *In Proc. of the ISERN meeting*, 1996.

[7] V. R. Basili, F. Shull, and F. Lanubile, "Building knowledge through families of experiments," *IEEE Trans. Softw. Eng.*, vol. 25, no. 4, pp. 456–473, 1999.

[8] R. Conradi, V. R. Basili, J. Carver, F. Shull, and G. H. Travassos, "A Pragmatic Documents Standard for an Experience Library: Roles, Documen, Contents and Structure," 2001.

[9] P. Mian, G. Travassos, and A. da Rocha, "A Computerized Infrastructure for Supporting Experimentation in Software Engineering," in *ESELAW 2005*, 2005.

[10] M. Solari and S. Vegas, "Classifying and analysing replication packages for software engineering experimentation," in *7th International Conference on Product Focused Software Process Improvement (PROFES 2006)-Workshop Series in Empirical Software Engineering (WSESE)*, 2006.

[11] M. P. Robillard, M. Nassif, and S. McIntosh, "Threats of aggregating software repository data," in *Proceedings - 2018 IEEE International Conference on Software Maintenance and Evolution, ICSME 2018*, 2018, pp. 508–518.

[12] F. J. Shull, J. C. Carver, S. Vegas, and N. Juristo, "The role of replications in Empirical Software Engineering," *Empir. Softw. Eng.*, vol. 13, no. 2, pp. 211–218, 2008.

[13] D. Mendez, D. Graziotin, S. Wagner, and H. Seibold, "Open Science in Software Engineering," *Contemp. Empir. Methods Softw. Eng.*, pp. 477–501, 2020.

[14] D. Graziotin, "open science policies," *ICSE'21*, 2021. [Online]. Available: https://ineed.coffee/open-science-policies. [Accessed: 15-Jul-2021].

[15] D. Méndez Fernández, M. Monperrus, R. Feldt, and T. Zimmermann, "The open science initiative of the Empirical Software," *Empir. Softw. Eng.*, no. 24, pp. 1057–1060, 2019.

[16] Code Ocean by IEEE, "IEEE Xplore / Code Ocean FAQs," *IEEE*, 2021. [Online]. Available: https://ieeexplore.ieee.org/Xplorehelp/faqs/code-ocean#what-is-ieee-xplore-code-ocean. [Accessed: 09-Jul-2021].

[17] IEEE DataPort, "Search Standard and Open Access Datasets | IEEE DataPort," *IEEE*, 2021. [Online]. Available: https://ieee-dataport.org/datasets. [Accessed: 09-Jul-2021].

[18] TechRxiv by IEEE, "TechRxiv preprint server - Browse," *IEEE*, 2021. [Online]. Available: https://www.techrxiv.org/?utm_source=Innovate&utm_medium=Blog_Post&utm_campaign=Innovate_Oct_2019. [Accessed: 09-Jul-2021].

[19] A. for C. M. ACM, "Artifact Review and Badging - Current," *Version 1.1*, 2020. [Online]. Available: https://www.acm.org/publications/policies/artifact-review-and-badging-current. [Accessed: 02-Jul-2021].

[20] ICSE 2021 International Conference on Software Engineering, "ICSE 2021 - AE - Artifact Evaluation - ICSE 2021," *43rd International Conference*, 2021. [Online]. Available: https://conf.researchr.org/track/icse-2021/icse-2021-Artifact-Evaluation.

[Accessed: 02-Jul-2021].

[21] M. A. Heroux, L. A. Barba, M. Parashar, and V. Stodden, "Toward a Compatible Reproducibility Taxonomy for Computational and Computing Sciences," 2018.

[22] NISO, "Reproducibility Badging and Definitions," 2021.

[23] F. Shull *et al.*, "Knowledge-Sharing Issues in Experimental Software Engineering," *Empir. Softw. Eng.*, vol. 9, no. 1–2, pp. 111–137, 2004.

[24] S. Vegas, N. Juristo, A. Moreno, M. Solari, and P. Letelier, "Analysis of the influence of communication between researchers on experiment replication," in *ISESE'06 - Proceedings of the 5th ACM-IEEE International Symposium on Empirical Software Engineering*, 2006, vol. 2006, pp. 28–37.

[25] J. Almqvist, "Replication of controlled experiments in empirical software engineering-a survey," 2006.

[26] B. Kitchenham *et al.*, "Evaluating guidelines for empirical software engineering studies," in *ISESE'06 - Proceedings of the 5th ACM-IEEE International Symposium on Empirical Software Engineering*, 2006, vol. 2006, pp. 38–47.

[27] A. Hevner and S. Chatterjee, "Design Science Research in Information Systems," Springer, Boston, MA, 2010, pp. 9–22.

[28] S. Abrahão and D. Mendez, "ICSE'21 Artifact Evaluation Track-Submission and Reviewing Guidelines," *ICSE'21*, 2021.

[29] ICSE 2021 International Conference on Software Engineering, "ICSE 2021 - AE - Artifact Evaluation - ICSE 2021," *ICE'21*, 2021. [Online]. Available: https://conf.researchr.org/track/icse-2021/icse-2021-Artifact-Evaluation#event-overview. [Accessed: 16-Jul-2021].

[30] J. A. Parejo, S. Segura, P. Fernandez, and A. R. Cortés, "EXEMPLAR: an Experimental Information Repository for SBSE Research.," *CMSEBA@MoDELS*, vol. 1340, pp. 35–41, 2014.

[31] Nature Portfolio, "Home | Protocol Exchange on Research Square," *Nature Portfolio*, 2021. [Online]. Available: https://protocolexchange.researchsquare.com/. [Accessed: 16-Jul-2021].

[32] 29th IEEE International Requirements Engineering Conference, "RE2021 - Artifacts - RE2021," *RE'21*, 2021. [Online]. Available: https://conf.researchr.org/track/RE-2021/RE-2021-artifacts#Call-for-Artifacts. [Accessed: 16-Jul-2021].

[33] 18th IEEE International Conference on Software Architecture, "Artifact Evaluation Track – ICSA 2021," *ICSA'21*, 2021. [Online]. Available: https://icsa-conferences.org/2021/call-for-papers/artifact-evaluation-track/. [Accessed: 16-Jul-2021].

[34] European Software Engineering Conference and Symposium on the Foundations of Software Engineering, "ESEC/FSE 2021 - Artifacts," *ESEC/FSE'21*, 2021. [Online]. Available: https://2021.esec-fse.org/track/fse-2021-artifacts. [Accessed: 16-Jul-2021].

[35] 54th IEEE/ACM International Symposium on Microarchitecture, "MICRO 2021: Artifact Evaluation," *MICRO'21*, 2021. [Online]. Available: https://www.microarch.org/micro54/submit/artifacts.php. [Accessed: 16-Jul-2021].

[36] C. V. C. De Magalhães and F. Q. B. Da Silva, "Towards a taxonomy of replications in empirical software engineering research: A research proposal," *Proc. - 2013 3rd Int. Work. Replication Empir. Softw. Eng. Res. RESER 2013*, pp. 50–55, 2013.

Una herramienta para el estudio de sentimientos en los mensajes de los desarrolladores y métricas de calidad

Jaime Sayago-Heredia [1]

[1] Pontificia Universidad Católica del Ecuador, Sede Esmeraldas, Ecuador
Espejo y subida a Santa Cruz Casilla 08-01-0065
jaime.sayago@pucese.edu.ec

Resumen. El desarrollo de software tiene una importante vertiente humana, por lo que se sabe que los sentimientos de los desarrolladores tienen un impacto significativo en varias cuestiones relacionadas con el desarrollo de software y que podrían afectar a la calidad, la productividad y el rendimiento de los desarrolladores. En este estudio, se ha comenzado el proceso para encontrar, comprender y relacionar estas afectaciones a la calidad de software. En un primer paso, se ha desarrollado un artefacto para la extraer y detectar los sentimientos en los mensajes de los commits presentes en GitHub junto con las métricas de calidad de SonarQube. Utilizamos la herramienta para extraer la toxicidad en los comentarios de los desarrolladores y métricas de calidad de proyectos de software. En futuros trabajos, se investigará a profundidad los factores que afectan a las emociones de los desarrolladores y si estos factores se relacionan con la calidad del código en el ciclo de vida de un proyecto de software. Además, se estimará la calidad del código en función de los sentimientos de los desarrolladores.

Palabras clave: Análisis de sentimientos, GitHub, SonarQube, Commits, Calidad del software, Ingeniería de software

1 Introducción

La investigación en el campo de la ingeniería de software ha aplicado cada vez más técnicas y métodos de otras áreas de investigación [1], como el análisis de sentimientos [2–5]. El análisis de sentimientos (también conocido como minería de opinión) se desarrolló inicialmente como un método automatizado para extraer la polaridad de los sentimientos de textos cortos publicados en línea, como las críticas de películas, las reseñas de productos, los *microblogs* y los *tweets* [6] que tuvo una gran aplicación en el mundo del marketing. En concreto, el análisis de sentimientos es el estudio de la subjetividad y la polaridad de un texto escrito manualmente (normalmente identificado como neutral positivo o negativo) [7].

El desarrollo de software tiene una importante vertiente humana, es evidente entonces, que los sentimientos del desarrollador tienen un impacto significativo en diversas cuestiones relacionadas con el desarrollo de software, como por ejemplo la calidad. Actualmente, los proyectos de desarrollo de software dependen de un gran número de programadores que colaboran entre sí realizando esfuerzos para el desarrollo de un sistema de software [8]. Estos esfuerzos para construir y mantener un proyecto software son continuos y estresantes para los desarrolladores, lo que se convierte en un problema difícil de solucionar [9]. Los investigadores están preocupados de que estos sentimientos podrían desencadenar en un código con errores y por consiguiente un código de mala calidad, como lo demuestran algunas publicaciones [5, 10, 11].

Los desarrolladores cada día se enfrentan a varios problemas y tienen que encontrar una solución que requieren niveles altos de conocimiento técnico. Para los desarrolladores, estos obstáculos para completar con éxito el desarrollo de un proyecto software puede resultar agotador y elevar el estrés [9] . Esto repercute posteriormente en su capacidad para autorregular sus sentimientos y su comprensión [12], por ejemplo: los *commits messages* tienen una gran cantidad de sentimientos negativos [6]. Estos mensajes contienen una expresión emocional (negativa o toxica), y que podría influenciar en la calidad del código, o bien ser un reflejo de que la calidad del código también influencia los sentimientos negativos de los desarrolladores. Por esto, es necesario analizar, comprender y relacionar los sentimientos negativos y la calidad del código de los desarrolladores, un campo de investigación importante y poco estudiado. Existen varias preguntas de investigación importantes que se plantean en esta investigación, por ejemplo: ¿Están los sentimientos de los desarrolladores relacionados con la calidad del código durante el ciclo de vida del proyecto de software?, ¿Están los sentimientos negativos de los desarrolladores relacionados con el aumento de los errores en un proyecto de software?, ¿Los sentimientos negativos afectan a la calidad del código o la calidad del código afecta a los sentimientos de los desarrolladores? El resultado, que se desea conseguir es responder a estas preguntas de forma empírica utilizando métodos directos e indirectos, y uno de estos métodos indirectos es el desarrollo de una herramienta para el análisis de una gran cantidad de datos y que ofrece la posibilidad de análisis estadísticos y comprobación de hipótesis. Los *commits messages* pueden utilizarse para extraer el sentimiento de los desarrolladores [4], funcionan como un recurso importante para analizar y comprender una posible relación entre el sentimiento del desarrollador y la calidad de código.

Hemos dado un primer paso desarrollando y proponiendo una herramienta de investigación (clasificador) para obtener el lenguaje toxico de los desarrolladores en los *commits messages*. El lenguaje tóxico puede estar presente en diferentes lugares en línea (ejemplo: Facebook), están presentes igualmente en los comentarios de los proyectos de software en GitHub. La toxicidad puede manifestarse de múltiples maneras, en el caso del desarrollo de software, a través de mensajes corroborando la falta de ayuda de un error o el tiempo que toman en solucionar un problema. Realizamos un caso de estudio piloto con algunos proyectos. Esta herramienta obtiene la toxicidad de los *commits messages* de los proyectos seleccionados desde GitHub (el mayor repositorio de software del mundo [13]) y de manera conjunta extrae las métricas de calidad de código correspondientes a los mensajes de los proyectos de software seleccionados. Nuestro trabajo realiza una contribución principal, verificando que la toxicidad de los mensajes pueden ser identificados a través de técnicas de Procesamiento del Lenguaje Natural (PLN) y obteniendo un corpus de datos con sentimientos negativos y toxicidad.

2 Justificación

La calidad del código es importante para los proyectos de software. El intento de medir la calidad del software ha llevado a la propuesta de varias métricas [14]. Investigaciones anteriores, centradas en los desarrolladores, han demostrado que las emociones de los desarrolladores de software pueden afectar a la calidad de las tareas, la productividad, la creatividad, la relación con el grupo y la satisfacción laboral, entre otras cosas [15]. Existen algunos trabajos que analizan los sentimientos en el ámbito de la ingeniería de software donde se analizan los sentimientos [2, 5, 10, 16–21], utilizando diferentes artefactos como GitHub[2, 6, 22], igualmente en Jira [18, 20, 23]. Otros estudios señalan algunas incertidumbres relacionadas con la aplicación infructuosa de las herramientas de análisis de sentimientos para la ingeniería del software [11, 24]. Las herramientas existentes requieren configuraciones para su uso específico o la adaptación para el contexto específico que se va a utilizar y eso puede ser crucial para el rendimiento de la herramienta [25]. Otros estudios [2–5] se han centrado en analizar y clasificar las emociones en los artefactos de software y, al mismo tiempo, en proponer estándares de emociones (tristeza, felicidad, ira, miedo, etc.) en los equipos de desarrollo. Guzmán et al.[2] propusieron un enfoque de análisis de sentimientos para las discusiones en listas de correo y herramientas de colaboración de software basadas en la web. Ding et al. [4] realizaron un análisis de sentimientos a nivel de entidad creando un conjunto de datos y una herramienta *SentiSW*. SentiSW es una herramienta de análisis de sentimientos a nivel de entidad y que consiste en la clasificación de sentimientos y el reconocimiento de entidades y clasifica los comentarios problemáticos con una precisión significativamente mayor que otras herramientas. Murgia et al. [3] analizaron a los artefactos de desarrollo y los informes de problemas para conocer si contienen alguna información emocional sobre el desarrollo de software a través de una herramienta automática para la extracción de emociones en artefactos de desarrollo de software. Cheruvelli y Da Silva [5] aplicaron una herramienta de análisis de sentimientos a los comentarios de seguimiento de problemas y observaron cómo las puntuaciones variaban para problemas sin reapertura, con una reapertura y con muchas reaperturas, sugieren que el sentimiento negativo se correlaciona con los problemas reabiertos, aunque el tamaño del efecto parece ser bastante pequeño.

Estos análisis se centraron en la búsqueda y localización de emociones a través de herramientas que no han sido creadas para el contexto de la ingeniería de software. Existen varias herramientas de análisis de sentimientos, tanto comerciales [25] como gratuitas [23]. Algunas herramientas de análisis de sentimientos aplicadas en ingeniería de software son:

— *SentiStrength* es la más utilizada en los estudios de ingeniería del software [2, 18, 26].
— NLTK es una herramienta de análisis de sentimientos basada en léxicos y reglas, cuyo núcleo es VADER (Valence Aware Dictionary and sEntiment Reasoner); VADER se adapta específicamente a los textos de las redes sociales incorporando un léxico de sentimientos extraído de contextos de microblogs y validado manualmente por múltiples jueces humanos independientes [27].
— Stanford CoreNLP se basa en una red neuronal recursiva, que se diferencia de otras herramientas por su capacidad para obtener el sentimiento de una frase basándose en cómo las palabras componen el significado de la frase, y no sumando el sentimiento de las palabras individuales. Se ha entrenado con críticas de películas [28].

Las herramientas descritas, encuentran algunas discrepancias en cuanto a su eficacia y coincidencia de resultados, lo que puede llevar a conclusiones diferentes, haciendo que no sean replicables cuando se utilizan diferentes herramientas de análisis de sentimientos [23]. En definitiva, varios autores reconocen [23, 25, 29] que existe una necesidad de construir herramientas de análisis orientadas a conjuntos de datos específicos para la ingeniería del software para que no pongan en duda la validez de los resultados de análisis de sentimientos.

Otros autores [10, 21, 30] se centraron en analizar los sentimientos y su impacto en la calidad del código a través de las tareas y las métricas de calidad del código (refactorización, clonación de código) utilizando diferentes artefactos de ingeniería de software.

En tal sentido, al no encontrar una herramienta que pueda extraer los sentimientos de los mensajes en los *commits* junto con las métricas de calidad del código, hemos implementado como primer paso una herramienta. A partir de esta base, continuar la investigación que pretende centrarse en analizar, comprender y relacionar la calidad del código y los sentimientos de los desarrolladores en un proyecto de software.

3 Solución propuesta

En el contexto del programa de investigación que se plantea, este deberá ser amplio para analizar, comprender y relacionar la calidad del código y los sentimientos de los desarrolladores. Así que; los esfuerzos a llevar a cabo son:

- Establecer un contexto en lo referente a conceptos, terminologías y enfoques de los sentimientos y calidad de código. Para compartir los resultados de la investigación en la comunidad de investigadores.
- Definir métricas y variables a través de diferentes enfoques para obtenerlas y que se utilizarán para la comprensión y relación de los diferentes enfoques y métodos existentes y que sirvan a nuestro tema de investigación.
- Proponer un artefacto que permita obtener el conjunto de datos necesarios para aplicar la métricas y variables definidas para la investigación.
- Desarrollar un caso de estudio aplicando el artefacto y variables definidas.
- Comprobar la hipótesis propuesta y que podría utilizarse para desarrollar mecanismos de mejora tanto a los desarrolladores como en los proyectos software.

4 Procedimientos metodológicos

Para el desarrollo de la investigación, están previstas varias actividades para construir la propuesta de comprensión y relación entre sentimientos y calidad de código:

- Estudio de mapeo sistemático: El primer paso es la realización de un SMS, para comprender en contexto el campo de investigación referente a los repositorios de código, donde se puedan identificar áreas de interés para llevar a cabo una investigación.
- Selección de métodos y enfoques de relación: En este paso está previsto realizar un análisis exhaustivo de los diferentes métodos y enfoques para comprender y definir las métricas y variables a utilizar para la comprensión y medición de la relación de los sentimientos y la calidad de código

— Propuesta de solución: A partir de estudios realizados y conjuntos de datos obtenidos generaremos artefacto para realizar el proceso de validación y que permita comprender e identificar una relación de los conceptos mencionados en nuestra propuesta de investigación.
— Caso de estudio: Al tener definidos los artefactos como las métricas a utilizar, se procede a evaluar la propuesta de solución con un caso de estudio aplicado a un conjunto de datos de gran volumen.

5 Resultados esperados

El programa de doctorado a través del tema de investigación propuesto se espera contribuir a la comunidad académica con lo siguiente:

1. Identificar las diferentes métricas y variables que vinculan a los sentimientos de los desarrolladores y la calidad de código.
2. Aportar a la comunidad de investigadores un conjunto de datos, que sirvan de base para futuras investigación que involucren sentimientos y calidad de código.
3. Proponer medidas y modelos que ayuden a disminuir los sentimientos negativos y toxicidad de los desarrolladores.

6 Estado actual de la investigación

La investigación se encuentra en una fase inicial. A pesar de esto se tiene algunos resultados como son un mapeo sistemático de la literatura sobre el análisis de repositorios de código, para identificar las principales áreas de interés para nuestra investigación [31] .Por otra parte, se construyó un prototipo del artefacto para la extracción de los sentimientos y métricas de calidad de código. A continuación, se describe la herramienta:

6.1 Descripción de la herramienta

La herramienta es una aplicación web. La herramienta integra y extrae los *commits messages* de la Api de GitHub que es la mayor plataforma en línea y contiene más de 3,4 millones de usuarios[32] y las métricas de la Api de SonarQube que es la herramienta más utilizada en el mercado para el análisis de la calidad del código [33]), se utilizaron para su desarrollo .Net Visual Studio, C#, HTML5 y la librería ML.NET que permite a los desarrolladores construir complejos pipelines de aprendizaje automático [34]. El primer paso es preparar el conjunto de datos que se utilizará para el análisis de sentimientos. Es importante entender el conjunto de datos. El sentimiento calculado desde el mensaje del *commit* consiste en un índice de toxicidad, el valor numérico del sentimiento proporciona una cuantificación. Es importante determinar y comprender las palabras para entender el contexto de la frase. Al utilizar las diferentes palabras, debemos diferenciar el contexto de la ingeniería de software para extraer los valores de sentimiento correctos del mensaje. La herramienta utiliza diferentes algoritmos y entrena modelos separados para encontrar el modelo de mejor rendimiento para el conjunto de datos [35]. La herramienta extrae la toxicidad de los sentimientos de los mensajes en el proyecto (GitHub) y de las métricas (SonarQube) y genera gráficas con análisis y estadísticas para cada uno de los proyectos. En la Fig. 1, podemos ver la herramienta en producción, en la opción de estadísticas (panel izquierdo) se describen varios análisis del proyecto seleccionado del estudio piloto. Los gráficos estadísticos que se observan en la herramienta son los *commits messages* por autor, las palabras más utilizadas, el número total de toxicidad de los mensajes. Los sentimientos negativos están representados por palabras negativas o tóxicas. Observamos en la herramienta, una distribución de la toxicidad y una clasificación por autor. La herramienta genera un conjunto de datos que puede ser exportado a diferentes formatos. Y la última opción de la herramienta muestra una distribución porcentual de la toxicidad de los *commits messages* del proyecto que pueden ser listados por autor.

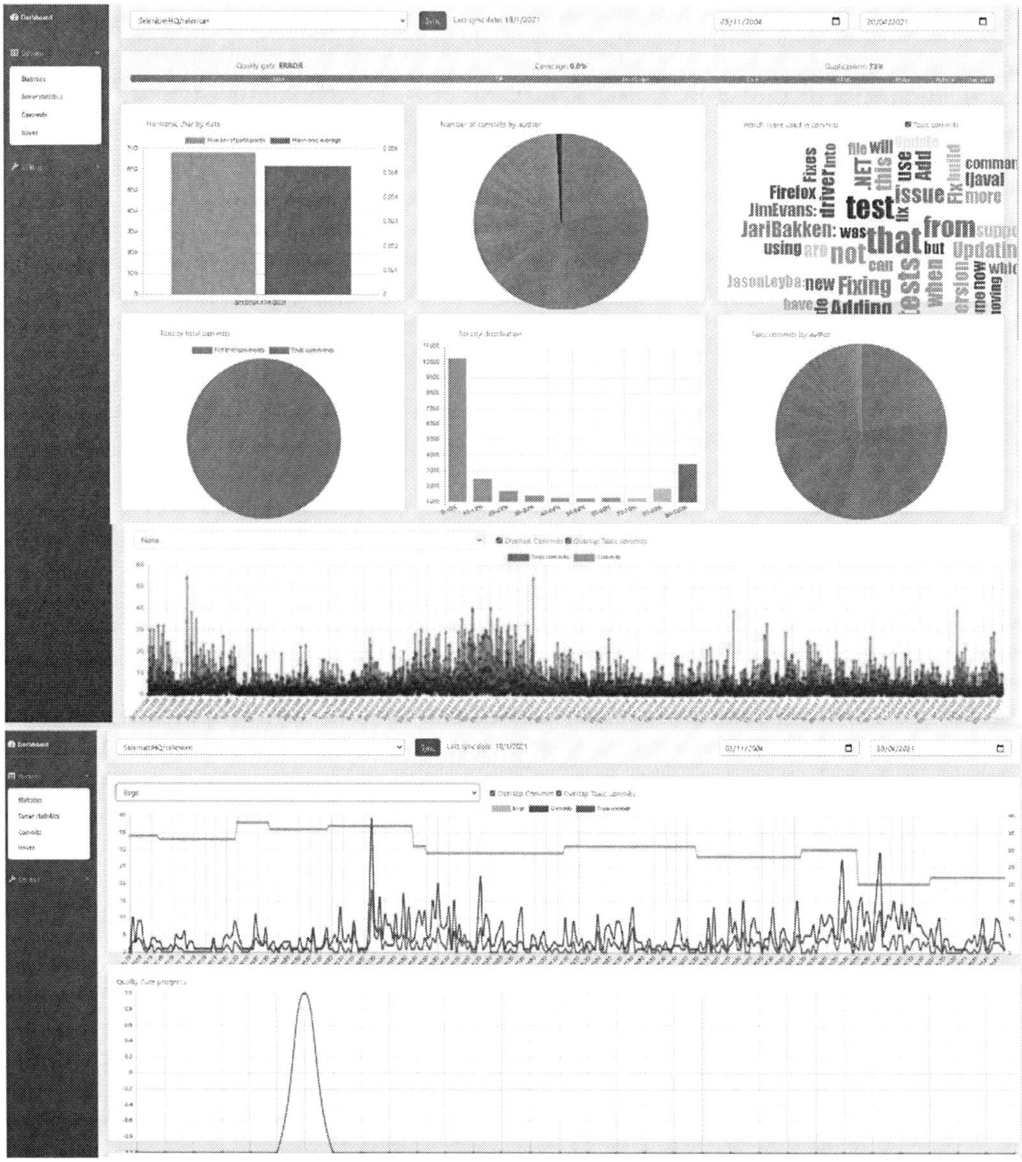

Fig. 1. Vista de la herramienta de análisis desarrollada.

6.1.1 Procedimiento para recogida de datos

Para obtener el conjunto de datos necesario para nuestro estudio piloto, utilizamos los seis proyectos. El conjunto de datos para cada uno de los proyectos se muestra en la Fig. 2. A partir de estos datos (112 variables), en los que se incluyó el número de sentimientos negativos, las métricas de calidad del código (por ejemplo, errores, complejidad, líneas duplicadas, entre otras) y las métricas de GitHub (por ejemplo, el total de commits, los desarrolladores (committers), los cambios, entre otros), los resultados se pusieron en una hoja de cálculo para el análisis estadístico. El conjunto de datos está disponible en línea para su revisión o replicación en https://github.com/jaimepsayago/SentimentsAnalysis.

El resultado preliminar fue que existe una correlación débil entre las métricas de los sentimientos negativos (tóxicos) de los *commits messages* y las métricas de calidad de código. Por lo consiguiente, se hace necesario continuar la investigación utilizando métodos directos e indirectos para obtener más variables y analizar, comprender y relacionar la calidad del código junto con los sentimientos de los desarrolladores en un proyecto software.

Analysis	From	To	Day	0-10	10-20	20-30	30-40	40-50	50-60	60-70	70-80	80-90	90-100	%Negative commits percetaje	Negative commits avarage	Total negative commits	complexity	open_issues	code_smells	bugs
3.9-SNAPSHOT	7/9/2020	8/9/2020	1	2	0	0	0	1	0	1	0	1	1	50%	0.41762094	6	11052	2665	2591	31
3.8-SNAPSHOT	23/7/2020	7/9/2020	46	6	0	3	0	3	1	1	1	2	0	29%	0.22066092	17	33078	7989	7767	93
3.7-SNAPSHOT	11/4/2020	23/7/2020	103	5	2	0	0	4	1	2	0	5	3	50%	0.41324793	22	55115	13390	12930	155
3.6-SNAPSHOT	19/3/2020	11/4/2020	23	6	1	0	1	1	0	1	1	3	2	43%	0.37714449	16	10867	2615	2526	31
3.5-SNAPSHOT	8/1/2020	19/3/2020	71	9	6	4	4	4	3	2	1	3	1	27%	0.19460395	37	75916	17670	17068	196
3.4-SNAPSHOT	8/1/2020	8/1/2020	0	0	0	0	0	0	0	0	0	0	0	0%	0	0	0	0	0	0
master	12/9/2020	2/10/2020	20	6	5	2	12	6	0	2	1	1	3	18%	0.154491	38	34112	6222	5914	308
2.19.1	27/8/2020	12/9/2020	16	10	4	3	14	5	2	6	3	1	9	36%	0.29351134	67	17066	3187	3052	151
2.19.0	23/5/2020	27/8/2020	96	37	18	10	69	18	0	20	6	4	14	22%	0.17602843	196	85744	6324	6032	316
2.18.0	22/3/2020	23/5/2020	62	41	27	17	46	21	4	19	16	13	17	31%	0.24194186	221	12799	1777	1642	135
2.17.0	31/12/2019	22/3/2020	82	41	25	19	32	16	3	26	20	12	14	36%	0.27097588	208	25191	1016	775	242
2.16.0	12/11/2019	31/12/2019	49	30	13	15	7	16	5	16	19	3	13	40%	0.31087803	137	11736	379	259	121
2.15.2	24/9/2019	12/11/2019	49	24	10	5	11	7	3	11	11	5	7	39%	0.29520128	94	7634	411	221	192
2.15.1	22/9/2019	24/9/2019	2	1	0	0	0	1	0	0	0	0	0	0%	0	2	3817	199	110	90
2.15.0	7/4/2019	22/9/2019	168	80	13	21	17	23	15	29	33	26	20	44%	0.33265667	277	21765	1032	671	365
2.13.0	9/3/2019	7/4/2019	29	7	2	3	4	3	3	2	5	1	4	44%	0.33337184	34	6955	388	301	91
2.12.1	9/2/2019	9/3/2019	28	17	3	2	3	6	2	8	5	2	3	39%	0.28308704	51	6930	390	302	92
2.12.0	1/1/2019	9/2/2019	39	36	12	11	6	5	2	6	10	9	6	32%	0.24838518	103	10161	563	432	138
2.11.2	26/12/2018	1/1/2019	6	2	0	2	1	0	0	0	2	1	0	37%	0.29781297	8	3295	170	127	46
2.11.1	23/12/2018	26/12/2018	3	7	2	3	0	2	0	0	1	3	0	22%	0.17815469	18	3274	171	127	47
2.11.0	15/11/2018	23/12/2018	38	27	3	3	3	2	2	4	10	6	8	44%	0.34818781	68	12339	800	613	191
2.10.2	13/11/2018	15/11/2018	2	4	0	1	0	0	0	0	1	0	1	28%	0.23982094	7	3029	279	228	49
2.10.1	11/11/2018	13/11/2018	2	2	0	2	0	1	0	1	2	0	3	54%	0.45209932	11	6067	558	456	98
2.10.0	14/10/2018	11/11/2018	28	24	7	1	5	4	2	3	6	9	5	37%	0.29792147	66	22603	2591	2183	423
2.9.0	9/10/2018	14/10/2018	5	2	0	1	0	2	0	5	0	2	2	64%	0.50722785	14	8191	978	822	165
2.8.1	29/9/2018	9/10/2018	10	3	1	2	1	3	2	1	4	0	2	47%	0.34999564	13	2722	326	274	55
2.8.0	[illegible]	[illegible]	[illegible]	[illegible]	[illegible]	[illegible]	[illegible]	[illegible]	[illegible]	[illegible]	[illegible]	[illegible]	[illegible]	[illegible]	[illegible]	[illegible]	[illegible]	[illegible]	[illegible]	[illegible]

Fig.2. Conjunto de datos usados para estudio piloto.

7 Trabajo Futuro

El desarrollo de software lo realizan seres humanos. El factor humano tiene sentimientos y lleva a ser un componente con un impacto significativo en varias cuestiones relacionadas con el desarrollo de software y puede afectar a la calidad, la productividad y el rendimiento de los desarrolladores. La calidad del software se mide para encontrar errores y problemas de software en la fase de desarrollo. Por lo tanto, la falta de esta puede desencadenar graves consecuencias para un software. En esta investigación argumentamos que es importante extraer los sentimientos de los *commits messages* y las métricas de calidad del software durante la fase de desarrollo de un proyecto de software. Como un componente significativo del programa doctoral y la investigación relacionada, informamos sobre un primer paso para extraer los sentimientos negativos de los mensajes de compromiso GitHub, junto con las métricas de calidad de SonarQube, que inicialmente dan como resultado una posible relación. Diseñamos una herramienta y la evaluamos su utilidad con seis estudios preliminares. Nuestros resultados son prometedores. La herramienta extrajo un conjunto de datos como paso inicial para continuar con la investigación doctoral. El trabajo futuro estará orientado a replicarlo con una mayor cantidad de proyectos software y variables adicionales utilizando diferentes enfoques, con el fin de obtener un análisis, comprensión y relación más profunda de los factores que afectan a las emociones de los desarrolladores y, a su vez, a la calidad del código en el ciclo de vida de un proyecto de software. Por consiguiente, utilizarse para diseñar medidas y modelos que ayuden a identificar a los factores que afectan a los desarrolladores y a la calidad del código y disminuir la cantidad de proyectos con niveles de toxicidad y sentimientos negativos.

Referencias

1. Novielli N, Calefato F, Lanubile F (2018) A gold standard for emotion annotation in stack overflow. Proc - Int Conf Softw Eng 14–17. https://doi.org/10.1145/3196398.3196453
2. Guzman E, Azócar D, Li Y (2014) Sentiment analysis of commit comments in GitHub: An empirical study. 11th Work Conf Min Softw Repos MSR 2014 - Proc 352–355. https://doi.org/10.1145/2597073.2597118
3. Murgia A, Tourani P, Adams B, Ortu M (2014) Do developers feel emotions? An exploratory analysis of emotions in software artifacts. 11th Work Conf Min Softw Repos MSR 2014 - Proc 262–271. https://doi.org/10.1145/2597073.2597086
4. Ding J, Sun H, Wang X, Liu X (2018) Entity-level sentiment analysis of issue comments. Proc - Int Conf Softw Eng 7–13. https://doi.org/10.1145/3194932.3194935
5. Cheruvelil J, Da Silva BC (2019) Developers' sentiment and issue reopening. Proc - 2019 IEEE/ACM 4th Int Work Emot Aware Softw Eng SEmotion 2019 29–33. https://doi.org/10.1109/SEmotion.2019.00013
6. Sinha V, Lazar A, Sharif B (2016) Analyzing developer sentiment in commit logs. Proc - 13th Work Conf Min Softw Repos MSR 2016 520–523. https://doi.org/10.1145/2901739.2903501
7. Pang B, Lee L (2008) Opinion Mining and Sentiment Analysis. Found Trends Inf Retr 2:1–135. https://doi.org/10.1561/1500000011
8. Boehm BW (1988) A Spiral Model of Software Development and Enhancement. Computer (Long Beach Calif) 21:61–72. https://doi.org/10.1109/2.59
9. Rezvani A, Khosravi P (2019) Emotional intelligence: The key to mitigating stress and fostering trust among software developers working on information system projects. Int J Inf Manage 48:139–150. https://doi.org/10.1016/j.ijinfomgt.2019.02.007
10. Singh N, Singh P (2018) How Do Code Refactoring Activities Impact Software Developers' Sentiments? - An Empirical Investigation into GitHub Commits. Proc - Asia-Pacific Softw Eng Conf APSEC 2017–Decem:648–653. https://doi.org/10.1109/APSEC.2017.79
11. Asri I El, Kerzazi N, Uddin G, et al (2019) An empirical study of sentiments in code reviews. Inf Softw Technol 114:37–54. https://doi.org/10.1016/j.infsof.2019.06.005
12. Hancock PA, Szalma JL (2008) Performance under stress. Perform Under Stress 1–389. https://doi.org/10.21139/wej.2017.013
13. Borges H, Hora A, Valente MT (2016) Predicting the popularity of GitHub repositories. ACM Int Conf Proceeding Ser. https://doi.org/10.1145/2972958.2972966
14. Al Mamun MA, Berger C, Hansson J (2017) Correlations of software code metrics: An empirical study. ACM Int Conf Proceeding Ser Part F1319:255–266. https://doi.org/10.1145/3143434.3143445
15. Votano J, Parham M, Hall L (2013) Understanding Affect in the Workshpace via Social Media. CSCW '13 Proc 2013 Conf Comput Support Coop Work 303–315
16. Novielli N, Girardi D, Lanubile F (2018) A benchmark study on sentiment analysis for software engineering research. Proc - Int Conf Softw Eng 364–375. https://doi.org/10.1145/3196398.3196403
17. Souza R, Silva B (2017) Sentiment Analysis of Travis CI Builds. IEEE Int Work Conf Min Softw Repos 459–462. https://doi.org/10.1109/MSR.2017.27
18. Ortu M, Murgia A, Destefanis G, et al (2016) The emotional side of software developers in JIRA. Proc - 13th Work Conf Min Softw Repos MSR 2016 480–483.

https://doi.org/10.1145/2901739.2903505
19. Kuutila M, Mäntylä M V., Claes M, et al (2018) Using experience sampling to link software repositories with emotions and work well-being. Int Symp Empir Softw Eng Meas. https://doi.org/10.1145/3239235.3239245
20. Kaur A, Singh AP, Dhillon GS, Bisht D (2018) Emotion Mining and Sentiment Analysis in Software Engineering Domain. Proc 2nd Int Conf Electron Commun Aerosp Technol ICECA 2018 1170–1173. https://doi.org/10.1109/ICECA.2018.8474619
21. Bharti S, Singh H (2019) Investigating developers' sentiments associated with software cloning practices. Springer Singapore
22. Pletea D, Vasilescu B, Serebrenik A (2014) Security and emotion: Sentiment analysis of security discussions on GitHub. 11th Work Conf Min Softw Repos MSR 2014 - Proc 348–351. https://doi.org/10.1145/2597073.2597117
23. Jongeling R, Sarkar P, Datta S, Serebrenik A (2017) On negative results when using sentiment analysis tools for software engineering research. Empir Softw Eng 22:2543–2584. https://doi.org/10.1007/s10664-016-9493-x
24. Sun K Exploiting the Unique Expression for Improved Sentiment Analysis in Software Engineering Text
25. Lin B, Zampetti F, Bavota G, et al (2018) Sentiment Analysis for Software Engineer-ing: How Far Can We Go. DlAcmOrg 94–104
26. Novielli N, Calefato F, Lanubile F (2014) Towards discovering the role of emotions in stack overflow. 6th Int Work Soc Softw Eng SSE 2014 - Proc 33–36. https://doi.org/10.1145/2661685.2661689
27. Wilson J, Hernández-Hall C (2014) VADER: A Parsimonious Rule-based Model for Sentiment Analysis of Social Media Text. Eighth Int AAAI Conf Weblogs Soc Media 18
28. Socher R, Perelygin A, Wu JY, et al (2013) Recursive deep models for semantic compositionality over a sentiment treebank. EMNLP 2013 - 2013 Conf Empir Methods Nat Lang Process Proc Conf 1631–1642
29. Howard MJ, Gupta S, Pollock L, Vijay-Shanker K (2013) Automatically mining software-based, semantically-similar words from comment-code mappings. IEEE Int Work Conf Min Softw Repos 377–386. https://doi.org/10.1109/MSR.2013.6624052
30. Behnamghader P, Alfayez R, Srisopha K, Boehm B (2017) Towards better understanding of software quality evolution through commit-impact analysis. Proc - 2017 IEEE Int Conf Softw Qual Reliab Secur QRS 2017 251–262. https://doi.org/10.1109/QRS.2017.36
31. Sayago-heredia J, Pérez-castillo R, Piattini M (2021) A Systematic Mapping Study on Analysis of Code Repositories. 0:1–42
32. Li L, Goethals F, Baesens B, Snoeck M (2017) Predicting software revision outcomes on GitHub using structural holes theory. Comput Networks 114:114–124. https://doi.org/10.1016/j.comnet.2016.08.024
33. Lenarduzzi V, Lomio F, Huttunen H, Taibi D (2020) Are SonarQube Rules Inducing Bugs? SANER 2020 - Proc 2020 IEEE 27th Int Conf Softw Anal Evol Reengineering 501–511. https://doi.org/10.1109/SANER48275.2020.9054821
34. Ahmed Z, Amizadeh S, Bilenko M, et al (2019) Machine learning at microsoft with ML.NET. arXiv 2448–2458
35. Sistema I, Pomoću P, Net ML (2019) DEVELOPMENT OF RECOMMENDER SYSTEMS USING ML . NET

Process mining and data mining integration frameworks for evidence-based business intelligence: a systematic review

Martín Rubio, Andrea Delgado, and Libertad Tansini

Instituto de Computación, Facultad de Ingeniería,Universidad de la República
{dario.rubio,adelgado,libertad}@fing.edu.uy

Resumen In the last decades there has been a democratization of the use of Information Systems promoting the digitalization of organizations and society in general. These systems support data management needs and allow organizations to model and automate their process and data to fulfill their purposes. Large volumes of heterogeneous data are being constantly produced and made available, but in order to be able to transform data into valuable information and knowledge, data science techniques including approaches such as data mining and process mining must be used. These approaches are usually considered independently, concealing relations between processes and organizational data that would help discovering improvement opportunities for organizations. We explored existing proposals of data mining and process mining joint application We carried out the search in IEEE Xplore, Springer, Scopus and Science Direct sources covering the period from 2000 to 2020. We initially retrieved 2.868 papers resulting in 10 primary studies selected for analysis. We used five categories for the analysis: (i) type of proposal, (ii) type of algorithms, (iii) data integration, (iv) mining approach, and (v) data quality. As key contributions of our SLR we can highlight the little progress in integrating both approaches, and the lack of comprehensive proposals to guide organizations on evidence-based business intelligence.

Keywords: Process mining · Data mining · Systematic review.

1. Introducción

En las últimas décadas se ha producido una democratización del uso de sistemas de información que dio lugar a la digitalización de las organizaciones y de la sociedad en general. Estos sistemas se encargan de cubrir las necesidades apoyando a la gestión de los datos que permiten a las organizaciones modelar su realidad y cumplir con sus propósitos. Constantemente se producen y se ponen a disposición grandes volúmenes de datos heterogéneos, pero para poder transformar los datos en información y conocimiento valiosos, se deben utilizar técnicas de Ciencia de Datos [1,11] (Data Science) que incluyan enfoques como la minería de datos [10] (data mining) y la minería de procesos [1] (process mining). Estos enfoques generalmente se consideran de manera independiente, ocultando relaciones entre procesos y datos organizacionales que ayudarían a descubrir oportunidades de mejora para las organizaciones. La Ciencia de Datos [11,1] es una disciplina conformada interdisciplinariamente que ha emergido en los últimos años como respuesta a la problemática de la gestión, análisis y descubrimiento de información en grandes volúmenes de datos, generados a gran velocidad y con gran variedad (las tres V) [8] considerando también la veracidad [17]. Entre las disciplinas que componen a la Ciencia de Datos se encuentran la minería de datos [10] y la minería de procesos [1], elementos de inteligencia de negocio [1,9] (business intelligence) para proveer soporte a las organizaciones en la toma de decisiones basada en evidencia.

La minería de datos [10] es una disciplina madura y consolidada que busca analizar grandes volúmenes de datos buscando reglas generales y patrones de comportamiento, así como proveer predicciones con base en los datos de entrada. Los modelos de aprendizaje utilizados pueden ser supervisados (existe un conjunto de datos etiquetados del cual aprender las respuestas correctas) o no supervisados (no existen dichas etiquetas). Las técnicas de minería de datos son clasificadas como descriptivas i.e. describen el conjunto de datos bajo análisis, o predictivas i.e. proveen predicciones sobre nuevos datos con base en datos existentes. El foco de la minería de datos ha sido tradicionalmente los datos organizacionales gestionados en sus sistemas informáticos de soporte.

Por otro lado, la minería de procesos [1] es una disciplina relativamente reciente que utiliza técnicas de minería de datos y otras, desde una perspectiva de procesos esto es, aplicada a datos de ejecución de procesos para descubrir por ejemplo los modelos de procesos asociados. Un proceso de negocio es un conjunto de actividades o tareas que son llevadas a cabo por las organizaciones en un entorno organizacional y técnico, para cumplir con sus objetivos [22]. El objetivo también es extraer conocimiento a partir de los datos, pero utilizando como fuente de datos las trazas generadas por la ejecución de los procesos en su entorno operativo. La minería de procesos provee tres enfoques de análisis: i) descubrimiento de modelos i.e. desde las trazas de ejecución (instancias) del proceso; ii) conformidad de modelos i.e. chequear relación entre modelos y trazas de ejecución; y iii) enriquecimiento (enhance) los modelos i.e. agregando información como análisis de performance de la ejecución de los procesos, cuellos de botella, duración de las instancias, promedios, etc.

La minería de procesos y la minería de datos suelen ser consideradas en forma aislada una de la otra, aplicándose en forma independiente y con objetivos finales disjuntos. Sin embargo, tanto las trazas de procesos como los datos organizacionales generados por los sistemas tienen una alta correlación, pertenecen a un mismo contexto operativo que refleja la realidad de las organizaciones, por este motivo resulta de gran importancia contar con herramientas que permitan analizar los datos desde ambas perspectivas en forma conjunta. Por ejemplo, con una visión complementaria se podrían extraer los diferentes tipos de trazas a partir de técnicas tradicionales de minería de procesos y luego mediante minería de datos analizar los datos organizacionales relacionados a cada traza. A la inversa, se podría partir de un análisis de los datos organizacionales utilizando minería de datos, y luego obtener cuales son las trazas que se relacionan con esos datos para estudiarlos con técnicas de minería de procesos.

En este trabajo, exploramos propuestas existentes en las que los enfoques de minería de datos y minería de procesos se tratan de forma integrada. La propuesta general de trabajo en que se enmarca la revisión sistemática presentada, tiene como objetivo la definición de un framework de Ciencia de Datos Organizacional denominado PRICED (for Process and Data sCience for oRganIzational improvEment) que fue posicionado en [6]. El framework integra minería de procesos y minería de datos, técnicas y algoritmos para el análisis de datos integrados de la ejecución de procesos y datos organizacionales, y herramientas, para proveer soporte a la mejora basada en evidencia en las organizaciones.

El resto del documento se organiza como sigue: en la Sección 2 se presentan conceptos clave, en la Sección 3 se describe el proceso de revisión y el protocolo definido. En la Sección 4 se realiza un análisis de los resultados obtenidos y en la Sección 5 se describen las amenazas a la validez. Finalmente en la Sección 6 se presentan las conclusiones.

2. Marco teórico

A continuación se introducen brevemente la minería de datos y la minería de procesos, que son las áreas de Ciencia de Datos en que se centra esta revisión.

2.1. Minería de datos

La minería de datos [10] proviene de una comunidad fuertemente ligada a las bases de datos, que busca extraer información desconocida a partir de grandes volúmenes de datos. Existen varias herramientas que ofrecen diversos algoritmos de minería de datos comoWeka [1] y RapidMiner[2]. Las técnicas de minería de datos se clasifican en descriptivas o predictivas.

Técnicas descriptivas Buscan relaciones que permitan caracterizar el conjunto de datos que se está analizando. Mediante la identificación de patrones que explican o resumen los datos, de esta manera se extraen propiedades de los datos para un posterior análisis. Una de las técnicas más utilizadas es el agrupamiento (clustering) donde se busca agrupar los datos de manera de obtener conjuntos que minimizan la distancia intra-conjuntos y maximizan la distancia inter-conjuntos, es decir conjuntos de datos similares según algún criterio establecido. Existen diversos algoritmos de agrupamiento siendo uno de los más populares el K-Means. Otro ejemplo de modelos descriptivos son los obtenidos con las reglas de asociación, donde se buscan dependencias y relaciones sobre atributos nominales.

[1] https://www.cs.waikato.ac.nz/ml/weka/
[2] https://rapidminer.com/

Técnicas predictivas Permiten crear modelos a partir de un conjunto de datos capaces de predecir resultados o comportamientos frente a nuevos casos. Entre las técnicas predictivas se destacan la clasificación y la regresión. En clasificación se busca crear modelos predictivos que permitan clasificar un conjunto de datos en clases discretas conocidas y los modelos de regresión buscan predecir un valor no discreto por ejemplo un número real. En clasificación se utilizan algoritmos de aprendizaje automático como árboles de decisión, redes neuronales, máquinas de soporte vectorial (support vector machine), K-vecinos más cercanos (K-nearest neighbours), entre otros. Por otro lado las metodologías de regresión permiten obtener modelos que predicen valores continuos, por ejemplo el precio de un inmueble según metros cuadrados.

2.2. Minería de procesos

La minería de procesos [1] surge en comunidades ligadas a procesos, donde se usan elementos de minería de datos para analizar datos más específicos de la ejecución de los procesos. Existen varias herramientas que implementan diversos algoritmos de minería de procesos, como ProM[3], Disco[4] y Celonis[5]. El principal insumo para la minería de procesos es el log de eventos (event log) de la ejecución de los distintos procesos. Un log de eventos corresponde a un sólo proceso y se compone de casos (instancias o trazas) únicos y cada caso se compone a su vez de una secuencia de eventos. Los eventos dentro de un log deben estar ordenados cronológicamente y además cada evento cumple con las siguientes propiedades: i) cada evento refiere a una única actividad ii) cada evento pertenece a un único caso iii) cada evento tiene asociado un recurso que lo originóy iv) cada evento tiene una marca de tiempo (timestamp) asociada a su ejecución.

Partiendo de estos logs de eventos se utiliza la minería de procesos [1] para descubrir conocimiento, con tres enfoques: descubrimiento (discovery), conformidad (conformance) y enriquecimiento (enhancement).

- **Descubrimiento**: a partir de las trazas en el log de eventos se infiere de forma automática un modelo que represente dichas ejecuciones, por ejemplo un modelo especificado en una red de Petri[15] o BPMN[16]. Existe una variedad de algoritmos de descubrimiento con distintos enfoques (heurísticas, algoritmos evolutivos, etc.) y que han sido mejorados y extendidos en las últimas décadas [2].
- **Conformidad**: Estas técnicas permiten comparar un modelo de proceso (descubierto, existente) contra la ejecución real en el log de eventos. Mediante distintos enfoques (ej. replay del log de eventos sobre el modelo, alineación de segmentos) permite conocer la concordancia entre el modelo y la ejecución, con indicadores como adecuación y precisión.
- **Enriquecimiento**: El objetivo es extender o mejorar un proceso utilizando la información de las trazas. Por ejemplo, utilizando las marcas de tiempo

[3] http://www.promtools.org/
[4] https://fluxicon.com/disco/
[5] https://www.celonis.com/

se puede conocer cuales son las actividades que toman más tiempo y que pueden significar un cuello de botella. También se pueden descubrir patrones de interacción entre las personas o recursos que realizan las actividades.

2.3. Evaluación de la calidad de los modelos

Tanto en minería de datos como en minería de procesos es necesario evaluar la calidad de los resultados obtenidos. Dependiendo del tipo de modelo existen diferentes medidas de evaluación que permiten conocer características de interés.

En minería de datos, para tareas de clasificación medidas habituales son la ***precisión*** [10] y ***cobertura (recall)***. La precisión se calcula como el número total de instancias del conjunto de pruebas clasificadas correctamente dividido el número total de instancias del conjunto de pruebas clasificadas como positivas. La cobertura (recall) se define como el número de instancias a las que una regla se aplica y predice correctamente. Para las técnicas de regresión, la evaluación más habitual es mediante el error cuadrático del valor predicho frente al valor esperado. En tareas de agrupamiento, las medidas suelen considerar la separación inter-grupos y la cercanía intra-grupos.

En minería de procesos son cuatro los criterios de evaluación que se utilizan habitualmente: ***adecuación (fitness o recall)***, ***simplicidad (simplicity)***, ***precisión (precision)*** y ***generalización (generalization)*** [1]. La adecuación de un modelo, es la capacidad de poder reproducir el comportamiento observado en el log de eventos. La simplicidad, busca representar el nivel de simplicidad del modelo. La precisión, es la capacidad de ajustarse sólo a las instancias similares a las presentes en los logs. La generalización mide la capacidad de generalizar el comportamiento al soportar ejemplos nuevos no presentes en los logs utilizados para obtener los modelos. Si solo se permite el comportamiento observado está sobre-ajustado (overfitting), o sub-ajustado (underfitting) si permite mucho más comportamiento sin real soporte. Esto también se observa en minería de datos.

3. Procedimiento de la revisión

El procedimiento de revisión sistemática seguido se basa en los lineamientos propuestos por Kitchenham [12][13], donde se propone una metodología que consta de tres grandes etapas: planificación, ejecución y análisis. A continuación se presentan las etapas de planificación y ejecución, mientras que el análisis y descripción de resultados se realiza en la sección 4.

3.1. Planificación

En esta fase de la metodología se definen los lineamientos generales de la revisión, como son la formulación de la pregunta de investigación y la definición de los criterios de inclusión y de exclusión para determinar los estudios primarios. También en esta etapa se definen las fuentes que se utilizarán para realizar las búsquedas y el periodo de tiempo para el cual se realizarán las búsquedas. La necesidad de la revisión sistemática se identifica en el contexto de la definición del framework en desarrollo, que fue delineado en [6]. El resultado de esta revisión permite identificar elementos clave en la integración de la minería de procesos y la minería de datos a ser considerados en el framework.

Pregunta de investigación Una de las actividades más importantes en una revisión sistemática es la formulación de la pregunta de investigación [12]. Por este motivo, la pregunta de investigación busca representar el objetivo de investigación que involucra el presente estudio, y se define como:

¿Qué propuestas de frameworks y/o enfoques de aplicación integrada de minería de procesos y minería de datos existen para brindar soporte al análisis de datos e inteligencia del negocio basada en evidencia en las organizaciones?

Partiendo de la pregunta de investigación, se diseñó la cadena de búsqueda de forma de obtener la mayor cantidad de resultados, si bien esto puede generar falsos positivos se reduce la posibilidad de no tener en cuenta estudios relevantes. Para esto se realizó un proceso iterativo, donde en cada etapa se buscó refinar y evaluar la cadena ejecutada en las distintas fuentes. Para la evaluación de estas etapas se utilizaron algunos estudios conocidos por los autores como grupo de control, y de esta forma medir la performance de la búsqueda en cada iteración. Se utilizaron los términos específicos de minería de procesos y minería de datos y no agregamos Ciencia de Datos o inteligencia de negocio ya que éstos últimos actúan de "paraguas" incluyendo otras disciplinas que no interesan en el contexto de esta revisión y aumentarían innecesariamente la cantidad de resultados no relacionados. La cadena de búsqueda fue definida como:

"process mining" AND "data mining" AND ("business process" OR "business process management") AND framework

Las palabras clave "business process" y "business process management" fueron incluidas ya que únicamente son de interés los enfoques de minería de datos que aplican o incluyen datos de procesos de negocio, no así los enfoques tradicionales que operan únicamente sobre datos organizacionales. El término framework se incluye en la cadena de búsqueda para enfocar los resultados en ese sentido, pero resultados que presenten propuestas menos abarcativas o no completamente definidos no son excluidos, por ejemplo con foco metodológico.

Criterios de inclusión y exclusión Los criterios de inclusión definidos incluyen: i) estudios posteriores al año 2000; ii) estudios escritos en inglés; iii) estudios con aplicación integrada de minería de datos y minería de procesos (frameworks, metodologías). Los criterios de exclusión definidos incluyen: i) estudios que sólo tratan sobre minería de procesos o sólo tratan sobre minería de datos; ii) estudios no accesibles en formato digital.En la Tabla 1 se presentan los criterios de inclusión y exclusión definidos.

Tabla 1: Criterios de inclusión y exclusión

Criterios de Inclusión	Criterios de Exclusión
Estudios con aplicación integrada de minería de datos y minería de procesos	Estudios que solo tratan de minería de procesos o solo de minería de datos
Estudios escritos en Inglés	Estudios no accesibles en formato digital
Estudios posteriores al año 2000	

Fuentes y período de búsqueda Para la revisión se utilizaron cinco fuentes principales de artículos científicos que permiten acceso web a los mismos, seleccionadas entre las fuentes generalmente utilizadas y su accesibilidad. Estas fuentes fueron seleccionadas en base a su cubrimiento de publicaciones internacionales tanto de conferencias como revistas de primer nivel en el área: Springer, IEEE Xplore, Scopus, y Science direct, que se muestran en la Tabla 2.

Tabla 2: Fuentes de búsqueda

Fuente	**Sitio web**
Springer	http://www.springer.com/
IEEE Xplore	https://ieeexplore.ieee.org/
Scopus	http://www.scopus.com/
Science Direct	http://www.sciencedirect.com/

Las búsquedas se realizaron durante los meses de noviembre y diciembre de 2019 cubriendo el período 2000 a 2019, al inicio del trabajo de investigación para analizar el estado del arte en la temática. En marzo de 2021 se actualizaron las búsquedas con el fin de renovar los resultados y contrastar avances.

3.2. Ejecución

La ejecución de la revisión consistió en llevar a cabo las etapas descriptas, lo que se describe a continuación.

Proceso de selección de estudios En la primer etapa de recuperación se ejecutaron las consultas en las diferentes fuentes, realizando las adaptaciones necesarias, obteniendo inicialmente 2868 artículos. En segundo lugar, el primer autor procedió a la lectura de títulos, resúmenes y palabras clave de cada uno para aplicar los criterios de inclusión/exclusión definidos, y descartar duplicados, resultando en un total de 32 estudios seleccionados, cuya selección fue confirmada por los otros dos autores independientemente.

En una tercera etapa los tres autores llevaron a cabo la lectura detallada de los estudios aplicando los criterios de inclusión/exclusión al texto de los artículos relevantes. En esta última etapa se descartaron 22 estudios obteniendo como resultado de la revisión 10 estudios primarios que contestan la pregunta de investigación planteada. En la tabla 3 se muestran las cantidades de estudios obtenidas en cada fuente seleccionada, relevantes y primarios.

Tabla 3: Resultados obtenidos en las distintas fuentes

Fuente	**Encontrados**	**Relevantes**	**Primarios**
Springer	859	15	7
IEEE Xplore	40	0	0
Scopus	1798	12	2
Science Direct	171	5	1
Total	2868	32	10

El criterio de exclusión por el cual se descartaron mas estudios fue el enfoque, donde se descartó un total de 9 estudios relevantes. Luego se descartaron 6 estudios porque solo trataban a la minería de procesos, seguido de 5 estudios debido a que solo trataban a la minería de datos. Los restantes dos documentos descartados se debieron a que no estaban accesible en las fuentes utilizadas.

4. Análisis de resultados

En esta sección se presentan los resultados obtenidos, en primer lugar la descripción general y en segundo lugar las categorías analizadas. En la Tabla 4 se presentan los estudios primarios y sus referencias en el marco de su análisis.

Descripción de resultados Las consultas realizadas en las fuentes retornaron un total de 2868 artículos, incluyendo artículos duplicados, de los cuales se identificaron los 10 estudios primarios que se presentan en esta sección. A pesar de cubrir el período 2000 a 2020 con las búsquedas realizadas, los estudios relevantes seleccionados inician a partir del año 2008. En la Figura 1 se presentan los estudios primarios por año de publicación.

La baja cantidad de trabajos primarios integrando las dos áreas confirma lo reciente de la integración de las disciplinas de minería de datos tradicional con la más nueva minería de procesos, siendo un área de investigación incipiente.

Análisis de los estudios primarios Los estudios primarios obtenidos fueron analizados desde cinco perspectivas que surgen a partir del contenido de las propuestas. Estas categorías son: los tipos de propuestas (framework, metodología), la presencia y origen de los algoritmos utilizados (minería de procesos, minería de datos), la integración de los datos utilizados (log de eventos, datos organizacionales), tipo de minería (Descriptiva, predictiva) y aspectos relacionados a la

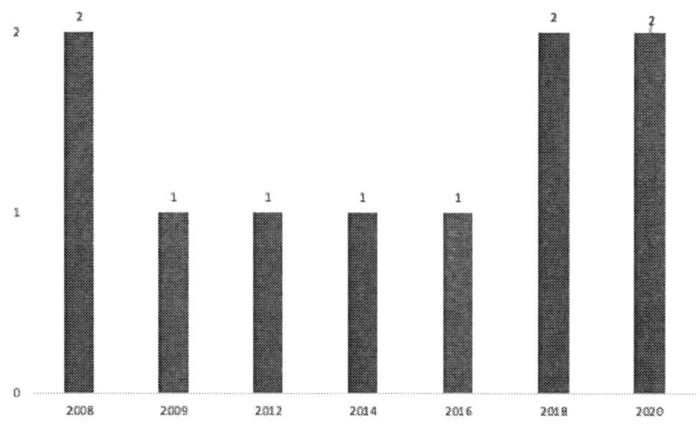

Figura 1: Años de publicación de los estudios primarios

calidad de datos en los enfoques de minería utilizados. En la Tabla 4 se presentan los estudios primarios y su aporte en cada una de las categorías analizadas.

4.1. Tipo de propuesta

Las propuestas de tipo metodológico pueden ser más concretas y específicas para algún tipo de escenario particular, donde puede enfocarse sólo en algunos aspectos del ciclo de vida de los procesos y datos. Tanto en [20] como en la primera parte de la metodología planteada en [7] el foco está centrado en logs de eventos de los procesos, con foco en agrupamiento de trazas. Con otra perspectiva [5] utiliza algunos datos del contexto e información de procesos para crear un modelo de estimación de calidad. En esta propuesta se presenta una primera etapa donde crean modelos que permiten predecir qué camino tomara una instancia en ejecución. Por otra parte [14] utiliza técnicas propias de data mining aplicadas directamente sobre logs de eventos de procesos, vinculado al ámbito de datos provenientes de una institución educativa.

Las propuestas que presentan frameworks tienen un planteamiento más abarcativo y profundo, donde puede ser considerado el contexto de donde provienen los datos, se toma en cuenta todo el ciclo de vida de los procesos y datos o se proponen generalizaciones que permiten aplicarlo en diferentes entornos. En [21] se propone un framework para monitoreo de procesos en tiempo real, para esto se combinan técnicas de minería de textos y clasificación. También con el objetivo de analizar procesos en tiempo real, la propuesta de [19] busca detectar desviaciones en flujos de eventos. Por otro lado, en [3] se presenta un framework para poder predecir la performance de procesos en cuanto al tiempo de ejecución y la cantidad de actividades que se ejecutaran en el mismo. En [24] se presenta un framework con lineamientos para obtener agrupamiento de trazas basados en atributos de los procesos. En [18] se presentan lineamientos con el fin integrar datos operacionales y el log de eventos de procesos de forma manual o semi-automática. También se pueden encontrar propuestas genéricas donde no importa el escenario concreto, por ejemplo [4] busca ampliar el espectro de algoritmos que se utilizan tradicionalmente partiendo de la estructura XML en las que los logs se almacenan comúnmente.

Tabla 4: Análisis de estudios primarios

Estudio	Propuesta		Algoritmos		Integración		Minería		Calidad
	F	M	PM	DM	Logs	Datos	D	P	
van Zelst et. al. [24]	●		●	●	●	●	●		
Križanić, S. [14]		●		●	●	●	●		●
Roudjane et al. [19]	●			●	●			●	
Ezpeleta et al. [7]		●		●	●		●	●	
Teinemaa et al.[21]	●			●	●	●		●	
Bevacqua et al. [3]	●			●	●	●	●	●	
Bui et al. [4]	●			●	●				●
Song et al. [20]		●	●	●	●		●		
Radeschütz et al.[18]	●				●	●			
Cardoso J. [5]		●		●	●	●	●	●	

4.2. Algoritmos

En cuanto a los algoritmos utilizados en las propuestas se categorizaron de forma de establecer si los mismos provienen de la minería de datos o de la minería de procesos. En esta categorización se encontró que la mayoría de los trabajos que explicita el uso de algún algoritmo, utiliza algoritmos que provienen de la minería de datos [14], [19], [7], [21], [3], [4], [20], [5], [24], aplicados a logs de eventos de procesos. Principalmente se destaca el uso de clustering y mayormente se utilizan variantes de K-Means con el objetivo de obtener conjunto de trazas para facilitar su posterior estudio.

En [14] luegò de obtener clusters utilizando K-Means aplican árboles de decisión para cada cluster con el objetivo de obtener una representación que permita un estudio más profundo de los datos. En [24] y [20] se hace mención además a algoritmos de minería de procesos, particularmente a algoritmos de descubrimiento . En ambos se descubren los modelos de procesos asociados a cada cluster de trazas para comparar su comportamiento a la luz del atributo seleccionado, en el segundo se aplica el algoritmo de minería heurística (heuristic miner).

4.3. Integración de datos

Los datos toman un rol primario tanto en minería de procesos como en minería de datos, ambos enfoques se basan en la utilización de datos de procesos y/u organizacionales por lo que un aspecto importante en la aplicación de ambas minerías es buscar la forma en que se integran los datos utilizados.Como tercera forma de análisis de los estudios primarios se consideró la fuente de datos utilizada y el nivel de integración de los datos asociados a los procesos, los datos asociados al proceso y al negocio en sí i.e. organizacionales.

Los estudios [4], [7], [19], [20] sólo consideran como fuente de datos a los logs de eventos de procesos, en cambio [3], [5], [14], [18], [21], [24] consideran en algún aspecto algunos datos asociados al contexto operacional (organizacionales). Cabe destacar que estos datos organizacionales suelen estar limitados a variables utilizadas en los procesos en sí, no considerándose en profundidad la información de negocio presente en otros sistemas. En contraposición, en [18] proponen diversas alternativas para la integración de datos organizacionales con los datos de procesos. En dicha propuesta se muestran alternativas manuales y semi-automáticas que permiten realizar esta tarea con el objetivo de integrar los datos para ser incorporados en un datawarehouse.

4.4. Tipo de minería

Los estudios se clasificaron según el principal enfoque de minería que utilizan: minería descriptiva y minería predictiva.

Las propuestas de minería descriptiva buscan el agrupamiento de trazas para facilitar y mejorar el análisis de los procesos. La mayoría de las aplicaciones de minería de procesos sobre logs de eventos se realizan para el descubrimiento modelos. Las técnicas utilizadas muchas veces dan como resultado lo que se denomina procesos spaghetti, con gran cantidad de nodos y relaciones que dificulta su interpretación y extracción de conocimiento. Este problema no sólo afecta a los resultados en el descubrimiento, sino que también en las aplicaciones enfocadas en la conformidad y mejora de procesos. Las propuestas en esta categoría toman logs de eventos de procesos y sus datos asociados, y buscan agruparlos de forma de obtener conjuntos más pequeños de trazas homogéneas, según algún criterio (i.e. atributo, como comportamiento, algún dato particular, etc), que faciliten el entendimiento y obtención de resultados. En este concepto se basan seis de los estudios primarios [3], [5], [7], [14], [20] y [24]

En este caso las propuestas utilizan la información existente para obtener modelos que permitan predecir el comportamiento frente a una nueva ejecución. Las predicciones se dividen en dos tipos, por un lado se busca predecir cuál será el camino o flujo que tomara un proceso y por otro la predicción de la performance que tendrá el mismo. Conocer qué camino dentro de un modelo tomará un proceso en momentos tempranos de su ejecución significa un gran valor para la toma de decisiones, permite evitar activamente cuellos de botella o anticiparse a situaciones antes de que estas sucedan. En este concepto se basan los estudios [7], [19] y [21]. De la misma manera que se puede predecir el camino que tomara una ejecución, se pueden crear modelos que permitan predecir el desempeño por ejemplo a nivel de costo o tiempo. En las propuestas [3], [21], [5], [19], [7] presentan diferentes técnicas que permiten llevar a cabo esta tarea.

4.5. Calidad de datos

Como se menciona en la sección anterior, los datos cumplen un rol fundamental en cualquier esfuerzo de minería para obtener información de interés para la organización. A la hora de trabajar con datos es clave que tengan características de calidad deseable, y para conocer la calidad de los mismos es necesario aplicar análisis de calidad de datos. Por tal motivo se buscó en los estudios relevantes la presencia de lineamientos en este sentido. Sólo en [4] y en [14] se explicita como parte del framework propuesto una etapa de pre-procesamiento donde puede considerarse el estudio de la calidad. En los otros estudios se asume que los datos cuentan con una calidad aceptable como para realizar los diferentes procesamientos y análisis, y no se explicita como, cuando y de qué tipo deberían ser los análisis de calidad de datos en la aplicación de las propuestas.

5. Amenazas a la validez

En esta sección presentamos las amenazas a la validez según [23]: construcción, interna, conclusión y externa.

Como amenaza a la validez de construcción la selección de fuentes o la cadena de búsqueda pueden no recuperar todos los artículos relevantes. Para minimizarlas, seleccionamos fuentes reconocidas en base a su cubrimiento de publicaciones internacionales tanto de conferencias como revistas de primer nivel en el área, y optamos por una cadena de búsqueda que maximizara la inclusión de artículos utilizando minería de procesos y minería de datos como términos clave incluyendo procesos de negocio como foco. Se realizaron búsquedas exploratorias en las fuentes y discusión entre los autores para ajustes previos.

La validez interna tiene como amenaza la reproducibilidad y el sesgo en la selección de estudios. Para minimizarlas el protocolo fue claramente especificado incluyendo las fuentes, la cadena de búsqueda y los criterios de inclusión / exclusión, y los resultados fueron discutidos entre los autores en cada etapa, para prevenir posible sesgo en la selección.

Como amenaza a la validez externa la cantidad y relevancia de los estudios seleccionados puede afectar la generalización de resultados. Para minimizar esta esta amenaza los artículos fueron seleccionados mediante los criterios de inclusión/exclusión definidos en el protocolo y discusiones entre los autores. Si bien la cantidad de artículos seleccionados en comparación a los recuperados puede parecer baja, el foco de la revisión está en la aplicación conjunta de minería de procesos y minería de datos, que es un área incipiente de investigación, por lo que consideramos que los resultados presentados representan el estado actual en nuestro mayor conocimiento. De todas formas podrían haber artículos no publicados o indexados al momento de las búsquedas que no estén incluidos.

La validez de las conclusiones se ve amenazada por la dependencia del punto de vista de los autores realizando la revisión. Para minimizar esta amenaza, la información recuperada de los artículos analizados es la indicada en cada propuesta y si en la extracción en las categorías identificadas había distintas visiones estas fueron discutidas entre los autores.

6. Conclusiones

En el presente trabajo se realizo un relevamiento de los artículos existentes que tienen como foco a la minería de procesos y a la minería de datos. El mismo fue realizado en forma de revisión sistemática y tuvo como resultado 32 estudios relevantes de los cuales 10 fueron seleccionados como estudios primarios. El estudio se centró en trabajos que proponían o mostraban ambos enfoques en forma complementaria e integrada. Según los resultados obtenidos, no hay un número importante de artículos publicados en la actualidad, registrándose entre uno o dos por año, lo cual confirma lo incipiente de la investigación el área.

En cuanto al contenido específico de las propuestas y el uso integrado de la minería de datos y de procesos, la integración de ambos enfoques se considera baja, ya que la mayoría de las propuestas se basan fuertemente en uno de los enfoques y utiliza el otro en alguna etapa puntual con un fin determinado y acotado. Principalmente se detectó la aplicación de algoritmos de minería de datos sobre logs de eventos de procesos, en forma previa al descubrimiento de modelos para agrupación de trazas homogéneas, o para predicción de distintos elementos del proceso considerando las trazas en los logs de eventos.

También puede destacarse que los estudios primarios aún en las propuestas más generales no se tomaba en cuenta todo el ciclo de vida de los datos, sino que se asumían dados sin tomar en cuenta un posible proceso de obtención de los mismos. También se asumen con una calidad aceptable como para trabajar con ellos sin indicaciones específicas de características de calidad deseables en la aplicación de los enfoques de minería. En este sentido, en el framework PRICED propuesto [6], se define claramente este ciclo de vida y las fases asociadas.

El trabajo de revisión sistemática presentado en este artículo, constituye la base para el trabajo actual y futuro de integración de propuestas y enfoques de minería de procesos y datos que estamos llevando adelante, en el marco del framework integrado. El objetivo es brindar soporte a las actividades que permitan transitar desde los datos de la operativa de los procesos y organizacionales asociados hasta la información brindada por los enfoques de minería de procesos y datos integrados que aporte valor y conocimiento al negocio, que permita detectar oportunidades de mejora.

7. Agradecimientos

Este trabajo es parte del proyecto "Minería de procesos y datos para la mejora de procesos en las organizaciones" financiado por Comisión Sectorial de Investigación Científica (CSIC), Universidad de la República (UdelaR), Uruguay.

Referencias

1. van der Aalst, W.: Process Mining: Data Science in Action, 2nd.ed. Springer (2016)
2. Augusto, A., Conforti, R., Dumas, M., La Rosa, M., Maggi, F.M., Marrella, A., Mecella, M., Soo, A.: Automated discovery of process models from event logs: Review and benchmark. IEEE Trans. Knowledge &Data Eng. **31**(4), 686–705 (2018)

3. Bevacqua, A., Carnuccio, M., Folino, F., Guarascio, M., Pontieri, L.: A data-driven prediction framework for analyzing and monitoring business process performances. In: Int. Conf. on Enterprise Inf. Systems (ICEIS). pp. 100–117. Springer (2012)
4. Bui, D.B., Hadzic, F., Potdar, V.: A framework for application of tree-structured data mining to process log analysis. In: International Conference on Intelligent Data Engineering and Automated Learning. pp. 423–434. Springer (2012)
5. Cardoso, J.: Applying data mining algorithms to calculate the quality of service of workflow processes. In: Intelligent Techniques and Tools for Novel System Architectures, pp. 3–18. Springer (2008)
6. Delgado, A., Marotta, A., González, L., Tansini, L., Calegari, D.: Towards a data science framework integrating process and data mining for organizational improvement. In: 15th Int. Conference on Software Technologies (ICSOFT) (2020)
7. Ezpeleta, J., Fabra, J., Álvarez, P.: On the use of log-based model checking, clustering and machine learning for process behavior prediction. In: 5th Int. Conf. Social Networks Analysis, Mgmt. and Security (SNAMS). pp. 209–214. IEEE (2018)
8. Furht, B., Villanustre, F.: Introduction to big data. In: Furht, B., Villanustre, F. (eds.) Big Data Technologies and Applications, pp. 3–11. Springer (2016)
9. Grossmann, W., Rinderle-Ma, S.: Fundamentals of Business Intelligence. Springer (2015)
10. Hernández Orallo, J., Ferri Ramirez, C., Ramirez Quintana, M.J.: Introducción a la Minería de Datos. Pearson Prentice Hall (2004)
11. IEEE: Task Force Data Science and Adv. Analytics. http://www.dsaa.co/ (2020)
12. Kitchenham, B.: Procedures for performing systematic revs. **33**(2004), 1–26 (2004)
13. Kitchenham, B., Charters, S.: Guidelines for performing systematic literature reviews in software engineering (2007)
14. Križanić, S.: Educational data mining using cluster analysis and decision tree technique: A case study. International Journal of Engineering Business Management **12**, 1847979020908675 (2020)
15. Murata, T.: Petri nets: Properties, analysis and applications. Proceedings of the IEEE **77**(4), 541–580 (1989)
16. OMG: Business Process Model and Notation (BPMN) v2.0 (2011)
17. Ong, K.L., De Silva, D., Boo, Y.L., Lim, E.H., Bodi, F., Alahakoon, D., Leao, S.: Big Data Applications in Engineering and Science, pp. 315–351. Springer (2016)
18. Radeschütz, S., Mitschang, B., Leymann, F.: Matching of process data and operational data for a deep business analysis. In: Enterprise Interoperability III. pp. 171–182. Springer (2008)
19. Roudjane, M., Rebaïne, D., Khoury, R., Hallé, S.: Real-time data mining for event streams. In: 22nd Int. Enterprise Distributed Object Computing Conference (EDOC). pp. 123–134. IEEE (2018)
20. Song, M., Günther, C.W., Van der Aalst, W.M.: Trace clustering in process mining. In: Int. Conf. Business Process Management (BPM). pp. 109–120. Springer (2009)
21. Teinemaa, I., Dumas, M., Maggi, F.M., Di Francescomarino, C.: Predictive business process monitoring with structured and unstructured data. In: International Conference on Business Process Management (BPM). pp. 401–417. Springer (2016)
22. Weske, M.: Business Process Management - Concepts, Languages, Architectures, Third Edition. Springer (2019)
23. Wohlin, C., Runeson, P., Höst, M., Ohlsson, M.C., Regnell, B.: Experimentation in Software Engineering. Springer (2012)
24. van Zelst, S.J., Cao, Y.: A generic framework for attribute-driven hierarchical trace clustering. In: International Conference on Business Process Management (BPM). pp. 308–320. Springer (2020)

Characterizing the Experience of Subjects in Software Engineering Studies

Rafael de Mello[1] [0000-0002-9877-3946] and Matheus Coelho[1]

CEFET/RJ, Rio de Janeiro, Brazil
rafael.mello@cefet-rj.br, matheus.coelho@aluno.cefet-rj.br

Abstract. Context: Empirical studies in software engineering are typically centered on human subjects, ranging from novice to experienced developers. The experience of these individuals is a key context factor that should be properly characterized for supporting the design of empirical studies and interpreting their results. However, the criteria adopted for characterizing the experience of subjects do not follow a standard and are frequently limited. Goal: Our research aims at establishing an optimized and comprehensive scheme to characterize the subjects' experience for studies in software engineering. Method: Based on previous work, we defined the first version of this scheme, composed of three experience attributes, including time, number of projects, and self-perception. In the last years, we applied the characterization scheme over four empirical studies, reaching the characterization of 79 subjects in three different skills. Results: We found that the attributes from our scheme are positively but moderately correlated. This finding suggests these attributes play a complementary role in characterizing the subjects' experience. Besides, we found that study subjects tend to enumerate the technical diversity of their background when summarizing their professional experience. Conclusion: The scheme proposed represents a feasible alternative for characterizing subjects of empirical studies in the field. However, we intend to conduct additional investigations with developers to evolve it.

Keywords: characterization · experience · human subjects · Empirical Software Engineering.

1 Introduction

Software Engineering is a sociotechnical field composed of several semi-automated and manual activities strongly influenced by human aspects at different levels [8]. Consequently, empirical studies in software engineering typically require the involvement of humans as subjects, ranging from novice students to experienced practitioners [4][9]. Empirical studies centered on practitioners include not only controlled studies but also studies intensive on qualitative data, such as opinion surveys [7], focus group sessions [10], case studies [21], and action research [11]. In most of these studies, it is common to gather some characterization data about the study subjects. In this way, characterizing their experience is often recognized as a relevant but also challenging task [17][20][9].

Among other utilities, characterizing subjects' experience is a key resource to support the design of empirical studies and to support the interpretation of their findings [17] [4]. For instance, researchers may use experience data to compose balanced pairs of developers for assigning code review tasks in the context of a controlled study [5]. This experience data may be also used to assess to which extent the experience in code reviews influenced the performance of each pair.

Despite the importance of properly characterizing the subjects' experience, one can see that characterization data gathered in empirical studies is frequently insufficient or underused, which may be partially explained by the lack of standardization of the characterization instruments used in the field. For instance, [4] identified that surveys in software engineering typically characterize subjects by few and frequently disconnected attributes from the perspective of the research topic. Consequently, characterization data- including experience- is barely used in the interpretation of the results. Besides, we argue that an inadequate characterization of the subjects' experience may lead to misinterpretations of the studies' results.

In this sense, one risky strategy is relying on a single attribute for characterizing experience. For instance, let us consider two co-workers named Johnny and Selena. Johnny has ten years of experience in reviewing code, while Selena has six years. Selena had worked reviewing code in a diverse portfolio of 20 projects, while Johnny worked with code review in 10 projects. When individually asked about their background, Johnny understands that he has more experience with code reviews than Selena. Besides, Selena understands that she has less experience in code reviews than Johnny. Now, let us consider that both professionals are volunteers in a controlled study on code reviews involving several other developers. If the researchers opted by characterizing the subjects' experience in code reviews only based on the number of projects, Johnny would be ranked under Selena. However, if the experience is grounded in self-assessment or years, Johnny would be ranked above Selena.

Although we should recognize that characterizing and comparing subjective context factors is challenging, the aforementioned example illustrates how a more comprehensive characterization, considering different perspectives, would improve interpreting the subjects' experience. However, one may see that researchers should avoid long characterization forms that would discourage the participation of subjects. In this paper, we propose the first version of a lightweight scheme for characterizing the experience of subjects from empirical studies in software engineering. This scheme is composed of three easy-to-assess attributes of experience: self-assessment (Likert scale), time (years), and number of projects. We also report in this paper a large-scale investigation on the feasibility of the proposed scheme. In the last five years, we applied a standard questionnaire based on this scheme to characterize the experience of 79 subjects from four empirical studies. In these studies, we used the scheme attributes to characterize the subjects' experience in software development and two more specific activities. Besides, the studies' subjects were asked to summarize their professional experience in software development.

The study results reveal that the scheme attributes are positively but moderately correlated. This finding suggests that researchers may combine these attributes for reaching a more comprehensive and reliable characterization of the developers' experience. Besides, we also found that developers tend to self-describe their experience based on other attributes addressing the diversity of their technical experience, such as enumerating the development activities performed and development technologies employed. Based on these findings, we conclude that the proposed scheme is feasible although we could improve its comprehensiveness. In this way, we are planning an in-depth investigation of the beliefs and values of researchers and developers about experience.

Section 2 presents the related work, in which we discuss approaches for characterizing the subjects' experience. Section 3 describes the settings of our feasibility study, also introducing the first version of our proposed scheme. Section 4 presents the results of our study, reporting its main findings. Section 5 presents a discussion of the study findings, reflecting on the strengths of the scheme proposed and possible opportunities for evolving it. Section 6 discusses threats to validity. Finally, Section 7 concludes the paper and indicates future work.

2 Related Work

As far as we are aware, our research is the first one assessing and comparing different perspectives for characterizing the experience of subjects in studies from the field. However, there are several related work addressing different aspects involved in the research motivation and design choices.

In [16], the authors discusses the role of context on interpreting the results of empirical studies from the field. In this way, they mapped a scheme in composed of omnibus dimensions and discrete context. Among the omnibus dimensions, the authors highlight the importance of properly characterizing the study participants. For this purpose, they exemplify some context factors used in empirical studies. However, none of them address the characterization of subjects' experience. In this way, one can see that merely labeling participants as students or professionals is insufficient. In [22], the authors investigated to which extent the performance of subjects ranked as students and professional developers are different. Based on their findings, the authors concluded that software engineering students may be used in empirical studies instead of professional software developers under certain conditions. In a more recent study [18], the authors recruited a group of students and a group of professionals for performing test-driven development tasks. Then, the authors measured and compared the quality of the tasks performed by these groups. As a result, they concluded that was no group reached better results than the other.

We also found related work proposing schemes for characterizing subjects in empirical studies. In [17], the authors proposed a scheme for characterizing subjects through their motivation (incentive) and experience. For measuring experience, the scheme rank subjects in five levels by combining their academic level with their time working in industrial projects. However, the working time is grounded in only three arbitrary ranges: less than three months, between three months and two years, and more than two years. After applying the scheme over the characterization data of previous experiments, the authors found a good level of agreement among the original classification and those resulting from the proposed scheme. Here, it is important to note that reaching high levels of agreement does not assure that both classifications are right. In other words, eventual misclassifications in the original studies may have been replicated or even intensified. Besides, one can see that the proposed scheme is insufficient to distinguish more experienced groups of subjects once any individual having more than two years of professional experience is considered highly experienced.

More recently, Falessi et al. [9] discussed the importance of empirical studies in software engineering going beyond a basic distinction between students and professionals, arguing that characterizing the subjects' experience is a key strategy for interpreting the results of empirical studies. After conducting qualitative studies with Empirical Software Engineering specialists, the authors proposed the R^3 scheme for characterizing the experience of subjects. This scheme advocates that experience should be characterized from from three perspectives: the subjects' *real* experience, the subjects' *relevant* experience and the *recent* experience. Although no formal set of experience attributes are defined, the authors exemplify the measurement of the different perspectives of experience by measuring the number of years of experience. However, they suggest using unbalanced intervals of years for ranking the level of experience. Besides, the authors also suggest arguing subjects about their participation in projects (industry, academic, open-source) as an additional criterion for assessing their real experience. In the end, the researchers should analyze the data collected from each subject to infer about its experience level. To support the characterization through R^3, the authors recommend taking preference to interviews rather than questionnaires. However, one can see that following this strategy may be unfeasible according to the nature of the sample and its size.

Different from the previous schemes proposed, our research aim at reaching a scheme combining few quantitative and qualitative attributes for reaching a more comprehensive characterization of experience. Besides, we intend to compose a characterization scheme composed of items easily gathered through characterization forms, avoiding the conduction of interviews. Finally, our research intends to support researchers in internally ranking and grouping subjects in empirical studies rather than classifying them through absolute levels of experience.

In this way, an important background from our research includes a previous investigation on the attributes used for characterizing subjects in surveys from the field [4]. For this purpose, it was conducted a literature review over surveys published in Empirical Software Engineering conferences until 2014. In these sources, they found 38 surveys published. After analysing their content, it was found that most of these studies (32) have individuals as the unit of analysis. From these, the most common information gathered from the subjects is their experience in the research topic. The indicators used for supporting this characterization include the experience level working in the research topic, number of projects, and number of publications. The authors recommend that the subjects' experience should be characterized by combining the overall experience in Software Engineering with the experience in the research topic. Besides, the characterization of subjects is one of the main activities of the conceptual framework proposed in [20]. In this work, it is recognized the lack of standardization on characterizing the subjects' experience. For mitigating this issue, it is recommended the adoption of the more frequent characteristics found in [4].

3 Study Design

Our research goal aims at characterizing an evidence-based scheme for supporting a comprehensive characterization of the experience of subjects from software engineering studies. By scheme, we define a set of attributes that complementary characterize the experience of each study subject. These attributes may be quantitative and qualitative ones but should be gathered through characterization forms. Besides, the scheme's attributes should be easily adapted for characterizing experience in different skills. The main expected benefit of our research is providing a hands-on resource to support the ranking and grouping of individuals in empirical studies from the field by their experience. Based on this goal and the more common perspectives/attributes observed in previous work (Section 2), we designed the first version of our characterization scheme, composed of the key attributes presented in Table1.

Table 1. Schema for Characterizing the Experience of Subjects.

Perspective of Experience	Attribute	Data Type
Time	Years of experience in the topic	Numeric
Projects	Number of Projects in the topic	Numeric
Self-assessment	Self-assessment of the experience in the topic	Likert scale (Very Low, Low, High, Very High)

One may see that *years of experience* and *number of projects* are quantitative attributes commonly used in empirical studies from the field. The self-assessment of experience intends to be a measurable qualitative attribute for gathering complementary and subjective aspects of experience. Therefore, our scheme is based on primitive measures for ranking subjects from the same study sample. In this way, we avoid arbitrarily establishing absolute categories or levels of experience once we believe they should be identified in the context of each study when needed. In the following subsections, we present the design of the empirical study conducted for evaluating the proposed scheme.

3.1 Research Questions

Considering our research goal and the proposed scheme, in this study we intend to answer the following research questions:

RQ1. *To which extent the different attributes used for ranking the experience of subjects from Software Engineering studies are correlated?*

RQ2. *Which attributes subjects from Software Engineering studies spontaneously adopt for self-describing their experience in software development?*

By answering RQ1, we want to observe the extent to which measuring subjects' experience by each attribute results in similar rankings. If two attributes result in highly similar rankings, they are probably redundant. Consequently, we could discard one of them could from the scheme proposed. By answering RQ2, we want to identify relevant perspectives that may be added to evolve the proposed scheme.

3.2 Population and Sample

Considering the goal of our research, the target population includes any software developer ranging from novice to very experienced ones. Once we need to gather characterization data, we opportunistically choose a sampling frame composed of participants from four empirical studies in Software Engineering conducted from 2017 until 2020. In all these studies, the subjects were invited by convenience. They are from different organizations and universities from Brazil, among students and practitioners. Two of these studies are controlled experiments on the manual identification of code smells [3] [5]. A third study investigated the social representations of the identification of code smells [1]. The fourth work is a controlled study investigating the incidence of confusing code [6]. One can see that the research topics of these investigations address code review tasks.

3.3 Instrumentation

We applied a standard set of characterization items for experience in the four studies, summarized in Table 2. These characterization questions aim at gathering experience data from the perspective of the scheme's attributes for the following three activities: *software development in general*, *programming in a particular language* and *code reviews*. We intentionally opted by investigating these activities once they address different characterization challenges. Software development is a considerably generic activity. Programming in a particular language is a more specific activity, although probably experienced by most of the subjects. On the other hand, the experience in code reviews may be concentrated in particular subgroups. We included the self-description question about the experience in software development to support answering RQ2.

Table 2. Characterization items for experience.

Perspective	Questionnaire Item	Data Type
Self description	Summary of experience with software development	Open
Self-assessment	Self-perception of experience with software development	Likert scale
	Self-perception of experience with (C/Java)	Likert scale
	Self-perception of experience with code reviews	Likert scale
Time	Years developing software	Numeric
	Years programming in (C/Java)	Numeric
	Years reviewing code	Numeric
Projects	Number of projects developing software	Numeric
	Number of projects programming in (C/Java)	Numeric
	Number of software projects reviewing code	Numeric

Besides the presented set characterization items, other ones were eventually added to address the scope of each study. To avoid bias, we designed each characterization form to gather data about each attribute in separated sections by following the same order presented in Table 2.

3.4 Data Analysis

After filtering the answers given from 79 subjects, we calculated the coefficient of correlation among the different attributes for each activity investigated (RQ1). Considering the heteroscedasticity and the sample size, we opted by applying Kendall's non-parametric correlation test [12] for each of the following pairs of distribution: *self-assessment x years of experience; self-assessment x number of projects; years of experience x number of projects.* For answering RQ2, we performed a single level of open coding over the self-description answers for identifying the attributes used by developers to describe their experience. Then, we ranked these attributes by frequency.

4 Results

Tables 3, 4, and 5 summarize the descriptive statistics of the experience attributes measured from the 79 subjects for each activity investigated.

The data about subjects' overall experience in software development in terms of years and projects indicates that these subjects range from novice developers to very experienced ones. Besides, the distribution of self-assessment reveals a trend on most of these developers assessing themselves as having a high level of experience (median=2, mean=1.91).

Table 3. Descriptive statistics of the developers' experience with software development.

Item	Self Assessment	Years	Projects
Minimum	0.00	0.00	0.00
1st Quartile	2.00	3.50	4.00
Median	2.00	5.00	7.00
Mean	1.91	7.25	11.25
3rd Quartile	2.00	8.50	13.00
Maximum	3.00	40.00	50.00

Table 4. Descriptive statistics of the developers' experience with programming in a particular language.

Item	Self Assessment	Years	Projects
Minimum	0.00	0.00	0.00
1st Quartile	1.00	1.00	1.00
Median	2.00	3.00	3.00
Mean	1.53	3.93	4.90
3rd Quartile	2.00	5.50	5.00
Maximum	3.00	20.00	30.00

Table 5. Descriptive statistics of the developers' experience with code reviews.

Item	Self Assessment	Years	Projects
Minimum	0.00	0.00	0.00
1st Quartile	0.50	0.00	0.00
Median	1.00	2.00	2.00
Mean	1.35	3.03	4.54
3rd Quartile	2.00	4.50	5.00
Maximum	3.00	20.00	40.00

The data about subjects' experience in a particular programming language reveals the distribution is considerably diverse in terms of time and number of projects. Besides, one can see the concentration of novices in the first quartile (0 to 1 years, 0 to 1 project). However, the distribution of self-assessment reveals a trend on these developers assessing themselves as having a high level of experience in this activity (median=2, mean=1.53). Finally, the distributions of experience in code reviews indicate an even higher concentration of novices in the first quartile (0 years, 0 projects), reflected in the self-assessment.

The distributions of experience analysed indicate that the study sample is considerably diverse for the different activities investigated. Besides, this diversity can be observed among the different attributes from the proposed scheme.

Therefore, we understand the collected dataset is favourable for supporting answering RQ1, which is discussed in the following subsection. RQ2 is answered in Section 4.2

4.1 RQ1: Comparing the Characterization Attributes

By answering RQ1, we intend to observe to which extent the different attributes used for ranking developers are correlated. Tables 6, 7, and 8 present the Kendall's correlation coefficients calculated for each pair of distributions evaluated. In total, we performed nine correlation tests involving the 711 answers given by the 79 subjects. In all the correlation tests performed, the p-values obtained were lesser than 0.0001.

Table 6. Kendall's correlation coefficients calculated for experience with software development.

Attribute	Self	Years	Projects
Self	-		
Years	0.5620	-	
Projects	0.4972	0.5601	-

Table 7. Kendall's correlation coefficients calculated for experience with a particular programming language.

Attribute	Self	Years	Projects
Self	-		
Years	0.6502	-	
Projects	0.6929	0.6616	-

Table 8. Kendall's correlation coefficients calculated for experience with code reviews.

Attribute	Self	Years	Projects
Self	-		
Years	0.6705	-	
Projects	0.6486	0.8362	-

Considering the nature of the study dataset (human aspects), we used the categorisation proposed by Dancey and Raidy [13] for interpreting the coefficients of correlation obtained. This categorization is reproduced in Table 9. Based on this, one can see that almost all Kendall's correlation coefficients calculated indicate moderately positive correlations among the attributes compared. The only exception is the strong correlation obtained for *years x projects* in *code reviews*. Based on these results, we may depict the following main finding:

Finding 1. *The experience of developers in terms of time, projects, and self-assessment are positively but moderately correlated.*

Table 9. Interpretation proposed for Kendall's positive correlations. Adapted from [13].

Kendall's tau	Correlation
1	perfect
0.7000-0.9999	strong
0.4000-0.6999	moderate
0.1000-0.3999	weak
0-0.0999	none

Besides, based on Finding 1 and the nature of Kendall's test, we may depict the following main finding:

Finding 2. *Ranking subjects' experience exclusively by years of experience, projects, or self-assessment leads to different results.*

4.2 RQ2: Self-Description of Experience

For answering RQ2, we asked the subjects to summarize their experience with software development. The answers resulted in 1,646 words. We performed a single round of open coding in these words to identify the set of attributes used by the developers for self-describing their experience. From the 79 respondents, 59 developers reported at least one characteristic of background. Table 10 shows the nine attributes coded, with their incidence among the 59 answers coded.

One can see that *time* was the single attribute mentioned by more than half of answers coded (30). However, the experience with *programming languages* was also largely mentioned (27). Curiously, the *number of projects*, another quantitative attribute from our scheme, was barely mentioned (3). The report of particular research projects (9) may be explained due several subjects investigated are also post-graduation students or experienced researchers. Most of them had worked with development activities at one or more research projects.

Different attributes revealed the concern of developers on enumerating the technical diversity of their software development experience. By development activities (16), we mean the cases in which developers listed activities they are used to perform, including different software engineering disciplines, such as requirements, design, implementation, and verification. In these cases, most of the

Table 10. Frequency (f) of the attributes used by developers to self-describing their experience in software development.

Attribute	*f*	%
Time (months/years)	30	50.85%
Enumeration of Programming Languages	27	45.76%
Enumeration of Development Activities	16	27.12%
Enumeration of Software Technologies	13	22.03%
Particular Research Projects	9	15.25%
Enumeration of Project Domains	7	11.86%
Particular Working Companies	6	10.17%
Number of Projects	3	5.08%
Experience with Entrepreneurship	2	3.39%

developers listed two or more activities. Similarly, several developers reported their experience in terms *programming languages* (27) and other*software technologies* (13) adopted. These technologies include particular frameworks, APIs, and operating systems. Therefore, the aforementioned results lead us to depict the following main findings:

Finding 3. *Software developers tend to quantitatively characterize their experience with software development in terms of time rather than in number of projects.*

Finding 4. *Software developers tend to enumerate their experience with software development through the diversity of their technical backgrounds.*

5 Discussion

The findings of our study indicates that both quantitative and qualitative sources of knowledge are relevant to reach a more comprehensive and accurate characterization of developers' experience. One could argue that once more attributes are adopted, the more comprehensive would be the characterization. However, fulfilling long characterization forms tends to be unfeasible when running studies in the field, especially when involving professional developers out of the researchers' network. Long questionnaires may discourage individual participation or even discourage potential supporters and sponsors, such as managers and local research and development representatives. Besides, applying a large number of questions- especially open ones- would demand considerable analysis effort from researchers, which could be unfeasible for large samples. Therefore, we should reach an optimized scheme for gathering relevant characterization data as much as possible.

In the first version of our schema, we combined two quantitative attributes (years and number of projects) with a single qualitative attribute (self-assessment), gathered through a standard Likert scale. The study findings indicate that these attributes effectively bring complementary perspectives for characterizing experience, especially those experience in more generic activities, such as software development. However, it is not clear to which extent they are sufficient. For instance, are there other attributes that worth composing the schema? On the other extreme, are self-assessments sufficient to synthesize all the subject experience?

Despite the exploratory nature of this first study, the analysis of the self-description answers (open questions) gives us some important hints for answering these questions. First, no other quantitative attribute than time was considerably reported. Second, the perception of technical diversity also emerged as a potentially relevant attribute. In this way, one possible direction for evolving the original scheme would be replacing the number of projects with self-assessment questions addressing the diversity of projects in terms of their domains, relevant technologies, and relevant activities.

However, the study findings indicate that we should perform a deeper investigation into what researchers and developers have in mind about the research topic before evolving the schema. In this sense, we are planning a new study using the theory of social representations from Social Psychology to support our research. This theory aims to establish an order that enables how groups of individuals guide themselves in their material and social world. Social representation is the collective elaboration of a social object by a particular community for behaving and communicating [15]. In this definition, a *social object* corresponds to an object socialized by two or more individuals from a community, such as the experience of software developers. Recent studies have shown the usefulness of the social representation theory for supporting both research and practice in software engineering [1] [2] [14].

6 Threats to Validity

Different characterization forms were designed to supporting each empirical study used in this investigation. This issue represents an important threat to the construct validity, once additional questions would influence the developers' answers. To mitigate this threat, we distributed the scheme items as presented in Table 2 at the beginning of each characterization form. Besides, we used proper settings to assure that developers would answer the questions addressing only a single perspective at a time.

Regarding the external validity, one can see that the four studies involved in this investigation address code reviews. Therefore, one may argue that the findings may do not apply to other research topics. However, it is important to note that we also characterized developers through a generic skill, i.e., software development. Besides, Section 4 shows that developers with different levels of experience and diverse skills participated in the study. Therefore, not only specialists in code reviews composed the study sample.

7 Conclusion and Future Work

Software Engineering research has several challenges addressing the support to empirical studies. One important challenge addresses the proper characterization of the studies' subjects, especially about their experience. The characterization of this experience may play a key role in the study design and in the interpretation of its results.

The scheme proposed in this paper for supporting the characterization of study subjects intends to be comprehensive but also simplified and easy to use for both researchers and subjects. The results of the empirical study reported in this paper suggest that our schema is feasible, but its comprehensiveness may be improved. However, it is still not clear the concrete changes that we should make. In this sense, we are designing an empirical study to investigate what researchers and developers have in mind about experience. We believe that this study would help us reach a more comprehensive characterization scheme still preserving its simplicity.

8 Acknowledgements

This work is funded by CNPq 152179/2020-8.

References

1. de Mello, R., Uchôa, A., Oliveira, R., Oliveira, D., Fonseca, B., Garcia, A., de Mello, F.: Investigating the Social Representations of Code Smell Identification: A Preliminary Study. In: 12th International Workshop on Cooperative and Human Aspects of Software Engineering (CHASE), pp. 53–60. IEEE press, Canada (2019)
2. de Mello, R., Uchôa, A., Oliveira, R., Oizumi, W., Souza, J., Mendes, K., Oliveira, D., Fonseca, B., Garcia, A.: IDo Research and Practice of Code Smell Identification Walk Together? A Social Representations Analysis. In: 2019 ACM/IEEE International Symposium on Empirical Software Engineering and Measurement (ESEM), pp. 1–6. IEEE, Brazil (2019)
3. de Mello, R., Oliveira, R., Garcia, A.: On the influence of human factors for identifying code smells: A multi-trial empirical study. In: 2017 ACM/IEEE International Symposium on Empirical Software Engineering and Measurement (ESEM), pp. 68–77. IEEE, Canada (2017)
4. de Mello, R., Travassos, G. : Characterizing Sampling Frames in Software Engineering Surveys. In: Proceedings of ESELAW 2015, pp. 68–77. Peru (2015)
5. Oliveira, R., Sousa, L., de Mello, R., Valentim, N., Lopes, A., Conte, T., Garcia, A., Oliveira, E., Lucena, C.: In: 2019 2017 IEEE/ACM 39th International Conference on Software Engineering: Software Engineering in Practice Track (ICSE-SEIP), pp. 33–42. IEEE, Argentina (2017)
6. de Oliveira, B., Ribeiro, M., da Costa, J. A., Gheyi, R., Amaral, G., de Mello, R., Oliveira, A, Garcia, A., Bonifácio, R., Fonseca, B.: Atoms of Confusion: The Eyes Do Not Lie. In: Proceedings of the 34th Brazilian Symposium on Software Engineering (SBES), pp. 243–252. IEEE, Brazil (2020)

7. Linaker, J., Sulaman, S., de Mello, R., Höst, M.: Guidelines for Conducting Surveys in Software Engineering. Technical Report. https://lup.lub.lu.se/record/5366801. Lund University (2015)
8. Lenberg, P., Feldt, R., Wallgren, L.:Behavioral software engineering: A definition and systematic literature review. Journal of Systems and Software (JSS), **107**, 17–37 (2015)
9. Falessi, D., Juristo, N., Wohlin, C., Turhan, B., Münch, J., Jedlitschka, A. and Oivo, M.: Empirical software engineering experts on the use of students and professionals in experiments. Empirical Software Engineering (EMSE) **23**(1), 452–489 (2018)
10. Kontio, J., Bragge, J., Lehtola, L.:The focus group method as an empirical tool in software engineering. Guide to advanced empirical software engineering, pp. 93–116. (2008)
11. dos Santos, P., Travassos, G.: Action research use in software engineering: An initial survey. In: 2009 ACM/IEEE International Symposium on Empirical Software Engineering and Measurement (ESEM), pp. 414-417. (2009)
12. Kendall, M.: A new measure of rank correlation. Biometrika **30**(1/2), 81–93 (1998)
13. Dancey, C., Reidy J.: Statistics without maths for psychology. Pearson education (2007)
14. de Mello, R., Costa, J. A., Oliveira, B. F., Ribeiro, M., Fonseca, B., Gheyi, R., Garcia, A., Tiengo, W.: Decoding Confusing Code: Social Representations among Developers. In: 13th International Workshop on Cooperative and Human Aspects of Software Engineering (CHASE), pp. 11-20. IEEE, Spain (2020).
15. Moscovici S.: Notes towards a description of social representations. European journal of social psychology **18**(3), 211–50 (1988)
16. Dybå, T. and Sjøberg, D., Cruzes, D.: What works for whom, where, when, and why? On the role of context in empirical software engineering. In: Proceedings of the ACM-IEEE international symposium on Empirical software engineering and measurement, pp. 19–28. (2012).
17. Höst, M., Wohlin, C., Thelin, T.:Experimental context classification: incentives and experience of subjects. In: Proceedings of the 27th international conference on Software engineering (ICSE), pp. 470–478. (2005).
18. Salman, I., Misirli, A. T., Juristo, N.: Are students representatives of professionals in software engineering experiments? In: 2015 IEEE/ACM 37th IEEE International Conference on Software Engineering (ICSE), pp. 666–676. IEEE (2015).
19. Meyer, A., Zimmermann, T., Fritz, T.: Characterizing software developers by perceptions of productivity. In: 2017 ACM/IEEE International Symposium on Empirical Software Engineering and Measurement (ESEM), pp. 105–110. IEEE (2017).
20. de Mello, R., Travassos, G.: Surveys in software engineering: Identifying representative samples. Proceedings of the 10th ACM/IEEE International Symposium on Empirical Software Engineering and Measurement (ESEM), pp. 1–6. Spain (2016)
21. Runeson, P., Höst, M.: Guidelines for conducting and reporting case study research in software engineering. Empirical software engineering **14**(2), 131–164 (2009)
22. Höst, M., Regnell, B., Wohlin, C.: Using students as subjects—a comparative study of students and professionals. Empirical Software Engineering 5(3), pp 201–214. Springer (2000)

How Tertiary Studies perform Quality Assessment of Secondary Studies in Software Engineering

Dolors Costal[0000-0002-7340-0414], Carles Farré[0000-0001-5814-3782], Xavier Franch[0000-0001-9733-8830], and Carme Quer[0000-0002-9000-6371]

Universitat Politècnica de Catalunya, Spain
{dolors, farre, franch, cquer}@essi.upc.edu

Abstract. Context: Tertiary studies are becoming increasingly popular in Software Engineering as an instrument to synthesise evidence on a research topic systematically. In order to understand and contextualize their findings, it is important to assess the quality of the selected secondary studies. **Objective**: This paper aims to provide a state of the art on the assessment of secondary studies' quality as conducted in tertiary studies in the area of Software Engineering, reporting the frameworks used as instruments, the facets examined in these frameworks, and the purposes of the quality assessment. **Method**: We designed this study as a systematic mapping responding to four research questions derived from the objective above. We applied a rigorous search protocol consisting of an automatic search over the Scopus digital library and a backward snowballing, resulting in 50 papers after applying inclusion and exclusion criteria. The extracted data were synthesised using content analysis. **Results**: A majority of tertiary studies perform quality assessment. It is not often used for excluding studies but for supporting some kind of investigation. The DARE quality assessment framework is the most frequently used, with customizations in some cases to cover missing facets. We outline the first steps towards building a new framework to address the shortcomings identified. **Conclusion**: This paper is a step forward establishing a foundation for researchers in two different ways. As authors of tertiary studies, understanding the different possibilities in which they can perform quality assessment of secondary studies. As readers, having an instrument to understand the methodological rigor upon which tertiary studies may claim their findings.

Keywords: Tertiary study, Quality assessment, Literature review.

1 Introduction

A tertiary study (TS) is defined as "a systematic review of systematic reviews" [1]. TSs are becoming increasingly popular in the Software Engineering (SE) field because they offer the possibility to integrate existing knowledge that has been previously synthesised in secondary studies [2].

As in any other type of systematic review, assessing the quality of the secondary studies selected in a TS is a recommended activity to fully embrace the subject of investigation [3]. Quality assessment (QA) of systematic reviews has been the subject of investigation in the past but, to the best of our knowledge, not in the specific case of TSs. Therefore, a number of questions arise, e.g., what are the QA frameworks adopted by authors of TSs?, how is the QA outcome used in the analysis part of TSs? This paper presents the results of a systematic mapping exploring these questions.

2 Background

Existing approaches from disciplines such as medicine and sociology with a long tradition of evidence-based research have influenced systematic reviews in SE, where the evidence-based paradigm has been adopted in the last fifteen years [3]. In the medicine discipline, there exist the quality criteria (QCs) proposed by the York University Centre for Reviews and Dissemination (CRD) Database of Abstracts of Reviews of Effects (DARE), which focuses on systematic reviews on health care interventions and services. A first version of the DARE QCs included four questions (DARE-4) [4] and, in 2008, they were extended to include an additional synthesis QC (DARE-5) [5]. DARE-4 and DARE-5 QCs are listed in Table 1; QC3 is only present in DARE-5. CRD uses those QCs to select reviews. In DARE-4, reviews have to meet at least three criteria, of which QC1 and QC2 are mandatory. In DARE-5, reviews have to meet at least four criteria of which QC1, QC2 and QC3 are mandatory.

Table 1. Quality criteria included in DARE

QC	Description
QC1	Were inclusion/exclusion criteria reported?
QC2	Was the search adequate?
QC3	Were the included studies synthesised? (not in DARE-4)
QC4	Was the quality of the included studies assessed?
QC5	Are sufficient details about the individual studies presented?

In the SE area, DARE-4 was initially adopted by Kitchenham et al. [1, 6, 7]. In 2011, Cruzes and Dyba [8] proposed to use DARE-5, arguing that it is critically important to evaluate whether a systematic review synthesizes primary studies.

In some of Kitchenham et al. works [6, 7, 9], the DARE QCs are refined. More concretely, a detailed rubric to evaluate each question achievement is defined (to Yes/Partly/No), a score is assigned to each degree of achievement (1/0.5/0), and scores can be aggregated. On the other hand, these studies did not use the QA for systematic literature review (SLR) selection because that would remove "SLRs relevant to practitioners and educators" and because "even if an SLR is of relatively low quality, it might still provide a useful starting point for academics [...] as long as all the relevant primary studies are fully cited" [7].

Budgen et al. [10] developed a TS to analyze the reporting of systematic reviews and extracted a set of practical lessons on how to achieve the DARE QCs. They pointed out that the DARE QCs do not cover all quality issues: "the DARE criteria address what should be reported rather than how it should be reported [and...] they do not attempt to cover all issues [...]. For example, while we might expect any secondary study to include an assessment of threats to validity, this is not actually something identified as being a part of the DARE criteria."

In addition, some authors argue that there exist proposals that present advantages over DARE for assessing the quality of systematic reviews [11]. More specifically, they advocate the use of AMSTAR having its first version 11 quality items [12] and its second one 16 [13].

3 Research Method

This study takes the form of a systematic mapping following the guidelines defined by Kitchenham and Charters [1]. As a first step, we confirmed the need for the review by checking that there are not similar studies with the same aim as our paper. We only found a literature study by Yang et al. [14] that investigates QA performed in secondary studies, i.e., assessing the quality of primary studies. This is a significant difference with our focus on secondary studies, because primary studies and secondary studies are fundamentally different: while primary studies are really diverse, secondary studies should all fulfil some methodological criteria that have become well-established in the SE community. Therefore, the quality of primary studies and secondary studies cannot be assessed in the same way (although some similarities may still exist, see Section 5).

3.1 Research Questions

We have used the GQM methodology [15] to derive our research questions. Based on the GQM goal template, the goal of this study is to analyze the state of the art in TSs to characterize how they assess the quality of secondary studies from the point of view of empirical researchers in the context of SE research literature. The research questions are:

- RQ1. What are the demographics of the selected TSs?
- RQ2. What are the frameworks and their variations applied to assess the quality of secondary studies in TSs?
- RQ3. What facets are examined by the criteria applied to assess the quality of secondary studies in TSs?
- RQ4. What are the purposes of assessing the quality of secondary studies in TSs?

3.2 Search Protocol

In this research paper, we took the following decisions that impact on the search protocol:

i. Perform automatic search.
ii. Use the Scopus digital library as the only resource. As stated by Krüger et al., it indexes papers of main publishers as ACM, IEEE, Springer and Elsevier [16].
iii. Restrict to papers written in English and published since 2004 in the SE area. Year 2004 was the publication date of the seminal paper on Evidence-Based Software Engineering [17].
iv. Perform backward snowballing on the selected papers [18].

We applied the following steps:

1. Design and pilot the search string in Scopus. We ended up with "TERTIARY STUDY" as the search string. To implement it in Scopus, we also fine-tuned the Scopus search parameters. For instance, we realized the importance of not restricting the Document Type, given that some TS published in journals are classified as Report instead of Article. Also, we decided to select "Computer Science" and "Engineering" as subject areas since SE papers could eventually fall in any of them. The final Scopus search string is in our replication package[1].
2. We executed the final search string over title, keywords and abstract with date 19-January-2021, resulting in 103 candidate papers.
3. We applied the inclusion criteria (IC) and exclusion criteria (EC) presented in Table 2 over title, keywords and abstract of these 103 papers, excluding 46 of them. IC and EC were applied by two team members to every paper, with the agreement not to exclude papers in case of doubt. Seven out of the 103 papers were conflictive, but after a plenary meeting, the team arrived at full consensus.
4. Later on, when analysing the 57 remaining papers, we excluded 10 additional works when the full text showed that they did not fulfil some IC or violated some EC. Exclusion was proposed by the team member in charge of extracting the data, and discussed and agreed upon in a plenary meeting.
5. Finally, we performed backward snowballing using as seed the 47 selected papers and we identified 3 additional papers once our IC and EC were applied. Therefore, this led to 50 TSs selected to analyse.

Table 2. Inclusion criteria (IC) & exclusion criteria (EC)

IC1	The paper is a tertiary study providing a survey of secondary studies in the SE field
IC2	The paper is published from 2004 onwards
IC3	The paper is written in English
EC1	The paper is superseded by (its RQs and selected papers are a subset of) a later version from the same team of authors
EC2	The paper describes the TS with very little detail, making its analysis unfeasible (because there are not enough data to answer RQs properly)
EC3	The paper is not available (even after contacting authors)

3.3 Data Extraction, Analysis and Reporting

We stored the result of the search in a GDrive spreadsheet, which was used in the rest of the study (shared as a replication package). Selected TSs are numbered [S01]-[S50]. We kept track of excluded papers for traceability reasons. We added as many columns as needed to extract the data required to answer the RQs (see sheets RQ1-RQ4 in the aforementioned spreadsheet). One team member was in charge of extracting the data for every individual paper; the set of papers were split into the team members at equal share. We held weekly plenary meetings to analyse progress and discuss issues as they emerged.

We used content analysis to synthesise codes from the extracted data [19]. Inductive coding prevailed, although we combined it with deductive coding in RQ3. In general,

[1] Replication package at Zenodo: https://doi.org/10.5281/zenodo.4742147

we paid attention to avoid researcher bias during analysis and reporting through several actions: working in pairs, supervision (i.e., a researcher validating results from another), weekly plenary meetings and explicit check of inter-rater agreement when we thought it was needed.

4 Results

4.1 RQ1. Demographics

Prevalence of QA. Fifteen out of the 50 selected TSs (30%) do not assess the quality of the secondary studies they included. Four of them claim that the applied search/selection procedure guarantees the good quality of the included secondary studies by either: limiting the set of venues where they are published [S16, S32], or obtaining them through an index like Scopus [S21], or requiring them to follow Kitchenham's guidelines [1] [S20]. The remaining 11 TSs do not mention this issue.

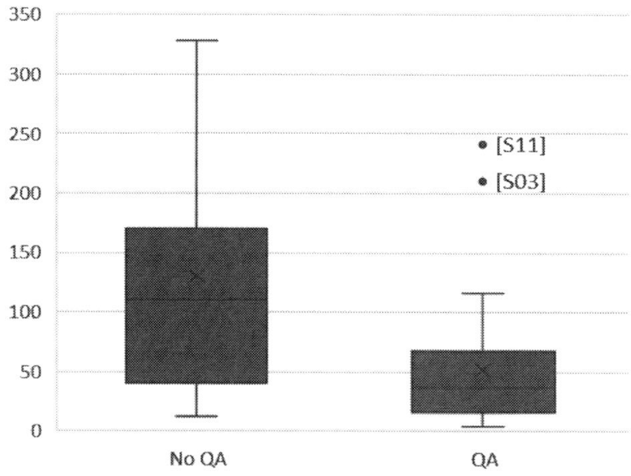

Fig. 1. Number of included secondary reviews in TS.

TS Types. From the analysis of the TSs, we observed that there are two main types as follows: (i) *SE-Area*: TSs that investigate the state of the research in a specific SE area; (ii) *Methodological*: TSs that focus on the methods and protocols followed by secondary studies in their development process.

Accordingly, 26 out of the 50 selected TSs (52%) are *SE-Area* and 24 (48%) are *Methodological*. Among the different SE areas addressed, Agile Software Development is the most recurring one, with 4 TSs, followed by Global Software Development with 3 TSs; and Education, Software Product Lines, and Software Testing, with 2 each. In the case of [S03], its SE area encompasses the whole SE field. Among the Methodological studies, four specific topics are subject of analysis by more than one TS: QA of Primary Studies, Types of secondary studies to consider, Search, Threats to Validity, and Synthesis. We labelled 5 *Methodological* TSs as *Generic*, in the sense that they cover several methodological topics at once.

Types of secondary studies. Eight TS papers considered only systematic literature reviews (SLRs), 1 paper [S03] only systematic mappings (SMs), 23 TSs papers both SLRs and SMs, 2 TSs only SLRS and Meta-analysis, and the remaining 16 considered more types (SLRs, SMs, Meta-analyses, Surveys, etc.).

Number of secondary studies. The average number of secondary studies per TS is 75. However, we observe disparities in the number of secondary studies considered when partitioning the 50 TSs into two groups: those that do not perform QA and those that do perform QA. The first group ("No QA" in Fig. 1) includes 15 TSs that are all *Methodological* but two. The second group ("QA" in Fig. 1) includes 35 TSs, 11 of which are *Methodological*, and the remaining 24 *SE-Area*. The two resulting box-plot diagrams shown in Fig. 1, where two outliers are made explicit, illustrate the clear difference between the two groups.

4.2 RQ2. Frameworks used in QA

QA framework. Most of the 35 papers reporting QA adopt an existing framework either directly or customizing it by adding or removing QCs. There are a few, i.e., 4 papers, that build their own custom-made QCs. In the former case, as we can see in Fig. 2, the framework chosen is DARE-4 or DARE-5 except for one study that customizes the AMSTAR framework. We can see that 25 out of the 31 studies adopting an existing framework apply it directly while 6 perform some adaptations. All adaptations consist of adding QCs to DARE-4 or DARE-5 except for one study that customizes AMSTAR by removing one criterion.

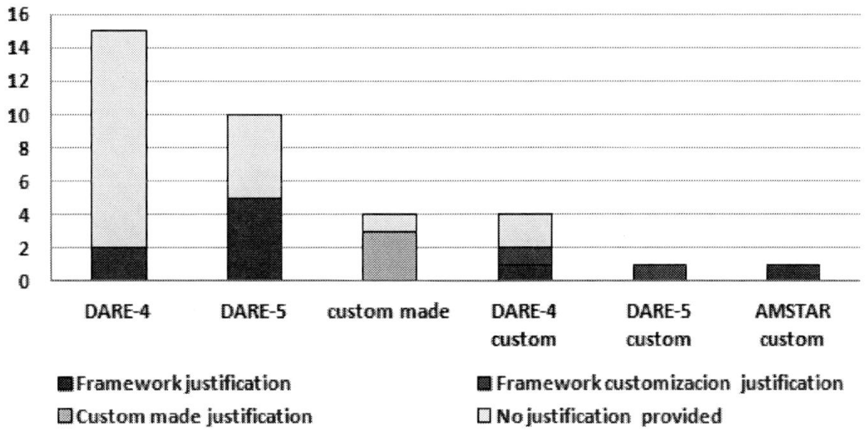

Fig. 2. Quality assessment frameworks

QA framework historical evolution. In the first years of the search period until 2015 all papers reporting QA used DARE-4 or DARE-5 directly with the single exception of a study from 2013 that defines custom-made criteria (1 out of 8). There is a turning point from 2015 onwards because in this latter period one third of the papers (9 out of 27) use QCs not present in DARE. Five studies customize DARE-4 or DARE-5 by adding QCs to them, three studies build custom made QCs and one adopts the AMSTAR framework which is more extensive than DARE.

Justification of the selection. Only 40% of the studies reporting QA (14 out of 35) provide a justification either for: (1) their framework choice, or (2) their framework customization, or (3) their custom-made approach. Each of them gives a single justification for only one of those aspects. The stacked bars in Fig. 2 depict the number of papers giving each kind of justification for each type of QA. We can see that the largest proportion of papers not providing justifications are those adopting the DARE-4 framework directly, i.e., 13 out of 15.

There are 9 papers that justify their framework choice and all of them argue about the good acceptance of the framework, except for [S24] that selects AMSTAR for its reliability since QA "requires the use of a valid and reliable tool" and for [S36] which also provides reliability arguments for their choice of DARE-5. There are 2 papers giving a justification for customizing a framework: [S14] mentions the need of adding missing aspects to DARE-4 and [S15] mentions the need of adapting DARE-5 to their specific study. Finally, 3 out of the 4 papers building their custom-made QCs provide explanations: 2 papers mention the need to adequate the QCs to their study research and paper [S08] says they have established their QCs to cover the four main areas of empirical research according to [20].

QA Measurement. Regardless of the QA framework applied, the 35 TSs with QA can be classified into three main types according to how they measure quality:

- *Aggregator*: 27 TSs aggregate the scores obtained from appraising each QC. Remarkably, all the QCs always have the same weight. All these 27 TSs but one summed the individual scores; [S10] used the arithmetic mean instead.
- *Non-Aggregator*: Five out of the 35 TSs that perform QA appraise each QC but do not aggregate the resulting scores.
- *Unknown*: Three TSs [S9, S22, S29] do not provide any information on how quality is assessed beyond stating that they use a DARE framework.

QC Appraisal. The 32 TSs (27 *Aggregator* + 5 *Non-Aggregator*) have different ways of appraising each QC:

- *Uniform Three-Value*: 24 TSs measure each QC using three possible values, usually "Yes", "Partially" and "No", which are then mapped into 1, 0.5, and 0, if they are aggregated.
- *Uniform Other Values*: Three TSs use two values, "Yes" and "No", for each QC; and [S24] assesses its list of customized AMSTAR criteria with five possible values: "Yes", "No", "Partially", "Cannot answer", "N/A".
- *Non-Uniform*: 4 TSs use a three-value score (e.g. 0, 0.5, 1) for some QC, and for the rest, they use a binary one (0, 1).

Breakdown of QC scores. The 32 TSs (27 *Aggregator* + 5 *Non-Aggregator*) can also be classified into three types:

- *Breakdown*: 23 TSs report the scores for each QC and secondary paper. Two of them include these breakdown scores in the supplementary material.
- *No Breakdown*: 9 TSs do not report any breakdown scores. Here we single out [S11, S38], which do not provide the breakdown for each secondary study but instead report the count of secondary studies for each possible score/QC.

4.3 RQ3. Facets examined in QA

Individual QCs. The 35 TSs that perform QA of secondary studies reported a total of 181 QC altogether. We induced 31 different codes from these 181 QC, see Table 3.

Table 3. Q3 Coding

Code id.	Topic	#TSs
QC1	Inclusion & exclusion criteria (DARE-4, -5)	32
QC2	Search coverage (DARE-4, -5)	32
QC3	Studies synthesized (DARE-5)	11
QC4	Quality assessment (DARE-4, -5)	33
QC5	Studies reporting (DARE-4, -5)	33
QC6	Statement of goal and RQs	4
QC7	Statement of RQs using PICOS	1
QC8	Inclusion of validity threats	2
QC9	Mitigation of bias	2
QC10	Traceability of QA into primary studies	1
QC11	Traceability of evidence into primary studies	1
QC12	Usage of QA and evidence in synthesis	2
QC13	Conclusions relying on evidence	1
QC14	Aggregation of results in synthesis	1
QC15	Weighting results during synthesis	1
QC16-20	Five additional detailed criteria in QA	1
QC21	Review supported by case study or survey	1
QC22	Type of systematic review	2
QC23	Adequacy of the research design	3
QC24	Team involved in selection & data extraction	1
QC25	List of included & excluded studies provided	1
QC26	Declaration of any conflict of interest	1
QC27	Focus on the scope of the study	2
QC28	Precise reporting of the findings	3
QC29	Precise reporting of research method	3
QC30	Value of the work made evident	1
QC31	Protocol design	1

Not surprisingly, the most used codes corresponded to the four DARE-4 criteria (32-33 occurrences each) with the additional synthesis criteria from DARE-5 coming next (QC3, 11 occurrences). Still, it is worth mentioning that some papers provided the definition of these five criteria in their own words. The rest of the codes, proposed in 10 TSs, were spurious, with only QC6 exceeding 3 occurrences.

Categorization of codes. Next, we categorized these codes into facets. We consolidated the phases of systematic reviews proposed in Kitchenham et al.'s works [1, 3] into a single classification schema, removing some steps or concepts we considered not related to QA (e.g., commissioning the review). We made this consolidation through dedicated meetings. We obtained 11 categories grouped into the three usual stages: Planning, Conducting and Reporting. We aligned this classification schema with the 31 codes, not allowing multiple categorization (we chose the category that we considered dominant for each code). In this step, we added 5 new categories and decomposed the single Reporting category into 6 more fine-grained categories. We finally obtained the classification schema shown in Table 4, with 21 categories, from which three of them did not have any code associated. At the end, a majority of 125 out of the 181 QA criteria reported correspond to the Conducting stage (69.1%), while only 12 correspond to Planning (6.6%) and the remaining 44 (24.3%) to Reporting.

Table 4. Categorization of QC codes. Ids: P, Planning; C, Conducting; R, Reporting

Id	Category	QA codes
P1	Identify the need for a review	--
P2	*Determine scope*	QC27
P3	Specify goal and RQs	QC6, QC7
P4	*Design research method*	QC21, QC23
P5	Develop protocol	QC31
P6	Validate protocol	--
C1	Search studies	QC2
C2	Select studies	QC1
C3	Assess quality	QC4, QC16-QC20, QC22
C4	Extract data	--
C5	Synthesise	QC3, QC12, QC14, QC15
C6	*Mitigate bias*	QC9
C7	*Involve the team adequately*	QC24
C8	*Extract conclusions*	QC13
C9	Analyse limitations	QC8
R1	*Statement of CoIs*	QC26
R2	*Reporting of research method*	QC29
R3	*Reporting of findings*	QC28
R4	*Description of studies*	QC5, QC25
R5	*Traceability into studies*	QC10, QC11
R6	*Evidence of value*	QC30

4.4 RQ4. Purposes of QA

In this research question, we used deductive coding. The coding scheme is an extension of QA purposes in [1] proposed by Yang et al. [14] to analyse SE secondary studies QA purposes.

Most TSs (23 out of 35) use QA for only one purpose, while six and four TSs use QA for two and three purposes respectively. Note that two TSs do not declare any purpose for doing QA.

Fig. 3 shows the percentages of TSs that use QA for each purpose (dark blue bars). More than half of the 35 TSs (60%) used QA to understand the quality of the secondary studies (*Investigation*), normally through a research question. Eight studies used QA results as additional IC/EC (*Selection*). Six studies used QA to guide recommendations for future research (*Recommendation*). Five studies used QA to ensure that selected studies exceed a quality threshold (*Validation*). The rest of purposes are gradually decreasing in application, and remarkably the three least declared purposes seem to be the most complex to carry out: use of QA for determining the strength of the inferences (*Interpretation*), for weighting the studies during synthesis (*Weighting*), and for explaining study results according to quality differences (*Differentiation*).

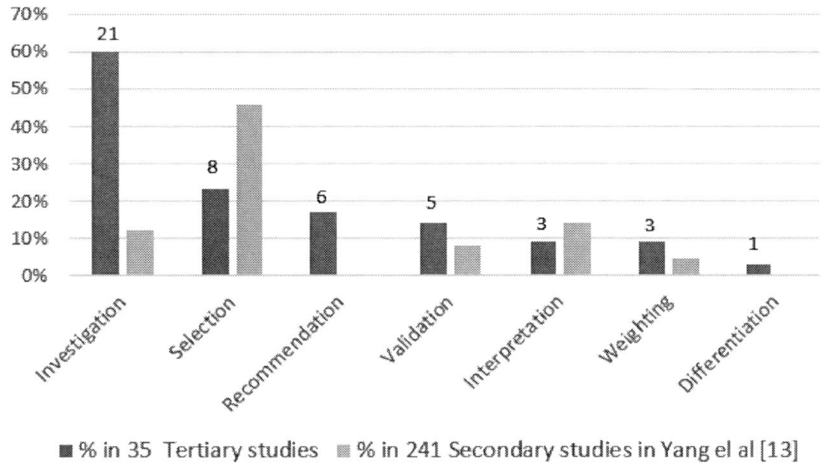

Fig. 3. Percentages of studies per purpose

5 Discussion

QA in TSs versus QA in secondary studies. Although QA in TSs and secondary studies is very different in nature, still we can compare the purposes of each, which have been analysed by Yang et al. [14], see Fig. 3. The differences show that the main purpose of QA in secondary studies is *Selection* of primary studies, far more than any other purpose, as shown in Fig. 3. This means that secondary studies use QA to ensure good quality of the primary studies analysed to synthesise the state of the art of a specific domain. In contrast, *Selection* of secondary studies is a purpose only in 23% of TSs, showing that authors of TSs seem to consider that secondary studies are relevant for a TS independently of their quality. This idea is corroborated in [S01, S04, S15, 7]. Conversely, secondary studies do not investigate the quality of primary studies to support any research goal as often as in the case of TSs; we argue that this is due to the intrinsic diversity of primary studies.

Impact of the type of TSs in QA. We have investigated further the influence of the TS type into our findings. Some results seem to point out that methodological TSs are less strict in assessing the quality of secondary studies than SE-area TSs. Almost all the TSs not performing QA are methodological (13 out of 15 TSs), and this is also the case of the two papers that do not state the QA purpose. A possible explanation is that methodological TSs focus on analysing in depth a particular aspect of the literature review process of the secondary studies included in the study and thus do not pay much attention to their quality, specially when there is a limited number of pages to report the study as it happens in conference papers, which is the case of 13 of the 24 mentioned methodological papers. Anecdotally, we remark that our own paper provides evidence related to this hypothesis! Another interesting observation is the greater number of secondary studies included in methodological TSs, which can be justified because they do not restrict to a particular area, therefore all secondary studies are likely to be candidates for inclusion.

Framework. Nearly three quarters of the studies reporting QA (71,4%) adopt DARE-4 or DARE-5 frameworks directly. All remaining studies (10 TSs) use QCs not present in DARE, mostly by adding QCs to DARE-4 or DARE-5 (in 5 TSs), but also by building custom made QCs (4 TSs), or by adopting the AMSTAR framework which is more extensive than DARE (1 TS). This trend is more pronounced from 2015 onwards as mentioned in Section 4.2. The justifications given by the studies that customize DARE are the need of covering missing aspects or adapting the framework to their specific study. Furthermore, as seen in Section 2, Budgen et al. point out that DARE does not cover all quality issues [10] and we can see in Table 4 that there are many phases of systematic reviews not covered by it. We refer to Section 6 for the first steps towards this direction.

Unclear purpose of QA in TSs. The answer to RQ4 shows a great diversity of purposes for which researchers assess the quality of secondary studies in TSs. The most popular purpose is *Investigation*, but in a deeper analysis of the TSs with this purpose, most of them used the result of QA as if it were yet another bibliometrics measure, reporting the numbers in more or less detail and adding a reflection on how the obtained score measures the quality of the work. Besides being a conservative approach, it suffers from the risk pointed out by Budgen et al. in reference to DARE: QA frameworks are only concerned with whether QA has been done, not how well it has been done [10]. For this reason, we argue that more insightful purposes such as *Interpretation*, *Weighting* or *Differentiation* should be adopted more often in TSs. In any case, selecting one purpose or another should be a logical consequence of some well-established goal.

6 Towards a Comprehensive QA Framework

RQ3's results and the discussion above point to the direction that it would be positive to have a comprehensive framework covering all phases of systematic reviews and then customizations would rather be to cut the criteria that should not be applied in a particular study reducing the need of authors to perform their own extension of a framework. In this section, we outline how this new framework proposal can be developed from the results of the present study.

This new framework, QUASY (QUality Assessment of SecondarY studies), is built in the following manner according to the categorization that we propose in Table 4:

- Given the wide acceptance of the DARE framework, categories C1-C3, C5 and R4 shall be based upon the DARE formulation. However, we acknowledge that some of the proposed works contribute to make these DARE's QC closer to the needs of TSs in SE, therefore we need to analyse whether these proposals are worth to be incorporated into the DARE formulation. For instance, QC25 could be incorporated into QC5 by requiring the list of studies to be provided in order to achieve the maximum score in the evaluation of R4 (Description of Studies).

- Those categories not addressed by DARE, but addressed by some of the studies found, shall be based upon the consolidation of the QCs elicited in this study. This concerns categories P2-P5, C6-C9, R1-R3 and R5-R6. For instance, the way in which S24 states QC31 ("Has the preliminary design of the research (i.e. the definition of research questions and the inclusion criteria) been correctly stated before starting the research?") seems a good starting point for category P5 (Develop Protocol), although we think that the protocol should include additional elements and thus the final formulation needs some work.

- Last, those categories for which we have not found any QC in the literature deserve special care in order to come up with solid proposals. Categories P1, P6 and C4 are in this situation. We have elaborated this novel part of our proposal in more depth and provide concrete proposals below, including score definition based on the guidelines of Kitchenham et al. [1, 3]:
  - **P1: Need for a review**. *Is the justification of the need for a review described and appropriate?* Score: *Yes*, a) the need for a study on the topic is duly argued, particularly if there exist relevant related studies on the same topic, which must be cited properly. *Partly*, the need for a review is not clearly justified or relevant related studies are not cited. *No*, the need for a review is not justified and no relevant related study is cited.
  - **P6: Validate protocol**. *Is the validation of the review's protocol described and appropriate?* Score: *Yes*, the review described explicitly how it was confirmed, prior to the execution of the protocol, that a) the search strings were appropriately derived from the research questions, b) the data to be extracted would properly address the research question(s), and if the data analysis procedure was appropriate to answer the research questions. *Partly*, some aspect (a, b, or c) is missing or all three are present but not addressed appropriately. *No*, the validation of the protocol is not explicitly described and cannot be readily inferred.
  - **C4: Data extraction**. *Is the review's data extraction process described and appropriate?* Score: *Yes*, a) the data extraction form is described explicitly, as well as b) the strategy for extracting and recording the data, and c) how the data extraction process was undertaken and validated, particularly when data required numerical calculations or were subjective. *Partly*, some aspect (a, b, or c) is missing or all three are present but not described with sufficient detail. *No*, the data extraction process is not defined and cannot be readily inferred.

The QUASY framework should also define scores in a consistent manner, and include a well-defined score aggregation mechanism.

7 Threats to Validity

The study does not include all published TSs on SE. The cause of this threat is that we used only one digital library. To understand the severity of the threat, we evaluated the coverage of Scopus. We conducted equivalent searches in Scopus, IEEE Xplore, ACM DL, SpringerLink, ScienceDirect and WoS on April 28th, 2021, obtaining 106, 22, 13,

24, 2 and 36 papers, respectively (details can be found in[2]). Once analyzed, only 5 papers were not found by the Scopus search: 2 of them not written in English, other 2 were published in journals not indexed in Scopus (SIGSOFT SEN and SIGCSE Bull.) and the last one was a paper indexed in Scopus whose area was not Computer Science nor Engineering. Therefore, none of these 5 papers were relevant for our study. Furthermore, we performed backward snowballing on the selected papers to mitigate this threat.

The study is not fully replicable. This threat is inherent to any literature review using digital libraries, due to their ever-changing nature. To mitigate this threat, we have documented in depth all aspects of our search process, including search string, parameters and dates, and have made all data available in a replication package.

Results may be biased by researchers' judgement. We mitigated this threat by intensive teamwork, e.g.: 1) we had weekly 90-minute plenary meetings to discuss relevant aspects of the research methods, results and analysis; 2) we discussed, and resolved offline through GDocs comments, minor discrepancies; 3) we did not exclude any paper without consensus of all researchers; 4) we intensively discussed all coding aspects through an iterative approach, processing the surveyed TSs by batches and reflecting on the coding after every batch.

8 Conclusions

In this paper, we have investigated the current state of the art on quality assessment (QA) of secondary studies as conducted in tertiary studies (TS). Our main conclusion is that, in spite of the great amount and increasing maturity of TSs in the SE discipline, there is a lack of a comprehensive framework covering all facets of quality, with a clear rationale to decide the most appropriate QA purpose according to the goal of the TS. In response to these shortcomings, we have used the results of this literature review as the basis to outline a comprehensive and rationalized first version of the new QUASY framework for secondary studies. Our future research aims at developing in full and validating this framework. Our long-term aim is to provide a consolidated framework similar to that proposed by Ampatzoglou et al. [21] for the assessment of threats to validity. The QUASY framework shall include also methodological aspects, for instance concrete advice on the QA purpose (cf. RQ4) in relation to the main objective of the TS in which the QA is conducted.

References

References [S01]-[S50] to TSs are in https://doi.org/10.5281/zenodo.4742147 (replication package at Zenodo).

1. B. Kitchenham, and S.M. Charters. 2007. Guidelines for performing structural literature reviews in software engineering (Version 2.3). Technical Report, Keele University and University of Durham.

---

[2] http://www.upc.edu/gessi/rep/Scopus-Coverage-Validation.xlsx

2. Raatikainen, M., Tiihonen, J., & Männistö, T. 2019. Software product lines and variability modeling: A tertiary study. Journal of Systems and Software, 149: 485-510.
3. B. Kitchenham, D. Budgen, and P, Brereton. 2015. Evidence-based software engineering and systematic reviews. Vol. 4. CRC press.
4. Centre for Reviews and Dissemination, Systematic Reviews (2007) http://web.archive.org/web/20070918200401/http://www.york.ac.uk/inst/crd/faq4.htm (accessed 23/12/2020).
5. Centre for Reviews and Dissemination, Systematic Reviews (2009) https://www.crd.york.ac.uk/crdweb/AboutPage.asp (acc, 18/12/2020).
6. B. Kitchenham, P. Brereton, D. Budgen, M, Turner, J. Bailey, and S. Linkman. 2009. Systematic literature reviews in software engineering–a systematic literature review. Inf. Softw. Technol. 51, 1, 7-15.
7. B. Kitchenham, R. Pretorius, D. Budgen, P. Brereton, M. Turner, M. Niazi, and S,G. Linkma. 2010. Systematic literature reviews in software engineering - A tertiary study. Inf. Softw. Technol. 52, 8, 792-805.
8. D.S. Cruzes, and T. Dyba, 2011. Research synthesis in software engineering: A tertiary study. Inf. Softw. Technol. 53, 5, 440-455.
9. J.M. Verner, P. Brereton, B. Kitchenham, M. Turner, and M. Niazi. 2014. Risks and risk mitigation in global software development: A tertiary study. Inf. Softw. Techn. 56, 1, 54-78.
10. D. Budgen, P. Brereton, S. Drummond, N. Williams, 2018. Reporting systematic reviews: Some lessons from a tertiary study. Inf. Softw. Technol. 95, 62-74.
11. N.Ali, and M. Usman, 2019. A critical appraisal tool for systematic literature reviews in software engineering. Inf. Softw. Technol, 112: 48-50.
12. B.J Shea, J.M Grimshaw, G.A. Wells, M. Boers, N. Andersson, C. Hamel, A.C. Porter, P. Tugwell, D. Moher, and L.M Bouter. 2007. Development of AMSTAR: a measurement tool to assess the methodological quality of systematic reviews. BMC Med Res Methodol.7, 10.
13. B.J. Shea, B.C. Reeves, G. Wells, M. Thuku, C. Hamel, J. Moran, D. Moher, P. Tugwell, V. Welch, E. Kristjansson, D.A. Henry. 2017. AMSTAR 2: a critical appraisal tool for systematic reviews that include randomised or non-randomised studies of healthcare interventions, or both, BMJ 358, j4008 .
14. L. Yang, H. Zhang, H. Shen, X. Huang, X. Zhou, G. Rong, and D. Shao. 2021. Quality assessment in systematic literature reviews: A software engineering perspective. Inf. Softw. Technol. 130, 106397.
15. V.R. Basili. 1992. Software modeling and measurement: the Goal/Question /Metric paradigm. University of Maryland at College Park, Technical Report.
16. J. Krüger, C. Lausberger, I. von Nostitz-Wallwitz, G. Saake, T. Leich. 2019. Search. Review. Repeat? An empirical study of threats to replicating SLR searches. Empirical Software Engineering 25: 627-677.
17. B. A. Kitchenham, T. Dyba, M. Jorgensen. 2004. Evidence-based software engineering. In Procs. 26th International Conference on Software Engineering, 273-281.
18. Wohlin, C., Runeson, P., Höst, M., Ohlsson, M. C., Regnell, B., & Wesslén, A. 2012. Experimentation in software engineering. Springer Science & Business Media.
19. Miles, M. B., Huberman, A. M., & Saldana, J. 2014. Qualitative data analysis: A methods sourcebook. Sage editions.
20. T. Dybå, and T. Dingsøyr. Empirical studies of agile software development: A systematic review. Inf. Softw. Technol. 50, 9-10: 833-859.
21. A. Ampatzoglou, S. Bibi, P. Avgeriou, M. Verbeek, A. Chatzigeorgiou. 2019. Identifying, categorizing and mitigating threats to validity in software engineering secondary studies. Inf. Softw. Technol, 106: 201-230.

Teaching Software Engineering Remotely to Teenagers in Social Vulnerability Conditions during the Coronavirus Pandemic: Challenges and Lessons Learned

Michelle Miranda[1], Arlanda Wisniewski[1], Álvaro Menezes[1], and Rafael Prikladnicki[1]

School of Technology - Pontifícia Universidade do Rio Grande do Sul (PUCRS), Porto Alegre, Brazil
{michelle.miranda,alvaro.menezes}@edu.pucrs.br,
arlandajws@gmail.com,
rafael.prikladnicki@pucrs.br

Abstract. The context of the Coronavirus Pandemic in the year of 2020 brought several challenges, including the professional and student adaptation to the virtual environment. This article brings a case study carried out within the software engineering teaching program, called Inclusive Accelerator, which is a short-term teaching course, aimed at socially vulnerable teenagers. As a purpose, we sought to identify the barriers found in the process of teaching software engineering in virtual environments, using a group of teenagers in situations of social vulnerability as the case study. A qualitative research was carried out through a case study using questionnaires and interviews as data collection tools, as well as the participant observation method carried out during the year of 2020 by the authors of this work. Five main challenges were observed in the results, such as: communication failures, reduced participation, time sharing with other responsibilities, lack of basic knowledge and social problems interfering with learning. We analyzed that these challenges were enhanced in distance learning education, due to the greater visibility of vulnerability contexts in remote education. We also realized about the importance of mapping the social markers that cross these contexts, such as geographic location, domestic infrastructure, internet access, which are beyond the question of teaching computing methodology. We believe that this work can provide reflections on the challenges to be faced in similar situations, expanding the discussion on diversity and inclusion of socially vulnerable groups within the area of software engineering education.

Keywords: Teaching software engineering · vulnerable teenagers · Virtual education.

1 Introduction

The year of 2020 brought several challenges, including the professional and learning adaptation to the virtual environment. For adaptation to happen, it is necessary to have openness to change, flexibility and an environment comfortable enough for creativity to emerge [10]. For example, Barr at al. [1] demonstrate that Software Engineering education may be successfully delivered online with some straightforward adjustments. However, Trinta et al [19], points that some students report difficulties in doing their programming homework, that main barriers were their psychological context, difficulties in balancing their course activities with their home tasks, as well as their job's demands.

This article brings a Case Study [13] carried out within the software engineering teaching program which presents itself as a short course, where teenagers in situation of social vulnerability have the opportunity to learn basic programming concepts with interpersonal skills [6]. The Program is a partnership through the Pontifical Catholic University of Rio Grande do Sul (PUCRS), and the industry, represented by the companies involved, which are: ThoughtWorks [16], Sicredi [14] and Globo [4].

Due to the beginning and worsening of the Pandemic it became necessary to search for possible and efficient alternatives to adapt the program's operation virtually. Thus, the objective of this research is to identify the barriers in the virtual teaching process. To achieve this goal, a questionnaire was used as a data collection method, and the use of the Participant Observation Method [8]. The results will be presented through the categorization of the identified barriers with the report of observed cases, enabling the sewing of such materials in order to provide a discussion on pertinent topics to those who are inserted in environments where inclusion and diversity are present.

As contribution, it is expected to provide reflection to the educational and social challenges of the Coronavirus Pandemic and assist similar cases, as well as similar projects and companies. Therefore, it is necessary to keep in mind when reading this article, that the study was carried out based on observation and reflection during the home office scenario, so the obtained results and discussions are guided by the challenges and consequences leveraged by the virtual scenario, which is becoming a present and striking reality, since the home office was regulated in Brazil in 2017 [5] and currently, highlighted by the Pandemic.

2 Social Vulnerability and Coronavirus Pandemic

Vulnerable groups of people are those that are disproportionately exposed to risks. According to Lancet [9], the socioeconomic effects highlight the increased risks of pregnancy in young girls, school dropout, as well as child abuse; people who live in highly dense communities with precarious or insecure housing, or poor sanitation are in risk to have malnutrition and health inequalities.

Toiviainen [17] affirms that by facilitating social inclusion of vulnerable teenagers and developing their skills related to socio-cultural, socio-economic and political dimension, educators need to take into account and understand multiple vulnerabilities, as well as students' diversities. The referred author states that the recognition of young people's diversity, rather than treating them as one common group with predetermined or assumed vulnerabilities and educational needs, becomes an important aspect of the role of educational professionals.

According to Trauth [18] social inclusion is a recognized area of information systems research, more specifically, social inclusion research has come to be seen as the effort to develop a greater understanding about aspects of human diversity, as they relate to underrepresented and underserved groups in relation to the development, deployment, management, use, and impact of information systems and technologies. The organizations must be socially inclusive and respect all aspects of human diversity.

However, diversity does not automatically promote social inclusion, rather, school administrators and educators need to create conditions that are safe and must accept all students [7]. If schools are truly committed to diversity and inclusion, teachers' roles and responsibilities need to proactively model socially inclusive behaviors, rely on practices that unite students with shared goals and activities, and manage situations when students are victimized, rejected, or have no friends.

During the 2020 Pandemic, 191 countries instigated nationwide school closures, affecting around 1.5 billion students worldwide [3]. In response to these schools' closures, many countries adopted online modalities (e-Learning) to ensure the continuity in learning. To individuals or groups experience vulnerability the social and economic conditions in which people live, learn, work, and play are the social determinants of health and educational disadvantage. The aforementioned author maintains that the more individuals are exposed to different forms of disadvantage, both social and material, the poorer are the health and developmental outcomes, especially related to education.

3 Study Context

3.1 Inclusive Accelerator Context

Inclusive Accelerator is a 4 months duration program that enable teenagers in social vulnerability conditions to have a first contact with software programming and agile methodologies, aiming at personal and professional development in technology [6]. Established as part of a spin-off from teaching and career development program with agile methodologies [15], the Program is carried out through a partnership that began in 2017 between the academy and the industry, primarily between PUCRS and Thoughtworks, currently having two more partners: Sicredi and Globo.

Currently, the Program consists of coordination, teachers, psychologist, mentors and monitors described as follow:

- *Coordination*: professors at PUCRS, employees at partner companies, including software developers and agile people. They form a group of approximately 6 people;
- *Teachers*: they are volunteer software developers from partner companies and are responsible for giving one or more classes to students according to

the teaching material previously prepared by the Program coordination. For each class, around 20 collaborating people make up the teachers' group;

- *Psychologist*: she works focusing on the students' personal development, performing one-on-one meetings according to the individual's demand, in addition to promoting the development of interpersonal skills, by providing welcoming and safe collective spaces for listening and speaking. She also helps the mentor network when necessary, especially with strategies to face the challenges of supporting the different realities of vulnerability;
- *Mentors*: there are two types of mentors: the first one consists of 2 PUCRS' Masters and PhDs' researchers in Computer Science. They provide support permanently during the classes for teachers and students in the classroom, and substitute teachers in case of necessity. The second type consists of the volunteers from the partner companies. They form a group of 15 software developers and provide extra class support for students by one-on-one meetings;
- *Monitors*: in each class 3 students are invited, who stood out during the course, to act in the next class as monitors. They normally participate in the course, but are encouraged to help their colleagues during practical tasks.

The Program has two teaching modalities: technical track composed of learning involving the introduction to logic programming, HTML, CSS and JavaScript.; socio-educational track that consists of preparation for work, interpersonal relationships and subjects' themes suggested by students such as racism, feminism, emotional dependence, among others. The contents of the technical trail are taught in order to highlight practices and philosophies of agile methodologies.

There are 3 stages for admission process: recommendation, interview and selection. The recommendations occur directly to the program team through companies, foundations and organizations' employees that carry out social work recognized by society. After these recommendations, interviews are conducted where the factors interested in technology and social vulnerability and diversity are the indicators that will influence the last selection phase.

3.2 Inclusive Accelerator in the Pandemic Scenario

The class of 2020 was composed of 15 students aged between 15 and 18 years old, with ten girls (including one trans girl) and five boys. Classified by racial ethnic diversity, eight students could be identified as white (mostly Hispanic or Latino) and seven as black people (black and brown). Due to the Pandemic, especially in the year of 2020, the Program received only one class lasting 8 months.

Since the foundation of the Program, classes have been held at PUCRS' computer labs and at the partner companies'rooms located in the university's technological park. However, due to the 2020 Pandemic, the course was interrupted for about 6 months, mainly due to lack of information on for how long the lockdown would continue and due to students' difficulties, such as lack of computers at home and internet access. It was necessary to switch the course to a virtual environment. The classes were taught through videos previously recorded and made available on a virtual teaching platform; the classes were attended simultaneously by all students at a pre-established time with mentors who made themselves available for possible questions from the students. To switch the students' difficulties, personal computers and mobile Internet devices were lent by the university to allow students to create their home teaching environment.

4 Research Method

We carried out a Case Study according the recommendations of Runeson and Höst [13]. This methodology consists of defining the research objective, the investigated case, revealing the research question, as well as the data collection strategy and the target audience. The objective is to identify the barriers in the teaching of software engineering in an online environment. The investigated case was a group of teenagers with social vulnerability, in the context of a global pandemic. This article aims to answer the following research question:

- **RQ1.** *"What are the barriers observed in the teaching of software engineering in an online environment in teams composed of teenagers with socially vulnerable groups in the context of this global pandemic?"*

The data was collected through interviews, a questionnaire and participant observation [8]. We also used the dialogic map method according to Conklin [2], as a strategy to systematize and analyze the results.The target audience of this case study was composed of members of the Program, these being students, monitors, mentors and teachers.

In order to answer RQ1, we use the data collected through a questionnaire, preserving the respondents' confidentiality. The questionnaire was semi-structured for mentors, monitors, teachers, the psychologist, and contained the following questions: (i) What was your involvement in the Program and how do you evaluate your experience and why?; (ii) Did you feel that there were barriers? If so, how did you manage to overcome them?; (iii) How do you assess your students' performance and why?; and, (iv) In your opinion, do you feel that there were barriers to the students you taught? If so, can you comment some of these barriers and how did the students overcome them?

The semi-structured questionnaire applied to students contained the following questions: (i) How was it for you to be part of the Program for one year?; (ii) How did you feel about the interruption of the Program due to the Pandemic?; (iii) What is your feedback on content and remote lessons?; (iv) What were the main difficulties you experienced during the Program?; (v) Did you feel any barriers that prevented you from participating in this Program?; (vi) In your opinion, what do you believe that the mentors or teachers could have done to support you to overcome these difficulties?; (vii) How do you evaluate your performance in the Program?; and, (viii) Are you interested in keep studying or working in the technology field?

We also used the notes recorded in a field diary as a data collection instrument, in which we collected data using the technique of Participant Observation [8]. The observations lasted a total of approximately 80 hours and were conducted with the consent of the participants in class sessions and technical monitoring.

5 Results

5.1 The barriers observed in the Inclusive Accelerator Program due to the Pandemic scenario (RQ1)

We obtained 5 responses between mentors, psychologist, and teachers; and also collected responses from 13 students in the Program. Participants were identified according to Table 1 1, keeping their secrecy. The results obtained were systematized into 5 categories, based on a thematic analysis of the participants' narratives, and then identified as barriers, which will be presented below.

Table 1. Table of Participants

	Type of participant
P1	Teacher
P2, P4	Mentor
P3	Psychologist
P4	Mentor
P5-P12	Student

Communication failures: failures in communication a significant barrier found in remote learning. With the reduction of physical contact, it was even more challenging to understand students' needs: *"With remote teaching, the absence of contact in the classroom to better read the students' interest or difficulties was as in a classroom. Sometimes it is possible to perceive the expression of "I am not understanding" when you explain something, and in the virtual environment you need students to have a degree of autonomy and maturity to say whether they are learning or not, and this is not simple"* (P4). The communication barrier also permeated elements such as insecurity, creation of affective bonds *"I came across mainly questions about the creation of a bond with the reduction of the senses (touch, smell, sight), since in this format, you can carry out displays of affection that were once so accessible to us, such as shaking hands, hugging, smelling the person who appears, and eye to eye"* (P3).

Although communication was also identified as a barrier to the remote content learning due to the changes in the dynamics of the classes held in the Program, which according to some participans, felt *"confused, did not understand anything"* (P9), having a face-to-face class, *"it would have been better because of the explanations. At first I was lost, I did not know where to start, I spoke with mentors and monitors" (P6)*, because *"due to the pandemic scenario the main barrier was communication with students and the observance of their performance, because many chose to study on flexible schedules, missing remote classes at fixed times. With this, it is understood that losing time with some students who may be underperforming and need more attention to clarify their doubts at the moment creates a communication gap"* (P2).

Reduced participation: in some cases the participation in the classes, or the lack of it, was directly related to the high or low performance. This low participation can be pointed out as a consequence of the change in the format of the classes due to the pandemic scenario, *"because most of the students feel discouraged during the course of the program. I believe that the main cause is family structure and situation, since in the face-to-face class we have a safe environment, immersed in technology and an escape to focus on, which is not always the case in students' homes"* (P3) and *"just a few students participated and I knew it was expected, but those students who participated were very engaged"* (P1).

The issue of participation in the Inclusive Accelerator Program was related to attendance at remote classes and delivery of the proposed exercises throughout the week. For some students, the performance ratio was measured more with the delivery of such exercises: *"My performance was on average. I feel I did not do well, but I did not do too badly. I just did not deliver all the exercises"* (P6) and *"I appreciated my performance, but it could be better. I could have tried to better manage my time for the delivery of the exercises"* (P8).

The performance was also directly related due to the change in routine, commitments due to the Pandemic and the emotional distress it brought, impacting different areas of the students' lives: *"I could have organized myself better. It was not how I wanted it to be, I was pretty average. The Pandemic discouraged me with everything, even my school studies, I wanted to quit, I just did not do it because my friends kept trying to encourage me"* (P7) and *"I tried hard, but I think that face-to-face classes were easier, because at home it was very tiring, many school activities, many tasks at home to perform"* (P11).

Some members of the Program believe that participation is a complex barrier to be analyzed mainly because *"each individual is unique and has unique responsibilities in their lives. There were students who were unable to commit to the program due to the most diverse circumstances"* (P3) and that, therefore, performance cannot be measured by the number of classes attended and the delivered exercises *"the performance meter can be delivering the correct exercises, or only delivered, however this may not correspond to the students' learning reality and not even taking into account the problems they are facing"* (P4).

Time sharing with other responsibilities: another barrier that was identified is related to the accumulation of responsibilities, in addition to the division of home space with work and family commitments, placing several people facing the time sharing of a certain activity with other demands in the period that would be dedicated only to the participation in the Program, as we can note on these narratives: *"It was complicated, there were weeks that I dedicated to the program and others to the school studies. It was all in a short time. In addition, I had other commitments. I preferred the classes in person because I would be focused on the program activity at that specific time. Sometimes I had to do a lot* *at the same time"* (P7); *"It was complicated to dedicate myself to the program at home, having to take care of the home tasks"* (P12) and *"some students had to split their time between school tasks and domestic activities, others found work during the program, and others the environment with several people at home since the lockdown did not allow concentration on the class"* (P2). In addition, *"Many had to start working because they had family members unemployed due to the Pandemic, others were unable to deal with their school study activities in parallel with the project activities, others had their personal difficulties increased"* (P3).

Lack of basic technical knowledge: the students' selection process of the Program does not require prior computer skills. In the previous editions, classes were given in a computer lab located at PUCRS, and had mentor people to assist in the handling and care of the equipment, answering the students' doubts. In addiction the University is responsible for any infrastructure need, such as computer maintenance and Internet access.

The switch of the classes to the remote environment required that the Program's coordination understand what the students' infrastructure needs were. However, even if such infrastructure was provided, some students observed difficulties in handling the technology on a daily basis when problems arose. For example, some students had no place to put their computers, others had no outlet, and other had a computer but had difficulty communicating their needs.

In addition, having the first contact with software engineering content and at the same time starting a new learning to use the video call or more interactive communication tools required unforeseen time in organizing the schedule: *"Mastering the equipment to do yoyr studies at home was a difficulty. In this Program, the computers are set up before class with all the programs installed. We had students who had difficulty learning how to turn on the computer and even more to set it up. Although the Program offered computers to study at home, Internet, the challenges of the home office were visible"* (P4) and *"My computer crashed, I stopped trying to solve it"* (P5) and *"I believe that the problem was with me because I had no experience with computer content to solve the problems, the remote context is new for me"* (P7). Access to the Internet in peripheral and rural regions was one of the greatest challenges among students: *"My Internet was very unstable, I was kicked from the classes several times because of this"* (P9) and *"In my neighborhood there was no way to access Internet to do the program"* (P10).

Social problems interfering with learning: the target audience of the Inclusive Accelerator Program are teenagers belonging to socially vulnerable groups, that is, teenagers who have more complex social well-being issues, but see in computing a possibility of changing their reality. However, the question of employability that was affected by the Pandemic, the demand for more enhaced attention to health care, the confinement caused by the social isolation that was necessary throughout 2020 in several countries and cities to contain the spreading of the Pandemic, highlighted some issues that guide aspects of vulnerability. Housing, employability, health, and anything else related to the teenagers' daily live may impact other social markers identified here as barriers, such as participation or time sharing, as mentioned: *"In addition to the barriers with technical language and programming learning, other personal problems such as job search to support the family's income, necessity to leave their houses, issues of gender identity and unemployment, were experienced by the students"*, *"There were a lot of things going on: leaving the shelter, looking for a new home, appointments at the church and periodic meetings with the social worker sometimes made me tired"* (P7), "It was difficult to study at home with other 16 people, I needed space for a remote learning" (P11) and *"It was difficult to study at home with so many household chores, taking care of elderly people at home such as my grandmother and my 100-year-old great-grandmother"* (P12).

5.2 Actions taken to minimize challenges

The following are some actions taken to minimize the mapped challenges. It is important to note that these actions were taken throughout the Program in the remote context during the Pandemic.

Communication was a barrier brought by several participants, so one of the actions taken by the team was the establishment of a fixed time to explain the content showed on the videos. Communication between students and technical staff was restricted to the exchange of official messages in an instant messaging application and individual mentoring sessions. There were attempts to use other communication tools that would allow students to interact with teachers to solve doubts, but it was noted that there was no adherence from the students. The solutions found to circumvent this barrier were to establish virtual monitoring schedules, use the communication channel already used by students, in addition to being available to exchange messages at alternative times.

In relation to what concerns the actions related to the participation, coordination and mentors met weekly to update on participation, engagement, student demands and teacher needs. The team began to realize that the participation was reduced from 15 students to around 4 to 7 present in the activities, among them were classes, delivery of exercises and individual mentoring. From this, one-on-one meetings with students were held to understand each context separately. The contact with students was made through text messages and phone calls, but there was not always a response and openness to dialogue. One of the ways mentors found to help the students' participation and consequently, their performance, was to be present at alternative times outside of course activities.

It became necessary, particularly in the remote context, to map the individual needs of each student and seek, as far as possible, to provide the materials and knowledge necessary for everyone to have access to classes. After carrying out this mapping of needs - including computers and Internet access - as weel as the dialogue with the enterprises, it was possible to provide all materials and devices for all students. Consideration was given to the fact that students could have difficulties in installing the necessary tools to enable them to communicate and access the classes. In order to help them, one f the coordinators held a class where the tools and instructions were introduced.

Seeking students' feedback was another practice carried out to face the barriers. In moments of individual dialogue with the students, the team endeavored to understand their demands and to adjust the actions both individually and collectively. There were positive feedback comments, among which we highlight those related to the support during the Program, and constructive comments regarding the lenght of the videos recorded, in which the students suggested shorter videos for a better understanding of the content.

In the scenario of teaching in virtual environments, there is a loss of physical contact, as eye-to-eye, handshake, which before was frequent and common. Reception, close monitoring and observation of subtle signs in the classroom, such as the students' facial expressions showing understanding or the lack of it, which were previously possible, since it became part of the past. Thus, the creation of bonds was impaired, as there was no face-to-face space for meetings or physical contact, in addition to the contract being made for the face-to-face course, that is, the students were not organized for the remote environment.

It was noted that the class of 2020 did not create the same type of bond that the previous classes built, because they had no previous experience with the virtual environment, and also because of the time shared with other activities during the course. The results indicate that the students had difficulties in managing the time dedicated to their activities, such as school, domestic, personal and professional, which generated an accumulation of activities, and even insecurity and self-assessments feelings with a high level of demand, even with the whole context of social vulnerability and in the midst of the Pandemic scenario.

6 Discussion

After contextualizing the Program and identifying the barriers encountered during the year of 2020 with virtual education, the discussion of the case became possible. It will be carried out through a narrative, where a dialogue will be promoted between the collected data - presented in the results - and the observations made, maintaining the barriers found as a guiding thread. In order to facilitate the exercise of reflection promoted by this study, two axes will guide this section: lessons learned and opportunities.

6.1 Lessons learned

Regarding basic technical knowledge and home office infrastructure, it was noted that it was necessary to map each student's access to technology and home infrastructure - computer, Internet access, and somewhere in the house to engage in work with privacy. In addition, because of the absence of computer lab technicians present in the remote environment, as well as because the Inclusive Accelerator Program is some students' first contact with computers, it was necessary to plan for an adjustment and learning period, providing students with greater autonomy in the problem-solving and learning process.

Regarding the systematization of the activities schedule and the study routine, several reports showed that the engagement in a virtual environment was reduced - when compared to the face-to-face environment - due to the excessive school, work and/or domestic demands. It was noted that in the face-to-face environment, where students were in an environment that was favorable for study and focus - in the presence of other students and teachers, with set time intervals between classes - engagement in the Program activities was different from how it was in the virtual environment. In the context of a pandemic with social isolation, remote education requires a dedicated place and time for activities and greater commitment from both the student and the support network, helping and supporting students at home when required. The flexibility of the syllabus provided by the Program at the beginning of the remote period was not successful, although there was an intention to offer greater autonomy to students. It was perceived that setting times for tutoring helped students to organize their timetables.

Another lesson learned is related to the aspects of social vulnerability and limitations of the Program. Although the Inclusive Accelerator's goal is to teach software development as a social program, it is important to realize, in addition to understanding what the infrastructure necessities are - better teaching methodology, recruiting technically trained professionals -, it is necessary to understand social aspects such as housing, employability, family, gender identity, and observe how these aspects pass through the students' learning, especially when they belong to vulnerable groups.

Concerning communication, the attempt to teach the use of new communication tools that aimed to facilitate the sharing of doubts and codes for problem solving, proved to be ineffective. Learning and using another communication tool was not successful, since the students continued using the instant messaging communication tool that they were already familiar with. That is, for the inclusion of a new tool, as well as the learning of any tool used for remote teaching, it seems to be necessary to provide a period in the timetable for onboarding.

6.2 Opportunities

One of the opportunities offered to the students in the Program is to develop themselves in the professional sphere - hard skills - as well as in the interpersonal sphere - soft skills. Through classes, discussions, contact with different realities and the students' identification with the Program's employees, the possibility of a strong individual and social impact on this experience is revealed.

According to Rosa [12], adolescence is the moment of transition from the family scene to the social scene, that is, the relationships of identification and insertion in the social group are worked out. People linked to the project interacted weekly with the students, helping to solve issues about the course technical subjects, doubts about careers in the computing area (courses and job market), in addition to supporting and assisting students with the experienced challenges, arose from the context of social vulnerability.

In the face-to-face setting of the course, communication was already a barrier. It is an inclusive program where the groups of employees belonging to industry and academy have privileged social realities, while the group of students have a social reality in contexts of social vulnerability, in addition of being a group composed of teenagers. The language used by the team is not the same as that of the students, mainly due to the highlighted difference in social contexts. Sometimes, the team used technical or formal terms that are not part of the students' vocabulary, creating a barrier for horizontal communication and bonding.

This contact has tested the team's openness and ability to work with inclusion, but in addition, it provided the possibility of identifying students with their mentors. For example, some students arrived at the project without dreams, without goals, without believing in their capacity, for social reasons or for experiencing structural prejudices that have not been dealt with. In the Program they met with mentors who had already gone through similar situations, opening the possibility of identification where students could perceive that it is possible to develop, grow, dream big and achieve their goals, whether in the area of technology or in another one.

Being the Inclusive Accelerator the result of a partnership between the academy and the industry, understanding the value of the presence of diverse people, as well as the promotion of affirmative actions for vulnerable groups in order to contribute to the elimination of biases and prejudices, are points of utmost importance within the Program. These issues have been worked in the Program with the participation of people who are currently in the industry or in the academy, and have a trajectory where social vulnerability had already been part of their stories, and also through the work of the psychologist, by providing spaces - both for the team and the students - for exchange, speech and acceptance so that stereotypes and complexes, which lead to veiled behaviors of structural prejudices such as racism, chauvinism, homophobia and many others, can be deconstructed.

7 Threats to validity

Petersen and Gencel [11] explain that the assessment of threats to validity is fundamental to guarantee the quality of empirical studies in Software Engineering. This study may have threats associated with data collection (theoretical validity, descriptive validity and generalization) or data analysis (interpretative validity and generalization).

Threats about data collection can occur through the participant observation method used as a strategy for data collection. This method involves continuous observation and interaction with the people involved in the research. We used a strategy to record the activities for later data collection, field diaries created by the researchers and virtual spreadsheets were used to record the data collected, both from both the questionnaires and by the participant observation.

The main limitations of this work are the difficulty of generalizing its results. The specific nature of the lives, environments, and therefore, the problems of the students (and also of the other participants of the Program), along with all the complications derived from the Pandemic situation, makes this experience FIT a specific moment of history in a specific place and with a specific set of people.

There were issues beyond the program's goodwill and intention to solve problems to ensure access to virtual activities. The Program had provided equipment such as computers, Internet access modem, trained teachers, mentors; however, there were limits when it came to working with vulnerable groups. One of the issues to be raised and that can be explored in a next study, is how to provide Internet access in peripheral and rural regions due to the lack of telephone services in these locations.

8 Conclusion

This article brought a case study carried out from data collection through questionnaires and participant observation with the purpose of identifying the barriers found in the remote teaching of Software Engineering for teenagers in situations of social vulnerability in the program Inclusive Accelerator. This study presented implications for the teaching of Software Engineering with social impact, which contributes to the understanding of the educational and social challenges of the Coronavirus Pandemic, which is still a current subject. Furthermore, it is an example of using qualitative research methods to address a research objective that could not otherwise be addressed.

The discussion brought a dialogue between the data collection and the observations carried out through a narrative, where lessons were learned and opportunities were discussed. The barriers were brought as a guiding thread to promote reflection, both for the team participating in the Program, and for similar projects, where inclusion and diversity are present.

The Pandemic context brought greater visibility to issues related to to the students' social vulnerability within their homes, which were previously not noticeable in the face-to-face format of the Program - for example, the infrastructure of their houses. It was necessary for the program to try to mitigate some challenges. Besides, although the focus of the Program is the teaching of Software Engineering within the field of computing, when it comes to teenagers in situations of social vulnerability, especially in a pandemic context, without human considerations (even if computing is understood as a motivating outlet for social change), it appears that the program has limited potential for transformation. Due to the importance and challenges related to the research problem of this article, we believe that the discussion of the subject can be carried out more broadly in future works, analyzing similar initiatives where there is a concern with inclusion of vulnerable populations, not only in the Software Engineering field, but also in Information Technology.

References

1. Barr, M., Nabir, S.W., Somerville, D.: Online delivery of intensive software engineering education during the covid-19 pandemic. In: 2020 IEEE 32nd Conference on Software Engineering Education and Training (CSEE&T). pp. 1–6. IEEE (2020)
2. Conklin, J.: Dialogue mapping: Building shared understanding of wicked problems. John Wiley & Sons, Inc. (2005)
3. Drane, C.F., Vernon, L., O'Shea, S.: Vulnerable learners in the age of covid-19: A scoping review. The Australian Educational Researcher pp. 1–20 (2020)
4. Globo: https://grupoglobo.globo.com/
5. Haubrich, D.B., Froehlich, C.: Benefícios e desafios do home office em empresas de tecnologia da informação. Revista Gestão & Conexões **9**(1), 167–184 (2020)
6. Heck, N., Knebel, P., Prikladnicki, R.: Aceleradora Ágil e Inclusiva: Unindo Conhecimento, Projetos e Pessoas para Construir um Futuro Tecnológico Justo. Fatos & Ideias (2019)
7. Juvonen, J., Lessard, L.M., Rastogi, R., Schacter, H.L., Smith, D.S.: Promoting social inclusion in educational settings: Challenges and opportunities. Educational Psychologist **54**(4), 250–270 (2019)
8. Kawulich, B.B.: Participant observation as a data collection method. In: Forum qualitative sozialforschung/forum: Qualitative social research. vol. 6 (2005)
9. Lancet, T.: Redefining vulnerability in the era of covid-19. Lancet (London, England) **395**(10230), 1089 (2020)
10. Pereira, C.S.P.R.: A emergência [e urgência] da criatividade na adaptação à sociedade contemporânea: uma proposta para a formação inicial de professores. Ph.D. thesis, Universidade de Lisboa (2020)
11. Petersen, K., Gencel, C.: Worldviews, research methods, and their relationship to validity in empirical software engineering research. In: 2013 Joint Conference of the 23rd International Workshop on Software Measurement and the 8th International Conference on Software Process and Product Measurement. pp. 81–89. IEEE (2013)
12. Rosa, M.D.: Adolescência: da cena familiar à cena social. Psicologia USP **13**(2), 227–241 (2002)
13. Runeson, P., Höst, M.: Guidelines for conducting and reporting case study research in software engineering. Empirical software engineering **14**(2), 131 (2009)
14. Sicred: https://www.sicredi.com.br/
15. Steglich, C., Lisboa, A., Prikladnicki, R., Marczak, S., da Costa Móra, M., Olchik, A., Heck, N., Rachid, Y., Ghidorsi, G.: Agile accelerator program: From industry-academia collaboration to effective agile training. In: Proceedings of the 34th Brazilian Symposium on Software Engineering. pp. 21–30 (2020)
16. ThoughWorks: https://www.thoughtworks.com/
17. Toiviainen, H., Kersh, N., Hyytiä, J.: Understanding vulnerability and encouraging young adults to become active citizens through education: the role of adult education professionals. Journal of Adult and Continuing Education **25**(1), 45–64 (2019)
18. Trauth, E.: A research agenda for social inclusion in information systems. ACM SIGMIS Database: the Database for Advances in Information Systems **48**(2), 9–20 (2017)
19. Trinta, F., Rego, P.A., Viana, W.: Teaching development of distributed software during covid-19: An experience report in brazil. In: Proceedings of the 34th Brazilian Symposium on Software Engineering. pp. 616–625 (2020)

Encuesta para analizar las necesidades con respecto al proceso de despliegue de las PyMES en Argentina

Marisa Panizzi[1,2,3][0000-0002-9699-1544], Marcela Genero[4][0000-0002-6868-7465], Rodolfo Bertone[1][0000-0003-0609-0310]

[1] Facultad de Informática, Instituto de Investigación en Informática LIDI (III-LIDI), Universidad Nacional de La Plata, La Plata, Argentina.
[2] Departamento de Ingeniería en Sistemas de Información, Universidad Tecnológica Nacional, Regional Buenos Aires, Argentina, Argentina.
[3] Instituto de Tecnología e Ingeniería, Universidad Nacional de Hurlingham, Hurlingham, Argentina.
[4] Departamento de Tecnologías y Sistemas de Información, Universidad de Castilla-La Mancha, Ciudad Real, España.
marisapanizzi@outlook.com; pbertone@lidi.unlp.edu.ar; Marcela.Genero@uclm.es

Resumen. En Argentina, la industria del software se compone mayoritariamente por Pequeñas y Medianas Empresas (PyMES). En la mayoría de estas empresas el despliegue no se realiza de manera sistemática lo cual impacta en la finalización del proyecto, en la no aceptación del sistema software por parte del cliente, sumado a que los errores se resuelven en el proceso de mantenimiento, estos inconvenientes generan retrabajo y baja calidad y productividad en el proceso. En este sentido, para obtener evidencia sobre el estado actual de la práctica del proceso de despliegue de sistemas de software en PyMES de Argentina, y en pro de incrementar la calidad y capacidad del proceso de despliegue en dichas empresas, se decidió realizar un estudio exploratorio basado en una encuesta. En esta encuesta participaron 195 profesionales de la industria del software que trabajan en PyMES. Los resultados reportan que la mayoría de las PyMES no cuentan con un proceso sistematizado para la ejecución del despliegue y que aún continúan presentándose dificultades en algunas de las actividades del proceso. Dificultades que se acentúan más en mircro y pequeñas PyMES. Se evidenció que la mayoría de los participantes convergen en la utilidad de disponer de un proceso de despliegue, en la necesidad de plantillas orientadoras para su ejecución y en la utilidad de la existencia de roles con las competencias adecuadas para su participación en este proceso. Estos hallazgos determinan que nuestro trabajo futuro inmediato se centrará en abordar estas necesidades.

Palabras clave: Procesos de software, proceso de despliegue de sistemas de software, encuesta.

1 Introducción

En Argentina, la industria del software se compone mayoritariamente por PyMES, representando casi el 80% del sector, lo que constituye un eslabón fundamental, en el sector, para el país y refuerza la necesidad de llevar adelante iniciativas que contribuyan con el desarrollo y mejora de competitividad de dichas empresas [1]. Este sector presenta un alto potencial para generar valor agregado al ecosistema productivo del país, promoviendo la generación de empleo calificado y evidenciando un crecimiento exponencial en los últimos años. De hecho, el notable desarrollo queda demostrado en el último informe publicado por el Observatorio de la Economía del Conocimiento (OEC) de Argentina [2]. Estas organizaciones descubrieron que es crucial mejorar sus procesos y métodos para ser competitivas en su negocio, aunque no cuentan con recursos y conocimiento suficiente para lograrlo. La única manera de lograr proyectos exitosos es mediante la definición, implementación y estabilización de los procesos de desarrollo [3]. El proceso de despliegue de sistemas de software es crucial en el ciclo de vida de desarrollo de software, de él dependen el cierre del proyecto y la aceptación del sistema de software por parte del cliente. En el despliegue se presentan inconvenientes como por ejemplo la falta de componentes (externos), descargas incompletas, la infraestructura heterogénea e incompatible, incumplimiento de calendarios, retrabajo por falta de pocas capacidades y competencias tecnológicas de las PyMES, capacitación y preparación inadecuadas de los usuarios finales entre otras [4, 5].

Por todos los inconvenientes enunciados anteriormente y con el propósito de incrementar la calidad y capacidad del proceso de despliegue, se decidió como objetivo de investigación a largo plazo, proponer un modelo de proceso de despliegue de sistemas de software que ayude a las PyMES a ejecutar el proceso de despliegue de los sistemas de información.

Con el propósito de recolectar evidencia sobre el estado actual de la práctica del proceso de despliegue de sistemas de software en PyMES de Argentina se decidió realizar un estudio exploratorio a través de una encuesta realizada según las directrices de Molléri et al. [6].

Este artículo se estructura de la siguiente manera: en la Sección 2 se describe la planificación de la encuesta, en la Sección 3 se describe su ejecución. Los resultados se presentan en la Sección 4. En la Sección 5 se presenta un análisis de las amenazas a la validez y finalmente, en la Sección 6 se exponen las conclusiones y trabajos futuros.

2 Planificación de la encuesta

Objetivos y preguntas de investigación. El uso de la plantilla de GQM (Goal-Question-Metric) [7] nos permitió formular el objetivo de la encuesta de la siguiente manera: *"**Analizar** el proceso de despliegue de sistemas de software **con el propósito de** conocer el estado actual de la práctica del proceso de despliegue de sistemas de software **con respecto a** descubrir las características del proceso de despliegue (sistematización de las actividades y tareas, roles y documentación) **desde el punto de vista** de profesionales de la industria del software".*

Las preguntas de investigación (PI) que guiaron esta encuesta son las siguientes:

PI1: ¿Qué características tienen las PyMES, distinguiendo las que disponen de las que no disponen de un proceso de despliegue?

PI2: ¿Qué inconvenientes se presentan en el proceso de despliegue?

PI3: ¿Cuáles son las características que tiene el proceso de despliegue?

PI4: ¿Sería deseable disponer de un proceso de despliegue bien definido?

Proceso de ejecución. Este proceso consta de: 1) Diseño de un formulario para llevar un registro sistemático de la ejecución de la encuesta. Este se compone de dos partes: a) Proceso de envío de la encuesta: cantidad de envíos y a quienes. y b) Proceso de seguimiento del envío: mails erróneos, cantidad de cuestionarios respondidos y fecha de respuesta, 2) Envío de la encuesta por correo electrónico. Se diseño un texto de presentación en el cual se menciona el propósito de la investigación, quiénes participan, tiempo estimado para responder la encuesta, agradecimiento por la colaboración y una invitación a que el encuestado difunda la encuesta entre sus contactos, 3) Revisión diaria de encuestas respondidas, 4) Extracción de las respuestas, 5) Revisión de si hay preguntas sin responder y 6) Extracción de los datos.

Población. La población a la cual se decidió enviar la encuesta son PyMES desarrolladoras de software y PyMES de otro sector que cuentan con un área de sistemas que desarrolla software para uso propio. Se utilizó la clasificación de PyMES en Argentina según la cantidad de empleados propuesta en [8].

Se utilizaron diferentes estrategias para seleccionar la muestra, todas a través de correo electrónico, una de ellas consistió en el envío de la encuesta de manera directa por parte de los autores. La otra estrategia consistió en el envío de manera indirecta a socios de consejos profesionales, polos tecnológicos regionales y PyMES vinculadas a determinadas Universidades. En el segundo caso, se previó una tarea de depuración de aquellas respuestas que no correspondan a PyMES.

Diseño de la encuesta. Se diseñó un cuestionario autoadministrado que se envió por correo electrónico a los encuestados y se utilizó la herramienta Google Forms.
Para el diseño del cuestionario se definieron tres categorías de preguntas junto con sus objetivos (ver Tabla 1). El cuestionario se compone de 23 preguntas de respuestas cerradas y 15 preguntas de respuestas abiertas. Dentro de las preguntas de respuestas cerradas, se emplean respuestas de tipo Sí/No, escalas de frecuencia y escalas de evaluación. También se contempla la categoría "Otros" para el caso de que no se cubran explícitamente todas las respuestas posibles. El cuestionario y la correspondencia entre las preguntas del cuestionario con las PI se encuentran en un apéndice [9] por restricciones de espacio. El cuestionario completo se encuentra disponible en https://forms.gle/ENQXYhv9yT2EtzfDA

Tabla 1. Categorías del cuestionario y sus objetivos.

Categorías	Objetivos
Participante	Identificar el perfil del participante de la encuesta, su rol y su antigüedad en la industria del software.
Empresa	Determinar las características de las empresas que participan en la encuesta, si es una PyME de desarrollo de software o de otro sector que cuente con un área de sistemas que desarrolla software para uso propio. La cantidad de empleados y su ubicación geográfica. Además, identificar las características de los proyectos de software como, por ejemplo, los dominios de los proyectos, los modelos de ciclo de vida que utilizan, así como también los frameworks o métodos que aplican y la existencia de algún tipo de certificación de calidad.
Proceso de despliegue	Conocer las características del proceso de despliegue de la práctica actual en las PyMES de Argentina.

Validación. Se realizó una prueba piloto con un grupo reducido de 10 participantes que permitió verificar el tiempo de respuesta inicial estimado de 15 minutos, quedando reducido a 10 minutos. También se logró validar la terminología empleada, los participantes de la prueba piloto confirmaron su claridad y legibilidad. Además, permitió modificar algunas palabras del cuestionario por errores involuntarios de tipeo.

3 Ejecución de la encuesta

Reclutamiento de los participantes. Se utilizaron bases de datos restringidas a las que se tuvo acceso mediante polos tecnológicos regionales, universidades, consejos profesionales, en este caso el envío de la encuesta se realizó de manera indirecta.
Además, de manera directa se envió a contactos de profesionales de la industria del software y ex alumnos de carreras de grado y posgrado de informática de uno de los investigadores.

Gestión de las respuestas. La gestión de la ejecución de la encuesta se realizó de acuerdo con el procedimiento definido en la sección 2.

Análisis de los datos. Para asegurar la calidad de los datos obtenidos de la encuesta se revisaron los datos con el propósito de encontrar errores en los datos (completitud y errores de tipeo). Se realizó un análisis de contenido de las respuestas de texto libre [10]; se codificaron las respuestas en categorías. Por último, se utilizó un análisis de clusters [11] para encontrar relaciones entre los resultados de respuestas de diferentes categorías de la encuesta.

4 Análisis e interpretación de los resultados obtenidos

En relación con los roles de los participantes de la encuesta (PE1 y PE1.a.), la mayoría de los participantes son desarrolladores (49 encuestados), en segundo lugar, líder de proyectos o jefes de equipos (44 encuestados) y, en tercer lugar, gerentes o dueños de producto (34 encuestados). En cuanto a la experiencia (PE2), la mayoría de los participantes cuentan con más de 10 años de experiencia en la industria del software (145 encuestados) y sólo 7 participantes tienen menos de un año de experiencia. El resto de los 43 participantes tienen entre 1 año y 10 años de experiencia.

PI1: ¿Qué características tienen las PyMES, distinguiendo las que disponen de las que no disponen de un proceso de despliegue?

Se encontró que 43 PyMES de sistemas cuentan con proceso de despliegue y 51 no cuentan con este. De las PyMES que desarrollan otra actividad y cuentan con un área de sistemas que desarrolla sistemas de software para su propio uso, 47 cuentan con un proceso de despliegue y 54 no cuentan con este (PE4 y PE15). Se encontró que la mayoría de PyMES que se dedican a otra actividad, son empresas de servicios (PE3),

Se observó que de las 94 PyMES de sistemas que participaron en la encuesta, la mayoría son micro (30) y pequeñas (35) (PE5). Para las PyMES que no son de sistemas se utilizó la misma clasificación de tipo de PyMES aplicada al tamaño de los equipos de desarrollo de software. En este caso se observa que en la encuesta participó un mayor porcentaje de PyMES medianas de tramo 2, resultando una distribución bastante homogénea para las tres categorías restantes.

La mayoría de PyMES participantes utilizan como modelos de ciclo de vida, el incremental o híbrido en sus proyectos de software, resultando una distribución de respuestas homogénea tanto para las PyMES que disponen o no de un proceso de despliegue (PE9 y P15). En relación con el uso de frameworks y métodos (PE10 y PE15), se encontró que Scrum es el framework más utilizado tanto por las PyMES que disponen o no de un proceso de despliegue.

PI2: ¿Qué inconvenientes se presentan en el proceso de despliegue?

Se descubrió que las PyMES que no disponen de un proceso de despliegue tienen mayor cantidad de dificultades respecto a las que disponen de uno (PE18, PE18.a. y PE15). Dentro de las dificultades que se presentan se encontró en primer lugar, un grupo de dificultades que se refieren a la gestión, como, por ejemplo, la estimación de tiempos (83 respuestas), resultando la más seleccionada por los participantes. En segundo lugar, las actividades que presentan dificultades y que son específicas del proceso de despliegue, se encontraron la capacitación a usuarios (78 respuestas), la migración (69 respuestas), la preparación del ambiente de instalación (67 respuestas), la instalación del producto software (65 respuestas).

De los aspectos afectados por las dificultades de las actividades del proceso de despliegue en función de si la PyME dispone o no de un proceso (PE19 y PE15), se observó que: a) un mayor número de aspectos afectados en las PyMES que no cuentan con un proceso de despliegue, b) los aspectos más afectados por las dificultades del proceso de despliegue se concentran en retrasos de tiempo y retrabajo.

PI3: ¿Cuáles son las características que tiene el proceso de despliegue?

Modalidad de instalación. Existe una tendencia en las PyMES a realizar la actividad de instalación de manera manual, resultando aproximadamente el 50 % mayor en las PyMES que no disponen de un proceso de despliegue respecto a las PyMES que disponen de este (PE12 y PE15).

Herramientas para la instalación. En función de si la PyME dispone o no de un proceso de despliegue (PE12.a. y PE15), se descubrió que las PyMES que utilizan herramientas de instalación son las que cuentan con proceso de despliegue. Las herramientas más utilizadas por estas PyMES son Jenkins, Gitlab y un software propio.

Roles. 129 PyMES no cuentan con roles específicos para el proceso de despliegue y 66 PyMES poseen roles específicos (PE13). El rol específico más utilizado es el de implementador (26 respuestas). Respecto a las respuestas de participantes que trabajan en PyMES que no cuentan con roles específicos (PE13.b. y PE13.c.), se observó que el rol más asignado al proceso de despliegue es el de desarrollador (85 respuestas).

Elementos del proceso de despliegue. De los elementos que componen el proceso de despliegue (PE15.a. y PE15.b.), se descubrió que los elementos más significativos son: actividades y tareas (73 respuestas), uso de herramientas y tecnología (70 respuestas) y documentación (59 respuestas).

Documentación. Un total de 115 respuestas indican que usan documentación en el proceso de despliegue y 80 respuestas indican que no (PE16). De las 115 PyMES que indican que usan documentación, se observa que: a) el mayor porcentaje utiliza la documentación en la actividad instalación (91 respuestas), b) en menor porcentaje se utiliza en el cierre del proceso (21 respuestas).

PI4: ¿Sería deseable disponer de un proceso de despliegue bien definido?

Utilidad de un proceso de despliegue. Del total de los participantes, 191 consideran de utilidad disponer de un proceso que permita la sistematización del proceso de despliegue (PE20). Utilidad que se ve más acentuada en los participantes con más experiencia en la industria del software.

Necesidad de roles. La mayoría de los participantes (191 en total) valoraron entre muy útil y útil, la necesidad de roles con competencias específicas para el proceso de despliegue (PE14). Los participantes con más de 10 años en la industria del software valoran de manera significativa la existencia de un rol específico con las competencias adecuadas para el proceso de despliegue (PE2 y PE14).

Utilidad de plantillas orientadoras. Se descubrió que prácticamente todos los participantes consideran de utilidad disponer de plantillas orientadoras para realizar el proceso de despliegue (PE17). Los participantes con mayor experiencia valoran de manera significativa la utilidad de este tipo de plantillas (PE2 y PE17).

Comentarios y sugerencias. De los participantes que aportaron comentarios (118), se identificó en primer lugar, la necesidad de automatización de algunas tareas del proceso de despliegue y en segundo lugar, la necesidad de roles capacitados y bien definidos así como también, de disponer de un modelo de proceso, guías o metodología para el proceso de despliegue. Las respuestas de los participantes con mayor experiencia en la industria (PE21 y PE2) remarcan la necesidad de automatización, la definición de roles específicos y bien capacitados, disponibilidad de un proceso o guías o una metodología (PE21).

5 Amenazas a la validez

Para analizar la validez de la encuesta se tuvieron en cuenta los tipos de validez propuestos por Wohlin et al.[12]:

- Validez de conclusiones. El tamaño de la muestra (195 encuestas) se considera pequeño para considerar los resultados estadísticamente aceptables. Por tratarse de un estudio exploratorio del estado actual de la práctica del proceso de despliegue de sistemas de software permitió cumplir con el propósito definido para esta encuesta. Además, se aplicó el proceso de manera sistemática y rigurosa para permitir que el proceso sea reproducible.
- Validez interna. Nuestra estrategia de reclutamiento de participantes podría haber sido sesgada por una alta probabilidad de similitud de perfiles y por profesionales sin experiencia. Si bien hay una variedad en los roles que participaron en la encuesta, la mayoría de los encuestados cuentan con más de 10 años de experiencia en la industria del software, pero para subsanar que algunos de los participantes no conozcan el tratamiento del proceso de despliegue dado en esta investigación, se les proporcionó dicha definición. Otro factor negativo podría haber sido la dificultad para comprender las preguntas, esto quedó resuelto con la prueba piloto realizada con 10 encuestados. Las motivaciones de los encuestados también podrían haber afectado las respuestas y, por lo tanto, los resultados de la encuesta, esto quedó resuelto porque en el mail que se envió junto con la encuesta quedó explicito el compromiso de compartir los resultados de la encuesta con los participantes.
- Validez externa. Se seleccionaron a los participantes de la encuesta de forma de que sean profesionales de la industria del software que se desempeñen en PyMES de Argentina. Esto permitió realizar observaciones sobre el estado actual de la práctica del proceso de despliegue de sistemas de software.

- Validez de constructo. Se definieron las preguntas de investigación de manera cuidadosa, así como también el esquema de las categorías de preguntas y los posibles valores de las respuestas. Todo el proceso ha sido consensuado entre los investigadores de manera que no sea sesgado el objeto de estudio. Otros aspectos que permitieron disminuir esta amenaza han sido que, en el mail de la invitación a los participantes, explicando claramente el propósito del estudio y del propio cuestionario. También se anticipó el anonimato al participante salvo que estuviese interesado en que lo podamos contactar para profundizar el cuestionario.

6 Conclusiones y trabajos futuros

A partir de la encuesta realizada a 195 profesionales de PyMES de Argentina, los principales hallazgos obtenidos para cada PI se detallan a continuación:

PI1¿Qué características tienen las PyMES, distinguiendo las que disponen de las que no disponen de un proceso de despliegue?

Las PyMES que son "micro" presentan una acentuada tendencia a no disponer un proceso de despliegue.

Tanto las PyMES que disponen o no de un proceso de despliegue utilizan como modelos de ciclo de vida, el incremental o híbrido en sus proyectos de software.

Scrum es el framework más utilizado tanto por las PyMES que disponen o no de un proceso de despliegue.

PI2¿Qué inconvenientes se presentan en el proceso de despliegue?

Dentro de las dificultades que se presentan de manera más acentuada en las PyMES que no disponen de un proceso sistematizado para el despliegue, se identifican la estimación de tiempos, la asignación de recursos humanos, la gestión de configuración y el cierre del despliegue. Así como también, la capacitación a usuarios, la migración, la preparación del ambiente de instalación, la instalación, las pruebas de aceptación, la documentación y el incumplimiento del cliente, requisitos técnicos, pruebas de instalación, la capacitación técnica y la carga de datos.

Los aspectos afectados por las dificultades en las PyMES que no disponen de un proceso de despliegue, los más frecuentes son los retrasos de tiempo y el retrabajo. En segundo lugar, se presentan la calidad del proceso y la insatisfacción del cliente y por último se presentan aspectos como la instalación incompleta, la falta de productividad, el cierre del proyecto, la reasignación de recursos humanos y la gestión.

PI3: ¿Cuáles son las características que tiene el proceso de despliegue?

El proceso de despliegue de las 90 PyMES que cuentan con dicho proceso tiene principalmente actividades y tareas. En un segundo lugar, presenta el uso de herramientas tecnológicas, en tercer lugar, el uso de documentación y por último una poca cantidad de PyMES utilizan prácticas, técnicas, métricas y métodos.

El rol específico más utilizado por las PyMES es el de "implementador.

115 PyMES utilizan documentación en el proceso de despliegue y en mayor medida se usa en la actividad de instalación.

PI4: ¿Sería deseable disponer de un proceso de despliegue bien definido?

Los participantes de la encuesta sugirieron mejorar el proceso de despliegue mediante la automatización y roles capacitados y bien definidos. La mayoría consideran de utilidad disponer de un proceso de despliegue, así como también de plantillas orientadoras para la ejecución del proceso.

A partir de los resultados de esta encuesta, se confirma la necesidad de un modelo de proceso de despliegue de sistemas de software que ayude a las PyMES, a realizar el despliegue de manera sistematizada mediante: a) la ejecución de actividades y tareas bien definidas, b) el uso de plantillas orientadoras, c) la asignación de roles específicos que cuenten con las competencias necesarias para ejecutar el despliegue y d) el uso de herramientas para automatizar algunas de las actividades del proceso. con el propósito de darle agilidad y automatización al proceso.

Por ello, nuestro trabajo futuro inmediato se centrará en abordar estas necesidades teniendo en cuento los hallazgos obtenidos en esta encuesta.

Agradecimientos. La investigación presentada forma parte de los siguientes proyectos: GEMA (JCCM, SBPLY/17/180501/000293) y AETHER-UCLM (MICINN, PID2020-112540RB-C42).

Referencias

1. Reporte anual 2018 sobre el Sector de Software y Servicios Informáticos de la República Argentina. OPSSI. Disponible en: https://www.cessi.org.ar/opssi (2018).
2. Ministerio de Producción y Trabajo. Presidencia de la Nación. Secretaría de la Transformación Productiva. Informe Argentina Productiva - Economía del Conocimiento. Disponible en: https://biblioteca.produccion.gob.ar/buscar/?fid=16 (2019).
3. Ianzen A., Mauda E.C., Paludo M.A., Reinehr S., Malucelli A. Software process improvement in a financial organization: an action research approach. Computer Standard & Interfaces, 36, pp 54–65 (2013).
4. Jansen S., Brinkkemper S. Definition and validation of the key process of release, delivery and deployment for product software vendors: Turning the ugly duckling into a swan IEEE International Conference on Software Maintenance, ICSM, art. no. 4021334, pp. 166-175 (2006).
5. Reascos I., Carvalho J. A., Bossano S. Implanting IT Applications in Government Institutions: A Process Model Emerging from a Case Study in a Medium-Sized Municipality. In: Proceedings of the 12th International Conference on Theory and Practice of Electronic Governance (ICEGOV '19), Melbourne, VIC, Australia, pp. 80-85 (2019).
6. Molléri J.S., K. Petersen K., E. Mendes E. An empirically evaluated checklist for surveys in software engineering. Information and Software Technology 119 (2020) 106240 (2020).
7. Basili V., y Rombach D. The TAME Project: Towards Improvement-Oriented Software Environments. IEEE Transactions on Software Engineering, 14(6) (1988).
8. Ministerio de Desarrollo Productivo. Nuevas categorías para ser PyMES. Disponible en: https://www.argentina.gob.ar/noticias/nuevas-categorias-para-ser-pyme (2018).
9. Panizzi M., Genero M., Bertone R. Apéndice. Encuesta para analizar las necesidades con respecto al proceso de despliegue de las PyMES en Argentina. Disponible en: https://doi.org/10.6084/m9.figshare.14946261.v1
10. Krippendorff K. Content analysis: An introduction to its methodology, 3rd edn. Sage Publications, Thousand Oaks (2012).
11. Matloff N. From Algorithm to Z-Scores: Probabilistic and Statistical Modeling in Computer Science. Disponible en: http://heather.cs.ucdavis.edu/~matloff/probstatbook.html (2009).
12. Wohlin C., Runeson P., Höst M., Ohlsson MC., Regnell B., Wesslén A. Experimentation in software engineering: an introduction. Springer (20

Replications on the use of Graphical Abstracts to Support Study Selection in Systematic Mapping Studies

Alex Fernando Bonora[1], Katia Romero Felizardo[1], Érica Ferreira de Souza[1], and Nandamudi Lankalapalli Vijaykumar[2]

[1] Department of Computer, Federal University of Technology - Paraná (UTFPR), Cornólio Procópio/ Paraná, Brazil
[2] National Institute of Space Research - (INPE), São José dos Campos/ São Paulo, Brazil
Federal University of São Paulo, São José dos Campos/ São Paulo, Brazil
alexbonora@alunos.utfpr.edu.br; katiascannavino@utfpr.edu.br; ericasouza@utfpr.edu.br; vijay.nl@inpe.br

Abstract. Context: Little is known about the relevance of using graphical abstracts to select studies within Systematic Mapping Studies (SMS). Only one study (renamed as "original study - OS") was conducted to evaluate the conduction of selection review activity manually and using visual graphical abstracts. **Aim:** This research aims to build a body of empirical evidence through replications on the use of graphical abstracts to support the selection of primary studies in SMS. **Method:** A total of five replication studies were performed. Each replication was organized in two sessions (training - 9 studies to be classified as included or excluded - and execution - other 20 studies) and two groups (G1 - reading abstracts of the studies; G2 - analyzing graphical abstracts versions of the same studies used by G1). Performance (time) and effectiveness (number of studies correctly/incorrectly selected) were assessed. Qualitative analysis from the opinion of participants was also carried out. **Results:** Confirming the results of the OS, our results suggest that graphical abstracts speed up the selection activity and increase the performance of reviewers. Moreover, graphical abstracts are useful, and reviewers are completely satisfied by using them. **Conclusions:** Graphical abstract is an innovative and positive alternative for supporting study selection in SMSs.

Keywords: Graphical Abstract and Systematic Mapping Studies and Replication.

1 Introduction

The term replication has come into use to refer to a systematic repetition of an original study to double-check its results [2]. This definition implies that replication must be explicitly related to a previous study. Replications increase the validity and reliability of the results yielded in an initial study [2]. Moreover, threats to the validity of a study can be addressed by the replication of this study.

Felizardo et al. [1] run one pilot study (renamed as "original study – OS") to evaluate the effects of using graphical abstracts to select studies during the conduction of Systematic Mapping Studies (SMSs) in Software Engineering (SE). The goals and the main contributions of the research presented in [1] were: (1) to compare performance (in terms of time taken); (2) effectiveness (in terms of correctness of the study inclusion/exclusion); and (3) to collect the opinion of participants on using conventional and graphical abstracts to select studies. This paper is an extension of [1].

For the purposes of the OS, Felizardo et al. [1] created a set of graphical abstracts. To assist the creation of graphical abstracts they proposed an approach using Concept Maps (CMs). In summary, Felizardo and the other collaborators [1] established a template based on CM and a set of guidelines to use this template to create graphical abstracts. The focus of Felizardo et al. [1] was not to carry out a study considering a large-sample. The study validated the template and the use of graphical abstracts based on CMs to support the selection activity of candidate studies. Therefore, one of the potential threats to the validity of the OS was related to the sample used (eight participants). It is often difficult to draw general conclusions from small-sample data. Therefore, the goal of this paper is to replicate the OS [1], involving a larger sample size of participants.

A summary of the OS is also presented herein, together with a comparison of its results and the results of the replications. The initial results of Felizardo et al. [1] have pointed out the value of graphical abstracts for selecting primary studies. Data from replications confirm that there are differences in performance and effectiveness for selecting studies manually or adopting graphical abstracts. An interesting finding is that participants widely pointed out that graphical abstracts are useful to support the selection activity, which is quite relevant information for researchers that intend to conduct SMSs.

The remainder of this paper is organized as follows: Section 2 describes related works on graphical abstracts. Section 3 reviews the study design, participants' task and metrics. Subsection 3.1 summarizes the results of replications. Conclusions are discussed in Section 4.

2 Related Works – Graphical Abstracts in Software Engineering

Graphical abstracts should concisely summarize the content of an article, through an image, to attract the reviewers' attention. Elsevier, which publishes the main Software Engineering (SE) journals, explains the purpose of a graphical abstract as "A graphical abstract should allow readers to quickly gain an understanding of the main take-home message of the paper and is intended to encourage browsing, promote interdisciplinary scholarship, and help readers identify more quickly which papers are most relevant to their research interests."[3].

Currently, the existing Elsevier guidelines for the creation of graphical abstracts are limited to technical information, such as the size of the figure, the minimum number of pixels, appropriate screen resolution, file types (TIFF, EPS, PDF, or MS Office). In this context, Felizardo et al. [1] have proposed an approach to creating graphical abstracts using CMs in SE. They established a template based on CM and a set of guidelines to use this template to create graphical abstracts. CMs are diagrams containing meanings, i.e., diagrams that have meaningful relationships and conceptual hierarchy. Unlike the diagrams mentioned above, the purpose of CMs is not to classify concepts but relate and organize them hierarchically.

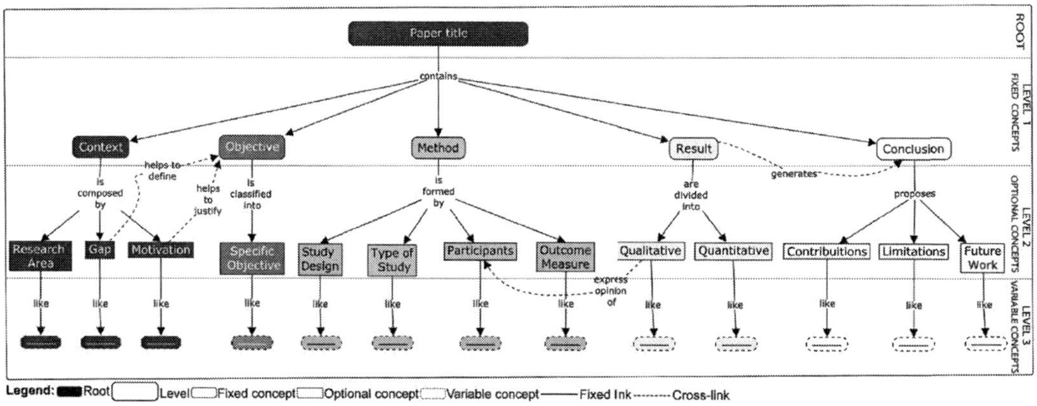

Fig. 1. CM template proposed by Felizardo et al. [1]

As shown in Figure 1, the CM template is a graphical and hierarchical view, containing parts of a scientific study (e.g., title, context, objective, method, result, and conclusion) as concepts and relationships between them. CM template contains the main concept (root) and other concepts related to this main concept are drawn. Concepts are also grouped into levels. The concept at the top is the most inclusive. More specific concepts are arranged hierarchically at the bottom. The lower the level is, the more details are described. The authors also proposed a set of guidelines to use their template to create graphical abstracts based on CMs. An exemplification of the use of the guidelines to create graphical abstracts and its evaluation are presented in Felizardo et al. [1].

Felizardo et al. [1] also evaluated the relevance of graphical abstracts based on CMs to support the selection of primary studies in SMSs. The current study also involves the use of graphical abstracts, however, its focus is to replicate

[3] https://www.elsevier.com/authors/journal-authors/graphical-abstract – Retrieved: 15/09/2020

Felizardo et al.'s study [1] to assess the relevance of using graphical abstracts for selecting primary studies in SE.

3 Replications: relevance of graphical abstracts for selecting primary studies

The Research Questions (RQ) of the original study [4](and that were also used in our replications) and their related hypotheses are:

- **RQ1:** *What type of abstract (textual or graphical) improve the performance of the study selection activity in SMS?*
  - ***H0:*** *Graphical abstracts has no effect on time taken to select studies.*
  - ***H1:*** *Graphical abstracts has a positive effect on time taken to select studies.*

- **RQ2:** *What type of abstract (textual or graphical) improve the effectiveness of the study selection activity in SMS?*
  - ***H0:*** *Graphical abstracts has no effect the number of studies correctly included/excluded.*
  - ***H1:*** *Graphical abstracts has a positive effect on number of studies correctly included/excluded.*

- **RQ3:** *What is the opinion of the participants in relation to the abstracts used?* – These questions will be carried out in a qualitative way.

The OS was organized in two sessions: training and execution. For training purposes, a small set of primary studies (Set 1 containing 9 primary studies, and their graphical abstracts) was used. To ensure that impressions and knowledge from the training would not interfere with the study, a different and larger set of primary studies (Set 2 with 20 studies and their graphical abstracts) was used for the execution stage. In summary, these sets of 29 graphical abstracts (Set1:9 + Set2: 20) were built for this study, based on SMS of Souza et al. [4] and randomly selected as Set 1 and Set 2.

Therefore, during the training session, the participants were given set 1 of studies to be analyzed (G1 – a list of abstracts; G2 – graphical abstracts), the inclusion and exclusion criteria, and a table to summarize the decision on whether to include or exclude a study. The design of the OS, previously described, was duplicated for replications without changes (2 groups, 2 sessions).

Qualitative analysis from the opinion of participants was carried out. The participants[5] in the five replications (85 in total) were not significantly differ-

[4] Laboratory package is available in:
https://www.dropbox.com/sh/qxea4866k48mt3l/AAAAKCvlt8gn-6hSRTzGnY0Ja?dl=0
https://www.dropbox.com/sh/lspjq3gtj3qc53p/AADLjS9Aq6Uz3QLleJfK_EfXa?dl=0

[5] The Informed Consent Form (ICF) used by us is available in
https://www.dropbox.com/preview/Public/Termo%20Consentimento.pdf?role=personal

ent from each other in terms of experience in conducting SMS (they had all conducted between 1–2 SMSs).

3.1 Results

This section reports the results of replications addressing our RQs. A summary of the results is shown in Table 1.

- ***RQ1: What type of abstract (textual or graphical) improve the performance of the study selection activity in SMS?***

Participants' performances were measured (see the second column of Table 1) to answer the first research question (RQ1). The time savings using graphical abstracts in replications was 7.40 minutes for each set of 20 studies. The answer to our RQ1 is that the use of graphical abstracts could speed up the selection activity.

Table 1. Summary of Results: Replications

Group	Time (min)	Cor. I	Cor. E	Cor. I and E	Inc. I	Inc. E	Inc. I and E
G1–ALL = 85	24.50	7.37	4.90	12.27	2.63	5.10	7.73
G2–ALL = 85	17.10	7.33	5.98	13.31	2.67	4.02	6.69
Legend: Cor. = Correct; Inc. = Incorrect; I = Inclusion; E = Exclusion							

We use the Wilcoxon-Mann-Whitney test to evaluate the group's values [3]. Wilcoxon-Mann-Whitney test[6] was used because results were not normally distributed. Moreover, we want to test whether one of the groups tends to have higher values (e.g. number of studies correctly included or excluded, etc) than the other group, or if they have the same median [7].

Regarding performance (RQ1), our results have shown that (see Table 2 – Performance) the use of graphical abstracts can improve the performance of the primary studies review activity (*p-value*$= 0.0001 < 0.05$). This means that the selection activity is faster using graphical abstracts.

- ***RQ2: What type of abstract (textual or graphical) improve the effectiveness of the study selection activity in SMS?***

Table 1 (see fifth column) shows averages of studies correctly included/excluded during the five replications. The answer to our RQ2 is that graphical abstracts could improve the effectiveness of selection study activity.

[6] For reproducibility purpose we adopted Action Stat, Version: 3.7, R Version: 3.3.2 as a statistical package.

[7] No statistical significance tests were used in OS due to the small sample employed (i.e., eight participants).

Table 2. Results for Man-Whitney test – Replications

Variable	*p-value*	Statistically Significant?
Performance	0.0001	Yes (p-*value* < 0.05)
Effectiveness – Correct Selection	0.0214	Yes (p-*value* < 0.05)
Effectiveness – Incorrect Selection	0	Yes (p-*value* < 0.05)

Regarding effectiveness (RQ2) (see Table 1), our results have shown that the use of graphical abstracts can improve the effectiveness of the primary studies review activity, i.e., increase the correct classifications and decrease the erroneous ones (p-*value* – Correct Selection $= 0.0214 < 0.05$; p-*value* – Incorrect Selection $= 0 < 0.05$).

- ***RQ3: What is the opinion of the participants in relation to the abstracts used?***

The replications also evaluated issues related to participants' opinions. A questionnaire with seven affirmative sentences was used. The sentences are detailed as follows:

- A1 – The abstracts are useful to select primary studies.
- A2 – The abstracts help me to select the primary studies.
- A3 – The abstracts make it easy for me to select the primary studies.
- A4 – The abstracts are easy to be read.
- A5 – I learned how to read the abstracts to select primary studies quickly.
- A6 – I like to read abstracts to select primary studies.
- A7 – I would recommend the reading of abstracts to another researcher conducting a systematic review.

The possible choices to these sentences vary from "strongly disagree" to "strongly agree", in a scale based on the Likert Scale method.

Table 3 summarizes participants' of replications 1–5 who agree or strongly agree with the seven affirmative sentences of our qualitative analysis.

3.2 Threats to validity

In conducting our replications, we identified some threats to validity, they are described as follows.

One of the potential threats to the internal validity of our replications is related to our assumption that the researchers who originally conducted the SMS made 100% correct decisions on the inclusion and exclusion of studies. However, SMSs conducted by different researchers on the same question sometimes led to different conclusions. Most of the classifications performed by the participants of replications match the classification conducted by the experts. For example, two studies were classified as included by the expert who conducted the SMS and all participants who participated in the replication. In the same way, the other three studies were classified as excluded by the expert and all participants.

Table 3. Summary of Results of Qualitative Questions

Sentence	*Manual Reading*	*Graphical Abstracts*
The abstracts are useful to select primary studies.	94%	92%
The abstracts help me to select the primary studies.	95%	96%
The abstracts make it easy for me to select the primary studies.	70%	91%
The abstracts are easy to be read.	48%	86%
I learned how to read the abstracts to select primary studies quickly.	48%	82%
I like to read abstracts to select primary studies.	52%	94%
I would recommend the reading of abstracts to another researcher conducting a systematic review.	78%	88%

One other study was originally classified as included by the expert and only one participant did not classify it the same way. Additionally, more than 90% of the participants agreed on the classification of the other five studies. Even so, we cannot affirm that all expert's opinions are correct.

Another threat to internal validity is related to the number of studies or graphical abstracts to be analyzed. A large number of studies could affect the motivation of the participants. We do not consider this threat serious since we limited the number of studies used as set 2 (20 studies).

One threat to construct validity was the participants' level of experience in KM/Software Testing. It is possible that the results could have changed if the participants of the replications had more research experience in the topic of the analyzed primary studies. Another threat was that the native language of the participants was different than the language of the study materials. The participants spoke Portuguese as their native language and the abstracts were written in English. The level of experience in English could affect the capability for selecting studies, especially for reading abstracts using the traditional approach. In graphical abstracts, there is little text to be read, only the concepts and links. Therefore, a new replication, with English-native speakers could be conducted to explore it.

It is also important to mention the replication of this study in a Systematic Literature Review (SLR). One of the main differences between SLR and SMS is related to the selection activity of the studies. The scope of an SMS is broader, and the selection criteria of studies are more general than in an SLR, where studies are selected/analyzed in a greater depth. It is difficult to draw general conclusions from our results, hence we cannot affirm that graphical abstracts also speed up the selection activity and increase the effectiveness of reviewers in SLRs. A new study is required to validate this assumption.

4 Conclusions

The main contribution of this research is five replications of a study to compare Ph.D. and Master students' performance, effectiveness, and participants' opinions in reviewing primary studies manually and using graphical abstracts. The results show that the answer to RQ1 is "The performance of the participants that used graphical abstracts is higher than that of the participants that used the manual method. The answer to RQ2 is "The effectiveness of the participants that used graphical abstracts is higher than that of the participants that used the manual method." Finally, the answer from RQ3 is that "The participants who use the graphical abstracts found the abstracts useful and they are completely satisfied by using them."

We concluded that graphical abstract is an innovative and positive alternative for supporting study selection in SMSs. As future work we intend to: (1) conduct a new replication with English-native speakers; (2) assess the use of graphical abstracts in SLR context.

References

1. Felizardo, K.R., Souza, E.F., Hesae, S., Vijaykumar, N.L., Nakagawa, E.Y.: Analysing the use of graphical abstracts to support study selection in secondary studies. In: Experimental Software Engineering (ESELAW Track). pp. 1–10 (2017)
2. Juristo, N., Gomez, O.: Replication of software engineering experiments. In: LASER Summer School. Lecture Notes in Computer Science, vol. 7007, pp. 60–88. Springer (2010)
3. Neuhäuser, M.: Wilcoxon–Mann–Whitney Test, pp. 1656–1658. Springer Berlin Heidelberg, Berlin, Heidelberg (2011)
4. Souza, E.F., Falbo, R.A., L., V.N.: Knowledge management initiatives in software testing: A mapping study. Information and Software Technology **57**(1), 378–391 (2014)

Increasing the say-do ratio of an agile team in a resource-shared environment using a traditional project management approach

Rodrigo Falcão[1 [0000-0003-1222-0046]], Frank Elberzhager[1 [0000-0002-8748-3927]], Sven Theobald[1 [0000-0001-7491-6431]], and Jannis von Albedyll[1]

Fraunhofer Institute for Experimental Software Engineering IESE
rodrigo.falcao@iese.fraunhofer.de

Abstract. Although Scrum declares that team members have to be dedicated to their teams during a sprint, in practice these team members are often shared throughout an organization. As a consequence, there is less focus on fulfilling the sprint plans. Instead of trying to enforce Scrum guidelines and having dedicated resources in each sprint, we accepted this organizational constraint and adapted our existing development process to take into account the fact that human resources will be shared during sprints. In this paper, we show how we used a set of traditional project management practices to adjust the sprint planning and monitoring processes in a resource-shared environment setting. We performed a 7-month case study in the context of the project Digital Villages, where five technical teams shared resources while working on eight products in parallel during the various sprints. The approach increased the overall say-do ratio of the team from 48% to 79%. Open challenges include further improvement of the say-do ratio in such environments and better predictability of it.

Keywords: agile development process · process improvement · scrum.

1 Introduction

Agile methods have been widely adopted in software development in recent years [18]. In contrast to traditional software development approaches, where a linear process is performed from the elicitation of product requirements to final delivery, agile methods favor short-term iterations in order to deal with uncertainty, and have been praised as the best fit for innovative projects [11] where neither the outcome nor the path towards the desired final product is clear. Among the existing agile practices, Scrum stands out by its widespread acceptance among practitioners when it comes to development processes. In 2014, 56% of agile practitioners used Scrum as their software development process, and this percentage has been increasing over time [12]. The same authors also demonstrated an increased interest of researchers in Scrum. Concerning problems in adoption, different causes have been presented and discussed. López-Martínez et al. [5] organized the existing reasons into four groups: people, project, process, and organization. By means of a systematic literature review, they concluded that most of the problems are people-related, including misalignment among teams and rotation of members of the team, among others. These are followed by problems related to organization, process, and project. The challenge of adopting Scrum may become harder depending on the particular setting of the company where Scrum is used. In fact, the real setting of companies can be so complex that in practice, it is very common for them to adapt methods and practices to their own context [3]. In our organization, for example, team members are usually shared among several projects at the same time. In one of these projects, where we adapted Scrum in order to develop eight software solutions, team members were also shared among different product teams in the same sprints (details in Section 3). Furthermore, there were interdependencies among product teams because the products belonged to the same digital ecosystem. Amid the different problems encountered in such a scenario, we highlight the low reliability of sprint commitment (details in Section 3). The reliability of sprint commitment is defined as the ability of a team to make a reliable statement about the backlog items that will be implemented at the end of the sprint [9]. It can be evaluated using the team's say-do ratio in each sprint. The say-do ratio is the ratio between what the team planned and what they actually did.

In this paper, we present how we used a traditional project management approach to adjust the sprint planning and monitoring processes in a resource-shared environment. The remainder of this paper is organized as follows: Section 2 discusses existing literature on the topic; Section 3 explains in more detail the context in which this study was carried out, describes the problems, and introduces the research questions; Section 4 describes the practices incorporated into the agile development process; Section 5 details how the approach was evaluated and presents its results and the discussion; and Section 6 finally concludes the paper with an outlook on future work.

2 Related Work

Mauch et al. [9] investigated the reliability of sprint commitments within the context of agile development across product families and found these influencing factors: quality of estimation, quality of capacity planning, awareness of the advantages of reliable sprint commitments, disturbances, and influences of non-agile teams. Awareness of self-responsibility is a key factor that influences the first three factors. The authors also report on a workshop concept to raise awareness for the advantages of reliable sprint commitments. Many companies enact hybrid processes combining agile and traditional development practices depending on their context [15] [2], either due to a lack of knowledge or by deliberate choice. Most research has rather focused on agile implementations in isolation, though there are many dependencies that influence the agility of an agile team [13]. For example, the exit or entry of people from/into the project has been identified as a factor impacting productivity [10], while having your team members dedicated full-time to your team was found to lead to higher focus and fewer interruptions. If the product to be developed becomes too large or too complex, more people have to be involved. For such cases, many scaling agile frameworks exist that help to align multiple teams for the development of a common product [14]. However, these frameworks assume fixed teams, each working on a different sub-part of a common system. There is not much work on multi-team and multi-project situations, i.e., situations where each member of a functional team is working on multiple sub-parts of a product (e.g., [8], [6] [7]).

3 Context, Problems, and Research Questions

In the project Digital Villages [16] at our institute, we elicited the different needs of people living in villages and created eight software-based solutions addressing problems regarding communication, public administration, local supply, and logistics. To streamline interoperability among these solutions and make them easier to implement, a digital platform was conceived as well. We refer to the complete team that worked in the project Digital Villages as "the global team". Given the innovative character of these solutions and the inherent uncertainties about their requirements, we decided to develop them using agile approaches, in particular Scrum, in order to refine them incrementally. We created and maintained a backlog of items to be developed for each product, refined them continuously, and organized our work in 2-week sprints. Developers with five different main skills were available to support the development of the solutions: backend, mobile client, web client, Wordpress development, and design & user experience. They were organized in what we refer to as "technical teams", comparable to Chapters in the Scaling Agile @Spotify approach [4]. Depending on the sprint goals, each product needed people from loose technical teams to support the development of the next increment, forming what we call "product teams". Frequently, the same person worked for different product teams within the same sprint. Furthermore, our institute has a balanced-matrix organizational structure, meaning that functional managers influence the assignment of resources to different projects at the same time. This resource allocation happens in a medium to long time range, like half a year or one year, whereas the allocation of a specific team member to a sprint happens *ad hoc* in a short time range. Two problems were found in this scenario with volatile product teams. First, the global team had an incontestably low say-do ratio, even though production-quality software had been developed. The volatile product team structure directly influenced the quality of the sprint due to the attention overhead required by context switching, which is usually overlooked. Referring to Tuckman's stages of group development, this situation means that a team would remain in the forming or storming phase most of the time, meaning it would never reach the desired state of performing [17]. This product team structure also compromises the ability to measure the product teams' velocity across multiple sprints, since the composition of product teams changes, the amount of time spent by each team member varies, or a combination of both. As a result, sprint plannings were often not fulfilled. Second, we also noticed that the say-do ratio varied too much, resulting in a lack of short-/mid-term predictability regarding the project plans.

In this context, three research questions were posed: "(RQ1) How can the say-do ratio of our team be improved?"; "(RQ2) How can the say-do ratio of our team become more stable?"; and "(RQ3) What influence does the number of issues[1] have on the fluctuation of the say-do ratio in our project?".

[1] The term "issue" refers to work items that are included in the sprint plans.

4 The Approach for a Resource-Shared Environment

We applied certain traditional project management practices to mitigate the impact of those problems while accepting the organizational constraint of working in our resource-shared setting. In general, the practices are not novel *per se*, but their application in the specific scenario of agile teams with shared resources is. In our setting, the figure of the Scrum Master becomes blurred, maybe due to the volatility of the product teams. So a process manager was designated to drive the implementation of the practices. This role was taken up by the first author of this paper.

Practice 1: Separate concerns in the sprint planning. Multiple planning sessions should take place in a resource-shared environment. Some concerns are better addressed within each product team, while others demand cross-team or cross-product alignment. These concerns include prioritization, resource-sharing, detailed planning, and alignment of plans. **Practice 2: Decrease the capacity of team members.** Team members should be asked to reduce their availability not only because of the expected overhead due to the regular sprint meetings, but also due to the frequent context switching (either from different products being developed within the project or from other projects). In our case, members were asked to reduce it by 25% (or more, for technical leaders). **Practice 3: Implement a sprint planning calendar.** The separation of concerns must be implemented through a sprint planning calendar with clear participants, subprocesses, activities, inputs, and outputs. In our concrete setting, we implemented the sprint calendar in three days. The first day focused on prioritization and resource sharing, the second day on the detailed plan, and the third day on the alignment of plans. **Practice 4: Involve product owners and technical leaders in the definition of sprint goals and priorities.** Given the interdependencies between product teams and technical teams, the decision about what to do in the next iteration should not be left solely to the product owners. This is necessary because some technical concerns may cut across different products, and in a resource-shared shared environment with interdependencies, a holistic view on the priorities is required in addition to single product-oriented views. **Practice 5: Involve product owners and technical leaders in the definition of resource sharing.** Based on the informed capacity of each team member for the next sprint, product owners and technical leaders have to agree on how these resources should be shared among the product teams. This decision is influenced by the priorities to which they have previously committed. This is a fundamental practice in a resource-shared environment and does not take place when team members can be dedicated to one product team. **Practice 6: Plan the details as a product team.** The need to focus on the *product teams* should be made explicit when it comes to detailing what has to be done in the sprint and how to get there. *Global team* planning meetings tend to be ineffective due to the large number of participants who have different foci and cannot capture the details of all products. Also, when *technical teams* gather to plan tasks, they may miss the overall goal that a certain product has in the sprint. **Practice 7: Estimate the usage of time.** Due to the fact that in a resource-shared scenario, the product teams are volatile, the strength of estimation techniques based on story points is reduced because they rely on the team's velocity, which can only be derived from a consistent team learning process over many sprints. Therefore, the usage of time as an estimation technique is better suited to such an environment.

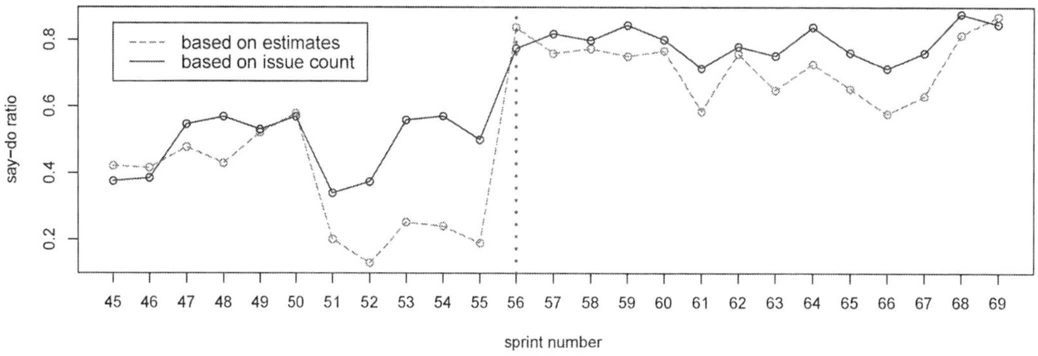

Fig. 1. Say-do ratio of the team based on issue count (solid line) and estimates (dashed line).

5 Evaluation: Case Study

We evaluated the effectiveness of the usage of the practices listed in Section 4 with a holistic case study[2] in the context of the project Digital Villages (the *case*). We collected data about the work planned and done by all team members (the *selection*) throughout the year 2019 (from sprint 45 to sprint 69). All data was collected in our issue-tracking software (indirect data collection) for managing our sprint activities. In total, 2841 issues were analyzed. Figure 1 shows the say-do ratio of all sprints in 2019. The practices were applied from sprint 56 on. Two different metrics can be used to calculate the say-do ratio: issue count (number of issues with the status *DONE* in the sprint divided by total number of issues in the sprint), and estimates (sum of all estimates of the issues with the status *DONE* divided by the sum of all estimates of all issues in the sprint). The results presented in this paper are based on issue count because this metric could be used consistently before and after the implementation of the practices (see details in Section 5.3). In this section, we present the evaluation of four hypotheses related to the research questions that are the focus of this paper (see Section 3). We used the GQM approach [1] to frame our investigation. Table 1 contains the goals (G_i), questions(Q_i), and metrics(M_i).

5.1 Hypotheses and results

Hypothesis 1: The say-do ratio of the resource-shared agile team increases when the practices are applied (RQ1). We found $M1 = 0.48$ *(M1)* and $M2 = 0.79$. Next, we verified whether the say-do ratio had a normal distribution using the Shapiro-Wilk normality test ($p - value = 0.01365$, $\alpha = 0.05$). Then we applied the Kruskal-Wallis test to compare the difference between the means. The null hypothesis (the means are equal) was rejected (p-value = 2.494×10^{-5}, $\alpha = 0.05$) ($M3$). **Hypothesis 2: The say-do ratio of the resource-shared agile team is more stable when the practices are applied (RQ2).** We found $M4 = 0.0088$ and $M5 = 0.0024$. Since the say-do

[2] In a strict sense, it should not be called "case study", since we were actively engaged in it. Here we use the term "case study" in a less restrictive way.

ratios did not have normal distribution, we applied the Fligner-Killeen's test to compare the difference. The null hypothesis (variances are equal) could not be rejected (p-value 0.1936, $\alpha = 0.05$) ($M6$). **Hypothesis 3: The number of planned issues in the sprints decreases when the practices are applied (RQ3).** We found $M7 = 129.27$ and $M8 = 101.35$. Next, we checked whether the distribution of the number of issues was normal using the Shapiro-Wilk Test, and the null hypothesis (normality) could not be rejected ($p - value = 0.4233$, $\alpha = 0.05$). Therefore, we used the Student's t-test to compare the difference between the means. The null hypothesis (means are equal) was rejected ($p - value = 0.0214$, $\alpha = 0.05$) ($M9$). **Hypothesis 4: There is a correlation between the number of issues and the say-do ratio (RQ3).** Since we identified a significant improvement in the say-do ratio and a significant reduction in the number of issues, we verified whether there is a correlation between the two variables. We counted the number of issues of each sprint (from sprint 45 to sprint 69) *(M9)* and the collected say-do ratios for the same sprints *M10*. As the say-do ratios were not distributed normally, we used Spearman's correlation coefficient to verify whether there is a correlation between the variables. The null hypothesis (there is no relationship) could not be rejected ($\rho(23) = -0.3643008$, p-value = 0.0734, $\alpha = 0.05$) ($M11$).

5.2 Discussion

The evaluation showed that the implementation of the practices did improve the say-do ratio of the global team. On the one hand, from the first time the practices were applied, the say-do ratio became notably better. On the other hand, over seven months of applying the practices, the global team never managed to fulfill 100% of the sprint plan, which suggests that maybe the practices have limited effectiveness and further improvement should call for more, or different, practices. It is worth noticing that "bad estimates" was perceived as a central cause for the low say-do ratio when we interviewed product owners and technical leaders, which is based on the assumption that they were not able to fulfill the plans because their estimates were flawed. However, significant improve-

Table 1. Goals, questions, and metrics. Each goal G_i refers to a hypothesis H_i.

GOAL	**G1**	**Improve the say-do ratio of sprints from the point of view of the global team in the context of the project Digital Villages**
Question	Q1	What is the say-do ratio of the global team of the project Digital Villages without the practices?
Metric	*M1*	*Average say-do ratio without the practices*
Question	Q2	Does the say-do ratio improve when the practices are applied?
Metric	*M2*	*Average say-do ratio with the practices*
Metric	*M3*	*Difference between the average say-do ratios*
GOAL	**G2**	**Reduce the variability of the say-do ratio from the point of view of the global team in the context of the project Digital Villages**
Question	Q3	What is the variability of the say-do ratio of the global team of the project Digital Villages without the practices?
Metric	*M4*	*Variance of the say-do ratio before the practices*
Question	Q4	Does the variability of the say-do ratio decrease when the practices are applied?
Metric	*M5*	*Variance of the say-do ratio after the practices*
Metric	*M6*	*Comparison of variance of the say-do ratio with and without the practices*
GOAL	**G3**	**Identify whether there is a reduction of the number of issues from the point of view of the global team in the context of the project Digital Villages**
Question	Q5	How many issues were included in the sprints of the project Digital Villages before the practices?
Metric	*M7*	*Average number of issues without the practices*
Question	Q6	Did the number of issues decrease when the practices were applied?
Metric	*M8*	*Average number of issues with the practices*
Metric	*M9*	*Difference between the average numbers of issues*
GOAL	**G4**	**Identify whether there is a correlation between of the number of issues and the say-do ratio from the point of view of the global team in the context of the project Digital Villages**
Question	Q7	How many issues were included in the sprints of the project Digital Villages before the practices?
Metric	*M9*	*Number of issues of all sprints*
Question	Q8	Is there a correlation between the number of issues and the say-do ratio?
Metric	*M10*	*Say-do ratios of all sprints*
Metric	*M11*	*Correlation coefficient between number of issues and say-do ratio*

ment was achieved without changing the estimation technique. Regarding the variance of the say-do ratio, we could not find significant difference after the implementation of the practices. Further investigation is needed to find out what can be done to reduce it, since a smaller variance would mean that the team has a more predictable say-do ratio.

The average number of issues observed with the practices was lower than before, which was expected to a certain degree since the practices focus on planning and monitoring. However it is important to note that the increase in the say-do ratio cannot be justified by the reduction in the number of issues per sprint alone. Additional investigation would be needed to reveal whether certain practices influenced the say-do ratio more than others (and if so, which ones in particular). For example, initial discussions within the project team indicate that the presence of the process manager played an important role in the effectiveness of the practices. We consider it important to add qualitative analysis on top of this research to better understand other impacts of the application of the practices. For example, during the seven months, there were no comments, neither from team members nor from managers, concerning a possible perception of lower productivity in the team, but this should be investigated in more detail.

5.3 Threats to Validity

Internal validity: The presence of the process manager alone, as a person working to ensure the fulfillment of the practices, may have acted as a confounding variable and influenced the say-do ratio. **External validity:** The evaluation was done in the context of a research project. Despite the fact that it was an applied research project where production-quality software was developed and deployed to thousands of users, the results may be different in a pure industrial setting. **Construct validity:** The global team was aware of the practices that were applied and knew that these practices aimed at improving the say-do ratio, so there may be possible interaction between testing and treatment. Besides, the implementation of the practices may have brought negative side-effects that were not captured in the analysis, which could explain, for example, why the average say-do ratio after the practices was not higher than 0.79. **Conclusion validity:** We used issue count to validate the hypotheses (as described at the beginning of Section 5). Since different issues have different sizes, a more accurate metric should take the estimates into consideration. However, prior to the implementation of the practices, most of the issues had no estimates documented in the issue-tracking software.

6 Conclusion

In this paper, we described how we adjusted our implementation of Scrum to deal with an environment where human resources have to be shared among different products and products within the same sprints. We had such a scenario in the context of the project Digital Villages, where we experienced low reliability of sprint commitment. We accepted resource-sharing as an organizational constraint and applied certain practices in the project for seven months. In our case study, we were able to verify their effectiveness in significantly improving the say-do ratio of the team. The incorporation of the traditional project management practices described in this paper can help practitioners to better plan and monitor sprints in a resource-shared environment. For researchers, we contribute empirical validation and indicate open questions for further investigation.

Acknowledgment

The project "Digitale Dörfer" is funded by the Ministry of the Interior and for Sport of the State of Rhineland-Palatinate (grant number "56:382 Digitale Dörfer").

References

1. Basili, V., Caldiera, G., Rombach, H.D.: The goal question metric approach. Encyclopedia of software engineering pp. 528–532 (1994)
2. Diebold, P., Ostberg, J.P., Wagner, S., Zendler, U.: What do practitioners vary in using scrum? In: XP 2015. pp. 40–51. Springer (2015)
3. Hoda, R., Kruchten, P., Noble, J., Marshall, S.: Agility in context. In: OOPSLA'10. pp. 74–88 (2010)
4. Kniberg, H., Ivarsson, A.: Scaling Agile @ Spotify with Tribes, Squads, Chapters Guilds. https://bit.ly/3hqmaKD, accessed: 2020-07-08
5. López-Martínez, J., Juárez-Ramírez, R., Huertas, C., Jiménez, S., Guerra-García, C.: Problems in the adoption of agile-scrum methodologies: A systematic literature review. In: CONISOFT 2016. pp. 141–148. IEEE (2016)
6. Lorber, A.A., Mish, K.D.: How we successfully adapted agile for a research-heavy engineering software team. In: 2013 agile conference. pp. 156–163. IEEE (2013)
7. Lorber, A.A., Tieszen, S.R.: A starting point for negotiations–delivering with a heterogeneous team. In: 2012 Agile Conference. pp. 148–155. IEEE (2012)
8. Marchenko, A., Abrahamsson, P.: Scrum in a multiproject environment: An ethnographically-inspired case study on the adoption challenges. In: Agile 2008 Conference. pp. 15–26. IEEE (2008)
9. Mauch, L., Steyer, M., Bursac, N., et al.: Agile baukastenentwicklung–chancen und herausforderungen bei der implementierung in der entwicklungspraxis am beispiel der zuverlässigkeit von sprintzusagen. In: DFX 2019, 18-19 September 2019, Jesteburg, Germany. pp. 291–302 (2019)
10. Melo, C., Cruzes, D.S., Kon, F., Conradi, R.: Agile team perceptions of productivity factors. In: 2011 Agile Conference. pp. 57–66. IEEE (2011)
11. Ries, E.: The lean startup: How today's entrepreneurs use continuous innovation to create radically successful businesses. Currency (2011)
12. Sharma, S., Hasteer, N.: A comprehensive study on state of scrum development. In: ICCCA 2016. pp. 867–872. IEEE (2016)
13. Theobald, S., Diebold, P.: Interface problems of agile in a non-agile environment. In: XP 2018. pp. 123–130. Springer (2018)
14. Theobald, S., Schmitt, A., Diebold, P.: Comparing scaling agile frameworks based on underlying practices. In: XP 2019. pp. 88–96. Springer (2019)
15. Theocharis, G., Kuhrmann, M., Münch, J., Diebold, P.: Is water-scrum-fall reality? on the use of agile and traditional development practices. In: PROFES 2015. pp. 149–166. Springer (2015)
16. Trapp, M., Hess, S.: Digital villages. In: Biological Transformation. Springer (2019)
17. Tuckman, B.: Developmental sequence in small groups. Psychol. Bull. **63**(6), 384–399 (1965)
18. VersionOne and Collabnet: 14th State of Agile Report. Available online: https://bit.ly/2QREgLn (accessed on 2021-05-07) (2020)

Estado da arte e da prática sobre catálogos de padrões de requisitos

Mariana C. Martins, Taciana N. Kudo, and Renato F. Bulcão-Neto

Instituto de Informática, Universidade Federal de Goiás, Goiânia, Brasil
maricrisostomo.martins@gmail.com, {taciana,rbulcao}@ufg.br

Resumo A prática de reúso por meio de padrões de requisitos de software (PRS) é uma abordagem para tratar problemas de qualidade das especificações, bem como auxiliar na melhora nos prazos de entrega. Para viabilizar o uso de PRS, faz-se necessária a construção e a divulgação de catálogos de maneira sistemática e organizada por domínios específicos. Nesse contexto, um mapeamento sistemático fornece uma visão geral da literatura e ajuda a descobrir novas oportunidades de pesquisa. Este artigo descreve o estado da arte e da prática de catálogos de PRS por meio de um mapeamento sistemático, que identificou 25 estudos primários sob as perspectivas de construção, validação, avaliação, manutenção, disponibilização e uso na prática desses catálogos. Há evidências de uma lacuna entre a teoria e a prática, em especial, dada a pequena quantidade de estudos que reportam a adesão da indústria ao reúso de requisitos por meio de catálogos de PRS. Para reduzir essa lacuna, propõe-se, dentre outros, maior suporte ferramental, validação de catálogos com especialistas e meios padronizados para sua disseminação.

Keywords: Padrão de requisito · catálogo · mapeamento sistemático

1 Introdução

Pesquisas afirmam que mais de 50% de projetos de software falham no cumprimento de prazos e orçamentos em função de especificações de requisitos de baixa qualidade, com requisitos errados, omitidos, conflitantes e ambíguos [21,33]. Consequentemente, a qualidade do produto de software final também é impactada.

Nesse contexto, padrão de requisito de software (PRS) é uma abordagem para reúso de requisitos, uma abstração que permite que partes genéricas de um requisito sejam reaproveitadas em outros projetos [35], gerando especificações com menor esforço e melhor qualidade.

Um estudo terciário sobre padrões de requisitos [15] propõe uma agenda de pesquisa como resultado da análise e síntese dos achados de quatro estudos secundários. Uma das seis linhas de ação dessa agenda de pesquisa é a disseminação de catálogos de PRS de modo sistemático, para que possam ser utilizados pela indústria de software. Porém, os esforços de desenvolvimento desses catálogos não estão devidamente mapeados e caracterizados em um estudo secundário, que possa orientar a realização de pesquisas nesse tema.

Sendo assim, este artigo descreve um mapeamento sistemático que visa caracterizar o estado da arte e da prática sobre catálogos de PRS. Através do rigor do mapeamento sistemático, busca-se obter estudos que tratem da construção, validação, avaliação, manutenção, disseminação e uso desses catálogos na indústria. O protocolo do mapeamento baseia-se em boas práticas [25], incluindo busca automática sobre quatro bases digitais, busca manual e *forward snowballing* [36] para ampliar a busca por estudos primários sobre catálogos de PRS. Da análise dos 25 estudos primários selecionados, evidencia-se a necessidade de reduzir a lacuna entre a teoria e a prática associadas a catálogos de PRS quanto à sua validação, avaliação, manutenção e disseminação.

O artigo está assim organizado: a Seção 2 apresenta trabalhos relacionados; a Seção 3 descreve o protocolo do mapeamento sistemático. As respostas às questões de pesquisa e os achados estão sintetizados na Seção 4. Por fim, relatam-se as ameaças à validade na Seção 5, e as considerações finais, na Seção 6.

2 Trabalhos Relacionados

Palomares et al. [21] mapeiam o estado da prática de reúso de requisitos, incluindo padrões de requisitos. Também identificam motivos pelos quais reúso de requisitos não é uma prática comum na indústria de software, como a não familiaridade dos profissionais com PRS em específico.

Barros-Justo et al. [3] identificam que elicitação, especificação, validação e gerenciamento são as atividades de Engenharia de Requisitos afetadas pelo uso de padrões de requisitos. Também apontam propriedades de processo e de produto de software que são impactadas pelo uso de padrões de requisitos e, em função disso, destacam a carência de métricas objetivas para esse fim.

Com foco em diferentes abordagens de reúso, incluindo padrões de requisitos, Irshad et al. [11] analisam os métodos de avaliação e a relevância e o rigor dos estudos empíricos encontrados. Como no estudo de Palomares et al. [21], destacam a escassez de estudos com validação na indústria de software.

Silva e Benitti [7] mapeiam os formatos utilizados para padronização da escrita de requisitos e concluem que formulários pré-definidos (*templates*) são os mais comuns. Outros trabalhos [21,11], entretanto, encontraram padrões escritos em linguagem natural, caso de uso e na forma de diagramas.

Apesar de terem mapeado dezenas de estudos primários, nenhum deles analisa o uso de padrões de requisitos em outras etapas do ciclo de vida de software, apesar da intrínseca influência de requisitos sobre elas. Essa análise encontra-se em um mapeamento sistemático [17] que descobre apenas oito estudos primários que investigam contribuições de padrões de requisitos em *design*, um em construção, um em teste e nenhum em manutenção.

Não é de conhecimento dos autores um estudo secundário que mapeie como desenvolver, validar, avaliar, evoluir e disponibilizar catálogos de PRS. Este estudo alinha-se à agenda de pesquisa de [15], que descreve que a produção e a disseminação de catálogos podem aproximar a teoria e a prática de PRS.

3 Protocolo do Mapeamento Sistemático

Um mapeamento sistemático da literatura (MSL) visa a categorização e classificação dos resultados obtidos em prol de uma visão geral de uma área de pesquisa [25]. Para fins de reprodutibilidade, um MSL inclui três etapas: planejamento, condução e publicação de resultados.

No planejamento, definem-se objetivo, questões de pesquisa (QP), estratégia de busca, *string* de busca, critérios de seleção e o formulário para extração de dados. Na condução, executa-se a estratégia de busca com a *string* definida, aplicam-se os critérios de seleção ao ler metadados de cada estudo, lê-se na íntegra cada estudo selecionado, preenche-se o formulário de dados e analisam-se os dados extraídos para responder às QPs. Por fim, a publicação dos resultados dá-se na forma de relatórios e/ou artigos.

O planejamento e a condução do MSL foram realizados com apoio da ferramenta *Parsif.al*, enquanto que a análise e a síntese dos dados extraídos deu-se por meio de planilhas do *Google Sheets*. A documentação do MSL teve apoio de ambas as ferramentas, incluindo a geração de gráficos. Informações adicionais sobre este MSL, incluindo o protocolo e detalhes dos resultados estão disponíveis[1].

3.1 Questões de Pesquisa e Palavras-chave

O objetivo deste mapeamento foi conhecer o estado da arte e da prática de catálogos de PRS. Para isso, foram elaboradas as seguintes questões de pesquisa com as suas respectivas justificativas:

QP1. Quais são os métodos para construção de catálogos? – para obter, de cada método, sua estratégia, os autores e eventuais ferramentas de apoio.

QP2. Como os catálogos são validados? – para identificar o mecanismo de validação de cada catálogo, conforme classificação proposta por Petersen et al. [25], o perfil dos validadores e eventuais ferramentas de apoio.

QP3. Como os catálogos são avaliados? – para identificar a abordagem de avaliação de cada catálogo, pela classificação de Petersen et al. [25], o perfil dos avaliadores, as métricas utilizadas e eventuais ferramentas de apoio.

QP4. Como os catálogos passam por manutenção? – para investigar como um catálogo de PRS evolui, como se dá o controle de suas mudanças e se existe apoio ferramental para isso.

QP5. Como os catálogos são disponibilizados para reúso? – para descobrir se há catálogos públicos, os diferentes meios de publicização desses catálogos e se há suporte ferramental.

QP6. Há evidência do uso prático de catálogos na indústria? – para mapear os estudos em que profissionais da indústria utilizam catálogos de PRS e reportam benefícios obtidos com essa prática.

Para responder às QPs, identificaram-se termos candidatos da *string* de busca, o que contou com a experiência dos autores no tema [17,15]: catálogo(s), padrão(ões) de requisito(s) e suas respectivas traduções e adaptações em inglês.

[1] Disponível para acesso em http://encurtador.com.br/nzNS7.

3.2 *String* e Estratégia de Busca

Visando equilíbrio entre abrangência e relevância dos resultados, buscas piloto com os termos candidatos foram feitas para definir as *strings* de busca a seguir:

("*catalog**") AND ("*requirement pattern**" OR "*requirements pattern**" OR "*NFR pattern*" OR "*FR pattern*" OR "*requirement template**" OR "*requirements template**")

("*catálogo*") AND ("*padrão de requisito**" OR "*padrões de requisito**")

A estratégia de busca inclui buscas automática e manual e a técnica de *forward snowballing* [36], a qual recupera artigos que citam os estudos considerados relevantes e que têm potencial de também sê-lo. Quanto aos filtros da estratégia de busca, filtraram-se estudos escritos em Português e Inglês, porém sem restrição quanto ao ano de publicação desses estudos.

A busca automática foi feita nas bases *Scopus*, *Engineering Village*, *ACM DL*[2] e *IEEE Xplore*. Para a busca manual, foram escolhidos o Workshop de Engenharia de Requisitos (WER) e o *Journal of Software Engineering Research and Development* (JSERD), ambos não indexados pelas fontes citadas.

3.3 Seleção dos Estudos Primários

Os estudos primários foram selecionados segundo sete critérios de exclusão (CE), de modo que se um estudo se encaixar em ao menos um CE, então é excluído do MSL. O único critério de inclusão (CI) é o que seleciona "*estudo que propõe, relata ou avalia um ou mais catálogos de padrões de requisitos de software*". Seguem os CEs aplicados a cada estudo identificado:

CE1. Estudo duplicado;
CE2. Texto completo indisponível gratuitamente na Web ou na Plataforma Periódicos CAPES;
CE3. Não está escrito nos idiomas Português ou Inglês;
CE4. Não foi publicado em periódicos ou anais de eventos científicos;
CE5. Não aborda requisitos de software;
CE6. Não aborda catálogos de PRS;
CE7. É uma versão preliminar ou resumida de outro já estudo incluso.

A Figura 1 apresenta a identificação de estudos e a seleção dos mesmos. Na busca automática (BA), foram identificados 60 estudos[3]. Na seleção inicial, 27 estudos estavam duplicados e nove foram excluídos, restando, assim, 24 estudos. Na leitura completa dos estudos, outros três foram excluídos, e 21 estudos foram selecionados como relevantes pela busca automática.

[2] Utilizou-se a configuração *The ACM Guide to Computing Literature*.
[3] Realizada em 27 de outubro de 2020.

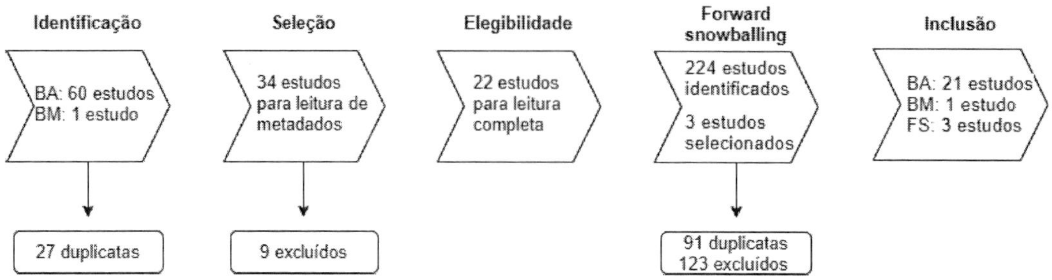

Figura 1. Processo de seleção dos estudos do MSL.

Como mostra a Figura 1, apenas um estudo foi encontrado na busca manual (BM) e considerado relevante. A técnica de *forward snowballing* (FS) foi realizada[4] sobre cada um desses 22 estudos, utilizando a lista de citações extraída da base *Scopus*. Encontraram-se 224 estudos, dos quais 91 eram duplicados e 123 foram excluídos por algum CE. Dez estudos permaneceram para leitura completa, dos quais três foram considerados para a seleção final. Portanto, selecionaram-se 21 estudos da busca automática, um da busca manual e três pelo *forward snowballing*, totalizando 25 artigos para extração e síntese de dados (E1 a E25).

De cada estudo lido na íntegra, extraíram-se as abordagens de construção, validação, avaliação, manutenção e publicização de catálogos, informações sobre uso na indústria, a adoção de ferramentas de apoio e os domínio de aplicação dos catálogos de PRS encontrados.

A Tabela 1 sintetiza os achados deste mapeamento. Os significados das siglas e símbolos presentes nessa tabela são fornecidos a seguir para facilitar a compreensão das informações extraídas.

- **ID** é o identificador do estudo;
- **REF** é a referência bibliográfica do estudo;
- **FER**, se existe (S) ou não (-) uma ferramenta para construção de catálogos;
- **CONS**, indica o método de construção do catálogo, i.e., Supakkul (S), Withall (W) ou não identificado (-);
- Em **Requisito**, se os requisitos do catálogo são não funcionais (NF), funcionais (F) ou não técnicos (NT);
- **VAL**, a abordagem de validação como experimento (EXP), estudo de caso (EC), prova de propriedades (PP) e simulação (SIM);
- **AVAL**, refere-se à avaliação do catálogo, e (P) para profissionais da indústria de software;
- **MAN**, refere-se à existência (S) ou não (-) de manutenção dos catálogos;
- **DIS**, o modo como o catálogo é disponibilizado, i.e., referências (R), site (S) ou não identificado (-).

[4] Executada em 29 de outubro de 2020.

Tabela 1. Síntese das descobertas do MSL.

ID	REF	Ano	FER	CONS	Domínio	Requisito	VAL	AVAL	MAN	DIS	Uso na prática
E1	[16]	2020	S	W	S-RES	F e NF	-	-	-		-
E2	[1]	2019	-	W	-	NF	-	P	-	-	-
E3	[12]	2018	-	-	-	NF	-	-	-	-	-
E4	[14]	2018	-	-	-	NF	EC	-	S	-	-
E5	[9]	2018	-	-	sistemas distribuídos	NF	-	-	-	R	-
E6	[27]	2017	-	W	-	NF	SIM	-	S	-	-
E7	[5]	2016	-	S	-	-	EC	-	S	-	-
E8	[2]	2016	S	-	sistema de informação	-	EC	-	-	-	-
E9	[28]	2016	-	S	-	NF	-	-	-	S	-
E10	[6]	2015	-	S	-	NF	-		-	-	-
E11	[30]	2014	-	S	-	NF	-	-	-	-	-
E12	[4]	2014	S	W	computação em nuvem	NF	-	P	-	R	consultores em segurança
E13	[8]	2014	-	S	Direito	-	-	-	-	-	-
E14	[13]	2014	-	W	-	NF	-	-	S	R	desenvolvimento de software sob medida
E15	[31]	2013	-	S	-	NF	-	-	S	R	-
E16	[10]	2013	-	W	gestão	NF e NT	-	-	-	S	-
E17	[24]	2013	-	W	gestão de conteúdo	F	PP	-	-	-	-
E18	[7]	2013	S	W	-	NF	EC	P	-	S	-
E19	[23]	2012	-	W	-	NT	-	-	-	S	TUDOR / CASSIS
E20	[22]	2011	S	-	-	NF	-	-	-	-	TUDOR / CASSIS
E21	[29]	2011	-	S	-	-	EXP	-	-	S	-
E22	[20]	2011	-	-	-	NF	-	-	-	-	-
E23	[26]	2009	-	W	licitações	NF	-	-	-	S	-
E24	[19]	2008	-	W	sistemas COTS	NF, F e NT	-	-	-	-	-
E25	[34]	2002	-	-	aplicação web	-	-	-	-	-	-

4 Síntese dos Dados

O método de síntese escolhido foi a síntese narrativa, com a análise quantitativa e qualitativa das respostas às questões de pesquisa deste MSL.

4.1 Resposta da QP1

Após extrair e analisar os métodos para construção de catálogos de PRS descritos nos 25 estudos, concluiu-se que dois métodos se destacam: as propostas de Withall [35] e Supakkul [32], respectivamente. Os estudos que abordam esses métodos de construção estão especificados na Tabela 2.

Na abordagem de Supakkul [32], os requisitos são representados como *softgoals* a serem satisfeitos. O processo de construção dos padrões é realizado quando um engenheiro refina um modelo adicionando incrementalmente um novo elemento e vinculando-o a um elemento existente. Para determinar a satisfatibilidade, as decisões são registradas e, à medida que um tópico é satisfeito, outros podem ser adicionados. A junção desses elementos forma uma estrutura conhecida como grafo SIG (*Softgoal Interdependency Graph*).

O método de construção de Withall [35] possui uma etapa de filtragem de requisitos a partir de especificações existentes, em que requisitos são classificados ou descartados. Em seguida, os requisitos são agrupados e, se necessário, decompostos, em requisitos mais simples. Na fase de análise, verifica-se a adequação do requisito mediante a frequência do mesmo nas especificações, que pode ter auxílio de especialistas de domínio para restringir o número de padrões candidatos. Depois, os padrões candidatos são convertidos em padrões de fato, podendo ser também agrupados. Por fim, os padrões são classificados de acordo com os esquemas e têm seus relacionamentos estabelecidos.

Tabela 2. Método de construção de catálogo de padrões de requisitos.

Método de Construção	Estudos
Baseado no método de Withall	E1, E2, E5, E6, E12, E14, E16, E17-19, E23, E24
Baseado no método de Supakkul	E7, E9-11, E13, E15, E21
Não identificado	E3, E4, E8, E20, E22, E25

De forma complementar, apenas cinco (E1, E8, E12, E18 e E20) dos 25 estudos reportam uma ferramenta de apoio à construção do catálogo. Além disso, dentre os domínios de aplicação para os quais os catálogos foram construídos, é possível identificar: sistemas de registro eletrônico em Saúde (S-RES) (E1), sistemas distribuídos (E5), sistemas de informação (E8), computação em nuvem (E12), Direito (E13), gerenciamento de conteúdo (E16 e E17), processos de licitação (E23), COTS (E24) e aplicações web (E25). Observa-se também que 17 dos 25 estudos tratam requisitos não funcionais, com destaque para os requisitos de segurança e transparência. Por outro lado, apenas dois trabalhos abordam requisitos funcionais em seus catálogos, e três tratam de requisitos não técnicos.

Portanto, como resposta à QP1, tem-se *a predominância dos métodos de Withall e Supakkul, o baixo suporte ferramental para construção de catálogos de PRS, uma diversidade de domínios de aplicação e maior número de estudos dedicados a padrões de requisitos não funcionais.*

4.2 Resposta da QP2

Apenas sete estudos descrevem a abordagem adotada na validação de seus catálogos de PRS, como mostra a Tabela 3. Observou-se uma diversidade de mecanismos de validação, que seguem o esquema de classificação de estudos discutido em Petersen et al. [25].

Tabela 3. Método de validação de catálogo de padrões de requisitos.

Método de Validação	**Estudos**
Estudo de caso com estudantes	E4, E7, E8 e E18
Experimento em laboratório	E21
Simulação	E6
Prova de propriedades	E17

Dentre esses sete estudos, quatro realizam validação com estudantes. No estudo E4, a validação deu-se com grupos de estudantes utilizando os catálogos para elicitação de requisitos, enquanto outros grupos efetuaram a elicitação sem o apoio de catálogos. No estudo E7, um estudante aplica o catálogo para proveniência de dados científicos em um sistema. Em E18, dois grupos de estudantes são utilizados (sendo um grupo de controle) e efetuaram a especificação de um sistema de livraria e de aluguel de automóveis com o auxílio de um catálogo.

O estudo E21 efetua a validação do catálogo sobre um grafo de argumentação, e algoritmos raciocinam sobre o grafo para determinar a validade relativa, verificando se os argumentos são aceitáveis ou se precisam de mais discussão. Em E6, efetua-se a validação com teste aleatório e conjunto de treinamento utilizando estatísticas Kappa, e os responsáveis determinam se o catálogo auxilia nos controles de segurança e privacidade. Por fim, o estudo E17 analisa aspectos do catálogo construído baseado em cobertura do esquema de classificação, cobertura do documento de especificação e generalidade do catálogo.

Portanto, em resposta à QP2, *poucos estudos reportam a validação de catálogos de padrões de requisitos, com diferentes abordagens de validação, sendo a maioria em ambiente acadêmico.*

4.3 Resposta da QP3

Ao extrair e analisar as abordagens de avaliação de catálogos, foram encontrados apenas três estudos que realizaram a avaliação, todos com profissionais da indústria. A classificação das abordagens de avaliação também seguem o esquema de classificação sugerido por Petersen et al. [25].

O E2 realizou avaliação com profissionais da metodologia ágil Scrum, utilizando diversos tipos de sistema, tais como registro de alunos, informação de cliente, empréstimo de biblioteca e controle de acesso ao aplicativo. Para avaliar a eficiência dos padrões de requisitos não funcionais (NFR), mediram o tempo que cada membro da equipe levou para especificar os requisitos, antes e depois de usar os padrões. Como resultado, descobriram que os padrões auxiliam na melhoria da eficiência da redação de requisitos. Para avaliar a eficácia dos padrões, primeiro verificaram a correção de todos os requisitos especificados quando os membros da equipe utilizaram os padrões. Os membros da equipe foram capazes de escrever os requisitos usando as representações corretas, aplicar o corretamente os padrões, e associar NFRs a padrões de requisitos funcionais (FRs).

O estudo E12 realiza a avaliação analisando aspectos do catálogo com consultores de segurança, e efetua uma análise baseada em projetos industriais a fim de, ter mais detalhes do catálogo, não esquecer nenhum aspecto. As conclusões dessa avaliação relatam: redução do esforço da documentação, ajuda na eliciação de requisitos com mais detalhes, apoio na identificação de ameaças e auxílio para tratar de questões importantes de segurança.

Em E18, aplica-se um questionário com seis profissionais com três a sete anos de experiência para verificar a contribuição do catálogo na redação e no reúso na atividades de especificação de requisitos.

Portanto, conclui-se que *há uma escassez de trabalhos que relatam a avaliação de catálogos de PRS e que a maioria dos estudos relevantes é classificada como proposta de solução para reúso de requisitos de um domínio de aplicação.*

4.4 Resposta da QP4

Apenas cinco dos 25 estudos (E4, E6, E7, E14, E15) abordam a manutenção dos catálogos de padrões de requisitos.

No estudo E4, a manutenção foi realizada a partir da reunião de 42 projetos. Foi feita uma limpeza dos dados e obteve-se em torno de 400 padrões. Buscaram um esforço de manutenção menor com aplicação do princípio de Pareto. No estudo E6 os autores apresentam uma extensão do catálogo mas não descrevem como ela acontece. No estudo E7 o refinamento do catálogo é por detalhamento da hierarquia de padrões. Identificam as perguntas e buscam o modelo conceitual para projetos. No estudo E14 os autores relatam que o catálogo foi mantido e melhorado mas não detalham como foi realizado. No estudo E15 é verificada a sintaxe e a semântica para efetuarem a manutenção.

Considerando que a maioria dos estudos primários não realizou validação e avaliação de seus catálogos, é de se esperar que *os estudos não se preocupassem ainda com a evolução desses catálogos.*

4.5 Resposta da QP5

Como apresenta a Tabela 4, quatro estudos citam trabalhos do grupo de pesquisa nos quais o catálogo é disponibilizado para acesso, como o estudo E5, que referencia um relatório técnico no qual o catálogo está publicado. A Tabela 4 destaca seis estudos que publicam catálogos em sites dos grupos de pesquisa para acesso. É o caso do estudo E19, que disponibiliza o catálogo sob uma licença *Creative Commons*, que permite o uso não comercial (e.g., pesquisa e experimentação), mas sem trabalhos derivados.

Tabela 4. Disponibilização do catálogo de padrões de requisitos.

Tipo de Publicação	Estudos
Referências	E5, E12, E14, E15
Site de grupo de pesquisa	E9, E16, E18, E19, E21, E23

Como resposta à QP5, portanto, *tem-se que a maioria dos estudos primários (15 de 25) não relata/disponibiliza formas de acesso aos seus catálogos de PRS.*

4.6 Resposta da QP6

Da análise dos 25 estudos relevantes, apenas quatro deles apresentam uso prático na indústria, como descrito a seguir.

Em E12, consultores de segurança utilizam um catálogo de PRS em cenários de desenvolvimento de aplicações de computação em nuvem. Como resultado, reportam que o catálogo auxilia: (i) na identificação e classificação de requisitos de segurança; (ii) na identificação de ameaças a ativos; (iii) na diminuição do risco de requisitos omissos; (iv) na redução do esforço de especificação. Porém, ressaltam que a estrutura dos PRS deve ser aprendida previamente.

O estudo E14 é conduzido por um departamento da *Poznán University of Technology* (PUT), que executa projetos de desenvolvimento de software sob medida, em parceria com a indústria. Um catálogo de PRS foi utilizado em sete projetos, dentre eles, de sistemas de gerenciamento de notas, construção de currículos, análise e coleta de dados do corpo docente e gestão de tarefas organizacionais. Como resultado, mais de 80% dos requisitos mantiveram-se estáveis e 90% dos participantes ficaram satisfeitos com a qualidade da elicitação, embora tenha requerido treinamento prévio no uso do catálogo.

Nos estudos E19 e E20, que envolvem o mesmo grupo de pesquisa, consultores autônomos utilizaram catálogos de PRS para elicitação e gerenciamento de requisitos nos domínios de licitação e gerenciamento de conteúdo em mais de 40 projetos. Esses profissionais são recebem treinamento para uso de métodos inovadores em contextos industriais, tais como o método de reúso por meio de catálogos de PRS. Esses catálogos foram produzidos pelo grupo do *Centre De Recherche Public Henri Tudor* (ou TUDOR), e os consultores são federados a uma rede de negócios, chamada CASSIS.

4.7 Discussão

O primeiro estudo primário sobre catálogo de padrões de requisitos data de 2002 (E25), enquanto que 22 dos 25 estudos foram publicados de 2011 a 2020.

Entretanto, apenas sete estudos validam seus catálogos e apenas três os avaliam, embora sejam com profissionais da indústria.

Ainda que existam dois métodos predominantes para construção de catálogos, esse processo ainda tem suporte ferramental limitado. Uma diversidade de domínios de aplicação desses catálogos foi observada. O desenvolvimento de ferramentas para apoio à construção de catálogos é um dos itens da agenda de pesquisa proposta em [15].

Dois grupos de pesquisa destacam-se: um encabeçado pelo brasileiro Julio Cesar Sampaio do Prado Leite [8,28,29,31,30,32], com foco em NFR, e outro liderado pelo espanhol Xavier Franch [19,22,23,24,26], que tem feito parcerias com a indústria para a adoção de PRS em seus processos de desenvolvimento.

Percebe-se que as preocupações com a manutenção dos catálogos encontram-se nos estágios iniciais. Além disso, não existe relato de repositórios de catálogos de padrões de requisitos organizados por pesquisadores do tema, de modo a disponibilizar esse catálogos de forma centralizada e organizada, outro item da agenda de pesquisa discutida em [15].

Todas essas informações trazem evidências de que construção, validação, avaliação, manutenção e publicização de catálogos de requisitos representam um espaço de oportunidades de pesquisa. Acredita-se que mais pesquisas relacionadas a esses tópicos ajudarão a amadurecer o uso de padrões de requisitos na prática da indústria de software, pois neste MSL apenas quatro estudos relatam o uso prático de catálogos.

Ou seja, para que se estabeleçam parcerias com a indústria, é necessário criar um arcabouço em torno de catálogos de PRS, em que hajam: (i) *ferramentas de apoio a sua construção*; (ii) *iniciativas de validação*; (iii) *definição de métricas para avaliação*; e (iv) *meios padronizados de publicização.*

5 Ameaças à validade

Sabe-se da dificuldade de encontrar estudos relevantes e selecionar evidências para um tópico de pesquisa durante a execução de um MSL.

O conhecimento dos autores sobre padrões de requisitos [17,15] foi essencial no planejamento deste MSL, em especial, na definição da *string* de busca apoiada por teste piloto. Também facilitou as seleções inicial (leitura de metadados) e final (leitura na íntegra) dos estudos, tendo sido realizada por duas pessoas: uma estudante de pós-graduação e um pesquisador atuante no tema do MSL.

Sabe-se também que outras fontes de busca poderiam ter sido utilizadas, como *ScienceDirect* e *WebOfScience*. Porém, a estratégia de busca híbrida mostrou-se abrangente ao encontrar: 21 estudos em três motores de busca (*Scopus*, *Engineering Village* e *ACM DL*) e uma base bibliográfica (*IEEE Xplore*), um estudo na busca manual em veículos não indexados pelas fontes da busca automática (WER e JSERD) e três estudos resultantes do *forward snowballing*.

Quanto às atividades de extração e síntese de dados, ambas foram cuidadosamente revisadas pelo orientador da pesquisa com o apoio de um terceiro pesquisador, de modo assim a atender o objetivo deste MSL.

6 Considerações Finais

Os resultados deste estudo secundário corroboram aqueles de trabalhos relacionados, como a lacuna entre academia e indústria dada a baixa adesão de profissionais a padrões de requisitos como abordagem de reúso, o pequeno suporte ferramental existente para construir catálogos de PRS e o interesse crescente da academia na última década, porém ainda com poucos estudos de validação.

Contribui-se também com detalhes sobre métodos de construção de catálogos, abordagens utilizadas para sua validação e avaliação em diversos domínios de aplicação, técnicas adotadas de manutenção e meios de publicização desses catálogos. Tais informações trazem evidências de que esses aspectos associados a catálogos de PRS ainda são espaço fértil de oportunidades de pesquisa.

Quanto às lacunas identificadas neste trabalho, os autores implementaram uma *ferramenta* de apoio à construção de catálogos de PRS [16], a partir da qual desenvolveram um catálogo para Sistemas de Registro Eletrônico em Saúde (S-RES) [18]. Usando como referência o manual de certificação de S-RES elaborado pela Sociedade Brasileira de Informática em Saúde (SBIS), a *validação* desse catálogo será realizada por especialistas em S-RES, que analisarão a corretude, completude e consistência dos PRS modelados em relação aos requisitos presentes nesse manual. A *avaliação* do catálogo deverá demonstrar, por meio de um experimento com profissionais, o suporte oferecido na especificação de requisitos de S-RES com menor tempo e esforço. Por fim, após validado, os autores planejam disponibilizar o catálogo à SBIS para que o divulguem *publicamente* em seu site, assim como o fazem com o manual de certificação de S-RES.

Deste modo, acredita-se criar condições necessárias para que a academia demonstre à indústria de software os potenciais benefícios de catálogos de PRS.

7 Agradecimentos

O presente trabalho foi realizado com apoio da Coordenação de Aperfeiçoamento de Pessoal de Nível Superior - Brasil (CAPES) - bolsa de pesquisa CAPES DS.

Referências

1. Amorndettawin, M., Senivongse, T.: Non-functional requirement patterns for agile software development. In: Proceedings of the 2019 3rd International Conference on Software and E-Business. p. 66–74. ICSEB 2019, ACM (2019)
2. Barcelos, L.V., Penteado, R.: Especificação de requisitos no domínio de sistemas de informação com o uso de padrões. In: Proceedings of XIX Ibero-American Conference on Software Engineering, CIbSE 2016, Quito, Ecuador. pp. 338–351 (2016)
3. Barros-Justo, J.L., Benitti, F.B.V., Leal, A.C.: Software patterns and requirements engineering activities in real-world settings: A systematic mapping study. Comput. Stand. Interfaces **58**, 23–42 (2018)
4. Beckers, K., Côté, I., Goeke, L.: A catalog of security requirements patterns for the domain of cloud computing systems. In: Proceedings of the 29th Annual ACM Symposium on Applied Computing. p. 337–342. SAC '14, ACM (2014)

5. de Castro Leal, A.L., Braga, J.L., da Cruz, S.M.S.: Cataloguing provenance-awareness with patterns. In: Fifth IEEE International Workshop on Requirements Patterns, RePa 2015, Ottawa, ON, Canada. pp. 9–16. IEEE CS (2015)
6. da Cruz, S.M.S., de Castro Leal, A.L.: Enhancing provenance representation with knowledge based on NFR conceptual modeling: A softgoal catalog approach. In: Provenance and Annotation of Data and Processes - 5th International Provenance and Annotation Workshop, IPAW 2014, Cologne, Germany. pp. 235–238 (2014)
7. Da Silva, R., Benitti, F.: Evaluation of a systematic approach to requirements reuse. J Univers. Comput Sci **19**(2), 254–280 (2013)
8. Engiel, P., Cappelli, C., do Prado Leite, J.C.S.: Eliciting Concepts from the Brazilian Access Law Using a Combined Approach. In: Proceedings of the 29th Annual ACM Symposium on Applied Computing. pp. 1001–1006. SAC '14, ACM (2014)
9. Fockel, M., Holtmann, J., Koch, T., Schmelter, D.: Formal, model- and scenario-based requirement patterns. In: Proceedings of the 6th International Conference on Model-Driven Engineering and Software Development, MODELSWARD 2018, Funchal, Madeira, Portugal. pp. 311–318. SciTePress (2018)
10. Franch, X.: Software Requirement Patterns. In: Proceedings of the 2013 International Conference on Software Engineering. pp. 1499–1501. ICSE '13, IEEE (2013)
11. Irshad, M., Petersen, K., Poulding, S.: A systematic literature review of software requirements reuse approaches. Inf Softw Technol **93**, 223–245 (Jan 2018)
12. Kamalrudin, M., Mustafa, N., Sidek, S.: A template for writing security requirements. In: Requirements Engineering for Internet of Things - 4th Asia-Pacific Symposium, APRES 2017, Melaka, Malaysia. Communications in Computer and Information Science, vol. 809, pp. 73–86. Springer (2017)
13. Kopczynska, S., Nawrocki, J.R.: Using non-functional requirements templates for elicitation: A case study. In: 4th IEEE International Workshop on Requirements Patterns, RePa 2014, Karlskrona, Sweden. pp. 47–54. IEEE CS (2014)
14. Kopczynska, S., Nawrocki, J.R., Ochodek, M.: An empirical study on catalog of non-functional requirement templates: Usefulness and maintenance issues. Inf. Softw. Technol. **103**, 75–91 (2018)
15. Kudo, T.N., Bulcão-Neto, R.F., Vincenzi, A.M.R.: Requirement patterns: a tertiary study and a research agenda. IET SOFTW **14**(1), 18–26 (2020)
16. Kudo, T.N., Bulcão-Neto, R.F., Vincenzi, A.M.R.: Uma ferramenta para construção de catálogos de padrões de requisitos com comportamento. In: Anais do WER20 - Workshop em Engenharia de Requisitos, São José dos Campos, SP, Brasil. Editora PUC-Rio (2020)
17. Kudo, T.N., Bulcão-Neto, R.F., Macedo, A.A., Vincenzi, A.M.R.: A revisited systematic literature mapping on the support of requirement patterns for the software development life cycle. JSERD **7**, 9:1–9:11 (2019)
18. Martins, M.C., Kudo, T.N., Bulcão-Neto, R.F.: Padrões de requisitos para sistemas de registro eletrônico de saúde. In: Anais do WER21 - Workshop em Engenharia de Requisitos, Brasília, DF, Brasil. Editora PUC-Rio (2021)
19. Mendez-Bonilla, O., Franch, X., Quer, C.: Requirements patterns for COTS systems. In: Proceedings - 7th International Conference on Composition-Based Software Systems, ICCBSS 2008. pp. 232–235 (2008)
20. Naish, J., Zhao, L.: Towards a generalised framework for classifying and retrieving requirements patterns. In: The First International Workshop On Requirements Patterns, RePa 2011, Trento, Italy. pp. 42–51. IEEE CS (2011)
21. Palomares, C., Quer, C., Franch, X.: Requirements reuse and requirement patterns: a state of the practice survey. Empir. Softw. Eng. **22**(6), 2719–2762 (2017)

22. Palomares, C., Quer, C., Franch, X.: Pabre-man: Management of a requirement patterns catalogue. In: RE 2011, 19th IEEE International Requirements Engineering Conference, Trento, Italy. pp. 341–342. IEEE CS (2011)
23. Palomares, C., Quer, C., Franch, X., Guerlain, C., Renault, S.: A catalogue of non-technical requirement patterns. In: Second IEEE International Workshop on Requirements Patterns, RePa 2012, Chicago, IL, USA. pp. 1–6. IEEE CS (2012)
24. Palomares, C., Quer, C., Franch, X., Renault, S., Guerlain, C.: A catalogue of functional software requirement patterns for the domain of content management systems. In: Proceedings of the 28th Annual ACM Symposium on Applied Computing, SAC '13, Coimbra, Portugal. pp. 1260–1265 (2013)
25. Petersen, K., Vakkalanka, S., Kuzniarz, L.: Guidelines for conducting systematic mapping studies in software engineering: An update. Inf Softw Technol **64**, 1–18 (2015)
26. Renault, S., Mendez-Bonilla, O., Franch, X., Quer, C.: A pattern-based method for building requirements documents in call-for-tender processes. Int. J. Comput. Sci. Appl. **6**(5), 175–202 (2009)
27. Riaz, M., Elder, S., Williams, L.A.: Systematically developing prevention, detection, and response patterns for security requirements. In: 24th IEEE International Requirements Engineering Conference, RE 2016, Beijing, China. pp. 62–67. IEEE CS (2016)
28. Sarmiento, E., do Prado Leite, J.C.S., Almentero, E.: Using correctness, consistency, and completeness patterns for automated scenarios verification. In: Fifth IEEE International Workshop on Requirements Patterns, RePa 2015, Ottawa, ON, Canada. pp. 47–54. IEEE CS (2015)
29. Serrano, M., do Prado Leite, J.C.S.: Capturing transparency-related requirements patterns through argumentation. In: The First International Workshop On Requirements Patterns, RePa 2011, Trento, Italy. pp. 32–41. IEEE CS (2011)
30. de Souza Cunha, H., do Prado Leite, J.C.S.: Reusing non-functional patterns in i_* modeling. In: 4th IEEE International Workshop on Requirements Patterns, RePa 2014, Karlskrona, Sweden. pp. 25–32. IEEE CS (2014)
31. de Souza Cunha, H., do Prado Leite, J.C.S., Duboc, L., Werneck, V.: The challenges of representing transparency as patterns. In: Third IEEE International Workshop on Requirements Patterns, RePa 2013, Rio de Janeiro, Brazil. pp. 25–30. IEEE CS (2013)
32. Supakkul, S., Hill, T., Chung, L., Tun, T.T., do Prado Leite, J.C.S.: An NFR pattern approach to dealing with NFRs. In: 2010 18th IEEE International Requirements Engineering Conference. pp. 179–188 (2010)
33. Tockey, S.: Insanity, hiring, and the software industry. Comput J **48**(11), 96–101 (2015)
34. Wahono, R., Cheng, J.: Extensible requirements patterns of web application for efficient web application development. In: Proceedings - 1st International Symposium on Cyber Worlds, CW 2002. pp. 412 – 418. Tokyo, Japan (2002)
35. Withall, S.: Software Requirement Patterns. Best practices, Microsoft Press, Redmond, Washington (2007)
36. Wohlin, C.: Guidelines for snowballing in systematic literature studies and a replication in software engineering. In: 18th International Conference on Evaluation and Assessment in Software Engineering, EASE '14, London, England, United Kingdom, May 13-14, 2014. pp. 38:1–38:10 (2014)

Uma Abordagem Orientada a Meta para Fundamentar e Orientar as Decisões do Product Owner em Projetos Scrum

Renato Mesquita[1], Fábio Penha[1,2], and Márcia Lucena[1]

[1] Universidade Federal do Rio Grande do Norte
Dep. de Informática e Matemática Aplicada
[2] Instituto Federal do Rio Grande do Norte

Resumo O *Product Owner* tem um papel importante dentro do *Framework Scrum*, assumindo a responsabilidade de interpor as necessidades do cliente através do *Product Backlog*, um artefato que consiste de uma lista de requisitos a serem desenvolvidos. Por essa relação direta do *Product Owner* com o valor do produto final, pesquisas têm explorado os desafios que o *Product Owner* enfrenta para conduzir suas atividades. Essas pesquisas são voltadas principalmente para atividades relacionadas ao planejamento, onde as tomadas de decisões são cruciais para o resultado final do produto. Os requisitos, na maioria dos projetos Scrum, são registrados na forma de histórias de usuário, que apresentam algumas limitações, como a ausência de informações para auxiliar nas tomadas de decisões de forma estratégica. Na Engenharia de Requisitos Orientada a Meta, os requisitos são descritos a partir das metas organizacionais, alinhando as necessidades do cliente com a estratégia organizacional, ao prover uma estrutura hierárquica dessas informações coletadas. Nesse sentido, este trabalho tem como objetivo apresentar um método para estruturar as informações organizacionais, inerentes ao produto ou serviço desejado, em uma disposição que favoreça a consciência estratégica do *Product Owner*, fundamentando e orientando nas tomadas de decisões. Para tanto, propomos uma abordagem Orientada a Meta inspirada no iStar, para ser usada em projetos Scrum. Além disso, realizamos um estudo avaliativo sobre a execução desta abordagem na indústria, apresentando evidências de que as informações, adicionadas e estruturadas pelo método, contribuem para fundamentar e orientar as decisões do *Product Owner*.

Keywords: Scrum · Product Owner · Product Backlog · Planejamento · GORE.

1 Introdução

Diante de ambientes dinâmicos, complexos e exigentes por respostas rápidas, métodos e práticas ágeis tem ficado em evidência devido a serem mais adaptativos e flexíveis que os tradicionais [1,2,7]. Para esta proposta, dentre os métodos ágeis, observou-se o *Framework Scrum* devido a sua relevância na indústria, o qual conta com o envolvimento de três papéis: *Product Owner*, *Scrum Master* e *Development Team* [24,42,21,31].

Segundo Yin et al. (2011), o relacionamento e a colaboração entre esses papéis são cruciais para o sucesso dos projetos *Scrum* [49]. A responsabilidade do *Product Owner* é representar o negócio e maximizar o valor do produto, gerenciando as necessidades do cliente através do *Product Backlog* [4,42]. Por esse motivo, o papel *Product Owner* concentra responsabilidades e informações cruciais para o processo de desenvolvimento, fazendo a comunicação entre as necessidades do cliente e o *Development Team*. Essas necessidades são planejadas e priorizadas no *Product Backlog* a cada *Sprint* [4,42], e geralmente descritas na forma de histórias de usuário, que representam os anseios do cliente [21,10,33,5].

A intensa responsabilidade atribuída ao *Product Owner*, observada pela incumbência de definir, planejar, especificar e priorizar requisitos a serem desenvolvidos, é um indicativo de que o sucesso das suas ações reflete no produto ou serviço, contribuindo decisivamente para a satisfação das metas do cliente. Metas que estão associadas aos requisitos incluídos no *Product Backlog* e que, ao serem desenvolvidos, permitirão alcançá-las. Por esse entendimento, diversos estudos têm explorado as atividades relacionadas ao *Framework Scrum* [28,20,16,45,25], como, por exemplo, o planejamento dos itens do *Product Backlog* e a sua priorização, compreendidas como atividades primordiais para o *Product Owner* [44,29,5,3,6].

Segundo Sverrisdottira et al. (2014), a tomada de decisão é considerada a tarefa mais árdua para o *Product Owner*. Diante de diversos interesses organizacionais, o *Product Owner* deve decidir qual item deverá ser incluído no *Product Backlog* e quando será priorizado [44]. Na análise de Drury, Conboy e Power (2012), o *Product Owner* enfrenta dificuldades para tomar essas decisões devido a ausência de informações estruturadas, produzindo um ambiente inseguro, podendo afetar o planejamento e a priorização da *Sprint* [44,14].

Soares et al. (2015) ratifica essa problemática ao relacioná-la com algumas dificuldades inerentes ao uso de histórias de usuário, como a falta de identificação de requisitos não funcionais; a falta de informações que proporcionem uma melhor consciência estratégica para realizar priorizações; e a ausência da representação de dependência entre os requisitos [43]. Diante dessas limitações, observou-se que a forma com que as necessidades do cliente são trabalhadas, quanto a sua concepção e análise, podem estar reprimindo uma tomada de decisão mais confiável.

A Engenharia de Requisitos Orientada a Meta (GORE) propõe que os requisitos sejam descritos a partir das metas organizacionais, uma vez que busca o alinhamento entre a estratégia organizacional e o produto ou serviço desejado. Neste contexto, os *stakeholders* possuem a consciência sobre o quê e porquê uma determinada necessidade deve compor o *Product Backlog*, ou quando deve ser priorizada [26].

O conceito de meta mostra ser importante para atividades inerentes à engenharia de requisitos [23,46], cujo a GORE é capaz de: (a) propiciar uma melhor investigação das opções de projeto, em termos análise, e detecção e resolução de conflitos [46,19,47,38]; (b) melhorar a compreensão sobre a completude dos requisitos [50]; e (c) prover rastreabilidade dos requisitos [37]. Através desses benefícios, a meta pode ser capaz de oferecer uma melhor consciência estratégica para que o *Product Owner* tomar decisões.

O objetivo deste artigo é proporcionar um ambiente de requisitos favorável à tomada de decisão do *Product Owner*. Inspirado no *Framework iStar*, uma abordagem de *Product Backlog* foi proposta com intuito de evidenciar as metas organizacionais, estruturando as informações para fundamentar e orientar as decisões. Para apresentação desta proposta, o artigo foi estruturado da seguinte forma: a seção 2 apresenta a metodologia adotada no trabalho; a seção 3 apresenta o modelo proposto na abordagem; a seção 4 apresenta os resultados da avaliação do trabalho, com sua aplicação em um ambiente real; e finalmente, a seção 5 apresenta as considerações finais e trabalhos futuros.

2 Metodologia

Para elaboração desta proposta, duas pesquisas bibliográficas foram realizadas com objetivos distintos; a primeira, identificar os desafios do *Product Owner*, enquanto a segunda, compreender como os requisitos são concebidos e inseridos no processo *Scrum*. Dentre os desafios identificados com relação as responsabilidades do *Product Owner*, a tomada de decisão é vista como destaque [4,5,3,6,45,25,21,35]. Norteada pelo o achado da primeira, observou-se que o *Product Backlog* conta com requisitos geralmente descritos em histórias de usuário, o qual é conhecido pela ausência de informações estruturadas, contribuindo para um ambiente inseguro para tomar decisões [22,10,12,43].

Compreendida a importância das metas e a sua explicitação dentro do processo *Scrum* [34,41,35,50,40], em relação ao aprimoramento da estrutura das informações para, como consequência, fundamentar e orientar as tomadas de decisão, foi proposto um método para a obtenção de um *Product Backlog* capaz de evidenciar as metas dentro do processo de desenvolvimento. O artefato gerado pelo método proposto, é baseado em conceitos da GORE e foi chamado de *Goal-Oriented Product Backlog*, devido a capacidade de relacionamento de histórias de usuário com metas.

A proposta foi aplicada na indústria com intuito de construir cenários reais de desenvolvimento, obtendo artefatos para serem utilizados em uma avaliação seguinte. Esses artefatos serviram para desenvolver e conduzir o questionário realizado com profissionais da indústria, que pode ser acessado através do endereço eletrônico https://github.com/renatomsoares/gpb/blob/main/questionario.pdf. O objetivo da avaliação foi encontrar um conjunto de evidências para reforçar o entendimento de que o *Goal-Oriented Product Backlog* proporciona informações mais estruturadas e capazes de fundamentar e orientar as tomadas de decisões do *Product Owner*.

3 Proposta

Na Figura 1 é possível observar uma representação do processo *Scrum* com a inclusão do *Goal-Oriented Product Backlog*, o *Product Backlog* proposto com conceitos da GORE, artefato de entrada para a *Sprint Planning*. O *Sprint Backlog*, obtido a partir da *Sprint Planning*, constitui-se de itens que foram selecionados mediante decisões tomadas pelo *Product Owner* durante o planejamento, para serem desenvolvidos. Dessa maneira, sabendo que o planejamento é fundamentado por um artefato de entrada e conduzido por decisões tomadas pelo *Product Owner*, é razoável considerar que a completude de informações do *Goal-Oriented Product Backlog* poderá proporcionar uma melhor construção do *Sprint Backlog*, assegurando que o novo incremento implementado e entregue ao final de cada *Sprint* atenda da melhor maneira possível os anseios do cliente.

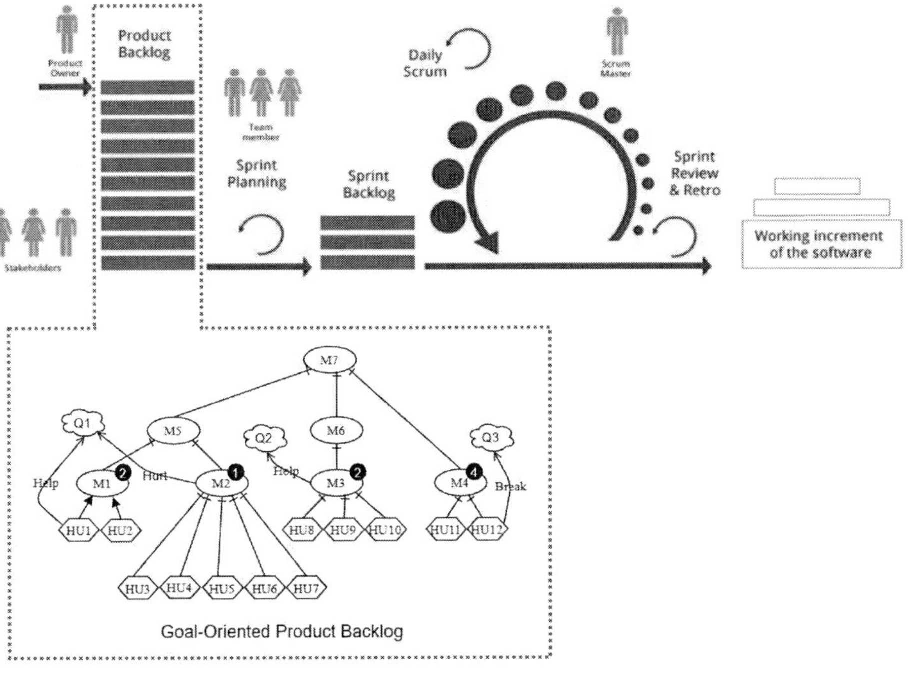

Figura 1. Representação do processo Scrum, adaptado com o *Goal-Oriented Product Backlog*. Fonte: Figura adaptada de Sverrisdottira et al. (2014) [44].

3.1 Goal-Oriented Product Backlog

Para desenvolver o *Goal-Oriented Product Backlog*, um subconjunto de elementos do *Framework iStar* foi utilizado com intuito de assimilar uma notação gráfica para o artefato proposto. A escolha do *iStar* é justificada por ser um *Framework* capaz de proporcionar uma apresentação das informações organizacionais, que contempla elementos e conceitos da GORE, utilizados nesta proposta, e pela capacidade de ajudar as partes interessadas na compreensão do problema como um todo. Embora alguns autores tenham criticado a sua notação gráfica [32], ou o gerenciamento dos modelos quando eles crescem [15], o uso do *iStar* tem se mostrado uma estrutura capaz de ajudar as partes interessadas, em termos de conduzi-las a uma melhor compreensão do contexto organizacional [8]. O *Framework* foi utilizado em sua versão 2.0, concebida com o intuito de simplificar a linguagem de modelagem. Nesse sentido, a comunidade *iStar* identificou um conjunto de elementos e conceitos principais amplamente aceitos a linguagem [13]. Além disso, a utilização de apenas um subconjunto de elementos do *Framework iStar*, nesta proposta, simplifica esta proposta.

O subconjunto de elementos utilizado é composto por: elementos intencionais de meta, qualidade e tarefa; e ligações de intenção de refinamento e de contribuição. A escolha desse subconjunto está fundamentada na finalidade do artefato proposto, de se beneficiar da orientação a metas, visando obter uma estrutura hierárquica das informações. Dessa maneira, os elementos contemplados nesse subconjunto são entendidos como suficientes para prover uma consciência organizacional desejada, hoje composta por itens de desenvolvimento, na maioria das vezes representados através de histórias de usuário.

Embora o iStar 2.0 tenha a definição de um quarto elemento intencional, o recurso, este não foi utilizado na proposta por não haver ligação direta de intencionalidade com as metas. Além disso, a ligação de qualificação, outro elemento presente no iStar 2.0 e que visa qualificar um elemento intencional do tipo tarefa, meta ou recurso, também não foi utilizada, partindo do entendimento de que a ligação de contribuição já é capaz de proporcionar informações sobre a influência de uma meta ou tarefa diante de uma qualidade desejada.

Além do subconjunto de elementos do *Framework iStar*, supracitado, também foi utilizada uma notação gráfica com o intuito de identificar a prioridade de uma meta no *Goal-Oriented Product Backlog*. Esta notação gráfica seguiu o mesmo padrão estabelecido por Liaskos et al. (2011), na priorização de tarefas [27], na qual a prioridade do elemento é determinada a partir de um rótulo numérico interno a um círculo. O elemento mais prioritário é aquele que contém o rótulo numérico mais baixo. Além disso, segundo o autor, o uso da técnica de definir a prioridade de nós folha, ou seja, de mais baixo nível, ao mesmo tempo, tem-se a determinação de um plano de satisfação do objetivo raiz.

3.2 Abordagem *Bottom-Up*

De modo a conduzir a criação do *Goal-Oriented Product Backlog*, foi elaborado o método *bottom-up*, com cinco passos, conforme podem ser observados na Figura 2. Essa abordagem parte de elementos de mais baixo nível, ou seja, de itens que constituem o *Product Backlog* da maneira em que ele foi concebido, admitindo que esses são descritos em histórias de usuário, por representar a natureza de requisito mais utilizada em projetos *Scrum*. Dessa maneira, foi considerado o formato de história de usuário proposto por Cohn (2005): como [papel] eu quero [fazer algo] para alcançar [uma meta] [11]. A escolha dessa formatação é justificada pelo seu amplo uso no ambiente ágil [9].

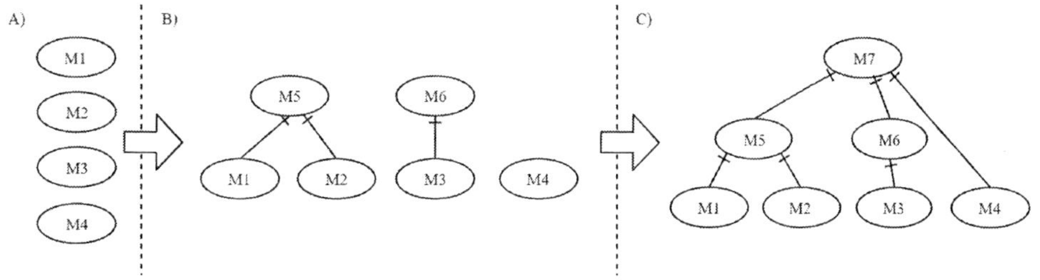

Figura 2. Abordagem *bottom-up* para a criação do *Goal-Oriented Product Backlog.* Fonte: Próprio autor.

Para iniciar o processo de criação do *Goal-Oriented Product Backlog*, o cenário imaginado possui um *Product Backlog* constituído por 12 histórias de usuário [HU1, HU2, ..., HU12], que deverão ser mapeadas em elementos do iStar, como **primeiro passo** deste método. Conforme pode ser observado na Figura 3, as histórias de usuário HU1 e HU2, foram mapeadas em elementos intencionais do tipo tarefa. Esse mapeamento é justificado pelo conceito do elemento tarefa onde, segundo Dalpiaz, Franch e Horkoff (2016), representa algo que deve ser realizado, geralmente com o propósito de se alcançar uma meta [13]. Da mesma forma, uma história de usuário deve ser realizada, no sentido de que a funcionalidade deve ser desenvolvida, para que uma meta organizacional seja alcançada.

Em seguida, partindo do pressuposto, segundo o formato da história de usuário proposto por Cohn (2005), de que cada história possui a definição de uma meta interna que deve ser alcançada [11], o **segundo passo** do mapeamento é elevar o nível dessa meta, fazendo com que a mesma passe a relacionar-se com a história de usuário através de ligações de refinamento.

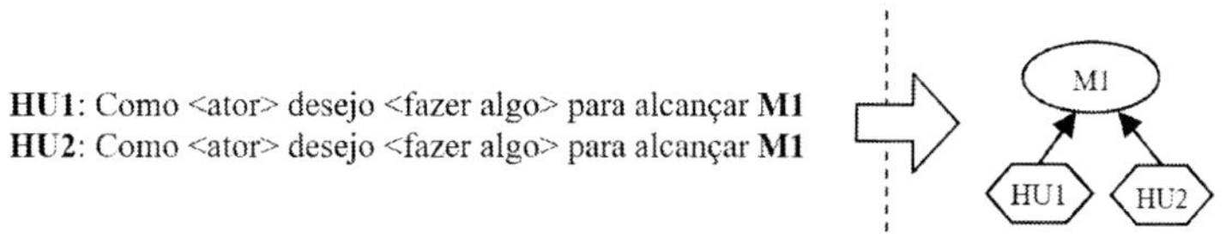

Figura 3. Representação da extração de uma mesma meta, presente em duas histórias de usuário, para elementos do *Goal-Oriented Product Backlog.* Fonte: Próprio autor.

Já na Figura 4, é possível visualizar a conclusão do segundo passo, com o mapeamento de todas as histórias de usuário. De forma adversa à HU1 e HU2, ligadas à meta M1 a partir de uma relação de refinamento do tipo OR, e que representam alternativas para o alcance de M1, as histórias HU8, HU9 e HU10 são consideradas obrigatórias para o alcance de M3, pois possuem refinamento do tipo AND.

Disposto do mapeamento das histórias de usuário com as metas nas quais estão relacionadas, o **terceiro passo** para a construção do artefato proposto consiste em elevar o nível de abstração dessas metas. Existem técnicas sofisticadas

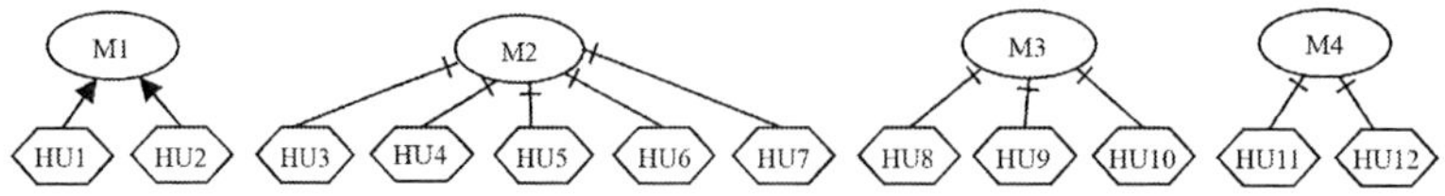

Figura 4. Resultado da extração de todas as metas das histórias de usuário. Fonte: Próprio autor.

para se chegar nessa abstração, como métodos que levam em conta heurísticas de mapeamento envolvendo cenários [39] ou, até mesmo, a sua formalização a partir de aprendizagem indutiva [48]. Porém, segundo Lamsweerde (2001), uma técnica simples e eficaz de se abstrair uma meta, apesar de contar com a expertise em termos de negócio, é fazendo perguntas "Por quê?", sobre as metas já existentes [46]. Para essa proposta, será utilizada o método de abstração mencionado por Lamsweerde (2001), pois, segundo o autor, os métodos mais complexos e formais são efetivos quando as especificações das metas são formalizadas.

Conforme pode ser observado na Figura 5, que está dividia em três seções: (A) representa as metas que foram geradas no passo anterior; (B) apresenta o resultado da abstração que foi realizada, onde as metas M1 e M2 foram abstraídas em M5, e M3 abstraída em M6; (C) apresenta outro nível de abstração, onde todas as metas raízes foram abstraídas em M7. Ao utilizar o método de abstração definido por Lamsweerde (2001) e fazer perguntas "Por quê?"para M1 e M2, se chegou na meta M5. Da mesma forma, ao fazer a mesma pergunta para M3, foi obtida a sua abstração M6. Em relação à meta M4 não foi encontrada uma abstração para ela, o que é possível de acontecer durante o processo de abstração. Por conseguinte, ainda em relação a etapa da seção B, quando for possível considerar que todas as metas raízes, ou de mais alto nível de cada subárvore (M5, M6 e M4), não podem mais ser abstraídas, é identificada uma meta raiz que representa a abstração de todas elas, nesse caso, M7. A intenção do processo de abstração é criar uma hierarquia capaz de relacionar as histórias de usuário a uma meta de mais alto nível.

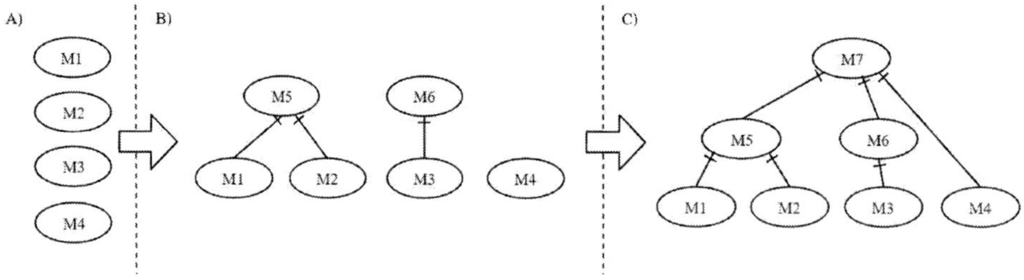

Figura 5. Representação da abstração das metas. Fonte: Próprio autor.

O **quarto passo** é a junção do que foi realizado anteriormente no segundo e terceiro passo. Sendo assim, conforme pode ser observado na Figura 6, os elementos de mais baixo nível, representados pelas histórias de usuário, podem ser mapeados com o elemento de mais alto nível especificado, representado pela meta M7.

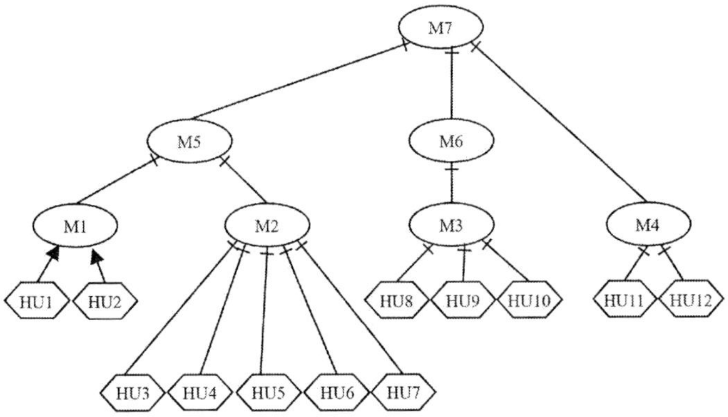

Figura 6. Representação da junção do que foi obtido no segundo e terceiro passo. Fonte: Próprio autor.

Por fim, já disposto de uma visão estratégica geral das histórias de usuário e seus relacionamentos com as metas organizacionais, o **quinto passo** consiste na definição das qualidades e priorização das metas, conforme pode ser observado na Figura 7. Segundo Heikkila et al. (2015), nas metodologias ágeis os requisitos não funcionais são frequentemente ignorados e dependem do conhecimento tácito dos *stakeholders* [17]. Dessa maneira, a qualidade, que pode ser considerada um requisito não funcional, e a prioridade das metas, embora sejam informações não especificadas nas histórias de usuário, é possível de que *Product Owner* tenha esse conhecimento através do seu contato direto com o cliente.

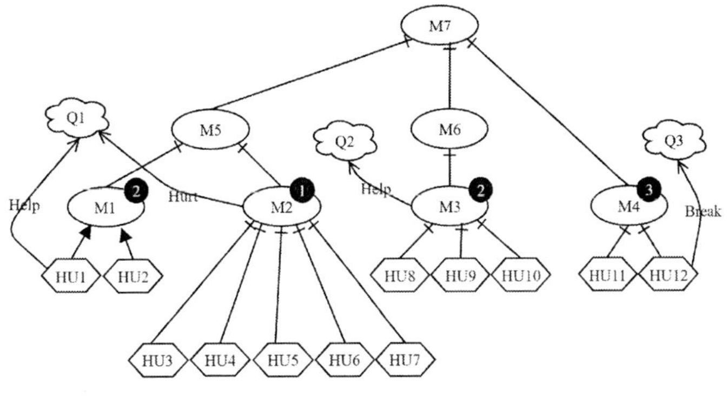

Figura 7. Representação da priorização e definição da qualidades relacionadas. Fonte: Próprio autor.

4 Avaliação da Proposta

Com o objetivo de aplicar o *Goal-Oriented Product Backlog* num cenário real de desenvolvimento de software, a proposta foi executada na indústria, num contexto em que o processo *Scrum* é adotado. A execução foi realizada no projeto Sistema de Inscrições em Dívida Ativa (SIDA) de uma instituição pública brasileira. A escolha do local de aplicação é justificada por, além da disponibilidade dos profissionais envolvidos para com o autor deste trabalho, a maturidade com a qual as práticas do método *Scrum* tem sido adotadas na instituição.

Preliminarmente, através de reuniões realizadas, foram elicitadas as necessidades do cliente. Essas reuniões contaram com a participação do *Product Owner* e do *Scrum Master* tendo, o primeiro, um amplo domínio sobre orientação a metas e, mais especificamente, conhecimento da proposta. Diante de uma percepção inicial, foi possível entender os objetivos do cliente, e a sua necessidade principal de sistematizar procedimentos, automatizando as etapas de inscrição dos débitos na dívida ativa, até então submetidos manualmente, via ofício. Com base no que havia sido levantado, em termos de necessidades do cliente, foi possível especificar as histórias de usuário e construir o *Goal-Oriented Product Backlog*, a partir da abordagem *bottom-up*. O artefato, em sua versão inicial e que foi posteriormente modificado no decorrer das *Sprints*, está apresentado na Figura 8. O artefato apresentado, apresenta o seu estado ao final do planejamento da primeira sprint. A cor azul foi utilizada na execução do projeto para identificar as histórias de usuário priorizadas no *Sprint Backlog*.

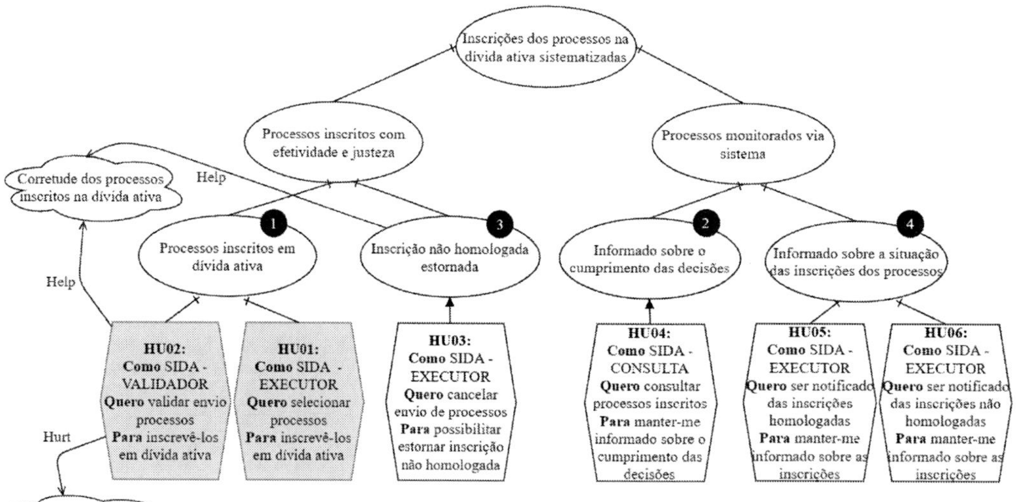

Figura 8. *Goal-Oriented Product Backlog* apresentando, em azul, o planejamento realizado para a primeira. Fonte: Próprio autor.

A partir da aplicação da proposta no projeto SIDA, foi possível obter indícios, em caso prático, que o *Goal-Oriented Product Backlog* pode contribuir de forma a orientar e fundamentar as tomadas de decisões do *Product Owner*. Dessa maneira, com o objetivo de encontrar um conjunto de evidências para reforçar o entendimento de que o *Goal-Oriented Product Backlog* é capaz de fundamentar e orientar as tomadas de decisões do *Product Owner*, foi realizado um estudo avaliativo baseado em artefatos produzidos no projeto SIDA. A Figura 9 apresenta a metodologia do processo avaliativo, que se iniciou com a aplicação da proposta, seguida do planejamento da avaliação, onde foi elaborado um questionário. O questionário, fundamentado nos artefatos gerados durante a aplicação da proposta, contou com a participação de 16 profissionais respondentes. Dentre esses, 100% já atuaram profissionalmente na área de desenvolvimento de software, 50% já executaram profissionalmente o papel de Product Owner e 37,5% conhece alguma técnica GORE. Por conseguinte, as respostas foram compiladas, enfatizando as questões subjetivas e buscando julgamentos representassem convicções voltadas para vivências práticas.

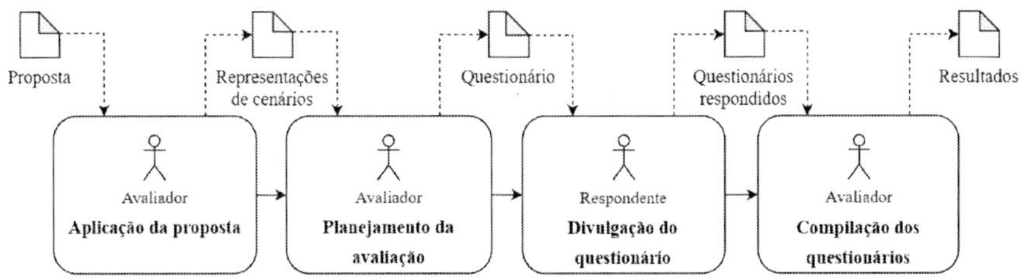

Figura 9. Metodologia de avaliação da proposta. Fonte: Próprio autor.

Para nortear o estudo avaliativo, foram elaboradas as seguintes questões de pesquisa: **(QP1)** O artefato *Goal-Oriented Product Backlog*, quando comparado com o *Product Backlog*, fornece uma melhor fundamentação e orientação para tomada de decisão do *Product Owner*?; **(QP2)** O *Goal-Oriented Product Backlog* pode ser útil ao *Product Owner* em algum momento do processo Scrum?; e **(QP3)** O artefato proposto proporciona algum benefício ao *Product Owner* quanto as suas tomadas de decisão?

Em relação a questão **QP1**, buscou-se compreender se o *Goal-Oriented Product Backlog* proporciona informações mais estruturadas em relação ao *Product Backlog*. De acordo com os resultados obtidos, 93,3% dos respondentes consideram que o artefato proporciona informações mais estruturadas ao apresentar as relações entre as histórias de usuário, e 80%, ao apresentar os requisitos não funcionais. Além disso, algumas afirmativas corroboram com o mesmo aspecto avaliado nesta questão, como o respondente que descreveu que o artefato "é permite observar os impactos das histórias de usuário através das relações existentes entre cada um dos elementos", além do que afirmou que "por meio das metas, é possível ter uma visão geral dos requisitos e as relações nele existentes".

Mesmo que sugerida a sua utilização nas reuniões de planejamento e revisão da *Sprint*, o uso do artefato não é restrito a essas fases do processo. Com base nisso, o questionamento da **QP2** objetivou, além de buscar uma compreensão sobre a importância do uso do artefato proposto durante essas reuniões, conhecer outras etapas do *Scrum* em que o *Product Owner* também possa ser beneficiado com a utilização do *Goal-Oriented Product Backlog*. Ao analisar os resultados, embora tenha sido possível encontrar evidências de que o artefato possa ser útil em todas fases do processo, os respondentes enfatizaram a sua utilização na reunião de planejamento. Um dos respondentes, afirmou que "o maior ganho pode ser obtido nas atividades ligadas ao planejamento, por permitir uma visão mais ampla do projeto", outro sustentou que o artefato "contribui no entendimento do projeto e na priorização das histórias de usuário, facilitando na construção do *Sprint Backlog*".

A literatura explicita diversos benefícios relacionando orientação a metas com um maior nível de informação. Nesse sentido, a partir da questão **QP3**, buscou-se compreender se as tomadas de decisões realizadas pelo *Product Owner* podem ser fundamentadas e orientadas pelo uso do *Goal-Oriented Product Backlog*. Diante disso, 85,7% dos respondentes consideram que artefato ajuda nas tomadas de decisões ao proporcionar um maior nível de clareza sobre o projeto, e 73,4%, ao identificar a necessidade por novos requisitos. Além disso, algumas afirmações evidenciam a importância do artefato em relação às tomadas de decisão, como a de que o mesmo "propicia uma maior clareza ao *Product Owner* por tornar as informações mais explícitas"e, que "por ser mais estruturado, diminui o nível de abstração de uma história de usuário, contribuindo para um melhor entendimento e organização". Além disso, um outro respondente considera que o *Goal-Oriented Product Backlog* ajuda na priorização dos requisitos a serem incluídos no *Sprint Backlog*, ao considerar que "o maior benefício é ter uma visão geral do projeto de forma prioritária, sendo fácil de identificar os requisitos de maior valor para o negócio".

5 Considerações Finais

Este trabalho levou em consideração as tarefas do *Product Owner* relacionadas ao planejamento das *Sprints*. Nesse cenário, a literatura mostrou evidências de que o *Product Owner* não possui informações estruturadas capazes de fundamentar e orientar as suas escolhas, dificultando suas tomadas de decisão durante o projeto. Diante disso, foi proposta uma abordagem Orientada a Meta para o *Product Backlog*, que estrutura as informações organizacionais com intenção de fundamentar e orientar as tomadas de decisões realizadas pelo *Product Owner*.

Para isso, uma abordagem para construção do *Product Backlog*, que consiste em conduzir a abstração das histórias de usuário para o nível de metas, foi apresentada. Em relação às principais contribuições deste trabalho, destaca-se o uso da orientação a meta para apresentar as informações estruturadas. A partir do estudo avaliativo realizado, foram encontradas evidências de que o *Goal-Oriented Product Backlog*, de acordo com as convicções dos respondentes, proporciona informações mais estruturadas ao *Product Owner* e torna o ambiente mais seguro para tomar decisões. Além disso, foi possível obter convicções de que os desenvolvedores e o *Scrum Master* também podem ser beneficiados com o uso da proposta, nas reuniões diárias e de retrospectiva, respectivamente.

Após as conclusões obtidas, foi possível identificar trabalhos futuros julgados como importantes e capazes de evoluir a pesquisa em diversas frentes, são eles: (i) exploração de uma abordagem *top-down* para a construção do *Goal-Oriented Product Backlog*, partindo de elementos de mais alto nível; (ii) expansão do estudo avaliativo para obtenção de convicções que representem uma amostra quantitativamente mais significativa; (iii) validar a proposta em outra metodologia ágil; e (iv) elaboração de um tutorial para a condução do processo *Scrum* com o uso do *Goal-Oriented Product Backlog*.

Adicionalmente, também é visto como importante o desenvolvimento de um aporte ferramental, capaz de instituir, de maneira prática, a proposta em projetos *Scrum*. Embora existam diversas ferramentas para a criação de modelos iStar, nenhuma é especializada para a seleção de elementos que constituem o *Goal-Oriented Product Backlog* [30,18,36]. Além disso, essas ferramentas foram elaboradas de forma independente, não possibilitando a integração com os eventos que contemplam o processo de desenvolvimento *Scrum*.

Referências

1. Aitken, A., Ilango, V.: A comparative analysis of traditional software engineering and agile software development. In: 2013 46th Hawaii International Conference on System Sciences. pp. 4751–4760. IEEE (2013)
2. Ambler, S.: Effective practices for extreme programming and the unified process. Ist. Ed. John Wiley & Sons, Inc (2002)
3. Bass, J., Beecham, S., Razzak, M.A., Canna, C.N., Noll, J.: Poster: An empirical study of the product owner role in scrum. In: 2018 IEEE/ACM 40th International Conference on Software Engineering: Companion (ICSE-Companion). pp. 123–124. IEEE (2018)
4. Bass, J.M.: Agile method tailoring in distributed enterprises: Product owner teams. In: 2013 IEEE 8th International Conference on Global Software Engineering. pp. 154–163. IEEE (2013)
5. Bass, J.M.: How product owner teams scale agile methods to large distributed enterprises. Empirical Software Engineering **20**(6), 1525–1557 (2015)
6. Bass, J.M., Beecham, S., Noll, J., Razzak, M.A.: All hands to the pumps: The product owner role in small companies lero technical report: 2017_1 (2016)
7. Bassi, D.: Experiências com desenvolvimento ágil. Master's thesis, Instituto de Matemática e Estatística da Universidade de São Paulo, São Paulo - Brasil (2008)
8. Carvallo, J.P., Franch, X.: An empirical study on the use of i* by non-technical stakeholders: the case of strategic dependency diagrams. Requirements Engineering **24**(1), 27–53 (2019)
9. Cockburn, A.: Agile software development: the cooperative game. Pearson Education (2006)
10. Cohn, M.: User stories applied: For agile software development. Addison-Wesley Professional (2004)
11. Cohn, M.: Agile estimating and planning. Pearson Education (2005)
12. Da Silva, T.S., Martin, A., Maurer, F., Silveira, M.: User-centered design and agile methods: a systematic review. In: 2011 Agile Conference. pp. 77–86. IEEE (2011)

13. Dalpiaz, F., Franch, X., Horkoff, J.: istar 2.0 language guide. arXiv preprint arXiv:1605.07767 (2016)
14. Drury, M., Conboy, K., Power, K.: Obstacles to decision making in agile software development teams. Journal of Systems and Software **85**(6), 1239–1254 (2012)
15. Estrada, H., Rebollar, A.M., Pastor, O., Mylopoulos, J.: An empirical evaluation of the i* framework in a model-based software generation environment. In: International Conference on Advanced Information Systems Engineering. pp. 513–527. Springer (2006)
16. Fitriani, W.R., Rahayu, P., Sensuse, D.I.: Challenges in agile software development: A systematic literature review. In: 2016 International Conference on Advanced Computer Science and Information Systems (ICACSIS). pp. 155–164. IEEE (2016)
17. Heikkilä, V.T., Damian, D., Lassenius, C., Paasivaara, M.: A mapping study on requirements engineering in agile software development. In: 2015 41st Euromicro conference on software engineering and advanced applications. pp. 199–207. IEEE (2015)
18. Horkoff, J., Yu, Y., Eric, S.: Openome: An open-source goal and agent-oriented model drawing and analysis tool. iStar **766**, 154–156 (2011)
19. Hui, B., Liaskos, S., Mylopoulos, J.: Requirements analysis for customizable software: A goals-skills-preferences framework. In: Proceedings. 11th IEEE International Requirements Engineering Conference, 2003. pp. 117–126. IEEE (2003)
20. Inayat, I., Salim, S.S., Marczak, S., Daneva, M., Shamshirband, S.: A systematic literature review on agile requirements engineering practices and challenges. Computers in human behavior **51**, 915–929 (2015)
21. James, M., Walter, L.: Scrum reference card. CollabNet Inc (2010)
22. Jaqueira, A., Lucena, M., Alencar, F.M., Castro, J., Aranha, E.: Using i* models to enrich user stories. iStar **13**, 55–60 (2013)
23. Kaindl, H.: A design process based on a model combining scenarios with goals and functions. IEEE Transactions on Systems, Man, and Cybernetics-Part A: Systems and Humans **30**(5), 537–551 (2000)
24. Kaur, K., Jajoo, A., et al.: Applying agile methodologies in industry projects: Benefits and challenges. In: 2015 International Conference on Computing Communication Control and Automation. pp. 832–836. IEEE (2015)
25. Larsson, M.: Usable Interventions for a Product Owner. B.S. thesis, University of Gothenburg (2013)
26. Lee, R.C.: The success factors of running scrum: A qualitative perspective. Journal of Software Engineering and Applications (2012)
27. Liaskos, S., McIlraith, S.A., Sohrabi, S., Mylopoulos, J.: Representing and reasoning about preferences in requirements engineering. Requirements Engineering **16**(3), 227 (2011)
28. López-Martínez, J., Juárez-Ramírez, R., Huertas, C., Jiménez, S., Guerra-García, C.: Problems in the adoption of agile-scrum methodologies: A systematic literature review. In: 2016 4th international conference in software engineering research and innovation (conisoft). pp. 141–148. IEEE (2016)
29. Lwakatare, L.E., Kilamo, T., Karvonen, T., Sauvola, T., Heikkilä, V., Itkonen, J., Kuvaja, P., Mikkonen, T., Oivo, M., Lassenius, C.: Devops in practice: A multiple case study of five companies. Information and Software Technology (2019)
30. Malta, Á., Soares, M., Santos, E., Paes, J., Alencar, F.M., Castro, J.: istartool: Modeling requirements using the i* framework. In: IStar. pp. 163–165 (2011)
31. Maximini, D., Maximini, Rauscher: Scrum Culture. Springer (2018)

32. Moody, D.L., Heymans, P., Matulevicius, R.: Improving the effectiveness of visual representations in requirements engineering: An evaluation of i* visual syntax. In: 2009 17th IEEE International Requirements Engineering Conference. pp. 171–180. IEEE (2009)
33. Moore, R., Reff, K., Graham, J., Hackerson, B.: Scrum at a fortune 500 manufacturing company. In: Agile 2007 (AGILE 2007). pp. 175–180. IEEE (2007)
34. Nuseibeh, B., Easterbrook, S.: Requirements engineering: A roadmap. In: Proceedings of the Conference on The Future of Software Engineering. pp. 35–46. ICSE '00, ACM, New York, NY, USA (2000). https://doi.org/10.1145/336512.336523, http://doi.acm.org/10.1145/336512.336523
35. Pichler, R.: Agile product management with scrum: Creating products that customers love. Pearson Education India (2010)
36. Pimentel, J., Castro, J.: pistar tool–a pluggable online tool for goal modeling. In: 2018 IEEE 26th International Requirements Engineering Conference (RE). pp. 498–499. IEEE (2018)
37. Pohl, K.: Process-centered requirements engineering. John Wiley & Sons, Inc. (1996)
38. Robinson, W.N., Volkov, S.: Conflict-oriented requirements restructuring. Departament of Computer Information (1996)
39. Rolland, C., Souveyet, C., Achour, C.B.: Guiding goal modeling using scenarios. IEEE transactions on software engineering **24**(12), 1055–1071 (1998)
40. Schnabel, I., Pizka, M.: Goal-driven software development. In: 2006 30th Annual IEEE/NASA Software Engineering Workshop. pp. 59–65. IEEE (2006)
41. Schwaber, K.: Agile project management with Scrum. Microsoft press (2004)
42. Schwaber, K., Sutherland, J.: The scrum guide-the definitive guide to scrum: The rules of the game. SCRUM. org, Jul-2013 (2013)
43. Soares, H.F., Alves, N.S., Mendes, T.S., Mendonça, M., Spínola, R.O.: Investigating the link between user stories and documentation debt on software projects. In: 2015 12th International Conference on Information Technology-New Generations. pp. 385–390. IEEE (2015)
44. Sverrisdottir, H.S., Ingason, H.T., Jonasson, H.I.: The role of the product owner in scrum-comparison between theory and practices. Procedia-Social and Behavioral Sciences **119**, 257–267 (2014)
45. Unger-Windeler, C., Klünder, J., Schneider, K.: A mapping study on product owners in industry: identifying future research directions. In: 2019 IEEE/ACM International Conference on Software and System Processes (ICSSP). pp. 135–144. IEEE (2019)
46. Van Lamsweerde, A.: Goal-oriented requirements engineering: A guided tour. In: Requirements Engineering, 2001. Proceedings. Fifth IEEE International Symposium on. pp. 249–262. IEEE (2001), http://ieeexplore.ieee.org/abstract/document/948567/
47. Van Lamsweerde, A., Letier, E.: Handling obstacles in goal-oriented requirements engineering. IEEE Transactions on software engineering **26**(10), 978–1005 (2000)
48. Van Lamsweerde, A., Willemet, L.: Inferring declarative requirements specifications from operational scenarios. IEEE Transactions on Software Engineering **24**(12), 1089–1114 (1998)
49. Yin, A., Figueiredo, S., da Silva, M.M.: Scrum maturity model. Proceedings of the ICSEA pp. 20–29 (2011)
50. Yue, K.: What does it mean to say that a specification is complete? In: Proc. IWSSD-4, Fourth International Workshop on Software Specification and Design (1987)

Modelagem de Requisitos não Funcionais em *Ambient Assisted Living*: Um Mapeamento Sistemático da Literatura

Maurício Manoel Coelho Júnior[1], Willy Silva Coutinho[1], Robson Lima de Alencar[1], and Fernanda Alencar[1]

Universidade Federal de Pernambuco, Departamento de Eletrônica e Sistemas, 50.740-560, Recife, Pernambuco, Brasil
{mauricio.coelhojr,willy.coutinho,robson.limaalencar,fernanda.ralencar}@ufpe.br

Resumo O aumento da expectativa de vida da população mundial é uma realidade, e quando combinado a quedas acentuadas e taxas de fertilidade, esses avanços na expectativa de vida podem levar a um rápido envelhecimento da população em todo o mundo. Tecnologias como *Ambient Assisted Living* (AAL) fornecem serviços que permitam às pessoas idosas viver uma vida independente, segura e saudável. Características, restrições e necessidades do usuário são requisitos não funcionais (Non-Functional Requirements - NFR) que exercem um papel fundamental na construção de sistemas, já que se forem esquecidos, podem aumentar consideravelmente o custo final de um sistema e até mesmo inviabilizar sua implementação. Deste modo, é apresentado uma visão geral da modelagem de NFRs em AAL e quais os principais NFRs para este domínio. Foi realizado um Mapeamento Sistemático da Literatura (*Systematic Mapping Study* - SMS) onde foram utilizados oito repositórios de publicação, obtendo-se 1071 estudos que foram filtrados com base num conjunto de critérios de inclusão/exclusão e qualidade, resultando em 22 estudos que foram utilizados para cobrir todo o material pertinente ao SMS. Foram mapeados quais os métodos e ferramentas utilizadas na modelagem de NFRs para AAL e os mais comuns NFRs utilizados para cada subdomínio. Baseado no resultado do SMS, existem indícios para explorar métodos e processos para modelagem de NFRs em AAL.

Keywords: Requisitos não Funcionais · Ambientes de Vida Assistida · AAL · Mapeamento Sistemática de Literatura · Modelagem · NFR Framework

1 Introdução

Segundo a Organização Mundial de Saúde (OMS) o número de pessoas com idade superior a 60 anos chegará a 2 bilhões de pessoas até 2050 [18], representando um quinto da população mundial. Segundo projeções do IBGE [13] a partir de 2040, 17% da população brasileira será de idosos. Na perspectiva de tecnologias direcionada a este público, pode-se destacar Ambientes de Vida

Assistida (*Ambient Assisted Living* - AAL) cujo objetivo é melhorar a qualidade de vida dos idosos, pacientes com condições crônicas e pessoas com deficiência, oferecendo autonomia/independência, conforto e segurança [8].

Do ponto de vista de soluções em AAL, é importante garantir que os NFRs sejam modelados, especificados e validados durante todo o ciclo de desenvolvimento. Nessa perspectiva, a garantia dos requisitos não funcionais e de sua modelagem deve ser considerada uma preocupação fundamental durante o desenvolvimento destes sistemas de *software*. Na literatura, pode-se identificar diversas iniciativas, com a intenção de melhorar e, de certa forma, garantir a qualidade desses sistemas. Muitas destas iniciativas têm discutido sobre o uso de modelos gerais de qualidade e a definição de atributos de qualidade [11]. No entanto, falta um panorama de como é feita a modelagem de NFRs nos sistemas AAL.

Este artigo é organizada da seguinte maneira: A Seção 2 apresenta a base conceitual para o desenvolvimento deste artigo e relaciona os principais conceitos: Engenharia de Requisitos, *Ambient Assisted Living* e *NFR Framework*. A Seção 3 apresenta o planejamento e condução da SMS. A Seção 4 apresenta os resultados da SMS com 22 trabalhos e uma análise sobre esses resultados. Finalmente, na Seção 5 é apresentada a conclusão e trabalhos futuros.

2 Fundamentação Teórica

2.1 Engenharia de Requisitos

De acordo com Abbott [6], um requisito pode ser uma função, uma restrição ou outra característica que deve ser fornecida ou atendida para satisfazer as necessidades do usuário do sistema que será desenvolvido. Já Sommerville [21] define que os requisitos de um sistema é uma descrição do que o sistema deve fazer, os serviços que o sistema fornece, e as suas restrições. O autor ainda classifica os requisitos de três maneiras: requisitos funcionais, requisitos não funcionais e de domínio, porém muitos autores preferem classificar os requisitos segundo os dois primeiro tipos: (i) Requisitos funcionais: Como o sistema deve reagir às entradas e como o sistema deve se comportar em algumas situações. Aplicam-se a funções específicas do sistema. (ii) Requisitos não-funcionais: São restrições das funções e serviços oferecidos pelo sistema. Podem ser restrições de tempo, de desenvolvimento, de processos e restrições por normas, aplicam-se ao sistema como um todo.

2.2 Ambient Assisted Living

O conceito de AAL está relacionado com um conjunto de produtos, serviços e sistemas que procuram manter a qualidade de vida e independência da população idosa e de indivíduos com necessidades de cuidados específicos [12]. Para Almeida et al. (2019) [7], AAL é um sistema crítico, e um dos fatores de sucesso para esses sistemas, é uma boa modelagem de requisitos não-funcionais [16]. Uma classificação dos sistemas AAL foi proposta no projeto BRAID [1] focando em quatro áreas de interesse do idoso: (i) **Vida independente**: auxilia as atividades da vida diária (por exemplo, lembretes médicos, monitoramento do estado de vida) e oferece suporte à mobilidade das pessoas (por exemplo, assistência para compras, cadeiras de rodas inteligentes); (ii) **Saúde e Cuidados na Vida**: auxilia os pacientes em atividades relacionadas à saúde, como o monitoramento remoto de saúde, assistência de emergência e assistência de exercícios; (iii) **Ocupação na Vida**: auxilia os idosos na continuidade de suas atividades profissionais; e (iv) **Recreação na Vida**: facilita a socialização e a participação dos idosos em atividades sociais, culturais e de lazer.

Broek [8] destaca que, em termos de funcionalidade, os sistemas de *software* AAL devem ser: a) personalizáveis, ou seja, adaptados às necessidades dos usuários; b) adaptável, ou seja, com capacidade de reagir às mudanças dinâmicas na disponibilidade de dispositivos/serviços, disponibilidade de recursos, ambiente do sistema ou requisitos do usuário; e c) antecipatória, ou seja, antecipar os desejos dos usuários na medida do possível, sem mediação consciente.

3 Mapeamento Sistemático da Literatura

Para realizar o SMS, foi acompanhado o processo proposto por Kitchenham e Charters [15], (i) Planejamento da revisão, (ii) execução da revisão e (iii) análise e divulgação dos resultados, mostrado na Figura 1 [17]. Nesta seção, são apresentadas as duas primeiras fases da SMS, na Subseção 3.1 é detalhada a fase de planejamento e na Subseção 3.2 é descrita a fase de execução.

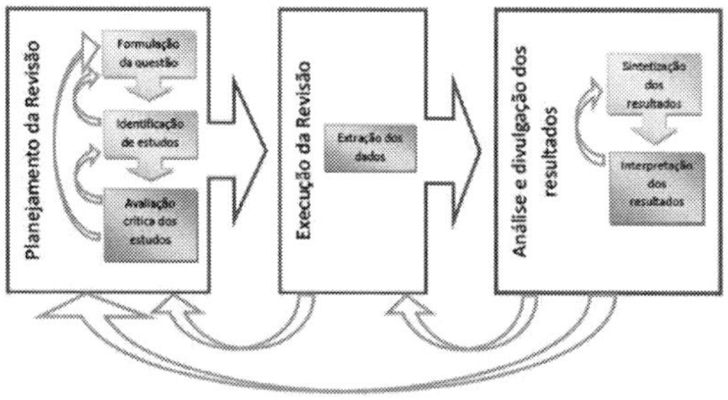

Figura 1. Processo do Mapeamento Sistemático da Literatura

3.1 Fase de planejamento

Nesta fase, foram definidos os objetivos da pesquisa e o protocolo SMS. Este protocolo contém: (i) objetivos de pesquisa e questões de pesquisa; (ii) estratégia de busca; (iii) critérios de seleção (ou seja, critérios de inclusão, exclusão e qualidade); (iv) procedimentos para seleção dos estudos; e (v) método de extração e síntese de dados.

Questões de Pesquisa Para orientar o planejamento desta SMS, foi adotada a abordagem *Goal Question Metric* (GQM) [22], que envolve três elementos:

(i) o objetivo a ser alcançado; (ii) um conjunto de perguntas que devem ser respondidas para alcançar o objetivo; e (iii) um conjunto de métricas necessárias para responder às perguntas. Em relação a SMS, o objetivo é apresentar uma visão geral de como é feita a modelagem de Requisitos não Funcionais em *Ambient Assisted Living* e quais são os principais NFRs abordados por subdomínio. Com base nesse objetivo, foram estabelecidas cinco questões de pesquisa, conforme Tabela 1.

Tabela 1. Questões de Pesquisas e suas Métricas

Questão de Pesquisa	Métricas
RQ1: Quais os subdomínios de AAL que o estudo suporta?	(1) Subdomínios AAL que apresentam os estudos; (2) Número de ocorrências de cada subdomínio AAL no estudo.
RQ2: Quais os requisitos não funcionais identificados?	(1) NFR que são importantes para sistemas de software AAL; (2) Número de ocorrências de cada NFR.
RQ3: Quais técnicas / métodos são usados para apoiar a modelagem e/ou especificação de NFR em AAL?	(1) Abordagens usadas para modelagem ou especificação de NFR em AAL; (2) Número de ocorrências de cada abordagem.
RQ4: Quais ferramentas são utilizadas na modelagem e/ou especificação de NFRs?	(1) Ferramentas usadas para modelar ou especificar NFR; (2) Número de ocorrências de cada ferramenta; (3) As ferramentas mais importantes.
RQ5: Quais são os problemas em aberto relacionados à área de pesquisa?	(1) Problemas em aberto apontados no estudo.

Estratégia de busca A construção dos termos de busca (Tabela 2) foi realizada seguindo uma estratégia composta pelos seguintes passos: (i) A partir de buscas, foram identificados os termos e palavras-chave; (ii) Sinônimos são identificados baseados em artigos conhecidos e relevantes na área de pesquisa; (iii) A string de busca é gerada a partir da combinação dessas palavras-chave e sinônimos.

Tabela 2. String de Busca

(("AAL"OR "Ambient Assisted Living"OR "ambient assisted"OR "ambient assistance"OR "assisted environment"OR "assistive environment"OR "AAL environment"OR "independent living"OR "assisted life"OR "intelligent living"OR "pervasive living"OR "assistive environments"OR "AAL environments"OR "assisted environments"OR "Assistive Software") AND ("quality model"OR "quality attribute"OR "non-functional property"OR "Non-Functional Requirements"OR "quality requirement"OR "quality models"OR "quality attributes"OR "non-functional properties"OR "non-functional requirements"OR "quality requirements"OR "NFR") AND ("specification"OR "model*"))

Fontes de busca A busca por trabalhos foi realizada por busca automática. Os três critérios para a seleção das fontes foram: disponibilidade de consulta dos artigos na web, presença de mecanismo de busca usando palavras-chave e; importância e relevância das fontes. A Tabela 4 apresenta as fontes utilizadas.

Critérios de Inclusão e Exclusão Os critérios de inclusão e exclusão devem identificar os estudos primários que fornecem evidências diretas sobre a questão da pesquisa. Eles devem ser testados para garantir que possam ser interpretados de forma confiável e classificar os estudos corretamente [15]. A Tabela 3 apresenta os critérios de inclusão e exclusão desta pesquisa

Tabela 3. Critérios de Inclusão e Exclusão

Critérios de Inclusão	Critérios de Exclusão
Os estudos devem ter sido publicados em periódicos, simpósios ou congressos das bases citadas	Artigos resumidos.
Os estudos devem ser escritos em inglês	Estudos duplicados (o único será considerado)
Os estudos devem estar disponíveis na web	Estudos que não abordam a relação com o foco do trabalho
Os estudos devem ser artigos completos.	O estudo redundante de um autor (será considerada a versão mais completa).
Estudos que abordam as relações com o foco de trabalho.	Livro ou capítulo de livro
Estudos primários	Estudos sem resumo disponível

Tabela 4. Bases de Dados Utilizadas x Total Artigos

Fonte de busca	URL para Acesso	Total
IEEE Xplorer	`http://ieeexplore.ieee.org/Xplore/home.jsp`	1
ACM Digital Library	`http://portal.acm.org/`	77
Sciencedirect	`https://www.sciencedirect.com`	487
PMC	`https://www.ncbi.nlm.nih.gov/pmc/`	107
Engineering Village	`https://www.engineeringvillage.com`	10
PubMed	`https://www.ncbi.nlm.nih.gov/pubmed/`	24
Springer	`https://link.springer.com/`	352
Scopus	`https://www.scopus.com/search/form.uri?display=basic`	13
Total		1071

Critérios para Avaliação de Qualidade Os critérios para avaliação de qualidade tem como objetivo aumentar a acurácia dos resultados de extração dos dados, ajudando a determinar a validade das inferências oferecidas, credibilidade e síntese coerente dos resultados [15]. Para responder às questões dos critérios de qualidade, o pesquisador pode usar os seguintes níveis de concordância (SIM = 1, PARCIALMENTE = 0,5 e NÃO = 0), conforme Tabela 5. Os estudos foram avaliados com base em 4 níveis de qualidade: Ruim (0 a 2,5), Regular (2,6 a 5,5), Bom (5,6 a 7,5) e Ótimo (7,6 a 10), e aprovados para a próxima fase os trabalhos com escala bom e ótimo.

Tabela 5. Critérios para Avaliação de Qualidade

#	Critério	Respostas
1	Existe uma explicação de por quê o estudo foi feito?	Y=1, N=0, P=0.5
2	Os autores deixam claro qual é o propósito do estudo?	Y=1, N=0, P=0.5
3	A abordagem proposta está claramente descrita?	Y=1, N=0, P=0.5
4	Há discussão sobre os resultados obtidos?	Y=1, N=0, P=0.5
5	Há uma apresentação clara dos problemas em aberto na área de estudo?	Y=1, N=0, P=0.5
6	O artigo apresenta alguma modelagem UML ou Orientada a Objetivos no estudo?	Y=1, N=0, P=0.5
7	O artigo apresenta de forma clara NFRs que apoiam ou tem impacto em AAL?	Y=1, N=0
8	O artigo descreve algum método para avaliação da proposta?	Y=1, N=0
9	O artigo apresenta técnicas ou métodos que apoiam a modelagem ou especificação de requisitos não funcionais?	Y=1, N=0, P=0.5
10	O artigo apresenta alguma especificação ou modelagem de NFR?	Y=1, N=0

3.2 Fase de execução

Nessa etapa, foi realizada a condução e análise dos estudos primários no período compreendido entre 01/02/2021 e 15/02/2021. Foram aplicados os critérios de inclusão e exclusão [5]. As buscas foram realizadas e os resultados (Tabela 4) passaram por cinco etapas de seleção, conforme a Figura 2 e o protocolo [5].

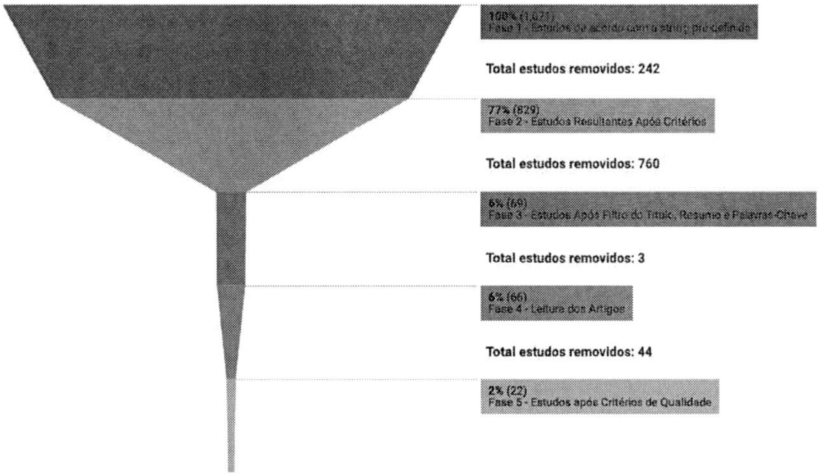

Figura 2. Fases da Revisão Sistemática

Na Fase 1, a pesquisa foi aplicada nos repositórios da **String** de busca. Para os repositórios ACM, Science Direct, Engineering Village, Scopus foram coletados os artigos no formato .bib. Para os repositórios US National Library of Medicine National Institutes of Health, PubMed foram coletados os arquivos no formato .ris e .nbib respectivamente, sendo necessário um *parser* para converter no formato .bib. Para a base Springer foi baixado os artigos no formato .csv e posteriormente executado um *script* para baixar o resumo de cada artigo. Também foram implementados *script* SQL para auxiliar no processo de mineração dos dados da SMS.

Na Fase 2, foi aplicado o critério de inclusão e exclusão [5] da lista baixada de artigos da fase 1. Para a Fase 3, foram lidos os campos título, resumo e palavra-chave dos artigos. Nesta fase foi feito um *script* para fazer a leitura semi-automatizada desses campos nos artigos. Na Fase 4, os artigos foram lidos integralmente e analisados com base na lista de verificação e de avaliação de qualidade. Por fim, na Fase 5, foram selecionados todos os artigos que foram classificados como bom e ótimo na escala de qualidade [5]. Todos os trabalhos selecionados em cada fase e o protocolo estão disponíveis online [5].

4 Resultados da Revisão

4.1 Fase de análise e divulgação dos resultados

Nesta fase, os estudos primários que atendiam ao propósito da SMS foram analisados criticamente e sintetizados no formulário [4] de aprovação dos trabalhos que preencheram os critérios de inclusão. Apresenta-se uma visão das características gerais dos estudos, bem como os resultados das questões de pesquisa [19]. Os gráficos foram extraídos a partir do *Dashboard* [3] criado para a SMS. A Tabela 6 apresenta os estudos selecionados após a fase de avaliação de qualidade. Foi disponibilizado um repositório online [5] com todos os artigos em suas respectivas fases.

Tabela 6. Trabalhos Selecionados

ID	Trabalho	Autor	Ano	Fonte
EP_01	A Quality Model for AAL Software Systems	Lina Garcés et al.	2016	IEEE
EP_02	Data and Information Quality Issues in Ambient Assisted Living Systems	McNaull et al.	2012	ACM
EP_03	Patterns for Identification of Trust Concerns and Specification of Trustworthiness Requirements	Mohammadi, Nazila Gol and Heisel, Maritta	2016	ACM
EP_04	Exploratory Study on the Use of Software Product Lines in the Development of Quality Assistive Technology Software	Martins et al.	2018	ACM
EP_05	Applying model-driven engineering to a method for systematic treatment of NFRs in AmI systems	Ruiz-López el al.	2013	Scopus
EP_06	Runtime models based on dynamic decision networks: Enhancing the decision-making in the domain of ambient assisted living applications	García-Paucar, Luis-Hernán and Bencomo, Nelly	2016	Scopus
EP_07	A semantic approach for designing Assistive Software Recommender systems	Elena el al.	2015	Sciencedirect
EP_08	Activities of Daily Living Ontology for Ubiquitous Systems: Development and Evaluation	Woznowski et al.	2018	PMC
EP_09	The SmartHabits: An Intelligent Privacy-Aware Home Care Assistance System	Grgurić et al.	2019	PMC
EP_10	Quality attributes and quality models for ambient assisted living software systems: A systematic mapping	Lina Garcés et al.	2017	Sciencedirect
EP_11	Ambient assisted living healthcare frameworks, platforms, standards, and quality attributes	Memon et al.	2014	PMC
EP_12	Enabling correct design and formal analysis of Ambient Assisted Living systems	Kawtar Benghazi et al.	2012	Sciencedirect
EP_13	A tailored smart home for dementia care	Amiribesheli, Mohsen and Bouchachia, Hamid	2018	Springer
EP_14	Using RELAX, SysML and KAOS for Ambient Systems Requirements Modeling	Manzoor Ahmad et al.	2012	Sciencedirect
EP_15	REUBI: A Requirements Engineering method for ubiquitous systems	Tomás Ruiz-López et al.	2013	Sciencedirect
EP_16	Development and evaluation of SOA-based AAL services in real-life environments: A case study and lessons learned	Erlend Stav et al.	2013	Sciencedirect
EP_17	A Quality Model for the Evaluation AAL Systems	Madjid Kara et al.	2017	Sciencedirect
EP_18	Quality Parameters as Modeling Language Abstractions for Context-Aware Applications: An AAL Case Study	Hoyos et al.	2017	Springer
EP_19	Ambient Intelligence in Assisted Living: Enable Elderly People to Handle Future Interfaces	Kleinberger et al.	2007	Springer
EP_20	Elicitation of Quality Characteristics for AAL Systems and Services	Omerovic et al.	2013	Springer
EP_21	Quality Assessment Approaches for Ambient Assisted Living Systems: A Systematic Review	Erazo-Garzon et al.	2020	Springer
EP_22	Ambient Assisted living system's models and architectures: A survey of the state of the art	Amina et al.	2020	Sciencedirect

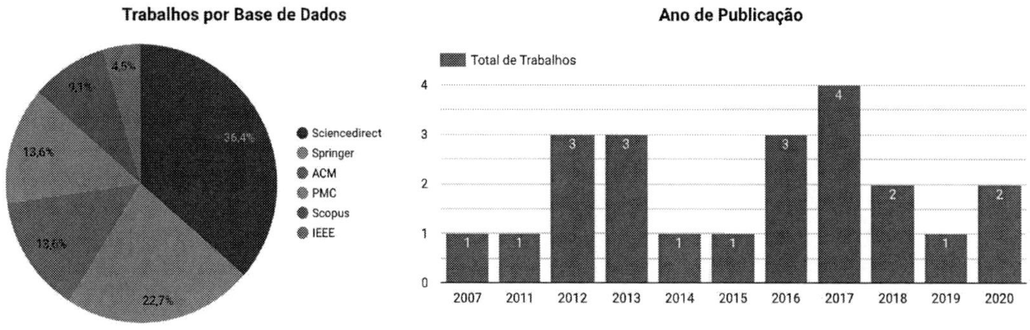

Figura 3. Estatísticas da SMS: Base de Dados e Ano de Publicação

São apresentados na Figura 3, os dados quantitativos referentes aos 22 estudos selecionados. Os estudos estão distribuídos da seguinte forma: 36,4% da base Science Direct, 22,7% para Spring e PMC, 13,6% para ACM, e 4,5% dos estudos para IEEE. Os estudos analisados nessa SMS foram publicados entre 2007 a 2020, conforme apresentado na Figura 3, com destaque para o ano de 2017 com quatro estudos e 2012, 2013 e 2016, estes com três estudos. Observa-se também que apesar de ser uma área importante, existem poucos estudos relacionados a modelagem de NFRs para AAL, visto que apenas foram encontrados um estudo em 2019 e dois em 2020.

RQ1 – Quais os subdomínios de AAL que o estudo suporta? Essa questão de pesquisa identifica os diferentes domínios da AAL nos estudos. A Tabela 7 apresenta uma listagem dos estudos associados ao seu subdomínio e percentual de cada subdomínio. Os subdomínios foram identificados tomando como base o projeto BRAID [1], que apresenta as áreas de interesse do idoso, sendo utilizado por Garces et al. [11] como subdomínios da AAL.

Tabela 7. Classificação dos trabalhos em relação aos subdomínios de AAL.

Trabalhos	Subdomínios de AAL	%
EP_02, EP_03, EP_05, EP_06, EP_12, EP_13, EP_14, EP_15, EP_19	Saúde e Cuidados na Vida	40,9%
EP_01, EP_08, EP_09, EP_10, EP_11, EP_16, EP_20, EP_22	Aplicado em todos os subdomínios	36,4%
EP_04, EP_07, EP_17, EP_18, EP_21	Vida Independente	22,7%

A tabela 7 apresenta a relação entre os estudos e os subdomínios de AAL, onde Saúde e Cuidado na Vida representa 40,90% dos estudos. Os estudos relacionados a Vida independente representam 30,56%. 22,7% dos estudos podem ser aplicados em todos os subdomínios. É importante destacar no subdomínio Saúde e Cuidados na Vida o trabalho EP_12, que define padrões e um processo formal de decomposição dos requisitos do sistema de modo a obter requisitos básicos, para uma validação composicional do sistema. Já os trabalhos EP_01 e EP_20 que podem ser aplicados em todos os subdomínios, onde o EP_01 aborda modelos de qualidade para sistemas AAL, estabelecidos e avaliados com base em evidências de diversos trabalhos publicados encontrados através da condução de um estudo de mapeamento sistemático. Já o EP_20 relata o processo e os resultados da obtenção de características específicas de qualidade AAL, baseado em arquiteturas de referência estabelecidas e no padrão de qualidade do produto de software ISO/IEC 9126.

RQ2 – Quais os requisitos não funcionais identificados? Os requisitos não funcionais identificados nos trabalhos foram classificados conforme as subcaracterísticas da ISO 25010/2011 [14], sendo detalhados na Figura 4. Observa-se que o modelo de qualidade do produto definido na ISO/IEC 25010 compreende as características de qualidade, por exemplo, a característica ***Security*** que é definida como o grau em que um produto ou sistema protege informações e dados para que pessoas, produtos ou sistemas tenham o grau de acesso aos dados apropriado para seus tipos e níveis de autorização; é composta pelas seguintes subcaracterísticas [14]: **Confidentiality**, **Integrity**, **Non-repudiation**, **Privacity** e **Authenticity**. A Figura 5 foi agrupada por características presentes na ISO/IEC 25010.

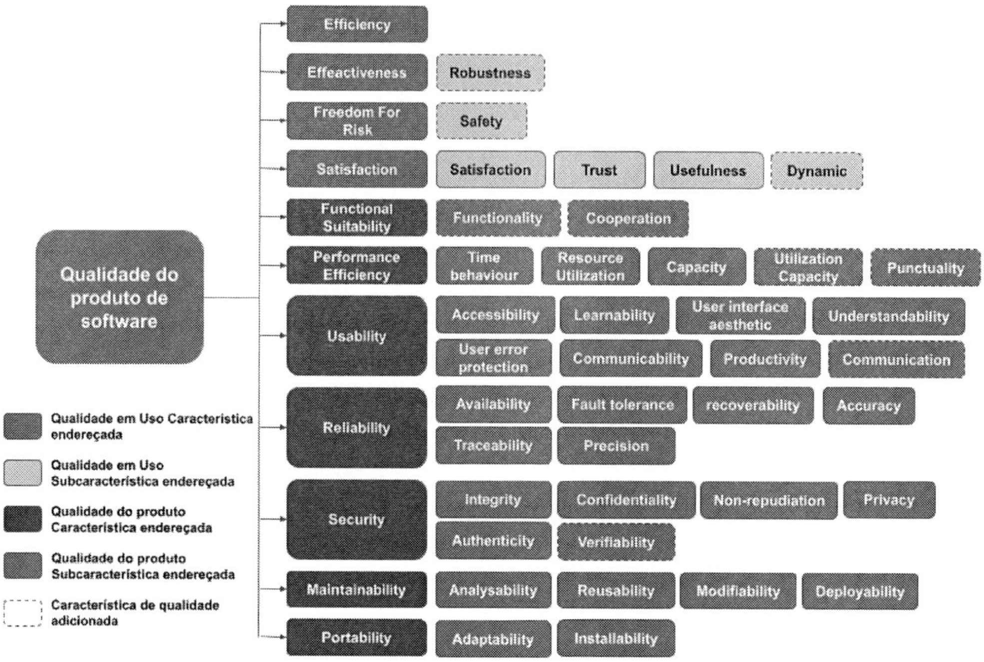

Figura 4. Análise de agrupamento dos NFR a partir da ISO/IEC 25010

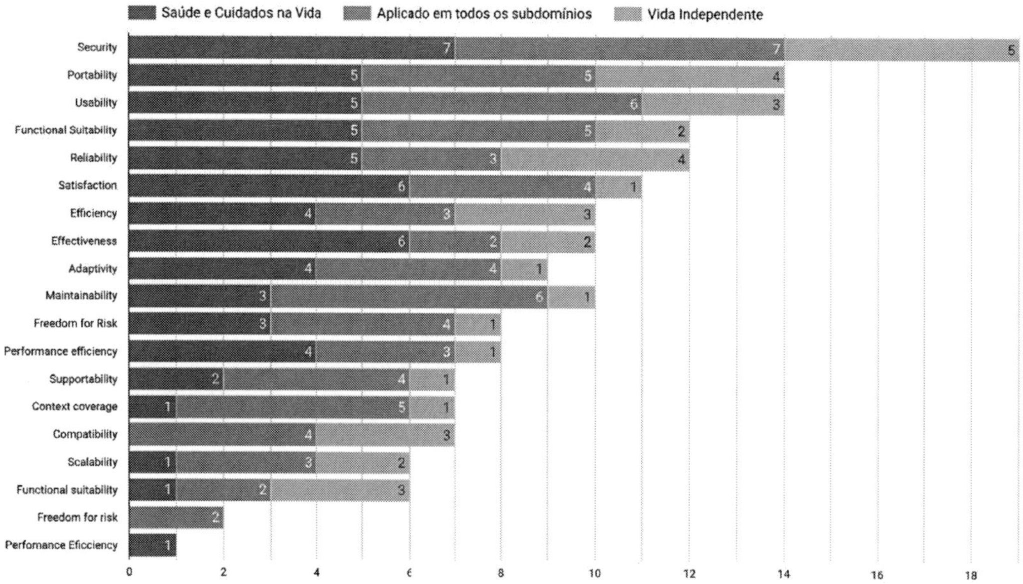

Figura 5. Requisitos não Funcionáis x Subdomínios AAL x Características

Durante a fase de leitura dos estudos, os NFRs ***Security*** (19 trabalhos), ***Portability*** (14 trabalhos) e ***Usability*** (14 trabalhos) apresentam reincidência contante nos estudos, levando-se a considerar que são NFRs que devem estar presentes em sistemas AAL. A ***Usability*** é definida como o grau em que um produto ou sistema pode ser usado por usuários especificados para atingir objetivos específicos com eficácia, eficiência e satisfação em um contexto de uso discriminado. E ***Portability***, é o grau de eficácia e eficiência com que um sistema, produto ou componente pode ser transferido de um *hardware*, *software* ou outro ambiente operacional.

NFRs como *Safety*, *Cooperation*, *Robustness*, *Communication*, *Verifiability*, *Utilization* emphCapacity, *Punctuality*, *Dynamic* foram encontrados nos estudos, porém não são verificados como uma característica dentro da ISO/IEC 25010. Por isso, foi sugerida uma nova sintaxe permitindo que esses NFRs sejam agrupados a partir de uma análise paralela com a definição de qualidade envolta de cada característica principal, usando o princípio de verossimilhança [20]. Assim, por exemplo, tomando como referência a taxonomia proposta por Garcês et al. [11], para o NFR ***Verifiability***, pode-se notar que tem uma relação estreita com a subcaracterística ***Integrity*** no sentido da necessidade de coexistência e de como ambos estão ligados a característica principal ***Security***.

Pode-se considerar os NFRs *Security*, *Usability* e *Portability* como críticos para o desenvolvimento, já que são transversais em qualquer subdomínio AAL e muitos destes sistemas não são desenhados considerando as necessidades especiais da população idosa. Outro ponto que não foi considerado nos trabalhos selecionados, é a falta de um catálogo ou um processo que indique, por exemplo, como o NFR de *Usability* é validado na modelagem.

Apesar de não ser referenciado diretamente, para o subdomínio Ocupação na Vida, pode-se associar o NFR **Freedom for Risk**, sendo definido como o grau em que um produto ou sistema mitiga o risco potencial para a situação econômica, a vida humana, a saúde ou o meio ambiente. É importante considerar que o risco é função da probabilidade de ocorrência de uma determinada ameaça e das consequências adversas potenciais deste evento.

Para o subdomínio Recreação na Vida, pode-se associar o NFR **Satisfaction** como crítico, já que é definido como o grau em que as necessidades do usuário são satisfeitas quando um produto ou sistema é usado em um contexto de uso especificado. É importante ressaltar que para um usuário que não interage diretamente com o produto ou sistema, apenas o cumprimento do objetivo e a confiança são relevantes.

RQ3 - Quais técnicas / métodos são usados para apoiar a modelagem e/ou especificação de NFR em AAL? Este tópico é importante para identificar quais técnicas, ou métodos foram utilizados na especificação de requisitos não funcionais nos trabalhos selecionados.

A Tabela 8 apresenta as técnicas/métodos identificadas em cada estudo. Com 45,50% dos estudos utilizando *Unified Modeling Language* (UML) ou uma extensão da UML para a modelagem de NFR, como o trabalho EP_15, que apresenta um método de Engenharia de Requisitos para a análise de Sistemas Onipresentes, baseado em metas que representam a influência do contexto e das situações adversas, proporcionando um procedimento de avaliação para auxiliar na tomada de decisão sobre a satisfação dos objetivos. Neste trabalho o autor cria uma extensão da UML para representar um gráfico de interdependência, utilizando o estereótipo no diagrama de classe para definir se o objeto é um

Tabela 8. Relação entre Trabalhos x Técnicas/Métodos para Modelagem

Trabalhos	Técnicas/Métodos	%
EP_02, EP_03, EP_05, EP_07, EP_10, EP_12, EP_15, EP_16, EP_20, EP_22	UML	45,5%
EP_01, EP_04, EP_09, EP_11, EP_13, EP_18, EP_19, EP_21	Outros	36,4%
EP_14	GORE	36,4%
EP_08, EP_17	Ontologias	4,5%
EP_06	OOA	4,5%

goal, *softgoal* ou *operationalization*. Apesar da utilização da UML que permitem uma menor curva de aprendizagem, o trabalho não fornece uma orientação base para a elicitação de requisitos, captura de NFR, preferências do usuário e contexto de uso na fase inicial do projeto. Não obstante, a rastreabilidade e geração de cenários dos modelos a partir de alterações no contexto ou preferências do usuário não são abordados neste estudo. Em 36,4% dos estudos utilizam-se outras técnicas/métodos para modelagem de NFR em AAL, por exemplo, os trabalhos EP_01 e EP_21 que apresentam um mapeamento sistemático para identificar os NFRs no domínio AAL, ou o trabalho EP_04 que apresenta uma revisão bibliográfica da literatura que visa investigar o uso de Linha de Produtos de Software para o desenvolvimento de tecnologias assistivas. Já 9,1% dos trabalhos usam de ontologias, exemplo é o trabalho EP_08 que apresenta uma ontologia hierárquica e requisitos importantes no desenvolvimento de sistemas para Atividades de Vida Cotidiana (*Activities of Daily Living* - ADL).

Por fim *Object-oriented analysis* - (OOA) e *Goal-Oriented Requirements Engineering* - (GORE) aparecem em 4,5% dos trabalhos respectivamente. O trabalho EP_14 apresenta o RELAX, uma linguagem de Engenharia de Requisitos (RE) para sistemas adaptativos, que podem introduzir flexibilidade nos NFRs para se adaptar a quaisquer mudanças nas condições ambientais, usando uma abordagem orientada a objetivos, baseada em Kaos, que estende o metamodelo SysML e a Linguagem Específica de Domínio (DSL) proposta no estudo. Esta questão de pesquisa mostra que muitos trabalhos têm procurado propor alguma extensão na UML para a modelagem de NFR em AAL, porém não foi encontrado nenhum trabalho que utilize, por exemplo, o gráfico de interdependência presente no NFR Framework [10], uma abordagem conhecida por fornecer um processo para modelagem de NFR.

RQ4 - Quais ferramentas são utilizadas na modelagem e/ou especificação de NFR? Esta seção foca especificamente nas ferramentas utilizadas nos estudos selecionados. Vale reforçar que as ferramentas não são especificamente técnicas ou métodos, o que deixa explícita a diferença entre esse tópico e o anterior. A Tabela 9 identifica as ferramentas em cada estudo.

Como apresentado na Tabela 9, foi identificado que 27,30% dos estudos não utilizam nenhuma ferramenta para auxiliar na construção de sua proposta. Já 22.7% dos estudos, utilizam ferramentas desktop, onde podem enfrentar problemas para modelagem e/ou especificação de NFR de forma colaborativa e online.

Tabela 9. Relação entre Trabalhos x Ferramentas

Trabalhos	Ferramentas	%
EP_02, EP_05, EP_13, EP_19, EP_20, EP_22	Não utiliza ferramenta	27,3%
EP_04, EP_06, EP_12, EP_15, EP_18	Ferramenta Desktop	22,7%
EP_03, EP_10, EP_11, EP_21	Análise Literária	18,2%
EP_07, EP_09, EP_16, EP_17	Ferramenta Web	18,2%
EP_08, EP_14	Outros	9,1%
EP_01	Não identificado	4,5%

Ferramenta Web representam 18,20% dos trabalhos, onde não foi identificado nenhuma referência em modelagem ou especificação de NFR com e/ou para reuso. Análise Literária aparece também com 18,20%, já que estes trabalhos utilizaram uma revisão bibliográfica para identificar os NFRs em AAL. Esta questão de pesquisa foi importante para mostrar que ainda não existe uma preocupação na construção ou automatização dos seus processos, com foco na modelagem colaborativa, disponível na plataforma web e que auxiliem na construção de modelos e especificação de NFR para o domínio e os subdomínios AAL com foco em reuso.

4.2 Ameaças à Validade

As principais ameaças identificadas para a validade deste SMS são descritas a seguir: (i) Extração de dados: Refere-se à forma como os dados foram extraídos dos estudos primários, visto que, nem todas as informações eram óbvias para responder às questões da pesquisa e alguns dados tiveram que ser interpretados. Além disso, em caso de desacordo entre os três revisores, uma discussão foi conduzida por um quarto revisor para garantir que um acordo total fosse alcançado. (ii) Confiabilidade de seleção: Com o objetivo de garantir um processo de seleção imparcial, definimos previamente as questões de pesquisa e elaboramos critérios de inclusão, exclusão e de qualidade. Acreditamos que as questões e critérios são detalhados o suficiente para fornecer uma avaliação de como o conjunto final de estudos primários foi obtido. Porém, é possível que estudos tenham sido excluídos na primeira etapa devido à falta de informações importantes nas seções de título, resumo e palavras-chave. (iii) Outra ameaça é a limitação de ferramentas suportando apenas arquivos no formato bibtex, excluindo arquivos do tipo (CVS, NBIB, TXT) disponíveis nas bases PubMed e PMC. Para resolver isso, foi desenvolvido uma ferramenta web para suportar arquivos de diferentes formatos e convertidos para o formato JSON (*JavaScript Object Notation*), sendo possível trabalhar com uma base de dados relacional.

4.3 Trabalhos Relacionados

O estudo proposto por Garcés et al. [11] apresenta um mapeamento sistemático da literatura com o objetivo de fornecer um panorama sobre o estado da arte em modelos de qualidade (QMs) e atributos de qualidade (QAs) importantes para o domínio AAL. Como resultado, o trabalho identifica e define os QAs mais comuns usados no desenvolvimento de sistemas AAL. O estudo também apresenta uma taxonomia com base na ISO 25010/2011 [14]. Apesar das contribuições deste estudo, não foi possível identificar técnicas e processos para modelagem ou especificação de NFR em AAL, principal foco deste SMS.

5 Conclusão e Trabalhos Futuros

Os sistemas AAL tornaram-se cada vez mais complexos, adotando múltiplos sub-domínios críticos, por exemplo, monitoramento de cuidados de saúde, suporte à mobilidade física, reabilitação de pessoas e assistência ao trabalho. Além disso, estes sistemas fazem parte da rotina de pacientes crônicos ou pessoas com deficiência, eles devem prevenir falhas que possam causar danos aos usuários finais. Apesar de importantes contribuições da comunidade para o desenvolvimento de sistemas AAL, existem poucos trabalhos que foquem na modelagem e especificação de NFR para este sistema. Nessa perspectiva, as principais contribuições deste trabalho são: (i) Foi apresentado um panorama contendo o estado da arte sobre abordagens, métodos e técnicas que tem sido utilizados na modelagem e especificação de NFR para AAL; (ii) Mapeamento dos principais NFRs baseado na ISO 25010/2011 [14] presentes nos sistemas AAL e em seus respectivos subdomínios; (iii) Atualização da Taxonomia AAL proposta por Garcês et al. [11], adicionando novos NFRs; e (iv) Transformação dos dados da SMS em *Dashboard* interativos com o uso da ferramenta Data Studio.

Como trabalho futuro, pretende-se desenvolver um método para modelagem de NFR em *Ambient Assisted Living*, fornecendo um tratamento sistemático que considere características que podem a modelagem. Apesar do uso da UML para modelagem de NFR apresentado nos estudos da SMS, o método proposto deve utilizar a técnica GORE, como o NFR Framework [9] para modelagem de NFR em AAL, já que a abordagem proposta por Chung já possui um processo definido, mas sem uma definição clara de como identificar domínio, subdomínios ou suporte ao reuso horizontal. É esperado deste método: **a)** Fornecer uma orientação base para elicitação de requisitos, captura de requisitos não funcionais, preferências do usuário e contexto de uso (características que impactaram no sistema); **b)** Mostrar o impacto do contexto nos objetivos que precisam ser cumpridos sempre que for necessário; **c)** Fornecer um procedimento algoritmo a fim de determinar quais decisões são as mais adequadas para a satisfação dos objetivos sob certas restrições (preferências do usuário) e **d)** Fornecer um catálogo com artefatos (NFR, Normativas Legais) para o domínio AAL. Também espera-se aplicar esta técnica em outro cenário de AAL, focado no subdomínio Ocupação na Vida e Recreação na Vida, áreas que podem vir a crescer muito com o envelhecimento de uma população ativa. Investigar através de uma revisão sistemática da literatura outros subdomínios ou classificações para AAL, e por fim, mapear as normativas legais para a área de AAL, já que estas normativas [2] podem ter um impacto na modelagem de NFR.

Referências

1. Braid project - bridging research in ageing and ict development (2012), https://cordis.europa.eu/project/id/248485
2. Aal guidelines for ethics, data privacy and security (2020), https://bit.ly/3t8cUOP, [Online; accessed 01-março-2021]
3. Dashboard da SMS. https://datastudio.google.com/s/p8wki5TufDU (2021), [Online; accessed 01-março-2021]
4. Formulário de Extração dos Dados da SMS. https://forms.gle/V6M5bK2PUMSczKB28 (2021), [Online; accessed 01-março-2021]
5. Repositório Online do Mapeamento Sistemática da Literatura. https://bit.ly/3te2uMS (2021), [Online; accessed 01-Fev-2021]
6. Abbott, R.J.: An integrated approach to software development. John Wiley & Sons, Inc. (1986), https://dl.acm.org/doi/10.5555/1098691
7. Almeida, A., Mulero, R., Rametta, P., Urošević, V., Andrić, M., Patrono, L.: A critical analysis of an iot—aware aal system for elderly monitoring. Future Generation Computer Systems (2019). https://doi.org/10.1016/j.future.2019.03.019
8. van den Broek, G., Cavallo, F., Wehrmann, C.: AALIANCE ambient assisted living roadmap (2010), https://dl.acm.org/doi/10.5555/1805924
9. Chung, L., Nixon, B.A., Yu, E., Mylopoulos, J.: Non-Functional Requirements in Software Engineering, vol. 5 (01 2000). https://doi.org/10.1007/978-1-4615-5269-7
10. Chung, L., Nixon, B.A., Yu, E., Mylopoulos, J.: Non-functional requirements in software engineering, vol. 5. Springer Science & Business Media (2012)
11. Garcés, L., Ampatzoglou, A., Avgeriou, P., Nakagawa, E.Y.: Quality attributes and quality models for ambient assisted living software systems: A systematic mapping. Information and Software Technology (2017). https://doi.org/10.1016/j.infsof.2016.10.005
12. Grguric, A.: Ict towards elderly independent living. Research and Development Centre, Ericsson Nikola Tesla (2012)
13. IBGE: Projeções e estimativas da população do Brasil e das Unidades da Federação. https://bit.ly/3uBmWbt (2021), [Online; accessed 01-march-2021]
14. ISO/IEC 25010: ISO/IEC 25010:2011, systems and software engineering — systems and software quality requirements and evaluation (square) — system and software quality models (2011)
15. Kitchenham, B., Charters, S.: Guidelines for performing systematic literature reviews in software engineering (2007)
16. de Macedo, P.C., de Cássia Catini, R., Neto, C.C.: Sistemas críticos, um guia para elicitação de requisitos de software. UNIVERSITAS (16) (2016)
17. Mian, P., Conte, T., Natali, A., Biolchini, J., Travassos, G.: A systematic review process for software engineering. In: ESELAW05: 2nd Experimental Software Engineering Latin American Workshop (2005)
18. OMS: "Ageing well" must be a global priority. https://bit.ly/3sOU7DJ (2014), [Online; accessed 01-August-2019]
19. Petersen, K., Vakkalanka, S., Kuzniarz, L.: Guidelines for conducting systematic mapping studies in software engineering: An update. Information and Software Technology (2015)
20. Simões, D.: Iconicidade e verossimilhança. Semiótica aplicada ao texto verbal. Rio de Janeiro: Dialogarts (2007)
21. Sommerville, I.: Software engineering 9th edition (2011)
22. Van Solingen, R., Basili, V., Caldiera, G., Rombach, H.D.: Goal question metric (gqm) approach. Encyclopedia of software engineering (2002)

Privacy Aware Blockchain Solutions: Design and Threat Analysis

Maria Fernanda Molina[1], Gustavo Betarte[1,2], and Carlos Luna[1,2]

[1] Área Informática, Pedeciba, Uruguay
[2] Instituto de Computación, Facultad de Ingeniería
Universidad de la República, Uruguay
fmolina.uy@gmail.com, {gustun,cluna}@fing.edu.uy

Abstract. The requirements established by data protection regulations pose specific challenges to the designers of information systems. In previous work we have studied the integration of *off-chain* capabilities into blockchain-based solutions, moving data outside the core blockchain network in order to comply with the security and privacy requirements of the European data protection regulation (GDPR). In this work we present in detail a methodological framework for the design of privacy aware solutions that are built using blockchain technology. We also put forward a systematic approach for performing a security and privacy threat analysis of such kind of solutions. We illustrate the use of the proposed methodological tools presenting and discussing both the design and the security and privacy assessment of a system that provides services to handle, store and validate digital academic certificates.

Keywords: blockchain, off-chain, GDPR, design principles, security and privacy, threat analysis.

1 Introduction

Blockchain is an incipient technology [8] that provides support to build decentralized systems in which transactions are processed without a responsible intermediary or authority. In [17] and [16] we discuss the challenges the European General Data Protection Regulation (GDPR) [9] requirements pose to the design and implementation of information systems that manage personal data and are built using blockchain technology. This technology meets by design some of the requirements of the Data Protection laws, such as the right of access to data by the owners, traceability, encryption and hash techniques as security by design mechanisms as well as transparency in data processing. On the other side, the technology has some general weaknesses: it is difficult to guarantee the confidentiality of information and the immutable nature of the blockchain prevents the deletion or modification of incorrect information. In permissionless blockchain networks, additionally, it is difficult to establish controls over access to information and to identify a responsable for information treatment. Thus, if blockchain technology is used for processing personal data, complementary mechanisms are needed for those processes to be GDPR-compliant.

We propose the use of off-chain mechanisms [5] to design and implement information systems with capabilities to enforce access control to personal data and to guarantee the confidentiality of the data managed by the system. More precisely we put forward the use of a high-level system architecture for hybrid blockchain and off-chain solutions.

We have also briefly presented in [17] a methodological framework that provides support for designing functionally correct and privacy aware solutions, systematically. In this paper we present and discuss in detail the design framework, including the use case model we have proposed for the high-level system architecture. Then we put forward a methodology for performing security and privacy threat analysis of blockchain solutions. We illustrate the use of the proposed design and analysis tools providing insights on the specification of a prototype of a system that provides services to handle, store and validate academics digital certificates. To analyze and validate the proposed design, we derive sequence diagrams from the use case diagrams presented for the high-level system architecture and perform a threat analysis that allows us to verify the adequacy of the framework to design privacy-aware solutions and to spot vulnerabilities that must be addressed at implementation time.

Contributions To the best of our knowledge, the design framework we present and discuss in this paper is a first attempt in providing formal support to the design of privacy-aware information systems that use blockchain technology. The specification of the digital certificates system addresses privacy and GDPR compliance aspects that have not been considered elsewhere. For example, in our design the verification of certificates is mediated by an access control mechanism, in contrast to other proposals, where this function is enabled without such type of control. Additionally, we believe the threat analysis methodology is in itself a contribution that can be used in the analysis of systems that manipulate personal data. Regarding the risk analysis itself, we do not know of analysis of that kind, except the one of fraudulent activities to make fake diploma described in [22], being performed over systems that manage digital certificates.

Related work The work reported in this paper builds upon the results presented in [17]. The high-level system architecture discussed is a direct consequence of the analysis of the GDPR requirements and the analysis of other proposed systems, like [13], [25] and [6]. The methodology for security and privacy threat analysis we present in this work makes use of concepts and procedures present in STRIDE [20] and the CNIL [4] methodology por privacy risk analysis.

As to the design of systems that store and manage digital educational certificates, there exist several solutions that have been proposed to deal with this problem, with different degrees of development. In particular, we have analyzed Latin American solutions like the Brazilian RAP System [7] and the Argentine System BFA [2]. In [22] the solutions *Blockchain for Education* and *EduCTX* are discussed. All these systems propose a hybrid solution, using the blockchain to perform the validation of the certificates by storing a hash of the certificate and, in some cases, some additional information. Some of those solutions use public blockchain networks and others private ones, but none of them implements access control mechanisms to perform the certificate verification process. In that process the candidate gives the employer his certificate (an act which is considered an implicit consent of personal data access) and the employer validates the provided certificate with the blockchain, typically comparing hash values. However, performing this verification implies access to personal data, since the hash of a personal data constitutes personal information, and therefore the execution of that procedure should be authorized by the data owner.

Paper organization The rest of the article is structured as follows. The high-level system architecture and the use case model are presented and discussed in Section 2. In Section 3 we put forward the methodology for security and privacy threat analysis we have developed. Then, in Section 4 we provide the specification of the digital certificates system and discuss the results of the threat analysis carried out on that specification. We conclude and discuss further work in Section 5.

2 A privacy-oriented design framework

We now proceed to introduce and explain in detail a framework, briefly described in [17], that provides support for designing functionally correct and privacy aware blockchain-based solutions.

2.1 System architecture

We propose the use of a high-level system architecture for hybrid blockchain solutions that incorporate off-chain mechanisms to store and protect personal data. The information stored off-chain is accessed through a link that is in turn stored in the blockchain together with a hash value that is used to ensure the integrity of the information.

Regarding the blockchain components this architecture comprises: i) an *access control network*, that stores the access control policy and, upon request, performs the corresponding authentication and authorization tasks; ii) an *audit network* that records all actions that have been performed, such as authorizations, access requests, modification and deletion of data; and iii) an *integrity network* in order to validate data stored off-chain. When data is stored in the off-chain network, a link can be stored in the blockchain network in order to locate the data and, together with this information, it can be stored an integrity control check mechanism, for instance using a hash function.

Additionally, a Gateway component is proposed for handling external communication towards the blockchain and off-chain, similar to how is done in the architecture proposed in [6]. As authorization mechanism we propose to use a Security Token Service, like the one proposed in [25].

2.2 The use case model

The model comprises eight use cases that cover the principal services we understand can be used to build a blockchain and off-chain based system compliant with well established security and privacy requirements.

In the definition of the use cases service requesters are associated to four GDPR-influenced roles, namely: i) the *data owner*, the user, owner of personal data (DO); ii) the *data controller* (DC), responsible for data processing; iii) the *data processor* (DP), to whom a data controller can delegate processing tasks; and iv) the *Receiver (recipient)*, a third party who wants to access personal data.

In what follows we shall describe in detail these use cases, that are represented in Figure 1.

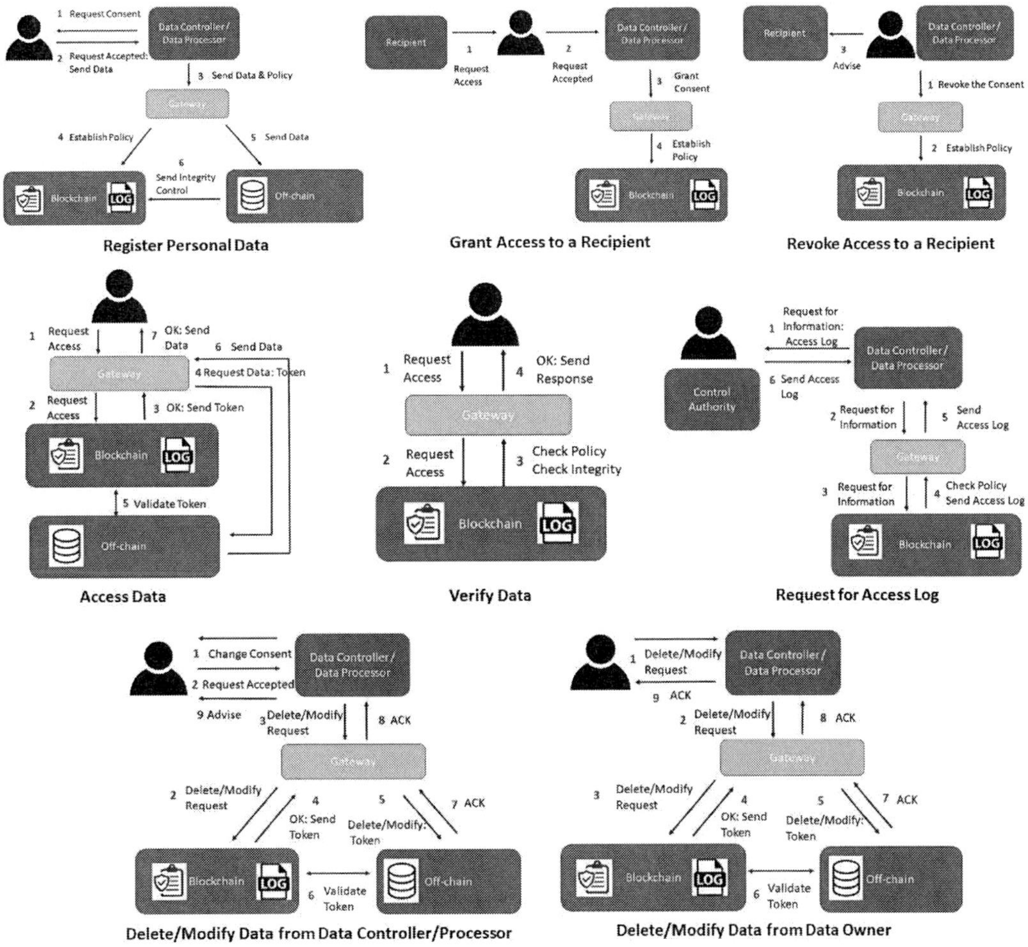

Fig. 1. Use case diagrams

Register personal data The first use case corresponds to entering the personal data into the system. In order to register personal data, either the DC or the

DP must first obtain authorization from the DO to record the information and establish a policy regulating the access to that information. This can be done by submitting a request signed by the user and either the DC or the DP. Then, the data is sent to the Gateway, that validates the access intent with the access control network blockchain. If the access policy authorizes the registration, the Gateway sends the data to the off-chain. Finally, the off-chain network communicates with the integrity network blockchain to store an integrity control (a hash of the personal data).

Grant access and Revoke access In order for a third party (recipient) to access the information, the DO and the DC or DP must authorize the request and send this authorization to the blockchain, so that the access policy is updated. This implies, therefore, registering the recipient in the system. It should be noted that the off-chain does not intervene in this flow since the data is neither accessed nor modified. The process of removing permissions involves updating the access policy stored on the blockchain. This action can be done by the DO, DC or DP. The blockchain validates the identification and access authorization before processing the requested change.

Data access and verification When a DO or recipient wants to access personal data, it has to send a request to the Gateway. The Gateway then sends the request to the access control blockchain network, which validates the access by reviewing the defined policy and, if the person requesting access is authorized, the blockchain delivers to the Gateway a token and the link to the data stored in the off-chain network. With this information, the Gateway can request access to the off-chain network, which in turn validates the token against the access control blockchain. If the Token is validated, the off-chain network returns the data and the Gateway sends the data to the requestor.

Once personal data is available in the system, the data owner or a third party might be interested in verify its integrity. We take the view that the processes of validating personal data and accessing the hash used to perform the validation are considered sensitive operations. Therefore, it is necessary to implement access control for this use case. To do that, the Gateway first validates access against the access control network blockchain. Once authorized, the integrity blockchain performs the integrity control of the data passed by the user. This is done by comparing the stored hash with the one presented by the user. It should be noted that in this use case it is not necessary to consult the off-chain.

Delete/Modify data from DO, DC or DP If the DO wishes to modify or delete his information, he can communicates it to the DC or DP who in turn can send the request to the Gateway. The Gateway verifies the policy against the access control network blockchain who sends a token to validate the access. The Gateway sends the request to the off-chain together with the token, so that the off-chain can verify it against the blockchain. If the token is validated, the off-chain network makes the change and adjusts the integrity check hash. In turn, either the DC or DP can modify or delete the information they have stored, giving notice to the data owner of the setting. Depending on the action to be taken and the context, it may be necessary to previously request the authorization of the DO. For example, we understand that in the case of deletion of information, it is only required to report the fact to the DO, while the modification of a data may require prior authorization.

Request for access Log Finally, the DO or an authority can request audit information from the DC or DP, who consult it with the blockchain. Before providing the information, the access policy must be reviewed.

3 A methodology for security and privacy threat modelling

The analysis of security and privacy risks of a computational system includes the study of aspects of hardware, software, operational practices and policies of the organization and application of the basic principles of protection of personal data. The basic methodological component of work that is typically applied to conduct one such risk analysis consists of the following steps: i) characterization of the context of the processing of personal data that takes place in the system; ii) creation of a catalog of the critical assets in this particular context and the security and privacy properties to be guaranteed; iii) identification of the threats to which these assets may be exposed; iv) assessment of the risks involved; and if required v) proposal of adequate measures to mitigate/treat critical level risks.

The execution of those procedures is carried out by making systematic use of the processes and catalogs of good or known practices provided by recognized methodologies for the analysis of privacy risks. In what follows we shall briefly describe a methodology that provides support for developing a security and privacy threat model for solutions that make use of blockchain technology to build privacy aware information systems.

3.1 Basic steps of the threat model

There exist several methodological proposals for the development of threat models. We shall follow the one proposed by OWASP [20], which consists of a process with six steps. The first step is to identify the *security and privacy properties* that should be guaranteed the system satisfies. In order to identify security objectives we use the CI4AM security mechanism [20], which proposes grouping security objectives into categories of confidentiality, integrity, availability, authentication, authorization, auditing and management. Additionally, we shall also require for *compliance* with the requirements of the GDPR, which relate to the processing of personal data. The second and third steps consist of *profiling* and *decomposing* the application. Once the components of the application have been identified we shall proceed to perform the *threat analysis*. This consists of determining, characterizing and classifying threats, possibly based on the attacker, the impacted assets and the attack method. Once the threats are detected it is required to identify the *vulnerabilities* the system has and that can be exploited by the threats analyzed. Finally, we *rank the threats* and define if each risk can be either accepted, mitigated, transferred or ignored.

3.2 Threat risk analysis

In order to achieve both a security and a privacy analysis we shall make combined use of the well-known Microsoft's STRIDE methodology [23] and the risk methodology defined by CNIL for privacy risk management [4]. STRIDE considers threats strictly from a security point of view, categorizing them into spoofing, tampering, repudiation, information disclosure, denial of service, and elevation of privilege. These threats are related to authentication, integrity, non-repudiation, confidentiality, availability and authorization security properties. CNIL considers threat groups related to processes, like unavailability of legal processes and change in processing. It also includes threat groups related to personal data, like illegitimate access to personal data (confidentiality), unwanted changes in personal data (integrity) and disappearance of personal data (availability).

Threat classes Some of the threats related to *unavailability of legal processes* that we consider affect GDPR compliance are legal problems derived from: i) *lack of responsibility for the treatment of personal data*; ii) *lack of processes to ensure the veracity or the consent of the treatment*; iii) *lack of processes for the correct treatment of data*; iv) *lack of processes to delete data*; and v) *failures in the information provided to the user.* Related to change in processing threats, we consider legal problems derived from vi) *failures in the processes to ensure the veracity or the purpose of the treatment*, vii) *failures in the processes to delete data*, and viii) *deficiency of controls over the treatment.*

Blockchain related threats can be summarised as those derived from i) *confidentiality issues*, since all transactions must be validated and processed by all the nodes of the network, all information necessary to perform this processing must be public, which undermines the confidentiality of the information. This issue in STRIDE can be categorized as information disclosure. Related to a tampering issues, we can consider ii) *immutability issues*, where the impossibility of modifying smarts contracts implies a problem of immutable bugs, because once a contract is published, it cannot be altered. Additionally, immutability is a problem for handling of personal data, as it contradicts the GDPR guidelines, and can be categorized as unavailability of legal processes threat. As a spoofing threat, we must also consider iii) *key management risk*, because blockchain is susceptible to theft of private keys, as digital assets could become unrecoverable [21]. Other type of issues that can be considered tampering threats are iv) *transaction security issues*, like the risk of double spending that is, spending the same money more than once [3]. There are others issues related to v) *consensus protocols* like unpredictable state issues. When a user sends a transaction to the network to invoke a contract, he cannot be sure of the state in which the contract will be when the transaction is executed. This is because in the interim, other transactions could alter the status of the contract, since no order is guaranteed in the execution of the transactions. Additionally we can consider the case known as 51 percent attack, related to what would happen if the network is dominated by a majority, like the cases [12] and [26]. Finally there are vi) *smarts contract security issuess*, like those described in [19] and [1].

We have also identified threats related to the use of off-chain tecnology, like i) *integrity issues*, thus in off-chain the storage goes to the hands of a third and not necessarily reliable party, a verification process is required to ensure the integrity of the information stored. We can also consider ii) *availability issues*, a property resolved by design in blockchain and difficult to guarantee in off-chain, since it has a single point of failure. Therefore, to improve availability, solutions can be sought where information is stored in a decentralized and redundant manner, such as IPFS [11] and SWARM [24]. Finally, we can find iii) *traceability issues*, as in off-chain audit is not resolved by design, so auxiliary mechanisms must be considered. This last threat could be categorized as unavailability of legal processes.

4 Applying the tools: a case study on digital titles

The IT services unit of the Universidad de la República, Uruguay, which is called SeCIU (Servicio Central de Informática) is in the process of studying alternatives for implementing and deploying a system that provides functionalities to handle, store and validate university certificates, like degree diplomas, using blockchain technology. The main objective of the solution is that (graduated) students are able to obtain their digital titles or certificates and deliver them to third parties (for example potential employers), which in turn could be able to validate the authenticity and legitimacy of those certificates using that same system.

Institutions all around the word have been concerned for a long time with finding good solutions to solve the problems related to educational certificates. There exists worldwide a severe problem of fake degrees, which is aggravated by the fact that, for instance, employers do not have the ability to validate the certificates a candidate present when applying to a job post. In the context of certification of studies, the blockchain technology has been visualized as the solution to counter the manipulation of fake certificates by providing an easy validation mechanism that provides integrity assurance.

4.1 The design of our solution

We have specified the expected behavior of the system using the GDPR-compliant constructs of the framework introduced in Section 2. In what follows we shall present and discuss the most relevant design decision we have taken. The complete specification of the solution can be found in [16].

In the first place, we have defined the following mapping from the data related roles presented in Section 2 to the institutions and individuals pertaining to the problem's domain: i) *SeCIU* is the *Data controller* (DC), the responsible for the personal data handled by the system; ii) the *School Registry Offices* are the *Data processor* (DP), working as delegates assigned by the SeCIU; iii) the *Candidates* are the *Data owner* (DO), the owners of personal data; and finally iv) the *Receiver (recipient)* are the employers or institutions that want to validate a certificate. Then, degrees and schooling (that corresponds to personal data) are stored in an off-chain network under the responsibility of the DC, and the operations of audit, access control and verification are carried out in a blockchain network that is accessed by School Registry Offices, students and authorized third parties, through a Gateway.

To validate the certificates, a hash of each certificate is stored in the blockchain, so that the validation system is based on the comparison of this hash with the hash of the certificate presented by the student. As was said, hash values should be considered personal data. Therefore, certificate verification should not be a public function and access to that operation should be controlled. In this respect, the authorities of the Universidad de la República decided to formally ask the Uruguayan Data Protection Agency, the *URCDP* (*Unidad Reguladora y de Control de Datos Personales*), whether it is valid, from the legal point of view, to implement a system where the verification of a degree diploma is public. The response of the URCDP was that such verification requires the consent of the individual that earned the diploma and therefore cannot be provided as an open and public function (Dictum 9-2018, Expediente 2017-2-10-000394).

Figure 2 depicts the data flow diagram (DFD) of the system, detailing the data and control flow that take place.

We have specified the behavior of the digital certificates system using refined versions of the generic use cases introduced in the use case model discussed in Section 2. In what follows we present and discuss the specification of the processes of the system. The corresponding sequence diagrams of some of this processes are described in Figure 3.

Registration Registration is carried out by the School Registry Offices. Thus, they are in charge of obtaining the authorization to manage data from its corresponding owner. The School Registry Offices send the data to the Gateway, which in turn sends the access control policy to the blockchain, following the process described in Section 2.

Grant and revoke access In order for a third party (an employer or another educational institution) to either access or verify a certificate, the student must give his consent and the system notified. This authorization will be stored in the blockchain network. The access authorization given by the student, though, can be revoked. This operation can be requested either by the student, the School Registry Office or the SeCIU.

Data access and verification In this case it is considered that the access to the certificates will be carried out only by the students. The student sends a request to the Gateway, which in turn requests access to the access control

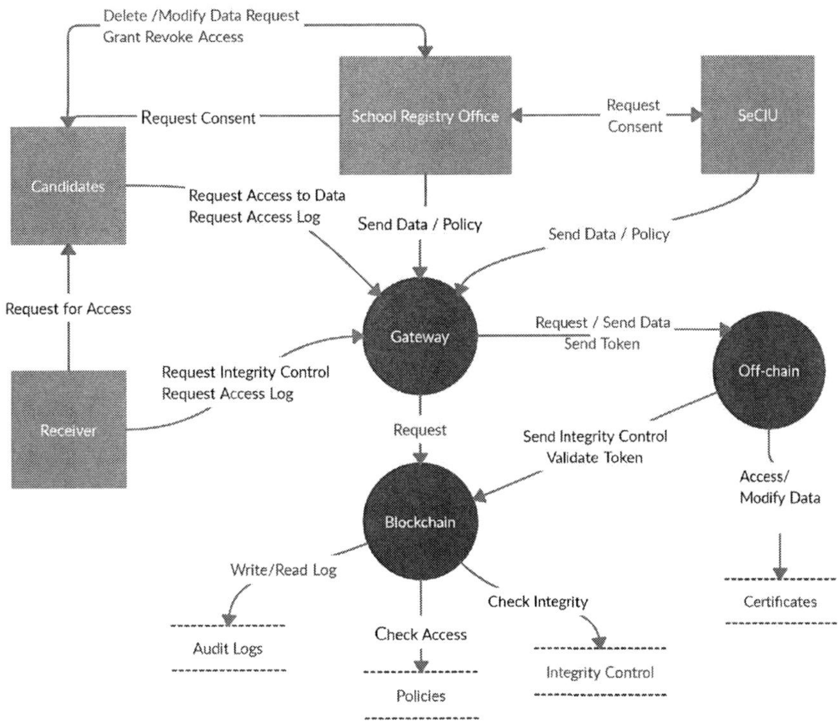

Fig. 2. Data Flow Diagram of the system

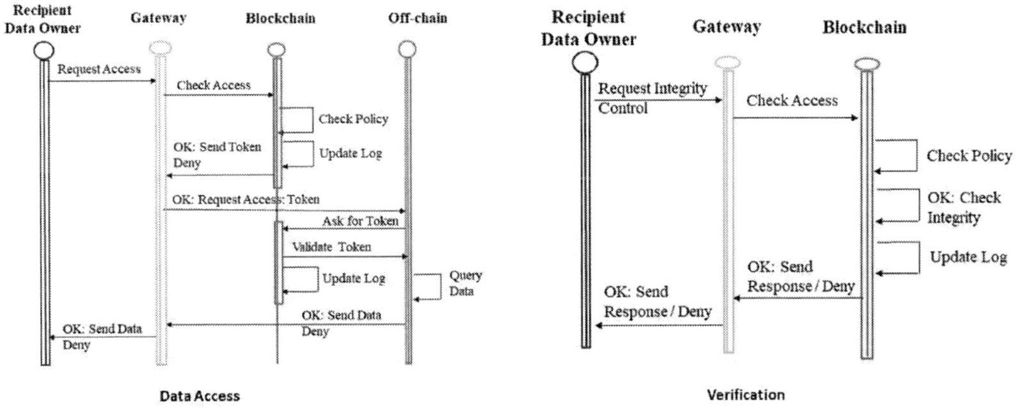

Fig. 3. POC sequence diagrams

blockchain network in order to validate the access policy. Authorization is done through a token, as described in Section 2. Employers or institutions that want to verify a certificate (that could have been delivered by the student), can do so by consulting the Gateway if the student previously made the corresponding authorization. For this reason the Gateway first verifies this access, before carrying out the integrity check.

Delete/Modify data from DO, DC or DP It could be the case that a student requests to modify stored information owned by him. That request is evaluated and processed by the corresponding School Registry Office, passing the request to the Gateway. The change involves checking the access policy, updating the information in the off-chain and updating the integrity control in the blockchain. Similarly, it may be SeCIU or the School Registry Office who must modify a student's data (for example, the correction of a grade). The cycle is similar to the previous one, but notice of the modification is also provided to the student.

4.2 Security and privacy threat modelling of the system

We shall illustrate the use of the proposed methodology discussing the definition of the security objectives and reviewing the threat analysis we have performed.

Security objectives We have identified the following security objectives:

- *Confidentiality:* protect certificates against unauthorized access and allow verification process only to authorized persons;
- *Integrity:* certificates must not be modified without authorization and must be verifiable using a validation process;
- *Availability:* availability of certificates, as well as the certificate verification system;
- *Authentication:* all participants, SecIU, School Registry Offices, students and employers must be identified and authenticated;
- *Authorization:* students must authorize companies or third parties who want their certificates to be validated and only students can see their certificates. Additionally, the SeCIU or the School Registry Offices must authorize changes in the access policy requested by the students. Finally, no person can access the information if it was not previously authorized by the system;
- *Auditing:* all accesses made, requested permissions and unauthorized access requests changes must be recorded;
- *Management:* the certificates are managed and stored by the SeCIU and the Gateway concentrates the interaction with the blockchain and off-chain.
- Finally as the *compliance* objective, the system processes must comply with GDPR requirements, like those related to responsibility for data processing, deletion and traceability of personal data and veracity and the consent of the treatment.

Threat risk analysis We have used the Microsoft Threat Modeling Tool [20] and STRIDE to identify threats and vulnerabilities of the designed system. We managed to derive 110 threats related to the STRIDE categories. In addition 18 threats related to either the use case described in [22] or to the use of blockchain and off-chain technology, as described in Section 3 were detected. From the application of the CNIL methodology [4] we identified 10 traditional threats related to the processing of personal data.

Out of the threats detected, 6 are considered not applicable, because either concern interactions with other universities, the manipulation of certificate translations or incorrect grading by the teaching body or School Registry Office, which are all cases not considered in the proposed solution. Finally, 3, related to Denial of Service threats, were not mitigated.

Mitigation measures In Table 1 we classify and discuss the threats that are mitigated by design, which amount to the 56% of the total identified. The rest of the threats can be mitigated by implementing mechanisms that guarantee, among others, traffic encryption, protection of user credentials, control measures for personnel of School Registry Offices and the use of cryptographic hash functions following the recommendations to avoid hash reversibility we have provided in [16]. All the analyzed threats are discussed in detail in [18].

Threats mitigated by design		
Type	**Threat examples**	**Possible mitigations**
Spoofing	An adversary may spoof a user and gain access to the Web Application [15].	Certificates are used to identify users.
Tampering	An adversary can modify the database and deny the action [15]. Student adds certificate or altere certificates [22]. Blockchain security issues that affect integrity.	Authentication and authorization are validated by the access policy blockchain. Aditionally, the integrity control protects against unauthorized changes of certificates.
Repudiation	Attackers can deny malicious acts and remove the attacks footprints leading to repudiation issues [15].	Authentication and authorization are validated by the access policy blockchain. Audit log and access policy stored in blockchain are immutable by design.
Information Disclosure	An adversary can gain access to sensitive data by performing SQL injection to certain pages or to the site as a whole [15]. Blockchain confidentiality issues.	Certificates are stored off-chain with not direct access provided to users. Authentication and authorization are validated by the access policy blockchain. Design the generation of hashes in a way that makes reversibility a hard problem [14]. Use permissioned blockchain and a commit-chain off-chain architecture [16].
Elevation of Privileges	An adversary may bypass critical steps or perform actions on behalf of other users. An adversary can gain unauthorized access to the database [15].	Authentication and authorization are validated by the access policy blockchain. Use permissioned blockchain and commit-chain off-chain architecture [16].
Unavailability of legal processes	Lack of responsibility for the treatment of personal data. Lack of processes to ensure the veracity or correctness of the treatment. Failures in the information provided to the user [4].	All operations are registered in the audit blockchain and this technology ensures by design the integrity of the audit and access policy. Use permissioned blockchain [16].
Change in processing	Failures in the processes to ensure the veracity or purpose of the treatment. Deficiency of controls over the treatment or the processes to delete data [4].	Information deletion is resolved by design, since the information is stored in the off-chain and there are specific use cases. All operations are registered in the audit blockchain and blockchain ensures by design integrity on audit logs and access policy.

Table 1: Threats mitigated by design

5 Conclusion and further work

We have presented a framework for the design of privacy-aware information systems that make use of blockchain technology. We have also put forward a methodology for performing security and privacy threat analysis of systems of that kind. We illustrate the use of the design framework and the threat analysis methodology on a realistic and not trivial digital certificates system. The design constructs are shown to be expressive enough to specify the required functionalities of that system. In particular, as result of the analysis we have carried out we observe that about half of the threats detected are mitigated by design. We emphasize that we did not find a threat modeling performed in the other existing solutions analyzed in Section 4, beyond the analysis of fraudulent activities to make fake diploma described in paper [22], that we have incorporated into our threat modeling.

An identified challenge to address in further work is the conception of the mechanisms to register and authenticate the third parties that shall interact with the digital certificates system. In particular, as SECIU would prefer not to provide and manage those mechanisms, a decentralized solution should be considered. Candidate solutions are the ones based on the use of decentralized digital identities to protect the identity and data of users, like the tools provided by Hyperledger Indy [10]. How well one such solution would integrate with the rest of the system preserving the privacy requirements requires further study.

References

1. Ethereum wiki, 2021. Available: `https://eth.wiki/en/howto/smart-contract-safety`.
2. bfa.ar. Blockchain Federal Argentina, 2020. Available: `https://bfa.ar/`.
3. U. W. Chohan. The double spending problem and cryptocurrencies. *Information Systems & Economics eJournal*, 2017.
4. CNIIL. Methodology for privacy risk management, 2012. Edition 2012.
5. J. Eberhardt and S. Tai. On or off the blockchain? insights on off-chaining computation and data. In *Service-Oriented and Cloud Computing*, pages 3–15, Cham, 2017. Springer International Publishing.
6. C. M. et al. Implementation of smart contracts using hybrid architectures with on and off-blockchain components. In *8th International Symposium on Cloud and Service Computing, SC2 2018, France.* IEEE, 2018.
7. R. C. et al. Uso não financeiro de blockchain: Um estudo de casao sobre o registro, autenticação e preservação de documentos digitais acadêmicos. In *Anais do I Workshop em Blockchain: Teoria, Tecnologias e Aplicações*, Porto Alegre, RS, Brasil, 2018. SBC.
8. European Commission. *Blockchain now and tomorrow*. Publications office, Luxemburgo, 2019.
9. General Data Protection Regulation. Regulation (eu) 2016/679. *Official Journal of the European Union*, 2016.
10. Hyperledger.org. Hyperleger indy, 2021. Available: `https://www.hyperledger.org/use/hyperledger-indy`.

11. IPFS. IPFS, 2020. Available: https://ipfs.io/.
12. E. G. S. Ittay Eyal. Majority is not enough: Bitcoin mining is vulnerable, 2018. Available: https://doi.org/10.1145/3212998.
13. C. Li, B. Palanisamy, and R. Xu. Scalable and privacy-preserving design of on/off-chain smart contracts. In *35th IEEE International Conference on Data Engineering Workshops, , China, 2019*, pages 7–12. IEEE, 2019.
14. T. Lyons, L. Courcelas, and K. Timsit. Blockchain and the gdpr. a thematic report prepared by the european union blockchain observatory and forumtitle. *European Union blockchain observatory and forum*, 2018.
15. Microsoft. Microsoft threat modeling tool, 2020. Available: https://www.microsoft.com/en-us/securityengineering/sdl/threatmodeling.
16. F. Molina, G. Betarte, and C. Luna. A blockchain based and GDPR-compliant design of a system for digital education certificates, 2020. Available: https://arxiv.org/abs/2010.12980.
17. F. Molina, G. Betarte, and C. Luna. Design principles for constructing GDPR-compliant blockchain solutions. In *4th International Workshop on Emerging Trends in Software Engineering for Blockchain, ICSE 2021*, 2021.
18. F. Molina, G. Betarte, and C. Luna. Threat analysis of an academic certificates management system, 2021. Available: https://gitlab.fing.edu.uy/privacy-aware-blockchain-solutions/blockchain-and-privacy/-/blob/master/Materials/Threat_Analysis-ACS.pdf.
19. T. C. Nicola Atzei, Massimo Bartoletti. A survey of attacks on ethereum smart contracts. *Universita degli Studi di Cagliari, Cagliari, Italy*, 2016.
20. OWASP. Owasp threat modeling, 2020. Available: https://owasp.org/www-pdf-archive/AdvancedThreatModeling.pdf.
21. P. Santhana and A. Biswa. Blockchain risk management – risk functions need to play an active role in shaping blockchain strategy, 2017. Available: https://www2.deloitte.com/content/dam/Deloitte/us/Documents/financial-services/us-fsi-blockchain-risk-management.pdf.
22. R. H. Saye. Potential of blockchain technology to solve fake diploma problem, 2019. Available: https://jyx.jyu.fi/bitstream/handle/123456789/64817/1/URN:NBN:fi:jyu-201906253406.pdf.
23. STRIDE. Stride methodology, 2020. Available: https://docs.microsoft.com/en-us/archive/msdn-magazine/2006/november/uncover-security-design-flaws-using-the-stride-approach.
24. SWARM. SWARM, 2020. Available: https://www.swarm.fund/.
25. N. Truong, Kai, G. Lee, and Y. Guo. Gdpr-compliant personal data management: A blockchain-based solution. *CoRR*, abs/1904.03038, 2019.
26. B. Wiki. Bitcoin weaknesses, 2020. Available: https://en.bitcoin.it/wiki/Weaknesses.

Automatically recovering students' missing trace links between commits and user stories

Sivana Hamer, Christian Quesada-Lopez, and Marcelo Jenkins

Universidad de Costa Rica, San Pedro, Costa Rica
{sivana.Hamer,cristian.quesadalopez,macerlo.jenkins}@ucr.ac.cr

Abstract. Trace links between commits and user stories can be used in educational software engineering projects to track progress and determine the students' contribution to projects' requirements. Thus, traceability can be helpful in courses for grade assessment, and project monitoring and improvement. Currently developers, including students in courses, manually link commits and issues using version control systems (e.g., Git) and issue tracking systems (e.g., Jira). However, manual trace links are often incomplete. In our study, we found that only 43% of the commits are linked to stories in the analyzed project. Therefore, there is a need to automatically or semi-automatically create trace links. This study aims to automatically recover trace links between commits and user stories requirements in an undergraduate student project with twenty students and four teams. We used unstructured data from messages, code and files of commits and stories to gather textual similarity measures. We evaluated the effectiveness of information retrieval (Vector space model, Latent semantic indexing and BM25) and machine learning (Random forests, Decision trees and Neural networks) techniques in recovering missing links using textual and process data. Machine learning models outperformed information retrieval models in precision, recall, and F-measure. Machine learning models were able to effectively recover missing trace links with an average of 93% precision and 94% recall, showing the applicability of the approach.

Keywords: software engineering education · traceability · link recovery · information retrieval · machine learning · mining software repositories

1 Introduction

Traceability supports, throughout the development life cycle, different software engineering tasks and activities such as verification and validation, change impact analysis, change management, and requirement completeness analysis [1]. The establishment and use of trace links have been applied and studied in a wide range of software development environments [2–5] and software artifacts [6–8]. Traceability practitioners in software projects have reported commonly using tracing for tracking the implementation of requirements and tasks, finding the origin and rationale of requirements, documenting requirements' stories, and analyzing requirements coverage in source code [9]. These benefits could also be applied to software development projects in education.

Links between changes and issues (i.e., features, bugs or enhancements) can be used to build prediction or localization models, characterize the impact of a change, assign bugs to developers, and map source code and features [10]. A common practice to establish manual trace links between changes and issues is tagging [11]. Source code changes (i.e., commits) are saved in version control systems (VCS) [12]. Meanwhile, issue tracking systems (ITS) collect bugs, enhancement requests, features and tasks [13]. To link issues with changes, developers tag (in the change) the identification of the implemented issue [14].

Tracing commits with user story requirements in student's software engineering projects would allow instructors and students to monitor requirement progress and completion. Roadblocks with requirement implementation can then be detected to be tackled by students or instructors providing additional feedback. Traceability could help determine a student's or team's contribution and can be combined with other information such as process [15] and quality [16] metrics. Trends in feature implementation could also be determined to find recurring patterns in the process or product. Therefore, the information gathered could help instructors determine improvement opportunities for courses and help grade assessment based on data.

Despite the benefits of establishing manual trace links, it has been reported that links are frequently inaccurate and untrustworthy [17]. Several studies, both in open source software and industrial projects, have also indicated that links between commits and issues are often incomplete [10, 11, 18]. Therefore, there is a need to establish automatic or semi-automatic trace links.

In this paper, we aim to automatically recover trace links between commits and user stories in students' software engineering projects. Therefore, we answer the following research question: What is the effectiveness of automatically recovering trace links between commits and user stories in student projects? We investigated missing link recovery in an undergraduate software engineering project with twenty students, 1,035 commits, and 230 committed or done stories. We analyzed to what extent students manually linked commits and user stories. Furthermore, we assessed a total of six information retrieval and machine learning techniques. Information retrieval methods used the messages, files and code of the commits and stories to create missing links. Additionally, machine learning techniques utilized both process and textual similarity information to recover the links.

The remainder of this paper is organized as follows. Section 2 describes related work. Section 3 details the proposed approach of our study. Section 4 presents and discusses the results. Section 5 describes the work's conclusions and future work.

2 Related Work

Several approaches have previously investigated recovering commits and issues.

Heuristic and information retrieval approaches have been previously applied. Śliwerski et al. [14] used syntactical and semantical heuristics to determine if a change fixed a bug. Wu et al. [19] applied ReLink, an algorithm that automatically learns from links between bugs and changes to recover missing links. ReLink uses the time, ownership, and textual features to determine the links. Nguyen et al. [20] proposed MLink, an approach that calculates, with Tf-Idf, code and textual similarity between bugs and bug-fixing changes. Hübner and Paech [21] used data from interaction logs, requirements, and source code in student projects. Hübner and Paech [5] further extend their approach by using the issue identifiers provided in the commit messages. We differ from these previous approaches by focusing on agile student projects. Additionally, we extend the results by also including probabilistic models which have been less studied for software traceability [22].

Other approaches have used machine learning techniques. Sun et al. [23] proposed FRLink, an approach that included non-source code documents and discards irrelevant source code files. FRLink extracts the textual similarity for the commit code, non-source code and logs, and issue reports with the vector space model. Then, FRLink classifies if the commits and issues are related using a binomial prediction model. Sun et al. [24] further improved their approach by considering unlabeled data with PULink. Rath et al. [11] used process and text-related features with machine learning techniques to generate missing links between the commits and issues (bugs and improvements). They calculated the textual similarity between commits and issues using algebraic information retrieval models with the commits messages and files, and issues summaries and files. Ruan et al. [10] utilized deep learning techniques to capture the semantic representation between commits' logs and code, and issues titles, texts and code. Therefore, our work extends previous approaches by generating more empirical evidence by validating machine learning trace recovery in another context (i.e., student projects). Furthermore, we also focus on requirements, another type of issue artifact. By studying another context and artifact, results of these approaches can be further generalized.

3 Proposed approach

3.1 Process

Figure 1 shows the process used in this study with four main stages: data extraction, data preprocessing, information retrieval modeling, and machine learning modeling. Commits from the version control systems (VCS) and user stories from the issue tracking system (ITS) are first extracted from their repositories. Next, the true commit-story and false commit-story trace links are recovered. Then, the unstructured data from the commits and user stories are preprocessed. The preprocessed data is then used with information retrieval techniques to extract the textual similarity between artifacts and retrieve the most relevant documents. Finally, machine learning models are trained and evaluated. The complete approach has been implemented in Python. Each step will be further elaborated in the following paragraphs.

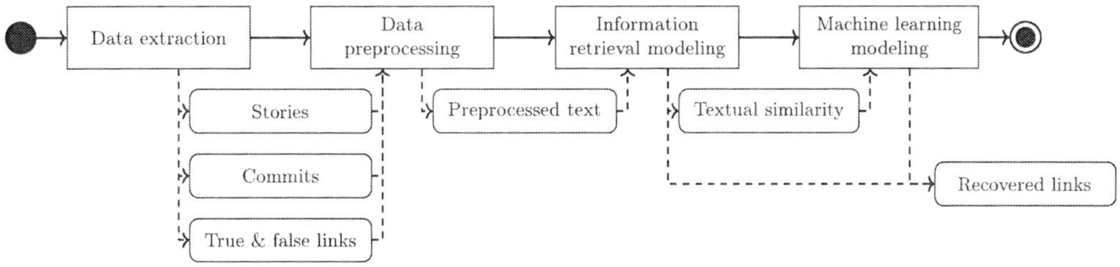

Fig. 1: Trace link recovery process

Data extraction. Many different artifacts are created during a software development project. In our study, we used the commits and requirements written as user stories.

Commit. For Git [25] a commit is a snapshot, a version of the repository at that moment. Each commit has a unique identifier and saves the changes to the files with the associated code. Furthermore, other metadata of the commit is saved, such as when the changes were made, the developer who made the change, and why the change was made in the commit message (subject and body).

User story. A user story is a type of requirement used in agile software engineering written from the perspective of the end-user in natural language [26]. User stories were written based on the Connextra template (I as a *role* want *function* so that *business value*) [27]. Furthermore, the user story also included a summary, acceptance criteria, user story points, sprints, creation time, termination time, and creator. The stories were saved in Jira [1], but some additional information, such as the assignees of each story, was saved in Excel. We consider the message of a story the summary and the description. This included the Connextra template and acceptance criteria.

The relationship between our selected artifacts is shown in Fig. 2. The squares represent artifacts. Relationships with an arrow represent linking, while squares represent containment. Commits have messages, a pair of subjects and bodies. Stories also have messages, which include their title and description. A user story can have multiple associated linked commits, and vice versa. Furthermore, a commit contains files that were changed and can be modified in multiple commits. These files save numerous code changes of addition, deletion, or modification.

Fig. 2: Relationship between commits and stories

[1] https://www.atlassian.com/software/jira

For both commits and stories, we mapped each developer and team to a unique identifier. To map the commits, we used a mailmap [2]. Meanwhile, the stories are mapped with a program based on a configuration file that maps the students' emails to the unique identifier. For both the commits and stories, students are also mapped with their respective team with a configuration file.

Finally, the trace links between the commits and user stories were recovered using previously used heuristics [10]. Trace links in the project were saved by tagging in the commits' message the associated story identifier. Therefore, we recover the true links by identifying the story identifier in a commit message. Meanwhile, false links are created for each commit with a true link. For each story not associated with the linked commit, a false link is created. Furthermore, to reduce the potential false links only commits that were committed between 7 days before the creation or after the completion date of the story [24]. Furthermore, stories had to be either committed to a sprint or done to be included as either a true or false link.

Data preprocessing. To select more representative terms using information retrieval models, the commits' and stories' unstructured data is linguistically preprocessed [28]. Particularly, the stories messages, and the commits messages, files and source code changes between snapshots. To preprocess the text, text normalization, camel and snake case words splitting, text tokenization, stop words removal, and morphological root stemming were applied. Words were stemmed using the Porter stemmer algorithm [29]. The nltk [30], ftfy [3] and Cucco libraries [4] were used to preprocess the text. As the text could be written in either English or Spanish, all the text was translated to English with google translate [31]. To process the commit files, we also included the full path. Furthermore, the files' extensions were removed and folders were split. Finally, to extract relevant terms from the source code from the commit, we eliminate source code keywords for CS, SQL and JS files [32].

Information retrieval modeling. Information retrieval models select and rank documents based on queries, and are classified into four main categories: probabilistic, algebraic and logical, informational theoretic, and bayesian [33]. In our case, we used these models to gather and rank the textual similarity between commits and stories. Most traceability information retrieval-based approaches have focused on using algebraic models, specifically the Vector space model [22]. In this paper, both algebraic and probabilistic models were analyzed. The examined models were the Vector space model (VSM) [34], Latent semantic indexing (LSI) [35] and BM25 [36, 37]. We used Gensim's [38] implementation of algebraic models. For BM25, we used the library Rank-BM25 [5]. The default configuration is used for all the models.

[2] https://git-scm.com/docs/git-check-mailmap#_mapping_authors

[3] https://github.com/LuminosoInsight/python-ftfy

[4] https://github.com/davidmogar/cucco

[5] https://github.com/dorianbrown/rank_bm25

The story's message is treated as the document in the model, while the commit's message, files and code are the queries. We index each of the different documents and the query is then processed to obtain the commit-story similarity score. Based on the similarity score given by the models, the relevant documents for a commit are the two highest, non-zero stories. For the queries with multiple entries (i.e., code and files), a total score is calculated based on four different strategies: maximum score, median score, average score, and the average of the top 5 scores. Models performance was evaluated based on the precision, recall and F-measure [28]. Precision is the fraction of retrieved documents relevant, recall is the fraction of relevant documents retrieved, and F-measure is the harmonic mean for the precision and recall.

Machine learning modeling. Our machine learning approach has four major steps: data selection, training and evaluation. For the data selection phase, the commits, stories, true and false links, and commit-story similarity scores are gathered from the previous steps. Previously, process and textual similarity sets have been used [11]. Therefore, we divide our features into the following sets:

Process. Incorporates process related information. We capture: (p_1) committer; (p_2) committer team; (p_3) story assignees; (p_4) teams assigned to story; (p_5) committer is an assignee (committer == an assignee); (p_6) committer team is an assigned team (committer == an assigned team); (p_7) story created date <= commit date; and, (p_8) commit date <= story resolution date. Features p_5, p_6, p_7 and p_8 are binary.

Similarity. Contains the textual similarity scores. We used: (s_1) commit message and story message similarity; (s_2) commit files and story message similarity; (s_3) commit code and story message similarity. Since we have multiple similarity scores, we select the highest performing information retrieval models for each similarity feature.

All. All the features ($p_1, \cdots, p_8, s_1, s_2, s_3$) from both the process and similarity set are selected.

Previously decision trees (DT), neural networks (NN) and random forests (RF) models have been applied to recover commit-issue trace links [10, 11]. Therefore, we trained and investigated these three different supervised machine learning classifiers. We used Scikit-learn's [39] implementation of machine learning models. Decision trees and random forests apply default hyperparameters. Meanwhile, the neural network adopts all the default hyperparameters except iterations with a value of 500 to achieve model convergence. As the datasets were severely unbalanced, data was balanced with sub-sampling using Scikit-learn. In order to mitigate the effects of randomness while training the model, every model and set is tested ten times. The classifier returns if the commit-story pair was either linked or unlinked. We evaluated each model's precision, recall and F-measure as they have been previously used to assess the performance of machine learning models for commit-issue link recovery [10, 11, 23].

3.2 Software project

We analyzed a third-year undergraduate software engineering project from the Universidad de Costa Rica. All students that participated in the project were included in our analysis. The project was developed for both the courses of software engineering and database. In these introductory courses students learn for the first time about software development methodologies and database development with their respective technologies. The students used Git to commit the code changes and Jira to save the user stories with some additional aspects saved in an additional excel. The students applied agile methodologies and developed a medical attention mobile application using Blazor, C# and SQL Server. The project was developed by twenty students divided into four teams decided by the students with scrums of scrums [6]. At the end of the project, students added 1,035 commits and 279 user stories in the backlog. 230 stories were committed to a sprint or done.

Students were required to manually tag while committing the identifier of the associated user stories and tasks. After the course ended, the number of manual links between the commits and user stories was calculated. Out of 279 user stories, 55 were linked to only one commit, 102 were linked to various commits, and 122 had no linked commits. Meanwhile, for the 1,035 commits, 353 were linked to only one story, 92 were linked to multiple stories, and 590 were not linked to stories. Therefore 56.3% of the stories were linked to commits, and 43% of the commits were linked to stories.

The number of commits with linked stories by student and team is shown in Fig. 3. Each bar represents the number of commits committed or stories assigned to the student or team. Each color of the bar represents the number of commits or stories that were not linked (0), linked to one artifact (1) or linked to multiple artifacts (n). There was significant variance in the number of commits linked to stories by students (Subfigure 3a) and teams (Subfigure 3b). The unlinked commits by students ranged from 22% to 95%. Furthermore, commits were not linked proportionally to their commits. For example, S14 had a total of 45 commits and had an average commit contribution. Despite not being a top contributor for commits, S14 had the lowest number of unlinked commits. In total, 16 students, representing 80% of the students, linked commits to more than one story. Thus it was a frequent practice to implement more than one functionality per commit. The differences of linking practices for commits are also present in the teams, with unlinked commits ranging from 37% to 83%. Meanwhile, the user stories assigned by students (Subfigure 3c) or teams (Subfigure 3d) had a higher degree of linking than commits, but still, there was considerable variability. For the assigned stories, 4% to 72% of stories were unlinked. The unlinked stories average was 33%. There were even two students who had linked at least one commit to their assigned stories. Still, there are 65 stories without an assignee. These unassigned stories were unlinked in 98% of the stories. 21% to 67% of the stories assigned to a team were not linked to a commit.

[6] https://www.agilealliance.org/glossary/scrum-of-scrums

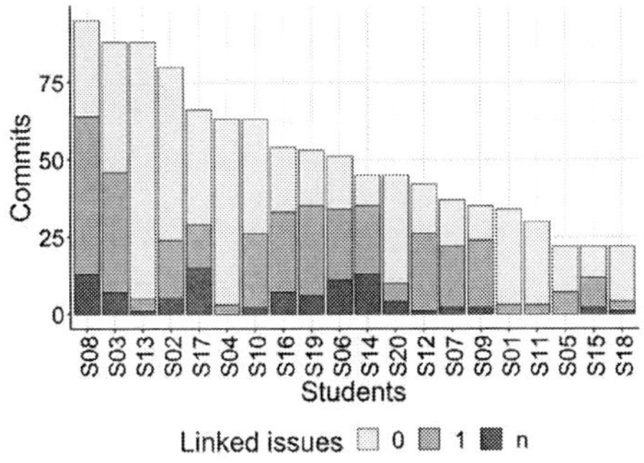

(a) Students' commits to stories

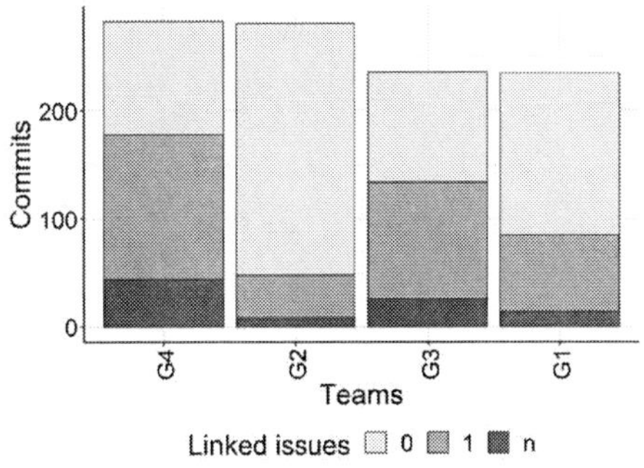

(b) Teams' commits to stories

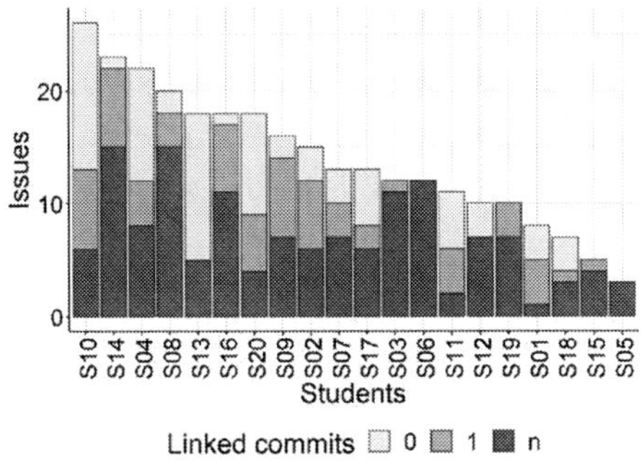

(c) Students' stories to commits

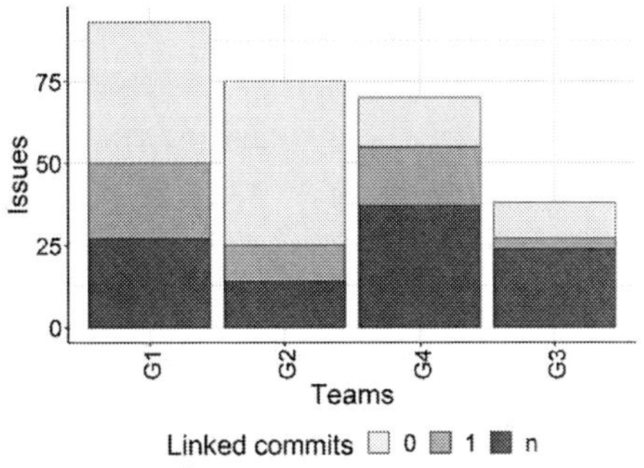

(d) Teams' stories to commits

Fig. 3: Manual links of students and teams

3.3 Threats to validity

There are several potential threats to the validity of our study. **External validity.** We studied an undergraduate software engineering project. A validity threat is related to how generalizable our results are to other projects, contexts and technologies. Thus, we cannot claim the generalizability of our results. As future work, we plan to evaluate additional undergraduate software engineering projects. **Internal validity.** The manual links were generated by the students' during the project as experts of the project. Thus we cannot guarantee the accuracy of the links. In order to mitigate the influence of grading in creating the links, the evaluation of the trace links was conducted after the project was finished. Only committed or done stories were used to create automatic trace links. There is a validity threat with regards to the selection of the stories used in the linking. To mitigate this threat we included any story that was committed or done in either Jira or excel. **Conclusion validity.** As information retrieval and machine learning models were used, a validity threat is concerned with how we evaluated the models. This threat was mitigated by using standard measures (precision, recall, and F-measure) for their evaluation. Furthermore, machine learning models were also balanced with sub-sampling. Finally, to reduce the effects of randomness while splitting the training and validation data, every model and set is tested ten times after splitting the data. **Construct validity.**

The constructed data set quality is a validity threat. To mitigate this threat, to construct the true and false links we used previously used heuristics.

4 Results and discussion

In this section, we detail (Subsection 4.1) and discuss (Subsection 4.2) the results of our study.

4.1 Results

Figure 4 shows the precision, recall and F-measure of the information retrieval models and sets. The x-axis represents the different models. The y-axis represents the value for each performance measure. The colors represent a different set. Each dot is a result for a model-set pair. The code and file sets have multiple dots per model-set pair as there are different strategies to calculate the total score. The best performing model was BM25 with the commit message, achieving an average precision of 32% and recall of 50%. Across all information retrieval models, the message attained the best results with 30% precision and 46% recall on average. Meanwhile, the files and code had similar performance. On average, files had 7% precision and 11% recall, and code had 6% precision and 10% recall. Furthermore, there was no singular strategy for selecting the total for files and code that had outperformed the performance of the models. Across all the models and sets, the recall was higher than precision. However, though the information retrieval models had a low performance, they were useful as they provided textual data for the machine learning models.

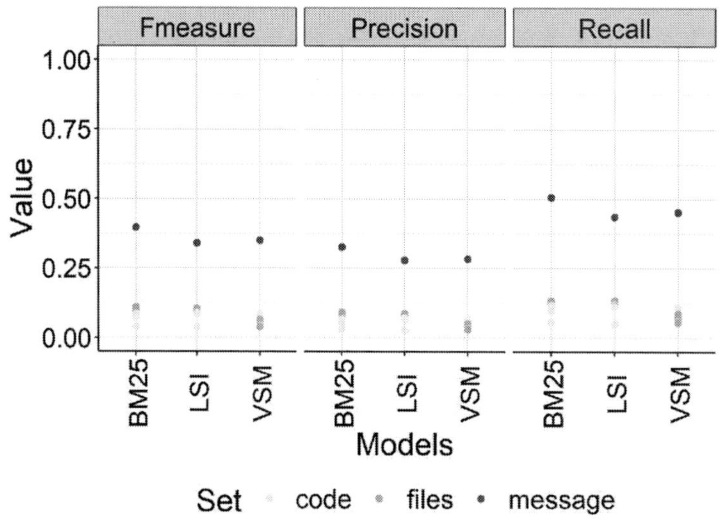

Fig. 4: Effectiveness of the information retrieval models

Figure 5 shows the precision, recall and F-measure of the machine learning models and feature sets. Each box plot represents the quartiles of the model-set pair. The RF model with the all set achieved the highest performance. The average precision was 93% and recall was 94%. Furthermore, the NN model with all the features obtained a very similar performance, with an average precision of 92% and recall of 94%. Still, both RF and NN had an average of 90% F-measure across the sets. Meanwhile, DT had an average 87% F-measure, thus were slightly less effective than RF and NN. Using all the features was the most effective set and it achieved 93% of precision, recall and F-measure on average. The process set was the second-best set with an average precision of 84% and recall of 98%. Specifically, the recall was very close to or was one for the process set. Lastly, the similarity set had the worst performance achieving an average precision and recall of 83%. Regarding the variance, the all set had a low variance. The all sets variance, on average, ranged between 1% to 2% for precision and recall. The similarity set variance was slightly more (on average) ranging between 3% to 5%. Lastly, using the process set, the variance was considerable across all models with an average 5% precision variance and 9% recall variance.

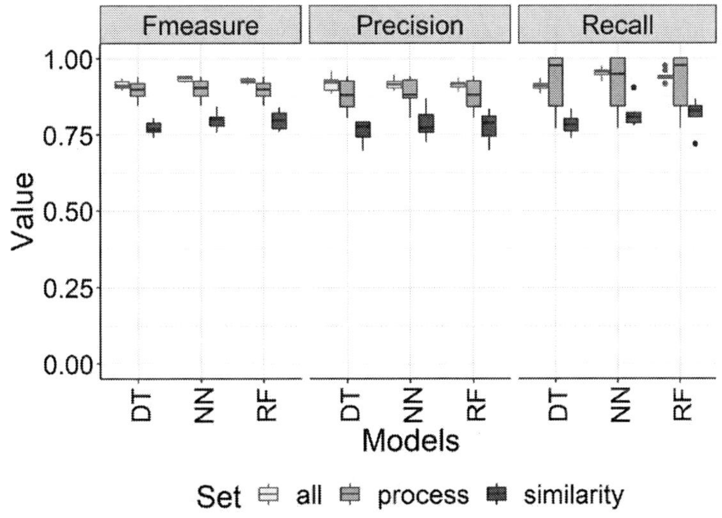

Fig. 5: Effectiveness of the machine learning models

4.2 Discussion

Our findings show that trace links were often incomplete in our project, which provides further empirical evidence of the need to create automatic or semi-automatic trace links. Previous studies reported that manual linking was approximately 48% of commits were not linked to issues, and ranged between 30% and 45% of issues were not linked to commits [10,11,18]. Our student undergraduate project had a similar percentage of missing commits links (43%), though the stories linked were slightly higher (56%) than the average reported by previous studies. We also found evidence that there is inequality in the linking process, with some students and teams students barely contributing to the manual linking. Hence, instructors must give further attention to verify if students are actually linking their commits, possibly with tool support.

We found that information retrieval models could achieve adequate precision by sacrificing the recall value. This seems to be in line with previous research results for information retrieval techniques in automatic link creation and maintenance, achieving low precision and higher recall [40]. However, these models did provide additional textual information to the machine learning models that helped improve their performance. The machine learning models attained high precision and recall, regenerating most commit-story links (true links) with few false links. Compared to other recent commit-issue approaches that accomplished and precision within the 90% using machine learning [10], we achieved similar results.

Our results are encouraging as machine learning approaches achieve good precision and recall in trace link recovery for student projects. Thus, instructors may further take advantage of traceability uses in their software development projects. With future validation, this approach may be used to help in semi-automatic or automatic link creation. Instructors could retrieve links automatically at any point of the project gathering insights from quantitive information about students' implementation trends during the process. Thus, the data gathered can be used to plan and monitor projects, helping grade assessment and improving the development process.

5 Conclusions

Manually creating trace links is often incomplete; therefore automatic or semi-automatic approaches are needed. Specifically, trace links are helpful in education as they can monitor projects, determine implementation contributions and help grade assessment. In this paper, we automatically recover trace links between commits and user stories in an undergraduate software engineering project. We applied our approach in a student project using agile methodologies with twenty students, 1,035 commits, and 230 committed or done stories. We found evidence that only 43% of the commits were linked to the stories. We evaluated both information retrieval and machine learning models to recover missing links. Algebraic and probabilistic information retrieval models achieved, in the best of the results, 32% precision and 50% recall. Even though information retrieval models did not achieve outstanding performance, they were helpful as they provided textual similarity information of the unstructured data. Thus, machine learning models, using a combination of textual and process data, achieved promising results. In the best case, these models reached 93% of precision and 94% of recall. The results demonstrate the applicability of the approach to recover links in projects to help monitor and evaluation of 'students' contributions during the development of the project.

In future work, we plan to extend our analysis to other undergraduate software engineering projects. Additionally, this work could be further expanded using different models and other data from the commits and issues. Further research is needed in creating automatic trace links in students' projects in-vivo to determine the accuracy and feasibility of the approach to create links. Additionally, creating tools to help monitor the projects' traceability. Further research could also gather students' and instructors' perceptions of the benefits and challenges of traceability in educational projects. Research can also be conducted to gather instructors' and students' benefits and current traceability challenges in an educational context. Additional research can also analyze students' trends between commits and issues to determine behavioral patterns. Finally, research can also validate trace link recovery in projects developed by the industry.

Acknowledgments. This research was partially funded by Universidad de Costa Rica, project No. 834-C1-011.

References

1. J. Cleland-Huang, O. Gotel, and A. Zisman, Eds., *Software and Systems Traceability.* London: Springer London, 2012.
2. H. U. Asuncion, F. François, and R. N. Taylor, "An end-to-end industrial software traceability tool," in *Proceedings of the the 6th joint meeting of the European software engineering conference and the ACM SIGSOFT symposium on The foundations of software engineering*, 2007, pp. 115–124.
3. P. Mäder, P. L. Jones, Y. Zhang, and J. Cleland-Huang, "Strategic traceability for safety-critical projects," *IEEE software*, vol. 30, no. 3, pp. 58–66, 2013.
4. D. Ståhl, K. Hallén, and J. Bosch, "Achieving traceability in large scale continuous integration and delivery deployment, usage and validation of the eiffel framework," *Empirical Software Engineering*, vol. 22, no. 3, pp. 967–995, 2017.
5. P. Hübner and B. Paech, "Interaction-based creation and maintenance of continuously usable trace links between requirements and source code," *Empirical Software Engineering*, vol. 25, no. 5, pp. 4350–4377, Sep. 2020.
6. R. Torkar, T. Gorschek, R. Feldt, M. Svahnberg, U. A. Raja, and K. Kamran, "Requirements traceability: A systematic review and industry case study," *International Journal of Software Engineering and Knowledge Engineering*, vol. 22, no. 03, pp. 385–433, May 2012.
7. R. M. Parizi, S. P. Lee, and M. Dabbagh, "Achievements and Challenges in State-of-the-Art Software Traceability Between Test and Code Artifacts," *IEEE Transactions on Reliability*, vol. 63, no. 4, pp. 913–926, Dec. 2014.
8. S. Winkler and J. von Pilgrim, "A survey of traceability in requirements engineering and model-driven development," *Software & Systems Modeling*, vol. 9, no. 4, pp. 529–565, Sep. 2013.
9. E. Bouillon, P. Mäder, and I. Philippow, "A Survey on Usage Scenarios for Requirements Traceability in Practice," in *International Working Conference on Requirements Engineering: Foundation for Software Quality.* Springer, 2013, pp. 158–173.
10. H. Ruan, B. Chen, X. Peng, and W. Zhao, "DeepLink: Recovering issue-commit links based on deep learning," *Journal of Systems and Software*, vol. 158, p. 110406, Dec. 2019.

11. M. Rath, J. Rendall, J. L. C. Guo, J. Cleland-Huang, and P. Mäder, "Traceability in the Wild: Automatically Augmenting Incomplete Trace Links," in *2018 IEEE/ACM 40th International Conference on Software Engineering (ICSE)*, May 2018, pp. 834–845.
12. S. Otte, "Version Control Systems," *Computer Systems and Telematics*, 2009.
13. D. Bertram, A. Voida, S. Greenberg, and R. Walker, "Communication, collaboration, and bugs: The social nature of issue tracking in small, collocated teams," in *Proceedings of the 2010 ACM Conference on Computer Supported Cooperative Work*, ser. CSCW '10. New York, NY, USA: Association for Computing Machinery, Feb. 2010, pp. 291–300.
14. J. Śliwerski, T. Zimmermann, and A. Zeller, "When do changes induce fixes?" *ACM SIGSOFT Software Engineering Notes*, vol. 30, no. 4, pp. 1–5, May 2005.
15. S. Hamer, C. Quesada-López, A. Martínez, and M. Jenkins, "Measuring students' contributions in software development projects using Git metrics," in *2020 XLVI Latin American Computing Conference (CLEI)*. IEEE, 2020, p. 10.
16. ——, "Measuring Students' Source Code Quality in Software Development Projects Through Commit-Impact Analysis," in *Information Technology and Systems*, vol. 1331. Cham: Springer International Publishing, 2021, pp. 100–109.
17. J. Cleland-Huang, M. Rahimi, and P. Mäder, "Achieving lightweight trustworthy traceability," in *Proceedings of the 22nd ACM SIGSOFT International Symposium on Foundations of Software Engineering - FSE 2014*. Hong Kong, China: ACM Press, 2014, pp. 849–852.
18. J. Polaczek and J. Sosnowski, "Exploring the software repositories of embedded systems: An industrial experience," *Information and Software Technology*, vol. 131, p. 106489, Mar. 2021.
19. R. Wu, H. Zhang, S. Kim, and S.-C. Cheung, "ReLink: Recovering links between bugs and changes," in *Proceedings of the 19th ACM SIGSOFT Symposium and the 13th European Conference on Foundations of Software Engineering*, ser. ESEC/FSE '11. New York, NY, USA: Association for Computing Machinery, Sep. 2011, pp. 15–25.
20. A. Nguyen, T. Nguyen, H. Nguyen, and T. Nguyen, "Multi-layered approach for recovering links between bug reports and fixes," in *Proceedings of the ACM SIGSOFT 20th International Symposium on the Foundations of Software Engineering, FSE 2012*, 2012.
21. P. Hübner and B. Paech, "Evaluation of Techniques to Detect Wrong Interaction Based Trace Links," in *Requirements Engineering: Foundation for Software Quality*, E. Kamsties, J. Horkoff, and F. Dalpiaz, Eds. Cham: Springer International Publishing, 2018, vol. 10753, pp. 75–91.
22. M. Borg, P. Runeson, and A. Ardö, "Recovering from a decade: A systematic mapping of information retrieval approaches to software traceability," vol. 19, no. 6, pp. 1565–1616, Dec. 2014.
23. Y. Sun, Q. Wang, and Y. Yang, "FRLink: Improving the recovery of missing issue-commit links by revisiting file relevance," *Information and Software Technology*, vol. 84, pp. 33–47, 2017.
24. Y. Sun, C. Chen, Q. Wang, and B. Boehm, "Improving missing issue-commit link recovery using positive and unlabeled data," in *2017 32nd IEEE/ACM International Conference on Automated Software Engineering (ASE)*, Oct. 2017, pp. 147–152.
25. S. Chacon and B. Straub, *Pro Git*. Apress, Nov. 2014.

26. S. Dimitrijević, J. Jovanović, and V. Devedžić, "A comparative study of software tools for user story management," *Information and Software Technology*, vol. 57, pp. 352–368, 2015.
27. M. Cohn, *User Stories Applied: For Agile Software Development*, ser. Addison-Wesley Signature Series. Boston: Addison-Wesley, 2004.
28. R. Baeza-Yates and B. Ribeiro-Neto, *Modern Information Retrieval.* ACM press New York, 1999.
29. M. F. Porter, "An algorithm for suffix stripping," *Program*, 1980.
30. S. Bird, E. Klein, and E. Loper, *Natural language processing with Python: analyzing text with the natural language toolkit.* " O'Reilly Media, Inc.", 2009.
31. M. Johnson, M. Schuster, Q. V. Le, M. Krikun, Y. Wu, Z. Chen, N. Thorat, F. Viégas, M. Wattenberg, G. Corrado, M. Hughes, and J. Dean, "Google's Multilingual Neural Machine Translation System: Enabling Zero-Shot Translation," *Transactions of the Association for Computational Linguistics*, vol. 5, pp. 339–351, Dec. 2017.
32. T. Vale and E. S. de Almeida, "Experimenting with information retrieval methods in the recovery of feature-code SPL traces," *Empirical Software Engineering*, vol. 24, no. 3, pp. 1328–1368, Jun. 2019.
33. G. Amati, "Information Retrieval Models," in *Encyclopedia of Database Systems*, L. Liu and M. T. Özsu, Eds. New York, NY: Springer, 2018, pp. 1976–1981.
34. M. Melucci, "Vector-Space Model," in *Encyclopedia of Database Systems*, L. LIU and M. T. ÖZSU, Eds. Boston, MA: Springer US, 2009, pp. 3259–3263.
35. G. W. Furnas, S. Deerwester, S. T. Dumais, T. K. Landauer, R. A. Harshman, L. A. Streeter, and K. E. Lochbaum, "Information retrieval using a singular value decomposition model of latent semantic structure," in *Proceedings of the 11th Annual International ACM SIGIR Conference on Research and Development in Information Retrieval*, ser. SIGIR '88. New York, NY, USA: Association for Computing Machinery, May 1988, pp. 465–480.
36. S. Robertson, H. Zaragoza, and M. Taylor, "Simple BM25 extension to multiple weighted fields," in *Proceedings of the Thirteenth ACM International Conference on Information and Knowledge Management*, ser. CIKM '04. New York, NY, USA: Association for Computing Machinery, Nov. 2004, pp. 42–49.
37. A. Trotman, A. Puurula, and B. Burgess, "Improvements to BM25 and Language Models Examined," in *Proceedings of the 2014 Australasian Document Computing Symposium*, ser. ADCS '14. New York, NY, USA: Association for Computing Machinery, Nov. 2014, pp. 58–65.
38. R. Řehůřek and P. Sojka, "Software Framework for Topic Modelling with Large Corpora," in *Proceedings of the LREC 2010 Workshop on New Challenges for NLP Frameworks.* Valletta, Malta: ELRA, May 2010, pp. 45–50.
39. F. Pedregosa, G. Varoquaux, A. Gramfort, V. Michel, B. Thirion, O. Grisel, M. Blondel, P. Prettenhofer, R. Weiss, V. Dubourg *et al.*, "Scikit-learn: Machine learning in python," *Journal of Machine Learning Research*, vol. 12, pp. 2825–2830, 2011.
40. O. Gotel, J. Cleland-Huang, J. H. Hayes, A. Zisman, A. Egyed, P. Grünbacher, and G. Antoniol, "The quest for Ubiquity: A roadmap for software and systems traceability research," in *2012 20th IEEE International Requirements Engineering Conference (RE)*, Sep. 2012, pp. 71–80.

Multi-objective Hyper-parameter Tuning for Software Effort Estimation

Leonardo Villalobos-Arias, Christian Quesada-López, Alexandra Martinez, and Marcelo Jenkins

University of Costa Rica, San Pedro de Montes de Oca, Costa Rica
{leonardo.villalobosarias, cristian.quesadalopez, alexandra.martinez, marcelo.jenkins}@ucr.ac.cr

Abstract. Studies of software effort estimation (SEE) have employed machine learning techniques to improve the accuracy of their predictions but concerns about the stability (and thus, replicability) of these models have been raised. In this study, we evaluate the impact of multi-objective hyper-parameter tuning on the accuracy and stability of five effort estimation algorithms: support vector regression (SVR), classification and regression trees (CART), and three versions of ridge regression (RR). Each model had two variants, for a total of 10: no data transformation and using logarithmig (Log). We compare the single- and multi-objective implementations of twelve hyper-parameter tuners, and evaluate their accuracy and stability on four subsets of the ISBSG R18 dataset. We evaluate the random search, flash, dodge, differential evolution, particle swarm optimization, tabu search, genetic algorithm (GA), one plus one GA, compact GA, bayesian optimization, harmony search, and hyperband tuners. The results indicated that, out of the 480 total (10 models × 12 tuners × 4 datasets) studied models, multi-objective tuning improved their stability on 159 cases (33%) and maintained it on 268 cases (56%), while improving accuracy on 60 cases (13%) and maintaining it on 247 (51%) cases. The effect of multi-objective tuning depended on the underlying model. For Log+SVR models, it was particularly effective, improving or maintaining accuracy in 65% of cases, and improving stability in 77% of cases. Multi-objective tuning also had a positive effect on CART and Log+CART models. In terms of accuracy, the most effective tuners were differential evolution, flash, genetic algorithm, and compact genetic algorithm when paired with Log+SVR.

Keywords: software effort estimation · hyper-parameter tuning · machine learning · multi-objective optimization · empirical study

1 Introduction

Software effort estimation (SEE), is an essential task of project management [6]. A key issue for software organizations is to accurately and consistently predict effort, as either overestimates and underestimates can result in missed business opportunities and threats for project development [14]. For these reasons, machine learning techniques have been used in SEE to create higher accuracy estimation models [8]. Recent SEE studies apply hyper-parameter tuning (the process of automatically finding optimal model hyper-parameters) [2, 35] for building accurate models [36].

Machine learning research on software engineering had centered around improving the accuracy of the model [8], but it has recently shifted its focus to include additional model qualities such as stability [29]. Stability refers to an effect that holds for different situations [16]. In the context of SEE, a stable model should have similar accuracy when replicated or tested on different datasets. On the contrary, an unstable model may produce inconsistent results under different circumstances [17]. The introduction of hyper-parameter tuning techniques can affect the stability and accuracy of the SEE models [26]. Fortunately, current defect prediction studies [29] demonstrate that tuned models are as stable as untuned models.

Our previous work has focused on the evaluation of hyper-parameter tuning approaches with respect to their ability to improve accuracy and stability [31–33]. Such approaches seek to minimize the average prediction error, but overlook the importance of producing effort estimates that lie in a consistent margin of error [21]. By incorporating multi-objective optimization, a hyper-parameter tuner could accomplish both objectives simultaneously.

In this paper, we investigate multi-objective tuning by optimizing the hyper-parameter search for both model accuracy and stability. Our aim is to determine how multi-objective tuning compares to single-objective tuning. To accomplish this, we evaluated 14 single-objective hyper-parameter tuners (including default parameters) and 12 multi-objective hyper-parameter tuners, applied to five machine learning algorithms, two transformations, and four datasets. We extended the scope of our most recent work [33] by evaluating additional hyper-parameter tuning approaches and incorporating multi-objective tuning. This paper is organized as follows: Section 2 presents related work; Section 3 describes the study design; Section 4 shows the results; and section 5 outlines the conclusions.

2 Related Work

Langsari et al. [13] employed a fuzzy multi-objective particle swarm optimization approach to find the optimal parameter values for the COCOMO II model, and compared these results to a COCOMO II model with traditional values. Their adjusted COCOMO model performed mode accurate estimations than the default model. Similarly, Azzeh et al. [5] investigated multi-objective particle swarm optimization to adjust the hyper-parameters of analogy-based estimation. Their results highlight the importance of simultaneously tuning all hyper-parameters and its noticeable impact to analogy based estimation. A study by Sarro et al. [21] introduced a dual-objective algorithm for effort estimation, which optimizes both the sum of absolute errors and the prediction confidence interval. They compared it with state of the art techniques. Their results show that the proposed approach outperforms state of the art techniques in terms of standardized accuracy, and that multi-objective approaches can improve model performance.

Recent literature on software engineering has studied the effectiveness of heuristics-based fast tuners as an alternative to exhaustive search. Agrawal *et al.* [1, 2] proposed the dodge as a novel optimizer that searches for "interesting" hyper-parameter combinations and avoids redundant settings. Fu *et al.* [10, 9] analyzed the effectiveness of a differential evolution algorithm applied to the tuning of defect prediction models. In the area of configurable software systems, Nair et al. [18] used flash tuner, a method that determines the most promising exploration points based on a prediction model. Xia et al. [35] evaluated both flash tuner and differential evolution algorithm in the context of effort estimation.

Researchers have also studied bio-inspired tuning methods. Ali et al. [4] used genetic algorithms, particle swarm optimization, ant colony optimization, and tabu, harmony, and firefly searches for feature selection and tuning. The study by Palaniswamy et al. [20] used particle swarm optimization and genetic algorithms to improve the performance of ensemble learners. Oliviera et al. [19] employed genetic algorithms for simultaneous tuning of hyper-parameters and selection of features in SEE models.

This study further investigates the use of multi-objective optimization in SEE in conjunction with many of the hyper-parameter tuners used in the literature.

3 Study design

The main objective of this study was to evaluate the impact of multi-objective optimization hyper-parameter tuning on accuracy and stability, in the context of SEE models. The following research questions were proposed to guide the study:

RQ1 What is the prediction accuracy and stability of single-objective hyper-parameter tuning?

RQ2 Does multi-objective hyper-parameter tuning improve the prediction accuracy and stability?

Figure 1 shows the model training and evaluation process used in this study. Each task on the process corresponds with a section in the paper. The process is supported by our our evaluation framework, which implements or adapts the machine learning techniques used in this study. This framework was built upon the scikit-learn library using Python 3.7, and supports three machine learning activities: (1) preprocessing, (2) training and evaluation, and (3) statistical analysis. Section 3.1 shows the dataset used in this study and preprocessing performed. Section 3.2 describes the process used to train and evaluate SEE models. Section 3.3 contains the studied algorithms that are combined to create SEE models, the evaluation metrics, and configurations for multi-objective optimization. The statistical analysis performed to the results of this study is detailed in section 4.

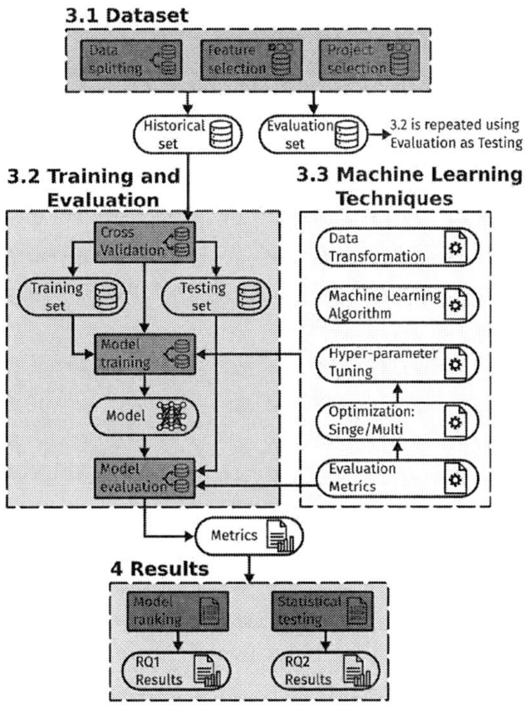

Fig. 1: Machine learning framework and process.

3.1 Dataset

We employed the International Software Benchmarking Standards Group Development & Enhancement 2018 Repository Release 1 (ISBSG R18) dataset. Based on previous research [8, 26, 32], we performed a three-step preprocessing that included data splitting, project selection, and feature selection.

Data splitting We splitted the data by their function point measurement unit, opting to use IFPUG 4+ and COSMIC. From these, we generated two datasets: one using total function points (FP), and another using the base functional components (BFC). This produced four datasets: IFPUG 4+ UFP (unified function points), IFPUG 4+ BFC, COSMIC FFP (full function points), and COSMIC BFC.

Project selection We selected projects that met these criteria: (a) data point quality A or B, (b) function point quality A or B if function point type is IFPUG 4+, (c) development type is "new development", and (d) projects with recorded effort values for the development team. The reason being that we were interested in investigating effort estimation of new projects using reliable project data, based on literature recommendations [8, 26].

Feature selection We selected those features that are both available and pertinent to the effort estimation process [8, 11]. Besides functional size features, the final feature set included Application Group, Architecture, Case Tool Used, Development Methodologies, Development Platform, Industry Sector, Intended Market, Language Type, Max Team Size, Team Size Group, Used Methodology, and Year of Project. We used Summary Work Effort as our target feature.

We randomly selected and removed 10% of the data in each dataset, to be used later in the evaluation (evaluation set). The remaining 90% of the data (historical set) was used in the training and evaluation activity. The evaluation set is used to review the metrics obtained in this study and discard problems such as overfitting and data mismatch.

3.2 Training and evaluation

We performed two evaluation runs using a set of 14 hyper-parameter tuners: one using single-objective optimization on prediction accuracy, and another using multi-objective optimization on prediction accuracy and stability. For the single-objective evaluation run, we used 5 machine learning algorithms, 2 transformation alternatives (log data transformation and no transformation), and 14 hyper-parameter tuners (including default parameters). A total of $5 \times 2 \times 14 = 140$ machine learning models were constructed by combining these configurations. For the multi-objective evaluation run, we only used 12 hyper-parameter tuners, plus the same 5 algorithms and 2 transformations as before. This yielded $5 \times 2 \times 12 = 120$ additional models. The two tuners excluded from the multi-objective run were default parameters and grid search.

We trained each model using 10 times 10-fold cross-validation, as suggested by previous research [27, 28]. To do this, we partitioned the dataset into 10 random groups of even size. Then we chose one partition as test set and the remaining nine as training set, and repeated this until each partition had been used once as testing set. The entire process was repeated ten times, for a total of 100 runs. All 100 partitions were randomly created beforehand to ensure that the 260 models were run over the same data. Each model instance was trained using its corresponding training set. Each hyper-parameter tuning internally performed a sub-partition using 10-fold cross-validation to adjust find optimal values. The model is re-trained with the selected parameter(s) using the entire training set. The evaluation metrics (section 3.3) are calculated on every testing set for a total sample of 100 metrics per model and dataset.

3.3 Machine learning techniques

Machine learning algorithms: Five machine learning algorithms were used to predict software effort values: classification and regression trees (CART) [7], support vector regression (SVR) [34], and three variants of ridge regression (RR) as a base for comparison [8]. The RR variants used were: normal ridge regression, ridge regression with percentile correlation as feature selection (CP+RR) [23], and ridge regression with threshold variance as feature selection (VT+RR) [3]. Table 1 shows the hyper-parameter search space, selected based on literature suggestions [27, 15]. Feature selection was not used for CART and SVR models,

Table 1: Hyper-parameter search space.

Model	Hyper-parameters' values
CART	min_samples_leaf = $\{1,2,3,...,20\}$; max_depth = $\{1,2,3,...,20\}$; min_impurity_decrease = $(10^x,\ x=\{-5,-4.5,-4,...,0\})$
SVR	$C = 1,5,15,30,\{50,100,\ ...\ ,450\},\{500,1000,\ ...\ ,15000\}$; kernel = {rbf, sigmoid}; $\gamma = (10^x,\ x=\{-3,-2.5,-2,...,-0.5\})$; auto, scale; $\epsilon = 10^x,\ x=\{-3,-2.5,-2,...,-0.5\}$
RR	$\alpha = 1,\{5,10,...,45\},\{50,75,...,500\}$
VT+RR	*threshold* $= 0,0.01,0.05,0.1,0.2,0.3,0.4,0.5$; α from RR
CP+RR	*percentile* $= \{10,20,30,\ ...\ ,90\}$; α from RR

as we determined in previous iterations of this experiment that the two studied feature selectors did not affect the accuracy and stability of the CART and SVR models. For tuning techniques that explore ranges of values (i.e., GA and DODGE), the minimum and maximum values were used for numerical features. Two varations of each model were used: one with no data transformation, and one with the logarithmic (Log) transformation.

Hyper-parameter tuners: Our evaluation comprised 14 different tuners used in SEE literature [33] and other research areas [36]. We employed the scikit-learn implementation of default hyper-parameters, random search (RS), and grid search (GS) as performance baseline. We also evaluated the flash (FS), dodge (DG), and differential evolution (DE) tuners, since recent SE literature has endorsed the use of such fast and effective optimizers [9, 18, 2]. As traditional tuners from the SEE literature, we selected particle swarm optimization (PSO), tabu search (TS), and three variants of genetic algorithms: traditional genetic (GA), one plus one (1+1), and compact genetic algorithm (CGA). We also evaluated algorithms used in other areas: Bayesian optimization (BO), harmony search (HS) and hyperband (HB). For each of the 14 methods, two variants were run: a single-objective variant (optimizing for standardized accuracy) and a multi-objective variant (optimizing for hyperspace). Grid search was not run using multi-objective optimization as it was too computer-intensive.

Evaluation metrics: The **accuracy** of the SEE models was measured using absolute residual metrics (based on the absolute difference between predicted and actual values): the median absolute residual ($MdAR$) and the standardized accuracy (SA) [25]. To measure the improvement on accuracy (with respect to default parameters), we used the improvement ratio (imp) [29]. On the other hand, the **stability** of the tuners was measured by the stability ratio [29] based on the standard deviation of the absolute residual (SdAR), and by the standardized stability (SD).

$MdAR$ and $SdAR$ correspond to the median and standard deviation of the absolute residuals, respectively. SA is computed as proposed by Shepperd and MacDonell [24], using the random estimation baseline model $MdAR_{p0}$ recommended by Langdon *et al.* [12]. Additionally, we included our own metric SD, similar to SA, for which the $SdAR$ is normalized using the standard deviation of random estimation baseline model, $SdAR_{p0}$. SD is calculated as $1 - SdAR/SdAR_{p0}$.

In order to calculate the metrics for the multi-objective approaches, we computed the average of the points in the Pareto front, as done in previous studies [21, 30] to compare single- and multi-objective methods. In real SEE applications, one of these points would be selected based on certain preference or decision. However, for the purpose of this study we wanted to consider all possible points and, to not favor specific solutions, we used the mean aggregated metrics.

Multi-objective optimization Implementations of hyper-parameter tuning algorithms are traditionally designed to (1) optimize only one metric and (2) return the best solution –usually one point in the search space. Thus, our tuners had to be adapted for multi-objective optimization. First, a composite metric was used to weight in both stability and accuracy. Second, the Pareto front of the search space was employed.

Multi-objective function: Random and grid search hyper-parameter tuners evaluate a set of points from the search space, either by random sampling or considering all possibilities. However, most of the hyper-parameter tuners in this study take a heuristic approach: they determine what is a 'good' (or 'bad') point in the search space, and select the next portion of the space to explore based on this information. A function (SA in our case) is then used to score each explored point in the space. For multi-objective tuning, the tuners maximized the function $(SA + 1) \times (SD + 1)$.

Evaluation of multiple solutions: The Pareto front of the searched values was identified. This set consists of all non-dominant solutions. A solution p_1 is said to dominate another solution p_2 if p_1 is equally good or better than p_2 for every metric. Conversely, a solution p_2 cannot be dominated by another solution p_1 if either p_2 has the same values as p_1 for each metric, or p_2 has at least one metric better than p_1. Thus, all points in the Pareto front offer different but equally viable trade-offs between accuracy and stability.

4 Results

4.1 Accuracy and stability of single-objective tuning (RQ1)

In order to rank the studied SEE models, we used the Scott-Knott algorithm [22], which employs hierarchical clustering to partition treatments into equivalent groups. This analysis was performed twice for each dataset: one for SA and one for SD. The Box-Cox transformation was applied to these metrics before the analysis, as Scott-Knott requires its input to follow a normal distribution. Ridge regression techniques were excluded from the analysis due to their low accuracy. Even hyper-parameter tuning did not improve the accuracy of ridge models. We refer to the ranks determined by the Scott-Knott analysis as dataset ranks.

A second Scott-Knott analysis grouped the techniques based on their overall performance. This analysis was applied on the ranks obtained from the first analysis, normalized to the $[0, 1]$ scale. For this, we used the transformation $1 - (r_i - 1)/(R - 1)$, where r_i is the rank of the i-th model and R is the amount of ranks. We refer to the ranks determined by the second Scott-Knott analysis as general ranks. Figure 2 shows the distribution of dataset ranks for each technique, grouped by their general rank.

The analysis on SA determined four general groups: the first group comprises tuned Log+SVR models, except traditional RS and GS tuners; the second group contains all tuned CART and Log+CART models as well as GS+Log+SVR and RS+Log+SVR; the third group has all tuned SVR models except those with CGA and DG; the fourth group contains the four untuned models, plus CGA+SVR and DG+SVR. Four models obtained the first dataset rank in all cases: CGA+Log+SVR, DE+Log+SVR, FS+Log+SVR, and GA+Log+SVR.

When performed on SD, the Scott-Knott analysis determined three general groups: the first group contains all tuned CART, Log+CART, and (CGA, DE, FS, GA, DG, DE, and GA)+Log+SVR; the second group includes the remaining tuned Log+SVR models, TS+SVR, RS+SVR, PSO+SVR, GS+SVR, and CGA+SVR; the third group comprises the remaining tuned SVR models and the four untuned models. Within the first group, four models obtained the first dataset ranking in all except IFPUG 4+ BFC, where they obtained the second ranking. These models are CGA+Log+SVR, DE+Log+SVR, FS+Log+SVR, and GA+Log+SVR.

From these groups, it can be observed that hyper-parameter tuning improved both the accuracy and the stability of CART, Log+CART, SVR, and Log+SVR models. For SVR, only the TS, PSO, GS and RS tuners improved both qualities. For CART and Log+CART models, all tuners provided similar improvements in both accuracy and stability. For SVR and Log+SVR, the choice of tuner affected the outcome, as demonstrated by the general groups. Overall, SVR benefited the most from DE tuning, and Log+SVR from DE, GA, CGA, and FS.

Table 2 shows the SA and SD scores, and highlights the most accurate models (with database rank 1 and 2). Log+SVR is shown as a reference point for untuned models. Hyper-parameter tuning provided significant improvements in mean SA in the top models with respect to its default counterpart. The gain in accuracy was at its peak in FFP datasets, ranging from 0.139 to 0.2 SA in COSMIC FFP, and from 0.123 to 0.168 SA in IFPUG 4+ UFP. Tuning in BFC datasets was less impactful, ranging from 0.089 to 0.116 SA in IFPUG 4+ BFC, and from 0.055 to 0.075 SA in COSMIC BFC. A similar pattern occurs in SD, where tuning had a larger improvement in stability on IFPUG 4+ UFP, ranging

Table 2: Mean *SA*, *SD*, and dataset rank of the most accurate models.

	SA				SD			
	IFPUG 4+		COSMIC		IFPUG 4+		COSMIC	
Model	FFP	BFC	FFP	BFC	FFP	BFC	FFP	BFC
CGA+Log+SVR	0.534	0.481	0.479	0.334	0.426	0.313	0.408	0.255
DE+Log+SVR	0.534	0.476	0.461	0.346	0.430	0.311	0.394	0.240
FS+Log+SVR	0.537	0.484	0.469	0.347	0.450	0.321	0.416	0.239
GA+Log+SVR	0.532	0.480	0.459	0.338	0.440	0.312	0.410	0.237
BO+Log+SVR	0.502	0.463	0.424	0.346	0.318	0.281	0.353	0.222
HB+Log+SVR	0.498	0.463	0.431	0.347	0.308	0.281	0.354	0.235
HS+Log+SVR	0.492	0.458	0.439	0.349	0.312	0.279	0.351	0.232
DG+Log+SVR	0.503	0.464	0.424	0.346	0.329	0.286	0.330	0.248
1+1+Log+SVR	0.496	0.459	0.418	0.344	0.315	0.282	0.365	0.231
PSO+Log+SVR	0.501	0.458	0.425	0.329	0.318	0.275	0.347	0.227
TS+Log+SVR	0.505	0.457	0.426	0.345	0.334	0.279	0.341	0.235
Log+SVR	0.369	0.368	0.279	0.274	0.216	0.222	0.209	0.212

Rank 1 Rank 2 Rank 3+

from 0.092 to 0.234 *SD*, and COSMIC FFP, ranging from 0.121 to 0.207 *SD*. In contrast, the effect was lower on IFPUG 4+ BFC, ranging from 0.053 to 0.099 *SD*, and COSMIC BFC, ranging from 0.01 to 0.043 *SD*.

Single-objective hyper-parameter tuning improved the accuracy and stability of CART and SVR based models, but had no effect on RR. In both accuracy and stability, the models with the highest metrics were Log+SVR tuned with differential evolution, flash, genetic algorithm, or compact genetic algorithm.

4.2 Accuracy and stability of multi-objective tuning (RQ2)

Comparing the performance of single- and multi- objective tuning was done by means of Wilcoxon signed-rank tests (at 0.05 significance level). These tests were performed for the two metrics *SA* and *SD*. Separate tests were done for each of the four datasets and 120 models, yielding a total of 480 tests for each metric.

Table 3 shows the win-tie-loss statistics on the results of the Wilcoxon signed-rank test, grouped by (a) tuner and (b) machine learning technique. These statistics are calculated by counting the results of each test: a *win* if the test determines a difference ($p < 0.05$) and multi-objective has a higher metric, a *loss* if the test determines a difference and single-objective has a higher metric, and a *tie* if the test determines no difference ($p \geq 0.05$). In total, multi-objective tuning scored 60 wins, 247 ties, and 173 losses in *SA*, and 159 wins, 268 ties, and 53 losses on *SD*.

All the multi-objective tuners had similar statistics. Regarding accuracy, the tuners maintained accuracy in 17 to 27 cases (out of 50 cases), and were able to improve it in 1 to 10 cases. However, they incurred in loss of accuracy in 9

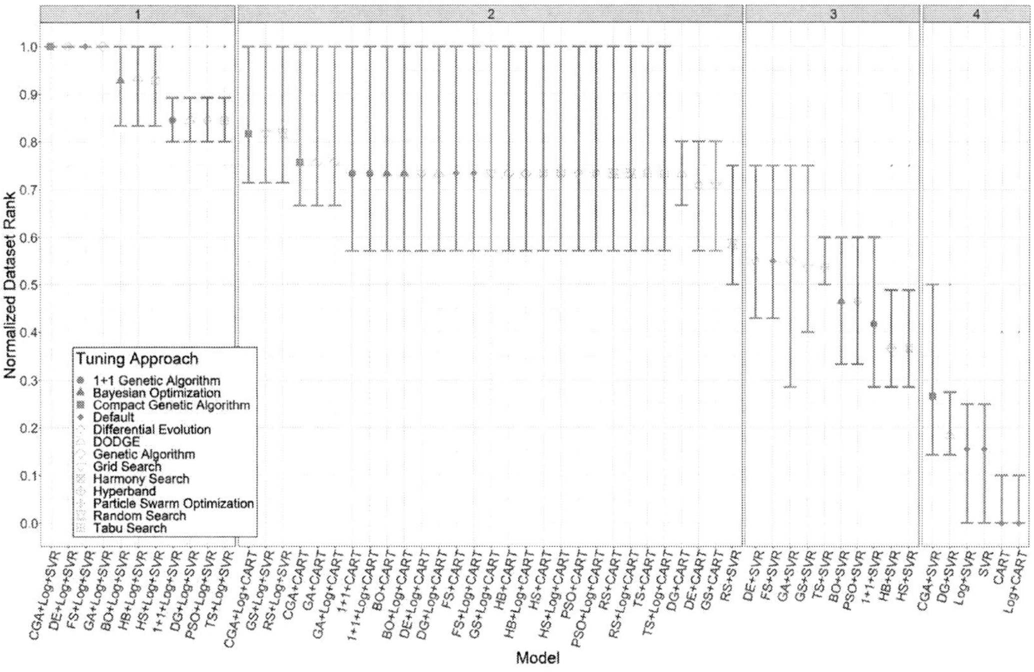

(a) Rank on SA.

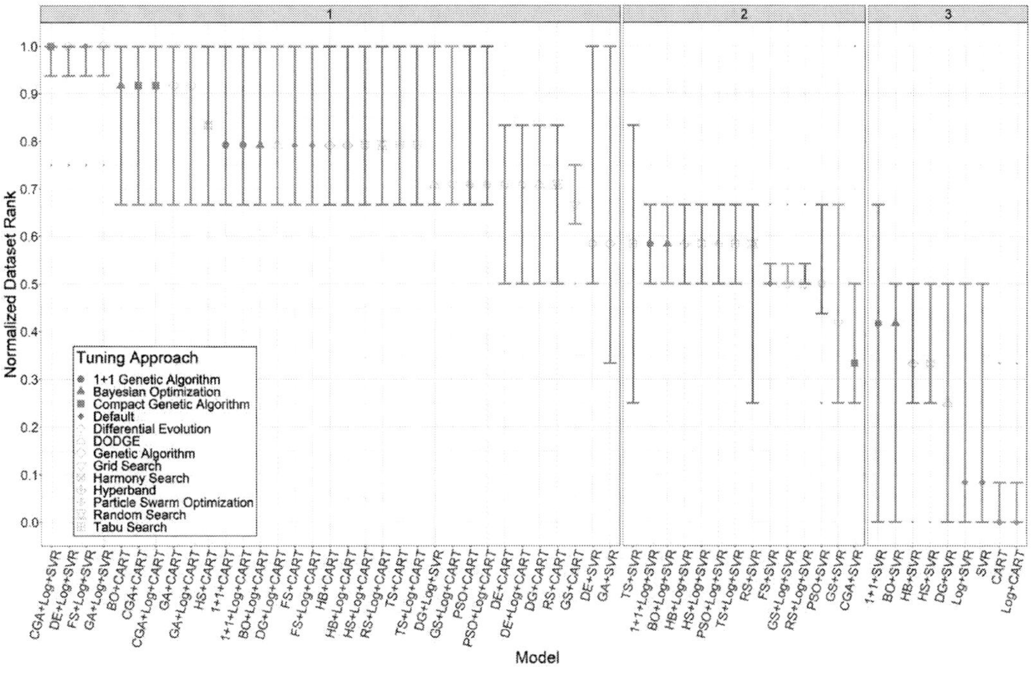

(b) Rank on SD.

Fig. 2: Distribution of dataset ranks for each SVR and CART model.

Table 3: Win-tie-loss statistics for multi-objective vs. single objective tuning.

(a) Hyper-parameter tuning

	SA			SD		
Tuner	W	T	L	W	T	L
1+1	6	25	9	20	18	2
BO	9	21	10	13	22	5
CGA	1	19	20	11	27	2
DE	1	21	18	6	29	5
DG	4	17	19	12	21	7
FS	1	27	12	12	21	7
GA	1	17	22	10	27	3
HB	6	18	16	18	18	4
HS	9	20	11	14	21	5
PSO	5	20	15	13	21	6
RS	10	21	9	16	21	3
TS	7	21	12	14	22	4
	60	247	173	159	268	53

(b) Machine learning technique

	SA			SD		
Model	W	T	L	W	T	L
SVR	2	14	32	29	15	4
Log+SVR	21	10	17	37	6	5
CART	4	44	0	8	37	3
Log+CART	6	40	2	10	38	0
RR	9	25	14	7	33	8
Log+RR	0	23	25	15	24	9
CP+RR	2	31	15	10	34	4
Log+CP+RR	2	13	33	12	29	7
VT+RR	10	29	9	15	26	7
Log+VT+RR	4	18	26	16	26	6
	60	247	173	159	268	53

to 22 cases (44% of cases in the worst scenario). The four tuners with highest accuracy from section 4.1 were those with the least improvement on accuracy. The CGA, DE, FS, and GA tuners registered only one win and up to 22 losses. Regarding their accuracy, each tuner improved in 6 to 20 cases, maintained it in 18 to 29 cases, and reduced it in 2 to 7 cases. Similarly, CGA, DE, FS, GA, and DG tuners obtained 12 or less wins. In general, tuners that were already good at optimizing models gained less from multi-objective optimization.

A difference in multi-objective performance is seen when analyzing the statistics by model. Multi-objective tuning has its largest effect on the Log+SVR model, with 21 improvements on accuracy and 37 improvements on stability, from the total 48 cases. However, there is potential hazard in 17 cases where multi-objective optimization resulted in loss. When applied to Log+SVR, the 1+1 and TS tuners scored 3 wins and 1 tie in accuracy, and 4 wins in stability, out of 4 cases. Similarly, the BO, HB, HS, PSO, and RS tuners obtained 4 wins for stability, but resulted in loss of accuracy in certain scenarios. GA, CGA, DG, and FS obtained the least gains from multi-objective optimization when applied to Log+SVR. We again observe that the best single-objective performers gained less from multi-objective optimization.

In the case of CART and Log+CART models, multi-objective optimization achieved more stable results. For both models, the tuners achieved 10 wins, 84 ties, and 2 losses on SA, and 18 wins, 75 ties, and 3 losses on SD. Although not particularly effective in improving either accuracy or stability, applying multi-objective tuning can be a net positive, as it would rarely result on either metric lowering and can potentially improve both metrics in certain cases.

The six RR and SVR model did not particularly benefit from multi-objective tuning, as accuracy was reduced in a maximum of 33 cases. With the exception of VT+RR, the amount of losses in SA outnumbered the amount of wins. The inverse can be observed for SD, with as high as 29 wins for multi-objective tuners. However, given that SVR and RR-based models had already some of the lowest accuracy scores in this study, we do not recommend multi-objective tuning for these models.

The metrics we obtained for the multi-objective tuners was an average of the Pareto front. In a real application, one of the hyper-parameter solutions in the front would be selected to construct the final model. Thus, multi-objective optimization has the aggregated value of producing multiple equally viable solutions.

Multi-objective hyper-parameter tuning had different effects depending on the model. For Log+SVR, tuning can boost stability at a potential loss of accuracy. In CART and Log+CART models, multi-objective tuning maintained or improved the accuracy and stability, except in 5 cases. Multi-objective tuning can also improve the stability of SVR and RR models, but it can lower the accuracy of the model.

5 Conclusion

In this study we evaluated the impact of multi-objective hyper-parameter tuning on accuracy and stability. Twelve single-objective and multi-objective tuners were compared over 5 machine learning algorithms, 2 data transformations, and 4 datasets.

The results of the study show that single-objective hyper-parameter tuning improves both the accuracy and stability on CART and SVR models, but had no effect on the studied ridge regression models. The most effective models, in both terms of stability and accuracy, were combinations of Log+SVR tuned using genetic algorithm, compact genetic algorithm, differential evolution, and flash. Multi-objective optimization offers a trade-off between accuracy and stability depending on the model. For Log+SVR, multi-objective tuning only improved the performance of the non-highest ranking tuners, such as random search. For models that use CART, multi-objective tuning resulted in improved or maintained accuracy and stability, with very few cases in which the multi-objective model performed worse. For SVR and ridge regression models, multi-objective tuning may provide improvements on stability, but at the potential cost of degrading their already low accuracy. Multi-objective optimization does offer multiple solutions that are equally viable, and a researcher or practitioner can select the hyper-parameter values that better suit their needs.

Future work includes exploring more datasets in the SEE literature, as well as replicating this study on further machine learning algorithms and data transformation methods. We are also interested in studying the effect of 'meta-tuning' the hyper-parameter tuners. For example, study how does a genetic algorithm tuner perform when parameters such as mutation and crossover rates are altered.

References

1. Agrawal, A., Fu, W., Chen, D., Shen, X., Menzies, T.: How to "dodge" complex software analytics. IEEE Transactions on Software Engineering (2019)
2. Agrawal, A., Yang, X., Agrawal, R., Shen, X., Menzies, T.: Simpler hyperparameter optimization for software analytics: Why, how, when? arXiv preprint arXiv:2008.07334 (2020)
3. Albon, C.: Machine learning with python cookbook: Practical solutions from preprocessing to deep learning. " O'Reilly Media, Inc." (2018)
4. Ali, A., Gravino, C.: Improving software effort estimation using bio-inspired algorithms to select relevant features: An empirical study. Science of Computer Programming **205**, 102621 (2021)
5. Azzeh, M., Nassif, A.B., Banitaan, S., Almasalha, F.: Pareto efficient multi-objective optimization for local tuning of analogy-based estimation. Neural Computing and Applications **27**(8), 2241–2265 (2016)
6. Boehm, B.W.: Software engineering economics. IEEE transactions on Software Engineering (1), 4–21 (1984)
7. Breiman, L., Friedman, J., Stone, C.J., Olshen, R.A.: Classification and regression trees. CRC press (1984)
8. Dejaeger, K., Verbeke, W., Martens, D., Baesens, B.: Data mining techniques for software effort estimation: a comparative study. IEEE transactions on software engineering **38**(2), 375–397 (2011)
9. Fu, W., Menzies, T., Shen, X.: Tuning for software analytics: Is it really necessary? Information and Software Technology **76**, 135–146 (2016)
10. Fu, W., Nair, V., Menzies, T.: Why is differential evolution better than grid search for tuning defect predictors? arXiv preprint arXiv:1609.02613 (2016)
11. González-Ladrón-de Guevara, F., Fernández-Diego, M., Lokan, C.: The usage of isbsg data fields in software effort estimation: A systematic mapping study. Journal of Systems and Software **113**, 188–215 (2016)
12. Langdon, W.B., Dolado, J., Sarro, F., Harman, M.: Exact mean absolute error of baseline predictor, marp0. Information and Software Technology **73**, 16–18 (2016)
13. Langsari, K., Sarno, R.: Optimizing effort and time parameters of cocomo ii estimation using fuzzy multi-objective pso. In: 2017 4th International Conference on Electrical Engineering, Computer Science and Informatics (EECSI). pp. 1–6. IEEE (2017)
14. Lederer, A.L., Prasad, J.: Causes of inaccurate software development cost estimates. Journal of systems and software **31**(2), 125–134 (1995)
15. Malgonde, O., Chari, K.: An ensemble-based model for predicting agile software development effort. Empirical Software Engineering **24**(2), 1017–1055 (2019)
16. Menzies, T., Shepperd, M.: Special issue on repeatable results in software engineering prediction (2012)
17. Mittas, N., Angelis, L.: Ranking and clustering software cost estimation models through a multiple comparisons algorithm. IEEE Transactions on software engineering **39**(4), 537–551 (2012)
18. Nair, V., Yu, Z., Menzies, T., Siegmund, N., Apel, S.: Finding faster configurations using flash. IEEE Transactions on Software Engineering **46**(7), 794–811 (2018)
19. Oliveira, A.L., Braga, P.L., Lima, R.M., Cornélio, M.L.: Ga-based method for feature selection and parameters optimization for machine learning regression applied to software effort estimation. information and Software Technology **52**(11), 1155–1166 (2010)

20. Palaniswamy, S.K., Venkatesan, R.: Hyperparameters tuning of ensemble model for software effort estimation. Journal of Ambient Intelligence and Humanized Computing pp. 1–11 (2020)
21. Sarro, F., Petrozziello, A., Harman, M.: Multi-objective software effort estimation. In: 2016 IEEE/ACM 38th International Conference on Software Engineering (ICSE). pp. 619–630. IEEE (2016)
22. Scott, A.J., Knott, M.: A cluster analysis method for grouping means in the analysis of variance. Biometrics pp. 507–512 (1974)
23. Shalev-Shwartz, S., Ben-David, S.: Understanding machine learning: From theory to algorithms. Cambridge university press (2014)
24. Shepperd, M.: Software project economics: a roadmap. In: 2007 Future of Software Engineering. pp. 304–315. IEEE Computer Society (2007)
25. Shepperd, M., MacDonell, S.: Evaluating prediction systems in software project estimation. Information and Software Technology **54**(8), 820–827 (2012)
26. Song, L., Minku, L.L., Yao, X.: The impact of parameter tuning on software effort estimation using learning machines. In: Proceedings of the 9th international conference on predictive models in software engineering. pp. 1–10 (2013)
27. Song, L., Minku, L.L., Yao, X.: The potential benefit of relevance vector machine to software effort estimation. In: Proceedings of the 10th International Conference on Predictive Models in Software Engineering. pp. 52–61 (2014)
28. Song, L., Minku, L.L., Yao, X.: Software effort interval prediction via bayesian inference and synthetic bootstrap resampling. ACM Transactions on Software Engineering and Methodology (TOSEM) **28**(1), 1–46 (2019)
29. Tantithamthavorn, C., McIntosh, S., Hassan, A.E., Matsumoto, K.: The impact of automated parameter optimization on defect prediction models. IEEE Transactions on Software Engineering **45**(7), 683–711 (2018)
30. Tawosi, V., Sarro, F., Petrozziello, A., Harman, M.: Multi-objective software effort estimation: A replication study. IEEE Transactions on Software Engineering (2021)
31. Villalobos-Arias, L., Quesada-López, C., Guevara-Coto, J., Martínez, A., Jenkins, M.: Evaluating hyper-parameter tuning using random search in support vector machines for software effort estimation. In: Proceedings of the 16th ACM International Conference on Predictive Models and Data Analytics in Software Engineering (PROMISE'20). ACM (2020)
32. Villalobos-Arias, L., Quesada-López, C., Martínez, A., Jenkins, M.: Hyper-parameter tuning of classification and regression trees for software effort estimation. In: Trends and Applications in Information Systems and Technologies: Volume 3 9. pp. 589–598. Springer International Publishing (2021)
33. Villalobos-Arias, L., Quesada-López, C., Martínez, A., Jenkins, M.: Técnicas de ajuste de hiperparámetros de algoritmos de aprendizaje automático para la estimación de esfuerzo: un mapeo de literatura. Revista Ibérica de Sistemas e Tecnologias de Informação (E42), 305–318 (2021)
34. Wen, J., Li, S., Lin, Z., Hu, Y., Huang, C.: Systematic literature review of machine learning based software development effort estimation models. Information and Software Technology **54**(1), 41–59 (2012)
35. Xia, T., Krishna, R., Chen, J., Mathew, G., Shen, X., Menzies, T.: Hyperparameter optimization for effort estimation. arXiv preprint arXiv:1805.00336 (2018)
36. Yang, L., Shami, A.: On hyperparameter optimization of machine learning algorithms: Theory and practice. Neurocomputing **415**, 295–316 (2020)

Developers' perception on the severity of test smells: an empirical study

Denivan Campos[1], Larissa Rocha[1,2], and Ivan Machado[1]

[1] Institute of Computing, Federal University of Bahia (UFBA), Salvador - BA, Brazil
[2] State University of Feira de Santana (UEFS), Feira de Santana - BA, Brazil
denivan.campos@ufba.br, larissa@ecomp.uefs.br, ivan.machado@ufba.br

Abstract. Unit testing is an essential component of the software development life-cycle. A developer could easily and quickly catch and fix software faults introduced in the source code by creating and running unit tests. Despite their importance, unit tests are subject to bad design or implementation decisions, the so-called test smells. These might decrease software systems' quality from various aspects, making it harder to understand, more complex to maintain, and more prone to errors and bugs. Many studies discuss the likely effects of test smells on test code. However, there is a lack of studies that capture developers' perceptions of such issues. This study empirically analyzes how developers perceive the severity of test smells in the test code they develop. Severity refers to the degree to how a test smell may negatively impact the test code. We selected six open-source software projects from GitHub and interviewed their developers to understand whether and how the test smells affected the test code. Although most of the interviewed developers considered the test smells as having a low severity to their code, they indicated that test smells might negatively impact the project, particularly in test code maintainability and evolution. Also, detecting and removing test smells from the test code may be positive for the project.

Keywords: Software Testing · Test Smells · Empirical Software Engineering

1 Introduction

Software testing is an essential strategy to ensure the quality of software systems. Creating and executing test code encompass activities that require a lot of effort and cost, especially when manually developed [13]. Nonetheless, the need to find defects early in the development cycle has increased the interest in employing unit testing practices [3].

In recent years, test code has become persistent and needs to evolve along with the production code to be more effective [3]. For example, at Google, the amount of code and the size of the test pool grows linearly to maintain the software quality. Google runs over 2 Million Lines of Code (LOC) and 150 million tests per day [8]. Keeping up this whole process of evolving and maintaining these test cases might be a time-consuming task. In addition, as the amount of tests grows, the effort invested in maintaining the tests can make it a costly activity. On the other side, creating and running unit tests can quickly capture and support fixing software failures introduced in the source code [13].

Despite their importance, unit tests might be subject to inappropriate design or poor implementation decisions. Such issues may lead to the insertion of smells in test code, the so-called test smells [2]. The presence of test smells makes test code more difficult to comprehend, more complex to maintain, and prone to errors [13, 18]. Software developers and testers are usually unaware of the concept of test smells [17].

Software projects commonly develop extensive sets of test cases to assure the quality of developed systems [16]. To this effect, automated support for creating test cases has gained momentum, and the software testing community has released many support tools lately [6, 11]. In addition, many tools are providing automated strategies to prevent, detect, and refactor test smells, as discussed by Aljedaani et al. [1].

Aligned with the need to understand whether and how harmful test smells are to a software project, many researchers have empirically evaluated the likely effects of test smells [7, 9, 17, 19]. In a recent study, Garousi et al. [7] enlisted the main negative consequences of the presence of test smell in test code: smells reduce tests changeability, stability, readability, and maintainability. Silva-Junior et al. [17] surveyed software testing professionals to understand and analyze how often they insert test smells into the test code and the reasons behind it. The authors showed that, independently of the professional experience, they are prone to insert test smells in their test code, even when using standard practices.

Although some studies claim that test smells might hinder code maintenance, there is still a lack of studies that capture the developers' perception of that issues. In this context, this study investigates how developers recognize test smells. We aim to empirically analyze how developers perceive the severity of test smells in the test code they develop. We refer *severity* to the degree to which a given test smell can negatively impact the test code. In addition to severity, we were also interested in investigating how the test code would behave after removing the test smells.

We conducted an empirical study split into three phases. In the first, we selected six open-source software projects from GitHub. The second phase consisted of interviews with the developers of the selected projects to investigate their perception of test smells. During the interviews, we introduced the definitions of each test smell and asked the developers whether they could refactor them. The third step was the analysis of the gathered data. To support this empirical study, we used the JNose Test [20] tool to identify the test smells in the selected projects.

In summary, our study brings the following contributions:

- an empirical study showing that most developers perceive test smells as low or middle in severity for their software projects;
- initial insights of the consequences of the test smells after refactoring.

2 Test Smells

Test smells are sub-optimal designs in the unit test code that the developer chose when implementing test cases [1, 7, 12, 15]. Deursen et al. [5] presents a catalog of 11 test smells and proposed refactoring strategies to remove them from the test code. Peruma et al. [15] extended that catalog and included another 12 new test smells inspired by bad practices in unit test-based programming. Other researchers identified other test smells types and analyzed the effects of various types on production and test code [9, 10, 13, 18, 22].

In this study, we analyzed eight types of test smells. We selected the most frequent ones in the test suites of the projects used in the study, which we briefly introduce next:

- **Assertion Roulette (AR):** It occurs when a test method contains more than one assertion statement without an explanation or parameter in the assertion method [5];
- **Eager Test (ET):** When a test method contains multiple calls to multiple production methods [5];
- **Empty Test (EpT):** It occurs when a test method does not contain executable instructions [15];
- **Lazy test (LT):** It occurs when multiple test methods call the same production method [5];
- **Redundant Assertion (RA):** When the test methods contain assertion statements that are always true or always false [15];
- **Constructor Initialization (CI):** It occurs when a test method implements a constructor. It is recommended that all the fields be initialized inside the *setUp()* method [15];
- **Unknown Test (UT):** When a test method does not contain assertions. An assertion statement describes an expected condition for a test method [15];
- **Sensitive Equality (SE):** It occurs when the test method makes an equality checking using the *toString* method [5].

2.1 JNose Test Tool

Aljedaani et al. [1] identified 22 tools for test smell detection. Most of the tools support the JUnit framework and Java programming language. For our study, we applied the JNose Test [20], as it elaborates on the state-of-the-art tool by providing users with an easy-to-use graphical interface that facilitates the detection of test smells. It analyzes Java projects that use Maven and JUnit Framework[3].

The JNose Test[4] is a web-based application that analyzes the quality of the test code by detecting test smells in the Java test code [20]. JNose Test detects 21 types of test smells by following the detection rules from the TsDetect tool [14]. The tool encompasses a set of rules to identify and quantify the types of test

[3] `https://junit.org/`

[4] `https://github.com/arieslab/jnose`

smells in each test class and supports the analysis of test smells through several project versions [20, 21]. Once started, the tool requires the user to configure the data entry to enable and specify one of the four types of analysis mode, *TestClass*, *TestSmell*, *TestFile*, and *Evolution*. JNose shows, as a result, the amount of LOC, methods, types, and amount of test smells in each test class of the project. With such a tool, it is possible to verify the test quality from an evolutionary perspective. It enables capturing metrics, and the occurrence of test smells through several project versions.

3 Research Methodology

We defined two research questions in this study:

RQ1. How do software developers consider the severity of test smells and their effects on test code quality? We aim to analyze how the software developers perceive the impact of the presence of test smells in test code, in terms of quality attributes such as comprehensibility and maintainability.

RQ2. What is the behavior of test code after refactoring test smells? We aim to analyze the changes in the test code after refactoring test smells.

3.1 Study Design

The design employed in this study consists of three phases: *Repository Creation*, *Interview*, and *Data Analysis*. Each phase comprises a set of steps, as Figure 1 shows.

Phase 1 - Repository Creation. This phase comprised the following steps:

- **Step 1**. *Filtering by JNose Test limitations.* In this step, we used a dataset composed of 21,482 projects available in public GitHub repositories. First, we manually filtered each of the repositories with the following criteria: projects written in Java, composed of at least two stars, with Issues, and test cases created with the JUnit framework (versions 4 or 5). The choice for projects written in Java and tests with JUnit was due to the JNose Test limitations. As a result, we obtained a sample with 4,452 public repositories.
- **Step 2**. *Filtering repositories by ownership.* In this step, we collected the URLs of the 4,452 projects and manually opened each one. We filtered the projects that contained e-mails with Brazilian developers. Then, we ran each of these projects in the JNose Test to validate them. As a result, we obtained a sample with 90 public repositories.
- **Step 3**. *Filtering repositories by responses.* In this phase, we sent out e-mails to the 90 selected projects. We received six positive replies, which composed our dataset.

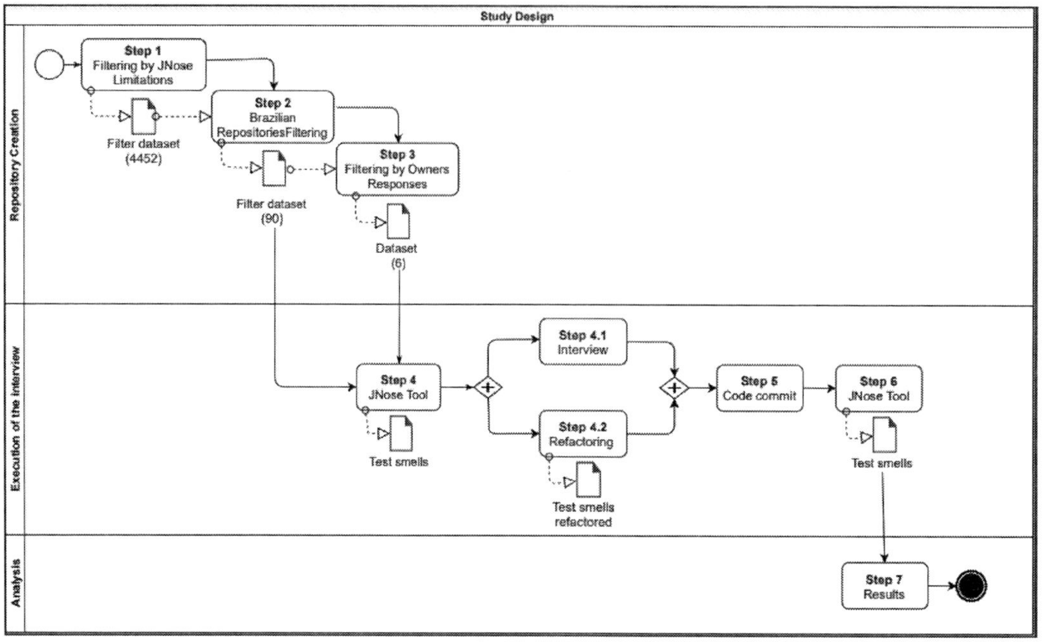

Fig. 1: Empirical Study Design

Phase 2 - Interview. The interview considered each of the developers individually. It comprised the following steps:

- **Step 4**. *Executing the JNose Test.* The first step was to execute the selected projects in the JNose Test [20] to gather evidence about the test smells identified in each project. Based on the yielded results (e.g., number of test smells present in each project), we created the protocol for the interviews.
- **Step 4.1**. *Carrying our the interviews.* Next, we proceeded with the actual interviews. First, we carried out the characterization of the participants, which included gathering information on their knowledge about creating and maintaining test cases. We created an online questionnaire using Google Forms and sent it to the interviewees. The interviews were held virtually, through Google Meet, and guided by the protocol created after detecting test smells in each of the projects. We presented the JNose Test to the participants during the interviews, explained that we ran the tool in their project, and presented the test smells we detected in each project. We also showed the most frequent test smells.
- **Step 4.2**. *Refactoring test code.* After analyzing the presence of test smells in the test code, they had to discuss (i) whether the test smells were harmful to their projects and (ii) whether they should refactor them. In this step, the developers had to refactor at least one test smell. We did not impose which test smell they must refactor. They could select any test smell they wanted.

- **Step 5**. *Commiting test code changes.* After refactoring, we asked the developers to commit the changes to their GitHub repositories. This step was essential to allow us to rerun the JNose Test on the refactored project.
- **Step 6**. *Rerunning the JNose Test.* In this final step, we reran the project in the JNose Test to compare the test classes before and after refactorings.

Phase 3 - Data Analysis. This phase comprises the analysis of gathered data, as follows:

- **Step 7**. *Results.* In this step, we present the results of our empirical study. This research has an exploratory character with a qualitative analysis. For open-ended questions that could combine multiple answers, the sum of percentages could be greater than 100%.

4 Results

4.1 Developers' Profiles

In this study, we interviewed the developers of each selected project. We next describe their background.

They all hold a Bachelor's degree (two in Computer Engineering, two in Electrical Engineering, and two in Business Information Systems), and two out of them have a Master's degree. They work in different Brazilian states: three of them work in São Paulo, and the others work in the states of Rio Grande do Sul, Bahia, and Santa Catarina.

Regarding their professional experience with software development, three had over ten years of professional experience, two had less than ten years, and one developer had less than five years. Among the three developers with more than ten years of experience, two of them also had more than ten years of experience in software testing. Among the two developers with up to 10 years of development experience, one also had a strong background in software testing. The others have between one and five years of experience in software testing.

4.2 Characterization of the selected projects

The six projects we analyzed vary in size - considering the number of LOC and the number of test methods, as Table 1 shows. The largest project is the `Fatiador` (the project aims to convert flat strings to Java objects and vice versa) with 162 test methods. For the `csv2Bib` (the project aims to convert `.csv` files into `.bib` or `.ris` files) and `Our Digital Bank` (the project provides an API to support the operation of a our digital bank) projects, we could only select two test smell types each.

Table 1: Selected projects

Project	LOC*	Test Methods	Test Classes	Project URL
Our Digital Bank	84	7	4	`https://bit.ly/3ABZui2`
csv2bib	98	5	2	`https://bit.ly/3xlHyXf`
CursoMassa	261	32	4	`https://bit.ly/3dQEwSV`
Dependency injection	390	23	5	`https://bit.ly/36h3ff3`
l2jserver	538	31	5	`https://bit.ly/3hInK9I`
Fatiador	2,362	162	17	`https://bit.ly/36gtS3F`

(*) Number of LOC in the test classes.

4.3 How do software developers consider the severity of test smells and their effects on test code quality? (RQ1)

We made an attempt to analyze how the developers would perceive the impact of the presence of test smells in test code. To accomplish that, we first considered the degree of severity of each test smell. Table 2 summarizes the data about the severity of the test smells identified in each project.

The *AR* test smell was the one which varied the most in terms of severity. Three projects presented variations for this test smell. The project `Curso Massa` (this project aims to support programming classes) presented 2 degrees of severity for the *AR* test smell: *low* and *middle*; the project `l2jserver` (this is a rewrite of the l2jserver project[5]) also presented 2 degrees of severity: *low* and *high*; and the project `Dependency Injection` (this project implements a dependency injection framework in Java with annotations) presented 3 degrees of severity: *low*, *middle*, and *high* severity.

In addition, the *UT* and *ET* test smells also presented differences in their perceived severity, ranging from *low* to *middle* and *low* to *high*, respectively. The remaining projects and test smells only presented a *low* severity degree.

Although most of the interviewees classified *AR* test smell as *low* severity, we observed small variations. For example, the developer of the project `Dependency Injection` analyzed 3 test smells of the *AR* type and gave a different classification for each. For this developer, *AR* could impact different her project in different ways.

We asked the developers about the test smells introduced in their respective projects. We wanted to know whether that test smells affect the maintainability of the test code. We next present the main findings.

Two projects (`Fatiador` and `csv2bib`) reported that no test smells found in the projects would affect the maintainability or cause any impact on the test code. Table 3 refers to the other four projects, and shows the that test smells *AR* is the test smell that has the most negative impact, followed by the test smell *ET* and *UT*.

For the `Curso Massa` project, the developer reported that the *AR* test smells would affect maintainability over time. Conversely, for *ET* and *LT* test smells,

[5] https://bitbucket.org/l2jserver/

Table 2: Degree of severity of test smells (TS) per project

Curso Massa		l2jserver		Dep. Injection		Fatiador		csv2bib		Our Digital Bank	
TS	Severity	TS	Severity	TS	Severity	TS	Severity	TS	Severity	TS	Severity
AR	Low	AR	Low	AR	Middle	SE	Low	AR	Low	AR	Low
AR	Low	AR	Low	AR	High	SE	Low	AR	Low	AR	Low
AR	Middle	AR	High	AR	Low	SE	Low	RA	Low	EpT	Low
ET	Low	ET	Low	ET	Low	AR	Low	RA	Low	EpT	Low
ET	Low	ET	High	ET	Low	AR	Low	CI	Low	UT	Middle
ET	Low	ET	Low	ET	Low	AR	Low	CI	Low	UT	Low
LT	Low	LT	Low	LT	Low	LT	Low	-	-	-	-
LT	Low	LT	Low	LT	Low	LT	Low	-	-	-	-
LT	Low	LT	Low	LT	Low	LT	Low	-	-	-	-

Legend: Assertion Roulette (AR), Eager Test (ET), Empty Test (EpT), Lazy test (LT), Redundant Assertion (RA), Constructor Initialization (CI), Unknown Test (UT), Sensitive Equality (SE).

the developer reported that they do not affect the maintainability of the test code. Thus, for the `Curso Massa`, `l2jserver`, `Dependency Injection` projects, the developers reported that the *AR* test smells have a negative impact on the test code. For the `l2jserver` and `Dependency Injection` projects, the developers reported that the *ET* test smells have a negative impact on the test code. Regarding the `Our Digital Bank` project, the developer considered that only the *UT* negatively impacts the test code.

Although they have informed that few test smells might negatively impact the code, 5 out of 6 developers reported that performing test smells maintenance in the test code would improve the comprehension and evolution of the system.

Table 3: Maintainability and impact of test smells (TS) per project

CursoMassa			l2jserver			Dep. Injection			Our Digital Bank		
TS	M	I	TS	M	I	TS	M	I	TS	M	I
AR	Yes	Negative	AR	Yes	Negative	AR	Yes	Negative	AR	No	-
AR	Yes	Negative	AR	Yes	Negative	AR	Yes	Negative	AR	No	-
AR	Yes	Negative	AR	Yes	Negative	AR	Yes	Negative	EpT	No	-
ET	No	-	ET	No	-	ET	No	-	EpT	No	-
ET	No	-	ET	Yes	Negative	ET	Yes	Negative	UT	Yes	Negative
ET	No	-	ET	No	-	ET	No	-	UT	Yes	Negative
LT	No	-	LT	No	-	LT	No	-	-	-	-
LT	No	-	LT	No	-	LT	No	-	-	-	-
LT	No	-	LT	No	-	LT	No	-	-	-	-

Legend: Maintainability (M), Impact (I).

4.4 What is the behavior of test code after refactoring test smells? (RQ2)

Before the interviews, we ran the JNose Test for each project. The tool generated a `csv` file containing the test smells identified in the projects. During the interviews, we asked the developers to refactor some test smells and next commit the changed test files to their GitHub repositories. Then, we introduced each test smell and asked if they could refactor them. After the modifications, we run the JNose Test for each project again, obtaining a new `csv` file with the latest results. We next present the results for each project.

Dependency Injection. We selected 9 test smells: 3 *AR*, 3 *LT*, and 3 *ET* to present to the developer. From the three *AR* test smells, he decided to refactor two out of them into two distinct test classes. He successfully removed the test smells from the test code. From the three *LT* test smells, he refactored one smell, but he did not remove it. Particularly, for the *LT* test smell, the developer should place the creation of an object in the *setUp()* method, but he linked the *LT* test smell to the use of external components, and to refactor, he made use of mocks. Hence, he performed incorrect refactoring. We also observed that the LOC and the number of test methods did not change after refactoring this project. The other test classes, methods, and smells remained without changes.

Curso Massa. We selected 9 test smells: 3 *AR*, 3 *ET* and 3 *LT*. The developer decided to refactor the *AR* ones. From the *AR* test smells refactored by the developer, only one was removed. The remaining *AR* were refactored but not removed. To refactor *AR* smells, it is necessary to include an explanation (message) in the first parameter of the *assertion* (e.g., `assertTrue([message,] boolean condition)`). The developer placed the message as the last parameter instead.

Csv2bib. We selected 6 test smells: 2 *AR*, 2 *RA*, and 2 *CI*. The developer decided to refactor 1 *CI* test smell. After refactoring, he removed the test smell. The *CI* test smell occurs when a test method implements a constructor. It is necessary to initialize all the fields within the *setUp()* method. Therefore, for that test smell, a possible refactoring would be to remove the constructor method since it had no instructions. However, the developer attempted to refactor the constructor method by including instructions for setting variables used in other test methods. The JNose Test continued to consider it a *CI* test smell. Since the developer modified the test class, the LOC and the number of test methods changed. For the `Run.java` test class, its LOC increased from 44 to 57, and the number of test methods risen from 2 to 5.

Fatiador. We selected 9 test smells: 3 *SE*, 3 *AR*, and 3 *LT*. The developer decided to refactor 2 *AR* smells from 2 different test classes: `DecimalWriter.java` and `IntegerWriter.java`. After refactoring, the developer successfully removed the two smells. For each test class, he added 1 LOC each (from 47 to 48 LOC and from 40 to 41 LOC), respectively. The other test smells did not present any change.

l2jserver2. We selected 9 test smells: 3 *AR*, 3 *ET*, and 3 *LT*. The developer refactored 2 *AR* and 1 *ET*. In addition, he also refactored other *AR* test smells not previously selected. For example, the `BitSetIDAllocator.java` test class contained 7 *AR* before refactoring. Although we asked him to refactor just 1 of them, he refactored 3 occurrences of this test smell. In total, he refactored 4 *AR* test smells for 2 different classes (`BitSetIDAllocator.java` and `CharacterIDProvider.java`), in which all of them were successfully removed after refactoring.

For the *ET* test smell, the developer chose to refactor the smell inside the `CharacterIDProvider.java` test class. Therefore, it was necessary to remove the multiple calls to the multiple production methods. However, the developer did not perform the necessary removals. Moreover, during the incorrect refactoring of the *ET* test smell, he introduced a new type of smell in the project, the *LT*, which occurs when multiple test methods call the same production method. Thus, 2 test classes (`CharacterIDProvider.java` and `WorldServiceImpl.java`) have changed. The first increased in 1 LOC, while the latter decreased by 1. For the number of test methods and other test smells, there was no change in behavior.

Our Digital Bank. We selected 6 test smells: 2 *AR*, 2 *Ept*, and 2 *UT*. The developer decided to refactor 1 *AR*, 2 *Ept*, and 2 *UT* test smells. This project contained 4 test classes. During the refactoring, the developer removed 2 of them. In addition, the `Validator.java` test class contained 35 LOC, and 90 LOC after refactoring. Also, the amount of test methods increased from 4 to 8. All the 3 types of test smells, *AR*, *UT*, and *Ept* presented different behaviors after refactoring: the amount of *AR* test smells increased from 2 to 9; the 2 *UT* refactored were successfully removed; and 2 *Ept* smells were refactored and removed. The project had 2 *Ept*, 1 was removed after refactoring and the other after removing one of the test classes. Additionally, after refactoring, the developer added other 9 test smells, 7 *IT* and 2 *LT*. From the analyzed projects, `Our Digital Bank` was the one that had the most changes in the test code, which had decreased the number of test classes, increased the number of test smells, and the number of LOC and test methods. After refactoring, two test smells that did not exist before in the project were added to the test code.

5 Discussion

In this study, we considered three degrees of severity (low, middle, and high) for the test smells. We used this approach to evaluate eight test smells (*AR*, *Ept*, *UT*, *ET*, *LT*, *CI*, *SE*, and *RA*). Five test smells were considered as *low* severity for all projects: *LT*, *SE*, *EpT*, *RA*, and *CI*. From the set of test smells the interviewees analyzed (48 test smells identified in their projects), 42 were considered as *low* severity (≈87,5%). Only 6 out 48 test smells varied in degrees of severity (≈12,5%), 4 *AR*, 1 *ET*, and 1 *UT*, spread over 4 projects.

The *AR* was the one that varied the most. It was perceived by the developers in the three severity degrees, while the *ET* and *UT* presented two different degrees. According to the developers, the *AR* test smell might harm test code maintainability. For example, one interviewee claimed that *"if someone else is going to test the system, they will not know why the test failed"*. Another interviewee also commented about the *UT* test smells, as follows: *"UT harms my code because it shows that it has unnecessary code, and triggers a function in my system that is not validated as it should".*

Although most test smells received a low severity degree, the developers reported that, in general, test smells might be indicative of problems and harmful to the test code. On the other hand, they claimed that their systems were relatively small, containing simple test cases, and therefore, the test smells may not have as much impact. For larger projects, on the other hand, they may affect more. Therefore, there is a need to conduct further studies to know if those and other types of test smells have a degree of severity that would be different.

According to the developers, fixing test smells may positively impact the test code by improving the quality of the test code, making it more comprehensible, and easing the system's evolution. Two out of six developers also believe that refactoring test smells can result in detecting more bugs. Although four developers claim that refactored test smells do not contribute to the detection of bugs.

Moreover, for one developer, the *LT* should not be considered a test smell at all. They argue that it might be necessary to have more than 1 test method testing the same production method. In this case, each test method has a different purpose concerning the production class method. For example, for a given test method, the focus may be to exclude something, while in another, it may be to change something else; and the developer cannot see how to perform the test methods in a single method.

6 Threats to Validity

Internal validity. We selected projects from 84 to 2,362 lines of code. This subset of projects may not represent industrial software systems, and therefore replications in this context are desirable. Although Deursen et al. [5] address 21 test smells, this study considered only 8. However, we selected the most frequent test smells in the projects, gathered from the JNose Test results.

External validity. The number of participants we found willing to participate in the interview represents a threat to the results. Nonetheless, we sent emails to 90 GitHub developers, and six replied. This sample is not representative, and we expect to replicate this study with a more significant number of participants. Although the results cannot be generalized, they represent a partial view of developers' practices. We believe that this preliminary study is significant and indicative of a trend in the area. In addition, we intend to investigate this topic further with a more considerable number of test smells and projects. We also present the step-by-step methodology of this work that may allow further replications of this study. Although most of the smells investigated in this study show low severity, we cannot generalize to other projects and other test smells.

Construct validity. The interpretation might influence the research results. Regarding refactoring, we did not provide information on how one developer should refactor test smells. We only provided them with definitions and how to detect each of them. The number of refactored test smells varied in each project because we asked the developers if they could refactor and then which one(s) they would like to refactor. The number of smells refactored depended on the developer's choice. As each project presented different test smells, it was impossible to compare the same test smell in all projects. Since the projects have not been in development for more than two years, this can threaten validity. However, after refactoring, all projects were committed to Github without any problems.

7 Related Work

Silva-Junior et al. [17] presented a study to understand whether test professionals insert unintentional test smells. They surveyed experts to analyze the frequency of use of a set of test smells during the creation and execution of the test cases. The survey was conducted with 60 professionals from different companies and approached 14 test smells widely studied in the literature. According to the authors, experienced professionals introduce test smells during their daily programming activities; they also can provide insights for a better comprehension of how and what practices can lead to the insertion of test smells in the test code. Our study extends such study by providing further information about the degree of severity of test smells and the consequence of refactorings from a developers' perspective.

Spadini et al. [19] present an investigation into the severity classification concerning four types of test smells and their impact on maintaining the set of tests implemented by the developers. The authors analyzed about 1,500 open source projects to obtain thresholds for the test smells' severity. The authors also integrated a tool for detecting test smells (*tsDetect*) in a prototype extension (back-end) of the *BetterCodeHub* (BCH), a web-based code quality analysis tool. In this study, 31 developers of the BCH project interacted with the prototype. They had to comment on the instances of test smells in the code base of 47 projects. As a result, the developers detected 301 test smells. In the developers' perception, *EpT*, *Sleepy Test*, and *Mystery Guest* present the highest priority as candidates for refactorings, while *Empty Test, Ignored Test*, and *Conditional Test Logic* were considered the smells with the most significant impact on the code maintenance. Unlike such study [19], in this work, we investigated the severity of 8 test smells through three degrees of severity and refactored the test smells from the developers' perspective. To support the detection of the test smells, we used the JNose Test [20].

Bleser et al. [4] conducted two empirical studies. The first observed the propagation of test smells on 164 open source SCALA projects available on GitHub. The authors implemented a tool called *SOCRATES* for automated test smells detection. In the second study, they analyzed the perception and capability of 14 developers in SCALA projects to identify test smells. As a result, test smells had a low propagation among test classes. The most frequently test smells were *Lazy Test*, *Eager Test*, and *Assertion Roulette*. Our work differs from such a study as we analyzed developers' perceptions regarding the degree of severity and the consequences of refactoring smells tests.

8 Concluding Remarks

This study aimed to analyze how developers perceive the severity of test smells on test code quality. To accomplish this goal, we selected a set of open-source software projects from Github and interviewed their developers. We also asked them to refactor their test code to remove test smells. Hence, we could observe, from their standpoint, how the developers could consider the effects of such removal.

The results indicated that test smell severity is highly dependent on the context. For example, for the same project, a given test smell may present different degrees of severity. Regarding test smell refactoring, our initial results pointed out that testers may not know how to refactor a test smell to remove it. In addition, we also identified that it is likely that the removal process could induce the inclusion of new test smells.

As future work, we plan to replicate this study with larger projects, including a more extensive set of test smells. We also plan to investigate the consequences of refactoring test smells further.

Acknowledgments. This research was partially funded by INES 2.0; CNPq grants 465614/2014-0 and 408356/2018-9 and FAPESB grants BOL0599/2019 and JCB0060/2016.

References

1. Aljedaani, W., Peruma, A., Aljohani, A., Alotaibi, M., Mkaouer, M.W., Ouni, A., Newman, C.D., Ghallab, A., Ludi, S.: Test smell detection tools: A systematic mapping study. In: Evaluation and Assessment in Software Engineering (EASE). p. 170–180. ACM (2021)
2. Bavota, G., Qusef, A., Oliveto, R., De Lucia, A., Binkley, D.: An empirical analysis of the distribution of unit test smells and their impact on software maintenance. In: 28th IEEE International Conference on Software Maintenance (ICSM) (2012)
3. Breugelmans, M., Van Rompaey, B.: Testq: Exploring structural and maintenance characteristics of unit test suites. In: WASDeTT-1: 1st International Workshop on Advanced Software Development Tools and Techniques (2008)
4. De Bleser, J., Di Nucci, D., De Roover, C.: Assessing diffusion and perception of test smells in scala projects. In: Proceedings of the 16th International Conference on Mining Software Repositories. p. 457–467. MSR '19, IEEE Press (2019)
5. Deursen, A., Moonen, L.M., Bergh, A., Kok, G.: Refactoring test code. Tech. rep. (2001), CWI (Centre for Mathematics and Computer Science), Amsterdam, Netherlands
6. Fraser, G., Arcuri, A.: Evosuite: Automatic test suite generation for object-oriented software. In: Proceedings of the 19th ACM SIGSOFT Symposium and the 13th European Conference on Foundations of Software Engineering. p. 416–419. ESEC/FSE '11, ACM, New York, NY, USA (2011)
7. Garousi, V., Küçük, B.: Smells in software test code: A survey of knowledge in industry and academia. Journal of Systems and Software **138**, 52–81 (2018)

8. Memon, A., Gao, Z., Nguyen, B., Dhanda, S., Nickell, E., Siemborski, R., Micco, J.: Taming google-scale continuous testing. In: IEEE/ACM 39th International Conference on Software Engineering: Software Engineering in Practice Track (ICSE-SEIP). pp. 233–242 (2017)
9. Meszaros, G.: xUnit test patterns: Refactoring test code. Addison-Wesley Professional (may 2007)
10. Meszaros, G., Smith, S.M., Andrea, J.: The test automation manifesto. In: Maurer, F., Wells, D. (eds.) Extreme Programming and Agile Methods - XP/Agile Universe 2003. pp. 73–81. Springer Berlin Heidelberg, Berlin, Heidelberg (2003)
11. Pacheco, C., Ernst, M.D.: Randoop: Feedback-directed random testing for java. In: 22nd ACM SIGPLAN Conference on Object-Oriented Programming Systems and Applications Companion (OOPSLA). ACM (2007)
12. Palomba, F., Di Nucci, D., Panichella, A., Oliveto, R., De Lucia, A.: On the diffusion of test smells in automatically generated test code: An empirical study. In: 9th International Workshop on Search-Based Software Testing (SBST). ACM (2016)
13. Peruma, A., Almalki, K., Newman, C.D., Mkaouer, M.W., Ouni, A., Palomba, F.: On the distribution of test smells in open source android applications: An exploratory study. In: Proceedings of the 29th Annual International Conference on Computer Science and Software Engineering. p. 193–202. CASCON '19, IBM Corp., USA (2019)
14. Peruma, A., Almalki, K., Newman, C.D., Mkaouer, M.W., Ouni, A., Palomba, F.: Tsdetect: An open source test smells detection tool. In: Proceedings of the 28th ACM Joint Meeting on European Software Engineering Conference and Symposium on the Foundations of Software Engineering. p. 1650–1654. ESEC/FSE 2020, ACM, New York, NY, USA (2020)
15. Peruma, A.S.A.: What the smell? an empirical investigation on the distribution and severity of test smells in open source android applications. Master's thesis (2018), Rochester Institute of Technology.
16. Reichhart, S., Gîrba, T., Ducasse, S.: Rule-based assessment of test quality. Journal of Object Technology **6**(9), 231–251 (2007)
17. Silva-Junior, N., Rocha, L., Martins, L.A., Machado, I.: A survey on test practitioners' awareness of test smells. In: Proceedings of the XXIII Iberoamerican Conference on Software Engineering (CIbSE). pp. 462–475. Curran Associates (2020)
18. Spadini, D., Palomba, F., Zaidman, A., Bruntink, M., Bacchelli, A.: On the relation of test smells to software code quality. In: IEEE International Conference on Software Maintenance and Evolution, ICSME. IEEE (2018)
19. Spadini, D., Schvarcbacher, M., Oprescu, A.M., Bruntink, M., Bacchelli, A.: Investigating severity thresholds for test smells. In: 17th International Conference on Mining Software Repositories. ACM (2020)
20. Virgínio, T., Martins, L., Rocha, L., Santana, R., Cruz, A., Costa, H., Machado, I.: Jnose: Java test smell detector. In: 34th Brazilian Symposium on Software Engineering (SBES). ACM (2020)
21. Virgínio, T., Martins, L.A., Soares, L.R., Santana, R., Costa, H., Machado, I.: An empirical study of automatically-generated tests from the perspective of test smells. In: 34th Brazilian Symposium on Software Engineering (SBES). ACM (2020)
22. Virgínio, T., Santana, R., Martins, L.A., Soares, L.R., Costa, H., Machado, I.: On the influence of test smells on test coverage. In: XXXIII Brazilian Symposium on Software Engineering (SBES). ACM (2019)

DEHIA: Una plataforma liviana para definir y ejecutar actividades con intervención humana basadas en workflows

Jose Arcidiacono[1][0000-0003-0300-5213], Patricia Bazán[2][0000-0001-6720-345X] and Alejandra B. Lliteras[3,4][0000-0002-4148-1299]

[1] Universidad Nacional de La Plata, Facultad de Informática, LINTI, Calle 50 esquina 120S/N, La Plata. Argentina
jarcidiacono@linti.unlp.edu.ar
2 Universidad Nacional de La Plata, Facultad de Informática, LINTI, Calle 50 esquina 120S/N 2° piso, La Plata. Argentina
pbaz@info.unlp.edu.ar
[3] Universidad Nacional de La Plata, Facultad de Informática, LIFIA, Calle 50 esquina 120S/N, 1° piso, La Plata. Argentina
[4] CICPBA, Calle 526 e/ 10 y 11, La Plata, Argentina
alejandra.lliteras@lifia.info.unlp.edu.ar

Abstract. En este trabajo se presenta el desarrollo de DEHIA una plataforma para crear, clonar y gestionar workflows de actividades de recolección de datos, que involucren la intervención humana, y cuya ejecución se realiza desde una aplicación móvil. La plataforma se despliega sobre una arquitectura distribuida y está integrada por tres componentes: 1- una plataforma Web, que permite a usuarios finales crear, clonar y gestionar sus propias actividades de recolección de datos en diferentes dominios; 2- una aplicación móvil para que voluntarios participen de la actividad de recolección de datos y 3- una API responsable de la comunicación entre las dos primeras componentes. Se aplica la solución a un caso de uso que aborda una alternativa tecnológica inclusiva y en este caso particular, con la expectativa de aportar a la labor social que el programa E-Basura realiza desde el año 2009. Sobre dicho caso de estudio, se aplicaron pruebas de usabilidad utilizando un formulario SUS. La propuesta de este trabajo espera abrir un espacio de debate en miras de la democratización y apertura de este tipo de actividad para ser empleado en diferentes disciplinas.

Keywords: Arquitecturas Distribuidas, Recolección de Datos, Workflows.

1 Introducción

En la actualidad, con la masificación en el uso de dispositivos móviles, diversas aplicaciones móviles son usadas para la recolección de datos con intervención humana, es decir, toma de datos que no son completamente realizados por sensores, sino que necesariamente requieren de una persona interactuando con la aplicación [1].

Entre los antecedentes de este tipo de aplicaciones móviles, se pueden considerar dos grandes grupos: 1- las aplicaciones móviles creadas ad-hoc y 2- las obtenidas mediante el uso de herramientas de autor. En el primer grupo, solucionan un problema específico y no son posibles de reusar en otros dominios. Su objetivo es la de satisfacer la necesidad puntual de un proyecto. Por ejemplo, en [2] el autor propone una aplicación para recolectar datos relacionados a ambientes acuáticos, en [3] los autores presentan “GeoVIN” una aplicación para recolectar datos ayudando a la sociedad a reconocer vinchucas. Por otro lado, en [4] los autores proponen una aplicación para recolectar datos del virus Zika en el mundo.

En el segundo grupo, por su parte, permiten a los usuarios finales crear sus propias aplicaciones móviles sin necesidad de tener conocimientos de programación, por ejemplo, en [5], los autores presentan a Zooniverse, una plataforma que, entre otras cosas, permite generar aplicaciones de recolección de datos para diversos dominios. En [6] se presenta EpiCollect+, otra herramienta de similares características, mientras que en [7] los autores presentan "MoLE" una herramienta de autor para generar actividades que podrían aplicarse también a la recolección de datos.

Por lo tanto, se observa que las herramientas de autor permiten a usuarios sin conocimientos de programación crear sus propias propuestas, lo que les otorga la libertad de generar una aplicación móvil acorde a sus necesidades sin depender de desarrolladores o expertos en tecnología.

En este sentido, se pueden identificar en las herramientas de autor, dos características que enaltecen su utilidad hacia los usuarios finales. Por un lado, permite que diferentes proyectos que involucran la actividad de recolección de datos comparten cierto tipo de tareas. Por ejemplo, es común que, para ciertas actividades, se necesiten tareas tales como, recolectar una foto del lugar donde se toma el dato y la posición geográfica del mismo o bien realizar la grabación de un audio. De este modo, alguno de estos tipos de tareas (que son parte de una actividad), podrían ser reutilizados para diferentes proyectos, sin la necesidad de definirlas una y otra vez para cada nuevo proyecto.

Por otro lado, la organización de las tareas como workflow [8] organiza las tareas de recolección de datos, siguiendo algún patrón de workflow [9] (por ejemplo, secuencial, libre, selección exclusiva y selección múltiple). Así, cada proyecto puede definir su propia estructura. Con el fin de reutilizar conocimiento, sería deseable las herramientas de autor permitan que estas estructuras se conviertan en plantillas o moldes, que puedan compartirse, basados, por ejemplo, en la buena experiencia de los usuarios, al momento de realizar las tareas estructuradas de cierta manera.

En este trabajo se propone una plataforma (DEHIA) para que usuarios finales definan, creen y ejecuten actividades que requieran de la intervención humana con el fin de realizar recolección de datos para su posterior análisis. Se presenta también un prototipo de la herramienta Web para permitir la creación de actividades y una aplicación móvil prototípica desde la cual se ejecuten las actividades creadas con la herramienta Web. Empleando los prototipos mencionados, se mostrará un caso de estudio donde sea posible diseñar, crear y ejecutar una actividad con el fin de concientizar en el reciclado de RAEE (Residuos de Aparatos Eléctricos y Electrónicos). Se entregará también un informe de usabilidad de dichos prototipos.

2 Trabajos relacionados

Existen numerosas herramientas para la recolección de datos, desde formularios en papel hasta soluciones tecnológicas complejas. En particular, se consideraron algunas herramientas de autor (para recolección de datos) las que permiten a usuarios finales la creación de formularios o workflows para que luego, otras personas, recolecten datos usando dispositivos móviles.

A continuación se describen cuatro de estas plataformas: EpiCollect5, Zooniverse, Open Data Kit (ODK) y MoLE. Las tres primeras fueron elegidas por ser soluciones ampliamente utilizadas y la cuarta por compartir el mismo enfoque de modelado de actividades [10] que la plataforma aquí presentada (DEHIA).

EpiCollect5 es la última versión de una herramienta desarrollada por el Imperial College de Londres [11]. Permite la creación de formularios de recolección de datos mediante un sitio web, y la ejecución de las mismas desde una aplicación móvil. Los resultados pueden visualizarse desde el sitio anteriormente mencionado. Permite una variedad de tipos de tareas que van desde la introducción de texto hasta la lectura de códigos de barras o QR. En cuanto a la planificación de las tareas, permite ramificaciones condicionales que se observan en la herramienta mediante opciones en cada tarea (no hay una vista general de la estructura). Permite exportar e importar actividades completas en formato JSON, aunque no se pueden reutilizar tareas individuales o planificaciones.

Zooniverse [12], es un portal de "Ciencia Ciudadana" [13] que invita a personas de la comunidad a participar de las investigaciones científicas en sus diferentes etapas. En particular, en muchos proyectos los participantes realizan análisis de datos a una escala a la que un investigador no podría llegar por su cuenta [5]. En esta plataforma se crean distintos proyectos, cada uno con una serie de workflows a realizar sobre un conjunto de elementos, generalmente imágenes. Un workflow está compuesto por un conjunto de tareas que van desde responder una pregunta hasta señalar algo en una imagen con herramientas de dibujo [14]. Las respuestas a las tareas ("clasificaciones") se envían desde el sitio web de cada proyecto, y en menor medida desde una aplicación móvil. También existe una API pública que admite clasificaciones desde otras fuentes, como una librería HTTP.

Open Data Kit[15] (conocido también como ODK) es una plataforma para la recolección de datos en entornos de recursos reducidos. Consiste en una herramienta de autor para crear formularios, que tiene una versión web y otra de escritorio. Además de la creación de tareas mediante drag-and-drop, la plataforma permite la importación de planillas de cálculo que permiten la creación de workflows de manera parametrizada. De las herramientas estudiadas es la que más tipos de tareas ofrece. La plataforma se completa con una aplicación móvil para resolver las tareas, un servidor que recibe los resultados y una aplicación de escritorio para ver los resultados.

MoLE[16] es una herramienta de autor de código abierto que permite a usuarios sin conocimiento sobre desarrollo móvil o programación, la creación de actividades mediadas por tecnología móvil [7]. La versión analizada incluye varios tipos de tareas como "elegir una opción" o "generar contenido multimedia", que pueden ser planificadas de forma lineal, libre o de grafo. MoLE cuenta con una aplicación móvil llamada “Resuelvo Explorando” [17] para resolver las actividades, y una API que recibe las respuestas.

En su herramienta de creación, todas las plataformas analizadas presentan las tareas de forma lineal, aunque pueden reordenarse mediante drag-and-drop (Epicollect5, ODK) y planificarse mediante condiciones o un grafo (este es el caso de MoLE). Ninguna de las herramientas presenta algún tipo de reutilización, a excepción de Epicollect5 y ODK las que permiten la reutilización de los workflows de manera completa.

Todas las plataformas cuentan además con una aplicación móvil para la resolución de las actividades. Esta resolución es similar en todos los casos, pero en cuanto al envío de respuestas, solo Epicollect5 y ODK permiten acumular respuestas para enviarlas cuando haya conexión.

En cuanto al servidor, Zooniverse y EpiCollect cuentan con servidores centralizados. Epicollect5 permite proyectos privados. ODK promueve el uso de servidores de los usuarios, así como lo permiten MoLE y Zooniverse por ser todos de código abierto [18].

De los trabajos analizados, se observa que no todos abordan la reutilización de tareas y de planificaciones (o workflows). Esta falta de reutilización, puede hacer que el conocimiento no circule y se difunda en la comunidad como sería esperado y que no todos se pudiesen beneficiar de las buenas prácticas de otros proyectos, por ejemplo, desde la perspectiva de la experiencia de usuario al conocer que una determinada forma de planificación conlleva ventajas por sobre otra.

3 DEHIA. Arquitectura y plataforma

DEHIA es una plataforma construida para que usuarios finales puedan diseñar, crear y gestionar actividades de recolección de datos que requieran de la participación de personas utilizando dispositivos móviles. Estas actividades están planificadas siguiendo el concepto de workflow. Además, incluye una aplicación móvil desde la cual los participantes recolectan datos para enviarlos a la plataforma.

A continuación se describen su arquitectura y sus componentes.

3.1 Arquitectura

La arquitectura de DEHIA es distribuida con microservicios. Esto quiere decir que un conjunto de componentes separados, incluso corriendo en distintos equipos, colabora para formar un sistema único. En particular, al tratarse de microservicios, estos componentes son pequeños servicios que se desarrollan y despliegan de forma independiente.

Se puede decir que la arquitectura de DEHIA tiene cuatro capas, como puede verse en la Figura 1:

- En la capa de clientes están los componentes que sirven de interfaz entre los usuarios (autores o usuarios *mobile*) y el resto de la plataforma (el servidor o API)

- En la capa de compuertas se tienen los componentes que redireccionan las peticiones de los clientes hacia los distintos servicios de la capa que sigue.
- La capa de servicios concentra la funcionalidad de la plataforma, dividida en varios servicios.
- En la capa de persistencia se tienen los mecanismos (sistemas de archivos, bases de datos) que hacen permanentes los datos utilizados por los servicios.

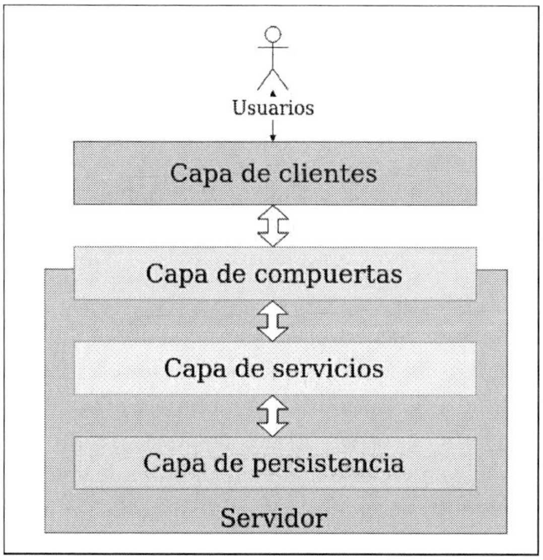

Fig. 1. Arquitectura por capas de DEHIA

3.2 Componentes

La plataforma DEHIA se compone de tres partes: la herramienta Web, que permite la creación y gestión de workflows de tareas; la aplicación móvil, que permite la ejecución de los mismos; y por último una API que recibe los resultados de la ejecución y persiste los datos.

Herramienta Web. Este componente, que consiste en un sitio Web, permite el acceso vía Inicio de Sesión de Google, además del acceso anónimo. Un usuario autenticado por el primer método es considerado un "autor" y puede crear y gestionar actividades, tareas y workflows (una actividad es un conjunto de tareas, donde cada tarea es un trabajo atómico: un workflow es una organización de tareas dentro de una actividad). En el segundo caso, el usuario sólo puede acceder al contenido público y descargar actividades.

Los autores pueden crear actividades, públicas o privadas, formadas por un conjunto de tareas que pueden ser de diversos tipos, entre ellas sacar una foto, elegir una opción o registrar coordenadas GPS. Los tipos de tareas están pensados para aprovechar las capacidades del dispositivo móvil en el que serán ejecutadas. Se pueden ver algunos de los tipos de tareas en la pantalla de selección de tareas de la Figura 2. Las tareas pueden ser definidas como opcionales u obligatorias.

Una vez creadas, o elegidas de entre las preexistentes, las tareas deben ser planificadas de una de tres maneras disponibles: secuencial, es decir que se ejecutarán una después de la otra de forma lineal; libre, es decir que se presentarán al usuario todas las tareas a la vez para que éste elija en qué orden realizarlas; o bifurcada, caso en el cual se planifica el orden de manera más compleja indicando condiciones para realizar determinadas tareas.

Fig. 2. Ejemplos de tipos de tarea

La planificación de tareas se realiza, desde la herramienta Web, mediante un editor gráfico que muestra las tareas como círculos y la relación anterior-siguiente con flechas. Las conexiones entre tareas (flechas) pueden ser simples, indicando una sucesión directa entre una tarea y otra, o condicionales, indicando que después de una tarea la siguiente se ejecutará sólo si se cumple una condición, que puede estar relacionado con lo respondido en la tarea anterior o con el camino tomado hasta el momento en la ejecución de la actividad (si pasó o no pasó por cierta tarea anterior). Las conexiones simples son flechas que pasan a través de un círculo, mientras que las conexiones condicionales se muestran con flechas que pasan a través de cuadrados.

Cuando se termina la planificación, el autor tiene la posibilidad de revisar la actividad o publicarla. En este último caso, la actividad pasa a estar disponible para la recepción de respuestas. Se puede entonces descargar la actividad al dispositivo móvil en formato JSON para su posterior ejecución. Si se desea dejar de recibir respuestas por un período de tiempo, se puede poner la actividad como cerrada temporalmente.

La misma herramienta web permite la visualización de los resultados de una manera simple, en forma de tabla. Se muestran como títulos de la tabla los nombres de las tareas, y cada columna es una respuesta enviada por un usuario desde la aplicación móvil.

Además de la creación de actividades se permite la consulta de otras actividades y tareas que sean públicas, y todas las actividades y tareas propias. Existe una funcionalidad que permite crear una segunda actividad a partir de una actividad específica, reutilizando su estructura de planificación. Es decir, que si la actividad original consistía de dos tareas seguidas de una bifurcación y luego dos más, una a cada lado de la bifurcación, la actividad nueva conservará esta propiedad pero se deberá rellenar la estructura con tareas nuevas.

Primero se indican las características de la actividad nueva (si es pública o privada, el idioma, etc) y luego se muestra una pantalla con la estructura a copiar y "huecos" para completar con tareas nuevas. En este punto se pueden elegir o crear las tareas que rellenan los espacios y se pasa a la etapa de planificación. En esta etapa la estructura ya está definida, pero las condiciones que dependen de las tareas específicas que había en la primera actividad deben ser ajustadas, como puede verse en la Figura 3. Hecho esto la actividad está terminada y lista para ser publicada.

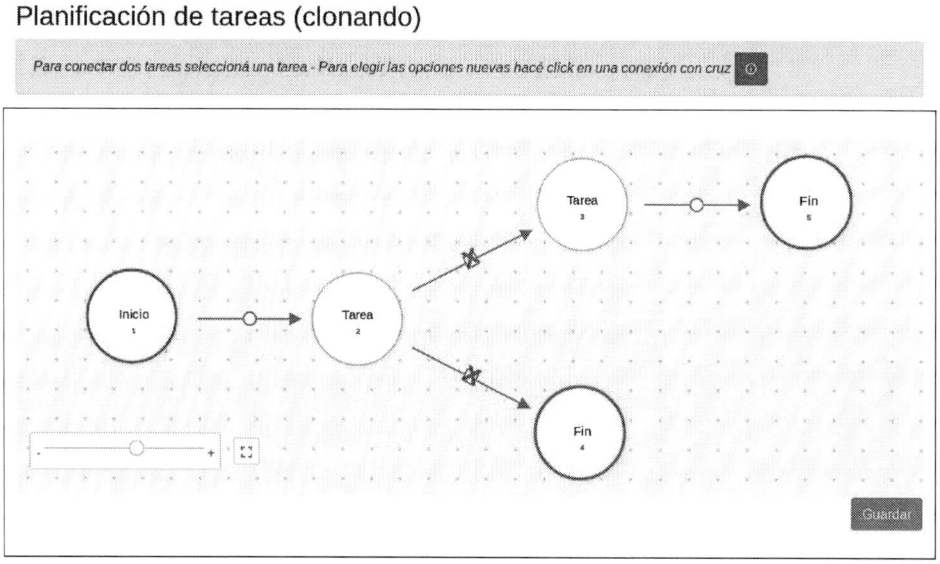

Fig. 3. Planificación de una actividad reutilizando la estructura (las cruces son las condiciones que deben ser ajustadas)

Aplicación móvil. Las actividades son descargadas en el dispositivo de cada usuario en formato JSON. Una vez abierta, la aplicación móvil detecta las actividades presentes en el dispositivo móvil y las muestra en una lista. La interfaz toma el idioma que se indica en la actividad (español o inglés) y se comienzan a mostrar las tareas de acuerdo a la planificación que tenga configurada (secuencial, libre o bifurcada). La interfaz se adapta a los tipos de tareas configurados en la actividad, mostrando pantallas tales como "elegir opciones" o "marcar posiciones en un mapa" por ejemplo, como puede verse en la Figura 4.

Fig. 4. Pantalla para tarea de localización

Una vez completadas todas las tareas obligatorias se procede a enviar los resultados. Notar que sólo se requiere internet para mostrar el mapa (existe la alternativa de escribir una dirección en texto) y al enviar las respuestas.

API. La API REST es la que brinda las funcionalidades que luego es mostrada por la herramienta Web. Estas funcionalidades incluyen la gestión de las actividades, tareas y planificaciones, el manejo de la autenticación y autorización en la aplicación, la recepción de respuestas desde la aplicación móvil y la devolución de los mismos de forma ordenada.

4 Caso de estudio y pruebas de usuario

Se tomó como caso de estudio una necesidad del Programa E-Basura de la Universidad Nacional de La Plata, el cual aborda la problemática de los Residuos de Aparatos Eléctricos y Electrónicos (RAEE) transformándolos en acciones para la inclusión digital, la equidad social y la protección ambiental [19]. Una de las áreas de trabajo del Programa consiste en la admisión de donaciones de elementos electrónicos en desuso para su posterior reacondicionamiento o descarte seguro [20]. Para coordinar la entrega del material se disponía de un formulario web [21]. En el encabezado del formulario se cuenta con diferentes secciones entre las cuales figura la sección de Datos de Contacto, al cargar este dato, la carga de datos que lo precede, varía de acuerdo a si es una donación particular o institucional.

Para este trabajo, se propuso una actividad basada en dicho formulario, utilizando la plataforma DEHIA y enriqueciendo el formulario original con tareas, como por ejemplo, para tomar una foto o grabar audio.

La actividad resultante tiene 22 tareas, algunas de ellas opcionales, e incluye saltos condicionales. La Figura 5 muestra el diseño conceptual de la actividad.

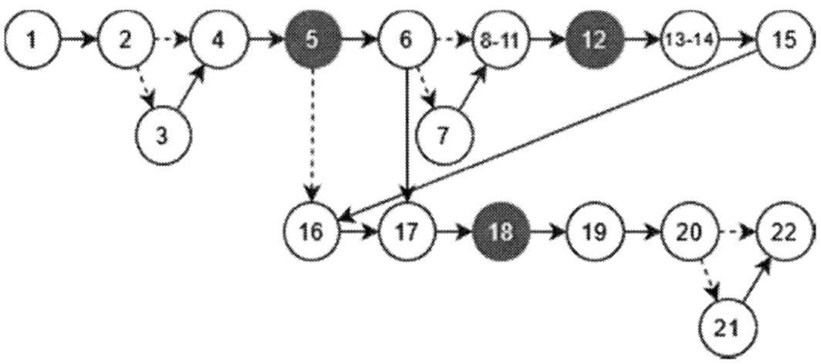

Fig. 5. Diseño conceptual de la actividad propuesta

En la Figura 5, las tareas opcionales se visualizan con relleno en gris, mientras que los saltos condicionales se muestran mediante líneas punteadas.

4.1 Creación de la actividad usando la herramienta Web

La actividad se crea indicando su nombre, su objetivo, idioma, entre otros campos. El tipo de planificación indica de qué manera se organizan las tareas. Para lograr una estructura como la del diseño conceptual visualizado en la Figura 5, se indica un tipo de planificación Bifurcada. La Figura 6 muestra la pantalla de creación de actividades.

A continuación se eligen o crean las tareas que van a formar parte de la actividad. Una tarea se crea indicando su nombre, una consigna, un tipo, un estado (público o privado) y un dominio.

Una vez creadas o elegidas todas las tareas, se procede a la planificación de las tareas. Para generar los saltos condicionales se necesita indicar la condición de salto.

El último paso consiste en poner la actividad como "Definitiva" y descargarla para comenzar a recibir respuestas.

Fig. 6. Pantalla de creación de actividades

4.2 Resolución de la actividad desde la aplicación móvil

Cuando se descarga una actividad en el dispositivo móvil (en formato JSON), ésta pasa a estar disponible en la pantalla inicial donde se elige la actividad a ejecutar (Figura 7)

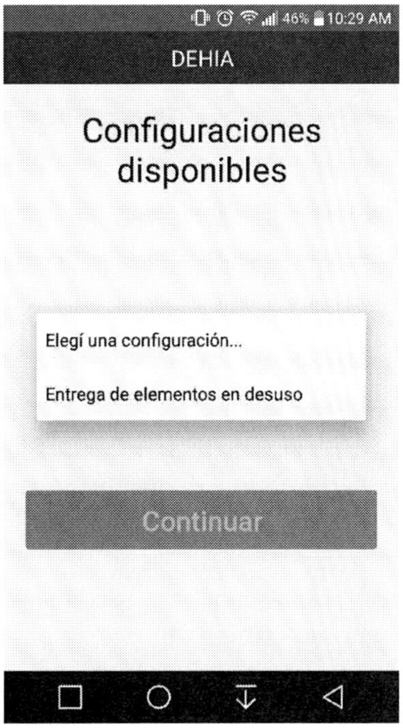

Fig. 7. Selección de actividades disponibles

De este modo, se ejecutan las tareas en el orden planificado. Una de las tareas que no figuraba entre los campos originales del formulario (tomar una foto) se muestra en la Figura 8.

Fig. 8. Tarea de tomar una foto

Una vez resueltas, por parte del usuario, todas las tareas no opcionales, pueden enviarse los resultados al servidor.

4.3 Pruebas de usuario

Se realizaron pruebas de usuario para medir la usabilidad de la herramienta Web de creación de actividades. Para tal fin se utilizó una encuesta que incluye un SUS (Simple Usability Scale), "un cuestionario simple de diez preguntas que provee una visión global de aspectos subjetivos de la usabilidad" [22].

La actividad se redujo a seis tareas representativas a fin de poder resolver la prueba en un tiempo razonable (no más de cuarenta minutos por participante). Se contó con participantes con diferente nivel de manejo de sistemas informáticos. Los usuarios no presentaron mayores dificultades para la resolución de la prueba y se tomaron en promedio, unos 16 minutos para realizarla. Los participantes más experimentados tomaron en promedio 13 minutos contra 19 de los no experimentados, lo cual se atribuye a la velocidad de tipeo de cada uno. En cuanto al resultado del SUS, se obtuvo un puntaje general de 70 (siendo aceptable "más de 68"). La mayor tasa de aceptación (nivel alto en el SUS) estuvo dada en los participantes menos experimentados, que son el público objetivo de la herramienta [18].

5 Conclusiones y trabajos futuros

El trabajo presenta una plataforma de recolección de datos que permite la creación de actividades, en múltiples dominios, por parte de usuarios sin conocimientos de programación. La plataforma incluye: una herramienta Web para el diseño y la creación de actividades, una aplicación móvil para resolver dichas actividades y un servidor que recibe las respuestas enviadas desde la aplicación móvil y que además, provee los resultados.

Se revisó el estado del arte de plataformas existentes que comparten un flujo de trabajo que consiste en [Diseñar →] Definir, → Ejecutar → Visualizar [23]. Se analizaron las funcionalidades y características específicas de cada herramienta de definición, aplicación móvil y servidor. Se observó que si bien cada plataforma tiene sus particularidades, hay una serie de características básicas en común a todas ellas, incluyendo la plataforma propuesta, como tipos de tareas soportadas, facilidades del editor de actividades, usabilidad de la aplicación móvil, etcétera. Cabe destacar que ninguna de las plataformas analizadas presenta la posibilidad de reutilización de tareas o actividades (aunque durante la redacción de este informe Epicollect5 agregó una funcionalidad para importar actividades completas) y solo MoLE y la plataforma propuesta permiten la visualización y edición gráfica de la estructura del workflow subyacente a la planificación de las tareas.

Para validar la propuesta, se desarrolló una solución prototípica que implementa una pequeña parte de la plataforma definida. Se detallaron los componentes específicos (clientes, servicios, compuerta, mecanismos de persistencia) que fueron elegidos para su implementación por formar parte del núcleo de la funcionalidad y que permitieran obtener una versión reducida pero completa en cuanto a sus prestaciones funcionales. Se ilustró la explicación de las características implementadas mediante un conjunto de capturas de pantalla del sistema en funcionamiento, que cumple con el flujo de trabajo ([Diseñar →] Definir, → Ejecutar → Visualizar) propio de este tipo de soluciones.

Se aplicó el prototipo al dominio de los RAEE (Residuos de Aparatos Eléctricos y Electrónicos) a través de una actividad para vehiculizar la donación de elementos en desuso para el Programa E-Basura y se realizaron las respectivas pruebas de usuario sobre los prototipos propuestos.

Se espera que la plataforma facilite el acceso a la recolección de datos a usuarios sin conocimientos de programación, favoreciendo la reutilización de esfuerzo y conocimiento de otros usuarios.

Entre los trabajos futuros previstos, mencionaremos que se puede separar en los aspectos funcionales de la solución y los aspectos arquitectónicos.

Entre los aspectos funcionales más importantes a extender se encuentran: 1-agregar un módulo para la ejecución de los workflows desde la plataforma Web, 2- sumar la edición colaborativa para la co-creación (diseño participativo) por un lado de las tareas y por otro de los workflows, 3- mejorar y ampliar el componente de visualización de datos

Respecto de los aspectos arquitectónicos, se pretende avanzar con mecanismos de persistencia más adecuados al volumen de datos utilizando (Elasticsearch), mecanismos de captura de los datos recolectados a través de dispositivos IoT, mecanismos de resiliencia que ayuden a la disponibilidad y mejoren la usabilidad, y también mecanismos de comunicación entre los servicios, que actualmente es sincrónica y se beneficiaría de un esquema dirigido por eventos.

Referencias

1. Arcidiacono, J., Lliteras, A. B., & Bazán, P. A. (2020). DEHIA, una plataforma para la generación y ejecución de actividades de recolección de datos con intervención humana aplicada en el Programa E-Basura. In *VI Simposio Argentino de Ciencia de Datos y GRANdes DAtos (AGRANDA 2020)-JAIIO 49 (Modalidad virtual).*
2. Cochero, J. (2018). AppEAR: Una aplicación móvil de ciencia ciudadana para mapear la calidad de los hábitats acuáticos continentales. Ecología Austral, 28(2), 467-479.
3. Balsalobre, A., Ceccarelli, S., Cano, M. E., Ferrari, W. A., Cochero, J., & Martí, G. A. (2018). GeoVin: Ciencia Ciudadana para aprender de las vinchucas de Argentina. In II Congreso Argentino de Ciencia Abierta y Ciudadana (CIACIAR)(Universidad Nacional de San Martín, 2 de noviembre de 2018).
4. Kelvin, A. A., Banner, D., Pamplona, L., Alencar, C., Rubino, S., & Heukelbach, J. (2016). ZIKATracker: A mobile App for reporting cases of ZIKV worldwide. The Journal of Infection in Developing Countries, 10(02), 113-115.
5. Simpson, R., Page, K. R., & De Roure, D. (2014, April). Zooniverse: observing the world's largest citizen science platform. In Proceedings of the 23rd international conference on world wide web (pp. 1049-1054).
6. Aanensen, David M., et al. "EpiCollect+: linking smartphones to web applications for complex data collection projects." F1000Research 3 (2014).
7. Lliteras A.B., Grigera J., Corporaal F.R.M., Di Claudio F., Gordillo S.E. (2020) A Flexible Web Authoring Tool for Building Mobile Learning Experiences. In: Pesado P., Arroyo M. (eds) Computer Science – CACIC 2019. CACIC 2019. Communications in Computer and Information Science, vol 1184. Springer, Cham
8. Sprinks, J., Wardlaw, J., Houghton, R., Bamford, S., & Morley, J. (2017). Task Workflow Design and its impact on performance and volunteers' subjective preference in Virtual Citizen Science. International Journal of Human-Computer Studies, 104, 50-63.
9. Kunze, Matthias, and Mathias Weske. Behavioural models: From modelling finite automata to analysing business processes. Springer, 2016.
10. Lliteras, A. B. (2015). Un enfoque de modelado de actividades educativas posicionadas que contemplan elementos concretos. Tesis de maestría. Facultad de Informática, UNLP.
11. "Epicollect5 - Free and easy-to-use mobile data-gathering platform.". Centre for Genomic Pathogen Surveillance. URL: https://five.epicollect.net/. Last accessed: 04-05-2021
12. "Zooniverse". Zooniverse. URL: https://www.zooniverse.org/. Last accessed: 04-05-2021
13. Bonney, R., Cooper, C. B., Dickinson, J., Kelling, S., Phillips, T., Rosenberg, K. V., & Shirk, J. (2009). Citizen science: a developing tool for expanding science knowledge and scientific literacy. BioScience,59(11), 977-984.

14. Trouille, Laura; Lintott, Chris J.; Fortson, Lucy F. Citizen science frontiers: Efficiency, engagement, and serendipitous discovery with human–machine systems. Proceedings of the National Academy of Sciences, 2019, vol. 116, no 6, p. 1902-1909.
15. "ODK - Collect data anywhere". ODK. URL: "https://getodk.org/". Last accessed: 04-05-2021.
16. "MOLE-Authoring-Tool". MoLE Github repository. URL: "https://github.com/cientopolis/MOLE-Authoring-Tool" Last accessed: 05-05-2021
17. Lliteras, A. B., Challiol, C., & Gordillo, S. E. (2017, October). Location-based mobile learning applications: a conceptual framework for co-design. In 2017 Twelfth Latin American Conference on Learning Technologies (LACLO) (pp. 1-8). IEEE.
18. Arcidiacono, J (2020). DEHIA: una plataforma liviana para definir y ejecutar actividades con intervención humana basadas en workflows. Tesina de grado. Facultad de Informática, UNLP. http://sedici.unlp.edu.ar/handle/10915/116617
19. "Programa E-Basura". URL: https://E-Basura.unlp.edu.ar/. Last accessed: 04-05-2021
20. "e-basura - Preguntas Frecuentes". Programa E-basura. URL https://e-basura.unlp.edu.ar/preguntas_frecuentes. Last accessed: 04-05-2021
21. "Formulario de entrega de elementos". E-basura. URL: https://encuestas.linti.unlp.edu.ar/index.php/369463/lang-es. Last accessed: 04-05-2021.
22. Brooke, J. (1996). SUS: a "quick and dirty usability scale". Usability evaluation in industry, 189.
23. Steinberg, M., Schindler, S. & Klan, F., (2019). Software solutions for form-based, mobile data collection – A comparative evaluation. In: Meyer, H., Ritter, N., Thor, A., Nicklas, D., Heuer, A. & Klettke, M. (Hrsg.), BTW 2019 – Workshopband. Gesellschaft für Informatik, Bonn. (S. 135-144). DOI: 10.18420/btw2019-ws-14

On the Challenges for Creating a Test Suite for Configurable Software Systems

Fischer Ferreira[1], João P. Diniz[1], Gustavo Vale[2], and Eduardo Figueiredo[1]

[1] Federal University of Minas Gerais (UFMG)
[2] Saarland University, Saarbrücken, Germany
{fischerjf, jpaulo, figueiredo}@dcc.ufmg.br, vale@cs.uni-saarland.de

Abstract. Configurable software systems allow developers to maintain a unique platform and address a diversity of deployment contexts and usages. Testing configurable systems is essential because configurations that fail may potentially hurt users and degrade the project reputation. Considering a gap of knowledge on creating tests for configurable software systems, we propose a list of ten challenges faced when performing test suites for configurable systems and dealing with a test suite for our dataset systems. Our list includes, for instance, the challenges of testing high coupled classes and of determining metrics for measuring the quality of the test suite. Our results can be seen as lessons learned on creating tests for configurable systems and they aim at supporting researchers and practitioners on this activity for configurable systems.

Keywords: Testing Configurable Systems, Software Faults, Feature Interaction, Challenges

1 Introduction

Configurable software systems (for short, *configurable systems*) are systems that can be efficiently extended, changed, or customized based on a set of features that fits specific customer needs [3]. Features allow configurable systems to have an optional or incremental unit of functionality [4]. The Web browser Firefox, Linux Kernel, and Android family are well-known examples of configurable systems.

Testing configurable systems is even more challenging than testing traditional software systems since instead of testing a product, configurable systems entail testing the set of all possible combinations of features. As the size of possible configurations to be tested grows exponentially, the testing effort becomes costly and often impractical [17, 21, 24]. Furthermore, dealing with all feature combinations may generate undesired feature interaction [31]. Unexpected feature interactions occurs when features that work correctly separately cause unexpected behavior when executing together with other features [31]. Given the recurring issues caused by unexpected feature interactions, several researchers have proposed approaches and techniques to deal with them [23, 26].

Although previous work concentrates on *the explosion of combinations* and *feature interactions* challenges, we present other challenges faced when testing configuration systems in practice. For instance, the challenges (1) on the creation of a test suite, (2) on measuring the test suite and its quality, and (3) on the identification of faults are often ignored. We defined ten challenges related to configurable software testing based through our experience when creating and extending the test suite for our dataset systems [11, 12]. Our main goal is to report the main challenges in the complete life-cycle of 30 open-source configuration systems [9–12]. Therefore, instead of focus on the well-known challenges present in the literature, we present challenges faced when creating, extending, assessing, and using test suites for 30 configurable systems. For brief, our list of challenges is:

1. *Creating from scratch and expanding test suites*
2. *Creating test cases in highly coupled classes*
3. *Dealing with the combinatorial explosion of configurations*
4. *Sampling configurations for test*
5. *Running the test suites*
6. *Assessing the quality of the automated test suites*
7. *Measuring the test suites*
8. *Dealing with false positives from tests*
9. *Tracking feature interaction faults*
10. *Finding technical debts in test cases of configurable systems*

We believe that presenting the faced challenges on the complete life-cycle of 30 configurable systems is just a starting point for researchers to deeply investigate each challenge and propose different ways to deal with them. Practitioners can also benefit from our work by looking at our solutions on each challenge and, hopefully, save time. At the end, we learned that testing configurable systems is related to the ability to automatically run test cases for all possible/desired configurations and identify faults efficiently. Furthermore, a high concentration of faults in a region of code (i.e., a method, class, or feature) might also be an indicative of technical debt in such region [10].

2 Background and Related Work

Configurable systems can be efficiently customized according to a set of features (configuration options) that satisfies different customer needs [32]. The source code that belongs to deactivated features is ignored in a determined configuration. To develop configurable systems, developers may choose between the two main strategies: *compile-* and *execution-time* [3].

In compile-time strategies, developers activate a set of features that is preprocessed in order to generate the final product [3]. This strategy can be divided into annotative and compositional approaches. Conditional compilation (CC) is a technique that uses the former approach [28], while Feature-oriented Programming (FOP) [4], Aspectual Feature Modules (AFM) [3], and Delta-oriented Programming (DOP) [29] are examples of techniques that implement the latter. The main difference among these approaches is that, in the annotative strategy, developers annotate their code (e.g., with `#ifdef`-like directives) to represent variation points, while in compositional approaches, developers implement each variation point in modularized components (e.g., features [4] in FOP, and deltas [29] in DOP). The LINUX KERNEL and the FIREFOX WEB BROWSER are examples of configurable systems developed with compile-time strategies.

In execution-time strategies, developers activate features that contain code blocks at execution-time [28]. Variability encoding is an example of execution-time strategy [3]. Similar to conditional compilation, developers should create conditional structures (e.g., `if/else` statements or ternary operator `?:`), and generate the so-called *meta-products* [34]. Then, developers should create configuration files determining features to be active in a target configuration. This way, all features can be activated or deactivated at execution time [21, 24]. ANDROID FAMILY is a (set of) configurable system(s) developed using variability encoding [24]. In this study, configurable systems are systems that the features code are enabled or disabled at runtime. We do not consider program parameters [3] and compile-time strategies to determine configurations.

2.1 Feature Interaction Problem

Feature interactions occur when features influence the behavior of other features. It becomes an issue when developers look at features together and find an unexpected behavior that does not occur when they look at features in isolation [31]. Unexpected behavior can introduce faults that manifest themselves in specific configurations. Feature interactions are among the greatest challenges in developing configurable systems [31] and enforces the need to create testing suites that cover all potential interactions [26]. These faults are usually caused by a problem with the interactions of two or more features.

```
public class WeatherReport {
  private Date date;
  private String temperature;

  public WeatherReport(Date currentDate, String
      currentTemperature){
    this.date = currentDate;
    this.temperature = currentTemperature;
  }

  public String createText(String c) {
    if (Configuration.SMILEY)
      c = c.replace(":]", getSmiley(":]"));
    if (Configuration.WEATHER)
      c = c.replace("[:weather:]", temperature);
    return c;
  }
}
```

Listing 1.1. Variability encoding example adapted from [24]

Listing 1.1 presents a traditional and simple example of feature interaction faults [24]. In this example, the `createText` method edits and returns a string *c*. Case only feature SMILEY is active, the method replaces *:]* by ☺. Looking at Listing 1.1, we see that both features use a string *":]"*. It may cause a feature interaction fault. To illustrate, let us consider that *createText* method receives as input the string *"[:weather:]"* (i.e., *c* = *[:weather:]*) and both features SMILEY and WEATHER are enabled. This way feature SMILEY will change string *c* to *[:weather*☺ and the code of feature WEATHER will not find the expected string *c* anymore, even thought it was exactly the expected input string before.

2.2 Related Work

There are dozens of papers that describe the challenge of testing configurable systems [21, 23, 24, 32]. However, previous work has focused on reporting the combinatorial difficulty explosion of the number of configurations to test and feature interaction faults. This section discusses two studies related to these challenges. The first discusses the difficulty in dealing with the combinatorial explosion of the number of configurations. The second discusses feature interaction faults.

Generating test configurations. Souto et al. [32] discusses the generation of test configurations in two different approaches through the sound test technique that generates all configurations. However, they argue that the approach does not scale to a system with many features. In addition, they discuss an alternative approach to test all possible configurations through sample testing. Their work aims to demonstrate the costs to test configurable systems and present a sample test solution to reduce this cost. Different from them, we demonstrate our personal observations based on previous empirical studies on other aspects related to the test phase. For this, we have listed seven challenges and our initial ideas for dealing with the challenges listed.

Feature Interaction Faults. Soares et al. [31] discusses aspects related to challenges arising from feature interaction faults by observing 35 primary studies. Through the observations of their work, it is possible to note the community's concern for decades about the problems related to the interaction of features. Our work demonstrates seven challenges related to the test phase, which are ultimately related to this major objective of identifying feature interaction faults.

3 Our Experience on Testing Configurable Systems

Considering that the lack of studies reporting and investigating the challenges on the complete life-cycle of testing configurable systems, we aim at filling this gap by **reporting the challenges we faced when creating, extending, assessing, using, and identifying faults on the test suites of 30 configurable systems** [11]. These challenges can benefit both researchers and practitioners since the creation, use, and maintenance of test suites are a fundamental step for testing configurable systems and our lessons learned can be used, for instance, as a starting point for future research.

Figure 1 provides an overview of the steps of our research, highlighting the lessons learned at each step. We also use the knowledge on creating test cases to propose the ten challenges in this paper. To achieve our goal, we performed a systematic mapping study (step 1), created and/or extended test suites for 30 configurable systems (step 2), empirically investigated testing strategies to generate a set of configurations to be tested (step 3 and step 4), and summarize the observed challenges during the life-cycle of testing configurable systems (step 5). Note that, despite we learned lessons in the first four steps, the focus of this paper is the last step. We spent an average of one year to complete the studies of Steps 1, 2, 3, and 4.

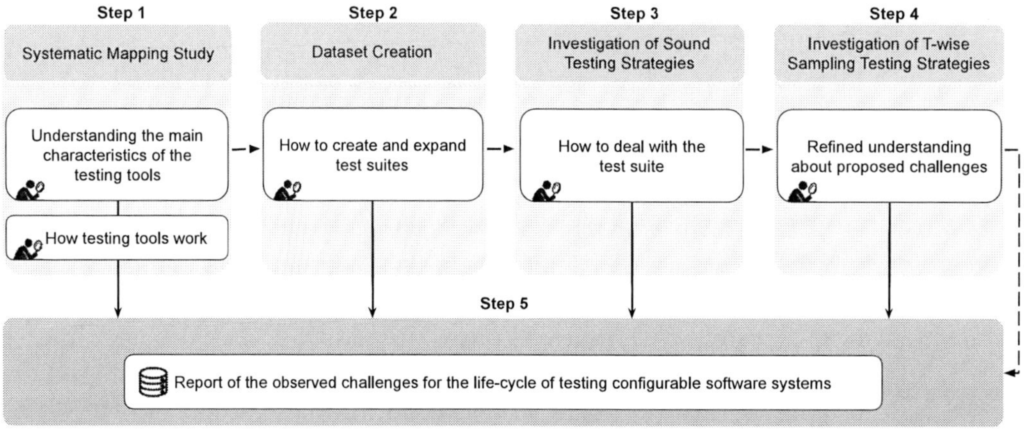

Fig. 1. Study steps

Step 1. We performed a systematic mapping study aiming at identifying the existing testing tools for configurable systems [9]. In this systematic mapping study, we (i) provided an overview of the state-of-the-art of testing strategies for configurable systems, (ii) analyzed the main characteristics of the testing tools for configurable systems, and (iii) presented the main strategies used to test configurable systems. We found a total of 34 tools and collected the main characteristics of testing tools for configurable systems. Through this step, we understand how the testing tools for configurable systems work and their main characteristics. In addition, Step 1 was essential to discover what are the main restrictions of testing configurable systems [9].

Step 2. We conduct an *ad hoc* literature review by analyzing survey papers on testing configurable systems and well-known datasets of configurable systems (e.g., SPL2go and SPLRepository) [11]. Despite we have found 60 configurable systems developed in Java-based programming languages, only 10 configurable systems have their test suite public available. Aiming at increasing this number, we create a test suite for further 20 systems. The creation of tests followed two stop criteria: (i) at least 70% of code coverage and (ii) at least 40% of the mutants killed. These two criteria aims at providing a high-quality testing dataset. At the end, we created test suites for 30 configurable systems. With the creation and expansion of the test suites for the dataset systems, we identified the main challenges faced. This the first dataset has been used by the community to research testing approaches in configurable systems [12].

Step 3. We conducted a comparative study [9], we evaluated the two main sound tools found in the systematic mapping studies: *VarexJ* [24] and *SPLat* [21]. The main goal of that study was to identify advantages and drawbacks on testing tools that use sound testing techniques. Hence, we measured the effectiveness and efficiency of *VarexJ* and *SPLat* to test seven systems acquired in the step 2. We only use seven configurable systems from our dataset due to the limitations of the non-scaling approach for systems with many features. We observed that, even though both tools use sound testing technique strategy, they generally did not present high intersection rates [9]. Alternatively, our experiments have shown that for configurable systems with up to 17 features, it was possible to use testing strategies that test all configurations.

Step 4. In this study [10], we compared variations of five t-wise sampling testing strategies, named *CASA* [16], *Chvatal* [18], *ICPL* [18], *IncLing* [2], and *YASA* [22]. We selected t-wise strategies because they ensure a degree of coverage for determining the set of configurations recommended by the strategy. At the end, we compared sixteen t-wise strategies (*CASA-T1*, *CASA-T2*, *CASA-T3*, *CASA-T4*, *Chvatal-T1*, *Chvatal-T2*, *Chvatal-T3*, *Chvatal-T4*, *ICPL-T1*, *ICPL-T2*, *ICPL-T3*, *IncLing-T2*, *YASA-T1*, *YASA-T2*, *YASA-T3*, and *YASA-T4*) and two baselines (*brute force* and *random selection*).

Step 5. We summarize the main challenges observed in the previous steps. These steps are the main outcome of this study and are presented in the next section.

4 Ten Challenges for Testing Configurable Systems

This section presents the ten main challenges observed when creating, extending, assessing, using, and identifying faults on the test suites of 30 configurable systems in our previous studies [9–12]. For each challenge, we present our solution. Each following subsection describes a challenge.

4.1 Creating from Scratch and Expanding Test Suites

Both creating and expanding a test suite for configurable systems are challenging because, when designing test cases, the requirements of the configurable system, the variability of features, and their functionality should be taken into account. That is, it has to be adjusted in terms of which test cases should be performed according to the state of the features (active/inactive) since it is not feasible to select each test for the configuration to be tested manually.

The test suite has to be automatically called and only the tests related to the current configuration must be performed. In this way, in the design of the test cases, we have to consider active feature for the test case to be executed. For that, a mechanism must be made in each test case to test the requirements using the specific active features. On the other hand, such a mechanism is necessary to prevent the test cases related to inactive features from being executed. If this occurs, the test result will be a false positive.

Solution. Listing 1.2 shows a test class for the example presented in Listing 1.1. In addition to the environment set up, it shows a test case testing the `createText` method when the feature WEATHER is active. For short, taking *"[:weather:]"* as input, it should provide *"30.0° C"* as output. Note that as we have only 2 features, it is easy to create test cases to cover all 4 possible configuration scenarios (i.e., 2^2). However, as the number of related features increases, it is not feasible anymore. To deal with that, we inserted a general configuration file loaded before the execution of the test suite. A further observation is that automated testing tools are not helpful on creating test cases, specially when expanding a test suite. Initially, we tried to use tools to automatically generate test cases (e.g., RANDOOP [27] and EVOSUITE [14]). However, after the generation of a small number of test cases, the subsequent new ones usually did not increase the test coverage as well as the percentage of killed mutants. As result, we suggest that testers use these tools carefully to only generate preliminary versions of their test suites.

```
public class WeatherReportTest {
  WeatherReport wr;
  @Before
  public void setUp() {
    wr = new WeatherReport("2019-11-13", "30.0°C");
  }

  @Test
  public void weatherTest () {
   if (Configuration.WEATHER)
    assertEquals(wr.createText("[:weather:]"), "30.0°C");
  }
}
```

Listing 1.2. Test Cases for the WeatherReport Class

4.2 Creating Test Cases in Highly Coupled Classes

To have a deep understanding on the projects of our dataset [11], we first needed to read the documentation. After, we spent a considerable time understanding their architecture and source-code. We noted that high coupling classes made the understanding challenging. It also reflected on the creation of test cases because we had to take care of relationships that, in the first moment, were hidden.

Solution. To overcome this scenario, we had to simulate some particular setup that in the first moment was challenging to achieve given high coupling among classes. After creating test cases for several projects, it became easier because we could reuse some strategies, or find some pieces of code that helped with feature interaction problems. We use MOCKITO [25] to allow the creation of mock object simplifying the development of tests for classes with dependencies of other classes [33].

4.3 Dealing with the Combinatorial Explosion of Configurations

The main challenge researchers and software companies face when developing configurable software systems is to test them. Indeed, adding configuration options yields a combinatorial explosion on the number of configurations to test. Therefore, it is impractical to test them all. For example, a configurable system with 320 features can yield more possibilities (i.e., software variants) than the number of atoms in the universe. It is an insuperable challenge to test all possibilities of configurations for systems with many features. While in traditional software systems there is only one configuration (a combination of features) to be tested, for configurable systems we need to run all tests in several different configurations.

Configurable software testing can be divided into two main parts, generating the configurations and running the automated test suite for these configurations. To generate configurations, we may use strategies that have been developed to test configurable systems [9]. These strategies can be classified into: variability-aware testing [21, 24] and configuration sampling testing [2, 32]. *Variability-aware testing strategies* explore dynamically all reachable configurations from a given test, by monitoring feature variable accesses during test execution. Concerning running the test suite for the generated configurations, it is possible to make a configuration partition and test the configurations by groups.

Solution. To test the most significant number of configurations in our study, we run all valid configurations for configurable systems with up to 17 features. However, for the other systems, we have created a configuration list for testing that is the union set all configurations run by the sixteen testing strategies (see Step 4, Section 3). Using multiple sampling strategies allows us to achieve a wide range of configurations at a low cost [10].

4.4 Sampling Configurations for Test

Even if testing all possible configurations of a configurable system is possible, the test suite's quality positively impacts the efficiency on observing faults. Generating the configurations and running the test suite is time consuming. Recall that the time consumption can consist of the sum of the time to generate configurations (by sampling strategies) and the time to run the test suite for the configurations [10]. The ideal scenario is to test all valid configurations but, in practice, the explosion of configurations for testing makes exhaustive testing prohibitively expensive and practically infeasible. Alternatively, developers may test a sample of valid configurations [2]. Several strategies for choosing a sample of configurations to test have been proposed. Some of them use information only from the *feature model* [2, 18], while others also use information from the source code [21, 32].

Solution. Nowadays, several sampling test strategies are available [2, 16, 18, 22], but, the choice of a testing strategy should be adapted to the time available for testing. Even using a sample strategy testing, the total testing time can take hours [10]. In this way, during the configurable system life-cycle, different test strategies can be used to meet the constraints of efficiency and effectiveness. For instance, *1-wise* strategies (e.g., *Chvatal-T1* and *ICPL-T1*) prioritize a minimal number of configurations and are able to find faults. On the other hand, if developers needs a more robust check and can wait longer, they can use strategies that return a greater number of configurations, such as *Chvatal-T4* and *ICPL-T3*. Testing few configurations in the test phase of configurable systems can be an effective alternative as a preliminary and superficial evaluation of the configurable system. However, a preliminary assessment may not discover all feature interaction faults, as these types of faults are harder to discover. In this way, using an efficient strategy can support testing for configurable systems.

4.5 Running the Test Suites

The number of configurations for testing determines the number of times the test suite runs. Therefore, configurable systems with hundreds of configurations result in hundreds of runs of the test suite. Hence, the process of running the suite for each configuration must be automated. Faults in configurable systems can occur in the same test case, but with different configurations. Therefore, there is no point in running the test suite several times if it is impossible to track where the faults occurred.

Algorithm 1 Test suite execution manager

Require: List of configurations selected for testing
Ensure: Test reports

```
totalConfigurations ← size(ListOfConfigurations)
config ← 1
while config ≤ totalConfigurations do
    c=nextConfiguration(ListOfConfigurations)
    setFeatures(c);
    Execute the test suite with configuration c
    config ← config + 1
end while
```

Solution. We created in our studies a way to record the output of JUnit's execution [19], always using as a pair the configuration for testing and the line of the test case where the fault was triggered. We use the processor defined in previous work to record JUnit's execution [9]. In this way, in the subsequent analysis of the faults report, we can quickly identify which configuration fails and which part of the test case code triggered the faults. Algorithm 1 shows a pseudo-code demonstrating how to run the entire test suite for each configuration selected for testing strategy.

4.6 Assessing the Quality of the Automated Test Suites

Despite of some techniques proposed for traditional systems to evaluate the quality of tests (e.g., mutation analysis technique), we still face with the challenge of testing multiple configurations in configurable systems.

Mutation testing is a fault-based technique commonly used to evaluate the effectiveness of software testing [20]. Even though it is a self cost technique, it has been empirically shown to be one of the most robust test selection criteria when compared to other measures, such as control flow and data flow-based testing [20]. Mutation testing consists of introducing syntactical changes, called mutations, into the source code and check whether the test cases distinguish them [8]. The resulting programs are called mutants. A mutant is killed if a test case observes the modification of the mutant from the original code. If the test suite cannot see changes, the mutant remains alive indicating that the test suite is not good enough to identify faults and developers should improve their test suite to kill surviving mutants.

Solution. To use this technique in a test suite for a configurable system, a viable alternative is to choose among the valid configurations, a single configuration that exercises a greater number of test cases. Then, it is possible to use a test case generation tool, such as PIT [6]. Through the generated mutants it is possible to check the quality of the test cases to kill the introduced mutants. New test cases can be created to kill living, non-equivalent mutants [8]. We use the mutant generation process described in the previous work [10].

4.7 Measuring the Test Suites

You cannot control something if you cannot measure it [7]. Hence, we needed to find ways to measure what the test suite covers. Metrics like code coverage and the number of test cases are not enough to know if the test suite covers a particular feature. The testers can prioritize the test for specific features because they have more accessible testing features and do not cover with testing other features in the same way. Therefore, we need to measure how the test suite covers the features.

Solution. Specific metrics to identify test suite coverage can also help the tester creating new test cases. For example, if a particular feature has higher priority for users of the configurable system, this feature should be heavily tested. In our studies, we measured the distribution of the test suite for each feature by calculating the variability points for each class and identifying which features reach the variability point. After, we checked which test cases can test each code fragment of the variability point. This way, we were able to estimate how the test suite tested the features.

4.8 Dealing with False Positives from Tests

The identification of false positives requires a manual verification effort. False positives occur mainly due to three problems: (i) poor test case design, (ii) lack of memory, and (iii) timeout. *Poor test case design.* The project of the test suite must consider all the features that are part of the tested functionality. Otherwise, the test case may fail for some configurations on which the target feature is not active. The problem is that this false positive can occur in only a few configurations, giving the impression of the feature interaction faults when a problem occurs in the test case design. Tests can also fail regardless of the configuration. These false positives are easier to identify, but they can cause problems when many faults have to be analyzed. A viable alternative is to correct the defects of these tests first since they fail in all configurations. Thus, with any sample configuration for testing, it is possible to identify these tests.

Lack of memory and Timeout. We analyzed the systems with several sample sizes. We noticed that when running the test suite for many configurations, the execution sometimes crashes due to a lack of memory. To identify problems with lack of memory, we identified the test reports provided by JUnit. To deal with this, we ran the test suite for batches of configuration. *Timeout.* Test cases can have problems with timeout definitions that can cause the test case to fail improperly. However, this type of fault is easily identified through the faults report provided by JUnit.

Solution. A viable alternative for identifying false positives in tests of configurable systems is to identify the failing configurations reported by the tests. Then, set the features according to the failed configuration, to the configurable system and execute only the failed test case. The analysis must occur initially to verify that all features are in the correct state. Otherwise, we checked if the computational state is correct. If no error is found in the configurable system code, the test case scenario should be reviewed.

4.9 Tracking Feature Interaction Faults

Identifying the origin of faults is challenging in configurable systems because the feature interaction must be considered. We perceived that the source code implementing some features are often tangled. We noticed two constraints needed to discover feature interaction faults. First, the sampling of configurations for testing must include at least one with feature interaction faults.

Second, at least one test case must identify the feature interaction faults. Failure to comply with these two constraints results in the tests' inability to observe faults. The first constraint takes up the challenge listed in Section 4.3 but, as discussed, it is impracticable to test all possible configurations for systems with several features. Features with feature interaction faults can appear in several valid configurations. However, if only one faulty configuration is found, it is sufficient to solve the problem reflected in several other configurations.

Solution. We observed in our study that a test case can fail several times in the same line of code but with different configurations. The developer solving the feature interaction faults of the configuration found will be correcting the faults in several other configurations that have the same feature combination. In this way, a viable alternative to identify feature interaction faults is to use testing strategies by sampling and creating compelling test suites to find faults.

Furthermore, we suggest to perform, for the list of configurations that caused faults, in each test case, the *frequent itemset mining analysis* [1]. A frequent itemset is defined as a set of items that occur together in at least a support threshold value of all available transactions . Therefore, we expect to identify which features and their respective states are most present in the faults. It is important to note that this technique can provide itemsets of different sizes, facilitating the analysis.

4.10 Finding Technical Debts in Test Cases of Configurable Systems

Patterns and catalogs have been used in software engineering to deal with challenges. As examples of catalogs, we can cite *design patterns* [15], *bad smells* [13], and *architectural patterns* [5]. We performed this last challenge to encourage the creation of standards and catalogs for testing configurable system. There are dozens of testing strategies that test by sampling [23, 10, 9]. However, there is still no consensus on which strategy to use under some constraints, such as time, the criticality of configurable systems, and the number of features.

In addition, a failure taxonomy could be created. In this sense, Soares et al. [30] proposed a list of types of feature interaction faults including Bad Annotation (the expression used in the annotation is incorrect), Wrong Object (an object used in place of another), Misplaced Variable Overwrite (the value of a variable is overwritten in a wrong place with a wrong value), Conditional Statement (incorrect implementation of conditional statements, using wrong or incomplete conditions), and Spread Code (piece of code spread over different features leading to unnecessary dependencies and problems related to code modularity).

Solution. Aiming at comparing sampling testing strategies and understanding the location of faults, we use our dataset and compare suggested configurations from variations of five t-wise testing strategies (see Step 4, Section 3). This comparison aims to find which strategies are faster, more comprehensive, effective on identifying faults, time-efficient, and coverage-efficient in this dataset and the reasons why a strategy fared better in one investigated property. As a result, we had a first step toward the identification of patterns and problems in code that may easy or hinder testing.

5 Final Remarks

This paper discussed ten challenges related to the life-cycle of tests for configurable systems. We summarized the challenges through our observations based on the background acquired from previous empirical studies. We believe that researchers and practitioners can benefit from the described challenges and can propose solutions for them making our challenges just a starting point for future research. As future work, we plan to investigate other challenges and different solutions related to tests of configurable systems.

ACKNOWLEDGMENTS

This research was partially supported by Brazilian funding agencies: CNPq (Grant 424340/2016-0), CAPES, and FAPEMIG (grant PPM-00651-17).

References

1. Agrawal, R., Srikant, R., et al.: Fast algorithms for mining association rules. In: Proceedings. 20th International Conference Very Large Data Bases, VLDB. vol. 1215, pp. 487–499. Citeseer (1994)
2. Al-Hajjaji, M., Krieter, S., Thüm, T., Lochau, M., Saake, G.: IncLing: Efficient Product-line Testing Using Incremental Pairwise Sampling . In: 15th Proceedings of the ACM SIGPLAN International Conference on Generative Programming: Concepts and Experiences (GPCE). pp. 144–155 (2016)
3. Apel, S., Batory, D.S., Kästner, C., Saake, G.: Feature-Oriented Software Product Lines – Concepts and Implementation (2013)
4. Batory, D.: Feature Models, Grammars, and Propositional Formulas. In: International Conference on Software Product Lines (SPLC). pp. 7–20 (2005)
5. Buschmann, F., Henney, K., Schmidt, D.: Pattern-oriented software architecture, on patterns and pattern languages, vol. 5. John wiley & sons (2007)
6. Coles, H., Laurent, T., Henard, C., Papadakis, M., Ventresque, A.: Pit: A Practical Mutation Testing Tool for Java. In: In 25th International Symposium on Software Testing and Analysis (ISSTA). pp. 449–452 (2016)
7. DeMarco, T.: Controlling software projects: Management, measurement, and estimates. Prentice Hall PTR (1986)
8. DeMillo, R.A., Lipton, R.J., Sayward, F.G.: Hints on test data selection: Help for the practicing programmer. Computer **11**(4), 34–41 (1978)
9. Ferreira, F., Diniz, J.P., Silva, C., Figueiredo, E.: Testing Tools for Configurable Software Systems: A Review-based Empirical Study. In: Proceedings of the 13th International Working Conference on Variability Modelling of Software-Intensive Systems (VaMoS). pp. 1–10 (2019)
10. Ferreira, F., Vale, G., Diniz, J.P., Figueiredo, E.: Evaluating T-wise Testing Strategies in a Community-wide Dataset of Configurable Software Systems. Journal of Systems and Software (JSS) (2021)
11. Ferreira, F., Vale, G., Figueiredo, E., Diniz, J.P.: On the Proposal and Evaluation of a Test-enriched Dataset for Configurable Systems. In: Proceedings of the 14th International Working Conference on Variability Modelling of Software-Intensive Systems (VaMoS). pp. 1–10 (2020)
12. Ferreira, F., Viggiato, M., Souza, M., Figueiredo, E.: Configurable Software Systems: The Failure Observation Challenge. In: 2020 24th ACM International Systems and Software Product Line Conference (SPLC) (2020)
13. Fowler, M.: Refactoring: improving the design of existing code. Addison-Wesley Professional (2018)
14. Fraser, G., Arcuri, A.: Evosuite: automatic test suite generation for object-oriented software. In: Proceedings of the 19th ACM SIGSOFT symposium and the 13th European conference on Foundations of software engineering. pp. 416–419 (2011)
15. Gamma, E.: Design patterns: elements of reusable object-oriented software. Pearson Education India (1995)
16. Garvin, B.J., Cohen, M.B., Dwyer, M.B.: Evaluating Improvements to a Metaheuristic Search for Constrained Interaction Testing. Empirical Software Engineering (ESE) (1), 61–102 (2011)
17. Halin, A., Nuttinck, A., Acher, M., Devroey, X., Perrouin, G., Baudry, B.: Test Them all, is it Worth it? Assessing Configuration Sampling on the JHipster Web Development Stack. Empirical Software Engineering (ESE) pp. 674–717 (2019)

18. Johansen, M.F., Haugen, Ø., Fleurey, F., Eldegard, A.G., Syversen, T.: Generating Better Partial Covering Arrays by Modeling Weights on Sub-product Lines. In: International Conference on Model Driven Engineering Languages and Systems (MODELS). pp. 269–284 (2012)
19. JUnit: JUnit (Accessed 16-Aug-2020), https://junit.org/junit5/
20. Just, R., Jalali, D., Inozemtseva, L., Ernst, M.D., Holmes, R., Fraser, G.: Are Mutants a Valid Substitute for Real Faults in Software Testing? In: Proceedings of the 22nd ACM SIGSOFT International Symposium on Foundations of Software Engineering. pp. 654–665 (2014)
21. Kim, C.H.P., Marinov, D., Khurshid, S., Batory, D., Souto, S., Barros, P., d'Amorim, M.: SPLat: Lightweight Dynamic Analysis for Reducing Combinatorics in Testing Configurable Systems. In: ESEC/FSE. pp. 257–267 (2013)
22. Krieter, S., Thüm, T., Schulze, S., Saake, G., Leich, T.: YASA: Yet Another Sampling Algorithm. In: Proceedings of the 14th International Working Conference on Variability Modelling of Software-Intensive Systems (VaMoS). pp. 1–10 (2020)
23. Medeiros, F., Kästner, C., Ribeiro, M., Gheyi, R., Apel, S.: A Comparison of 10 Sampling Algorithms for Configurable Systems. In: In 38th International Conference on Software Engineering (ICSE). pp. 643–654 (2016)
24. Meinicke, J., Wong, C.P., Kästner, C., Thüm, T., Saake, G.: On Essential Configuration Complexity: Measuring Interactions in Highly Configurable Systems . In: 31st Proceedings of the International Conference on Automated Software Engineering (ASE). pp. 483–494 (2016)
25. Mockito: Mockito (Accessed 16-Aug-2020), https://site.mockito.org/
26. Oster, S., Zink, M., Lochau, M., Grechanik, M.: Pairwise Feature-interaction Testing for SPLs: Potentials and Limitations. In: 15th Proceedings of the International Software Product Line Conference, Volume 2 (ISPLC). p. 6 (2011)
27. Pacheco, C., Ernst, M.D.: Randoop: feedback-directed random testing for java. In: OOPSLA Companion. pp. 815–816 (2007)
28. Post, H., Sinz, C.: Configuration Lifting: Verification Meets Software Configuration. In: Proceedings of the 23rd IEEE/ACM International Conference on Automated Software Engineering (ASE). pp. 347–350 (2008)
29. Schaefer, I., Bettini, L., Bono, V., Damiani, F., Tanzarella, N.: Delta-oriented Programming of Software Product Lines. In: International Conference on Software Product Lines. pp. 77–91 (2010)
30. Soares., L.: Feature Interactions in Highly Configurable Systems: A Dynamic Analysis Approach with VarXplorer. Ph.D. thesis, Federal University of Bahia (UFBA) (2019)
31. Soares, L.R., Schobbens, P., do Carmo Machado, I., de Almeida, E.S.: Feature Interaction in Software Product Line Engineering: A Systematic Mapping Study. Information and Software Technology (IST) **98**, 44–58 (2018)
32. Souto, S., d'Amorim, M., Gheyi, R.: Balancing Soundness and Efficiency for Practical Testing of Configurable Systems . In: In 39th Proceedings of the International Conference on Software Engineering (ICSE). pp. 632–642 (2017)
33. Spadini, D., Aniche, M., Bruntink, M., Bacchelli, A.: Mock objects for testing java systems. Empirical Software Engineering (3), 1461–1498 (2019)
34. Thüm, T., Schaefer, I., Apel, S., Hentschel, M.: Family-based Deductive Verification of Software Product Lines. In: Proceedings of the 11th International Conference on Generative Programming and Component Engineering (GPCE). pp. 11–20 (2012)

A Unifying Approach to Breakpoint Specification

Christoph Bockisch[1], Stefan Schulz[1], Viola Wenz[1], and Arno Kesper[1]

Philipps-Universität Marburg, 35039 Marburg, Germany
{bockisch,schulzs,wenzvi,kesperar}@mathematik.uni-marburg.de

Abstract. Breakpoint-based debugging is a well-known and widely used approach supported extensively by modern IDEs, and research frequently provides new, more advanced approaches. However, such mechanisms typically focus on one feature and disregard the interaction with existing ones. In this paper, we first provide an overview of existing breakpoint mechanisms and organize them in a design space. Next, we propose a unifying mechanism for breakpoint specification, which regards program executions as streams of XML elements. Breakpoints are specified as XQuery expressions over this stream. We define the format of this XML stream as a DTD and present a mapping of the existing breakpoint mechanisms to XQuery. While our prototypical implementation shows that a naïve implementation is prohibitively slow, a selective generation of a minimal XML stream is possible when the XQuery expressions are known in before the execution. In that case, we argue that our model can also have a practical application beyond the ability to investigate different advanced breakpoint mechanisms jointly.

Keywords: Debugging · Breakpoint Design Space · Unified Breakpoint Model

1 Introduction

Debugging of software systems is an important task as it helps us delivering functionally correct software and fixing field bugs. In fact, according to a recent study [13], most developers spend at least 20% to 40% of their working hours on debugging. The most prevalent debugging technique is symbolic debugging, where developers can specify breakpoints. Essentially, these are conditions under which the execution of a program must be paused, to facilitate the inspection of the current program state. Typical breakpoints feature a "base event" related to a program element such as *reaching a specified code line in the execution*, *accessing a specified field*, *loading a class* or *throwing an exception*. Usually breakpoints can be further refined using dynamic conditions like predicates that must evaluate to true, or a hit count that must be reached, for the execution to be suspended.

Beyond these broadly supported ways for specifying breakpoints, several authors have explored more advanced and powerful breakpoint mechanisms. The approaches that we are aware of are mainly motivated by aspect-oriented programming (AOP) [11] or related language technologies. In AOP, a central task is to select events at run-time to enable, e.g., executing additional functionality.

Suspending the execution can be seen as such additional functionality (cf. [5,4,18]). These approaches in particular, and AOP languages in general, each provide their own ways of selecting execution events, which typically overlap, but cannot be combined. This is because AOP languages strive for efficient execution and only offer optimized selection mechanisms for specific types of events.

The richness of research on trace-based debugging [10,14,3,17] sugests that conventional breakpoint-based debugging is not always sufficient. The motivation behind this approach is that online debuggers are not suited to efficiently solve certain kinds of bugs. For example, cause/effect chasms [7] are particularly hard to debug, since the distance (in space or time) of the defect to its root cause is large [13]. The idea of trace-based debugging is to record the execution of a program in order to replay it at a later time. These traces may, for example, be used to reconstruct the execution and to step through it forwards as well as backwards. One can navigate to the starting point by using some form of query over the trace, which is comparable to setting a breakpoint in online debugging.

In this paper, we present a unifying approach to declarative breakpoint definition that subsumes existing techniques for online debugging, as well as opens up new possibilities. Our approach is based on viewing the execution of a program as tree where the inner nodes are method executions and the leaf nodes are statements like field and variable accesses, or calls to methods whose execution is excluded from the trace. Breakpoints are then formulated as queries over the tree. When a statement is executed that corresponds to a node in the query's result set, the execution is suspended.

In our prototype, we use the XML formalism to represent the execution trace as a tree, which allows us to use XQuery to formulate breakpoints. The nodes are represented as XML elements and the context of the statement execution, such as argument values or the value assigned to a variable, are represented as attributes. Thus, breakpoints may be selected using the full computational power of XQuery, accessing all contextual information that is exposed in the XML document. In total, this paper makes the following contributions:

- We have thoroughly analyzed existing breakpoint mechanisms in state-of-the-art IDEs, and organized them in a *design space for breakpoint specifications*.
- We define an XML-based format for execution traces that contains enough information to support all identified breakpoint mechanisms.
- While some restrictions on XQuery expressions are necessary to facilitate simultaneous evaluation, we show that the expressiveness of XQuery opens new possibilities for breakpoint definitions.

2 A design space of breakpoint concepts

Breakpoint debugging allows programmers to define conditions under which the program execution is suspended. The developer then has the chance to explore the current program state. Most modern IDEs offer some form of breakpoint debugging. Since it is our goal to provide support for as many different breakpoint options as possible, we will at first analyze the existing types of breakpoints.

In order to gain an overview of current types of breakpoints we analyzed the three most commonly used Java IDEs[1] Eclipse, IntelliJ and NetBeans, as well as the literature on advanced breakpoint mechanisms [5,4,18]. We were able to identify the general design space of breakpoint definitions, shown in Figure 1, that accommodates for all primitive concepts that we found. Since specifying breakpoints bears a lot of similarity to aspect-oriented programming, which also shows in the fact that the advanced breakpoints are inspired by AOP, it is no surprise that the design space resembles a subset of the design space of aspect-oriented programming languages (cf. [12, Chapter 2]).

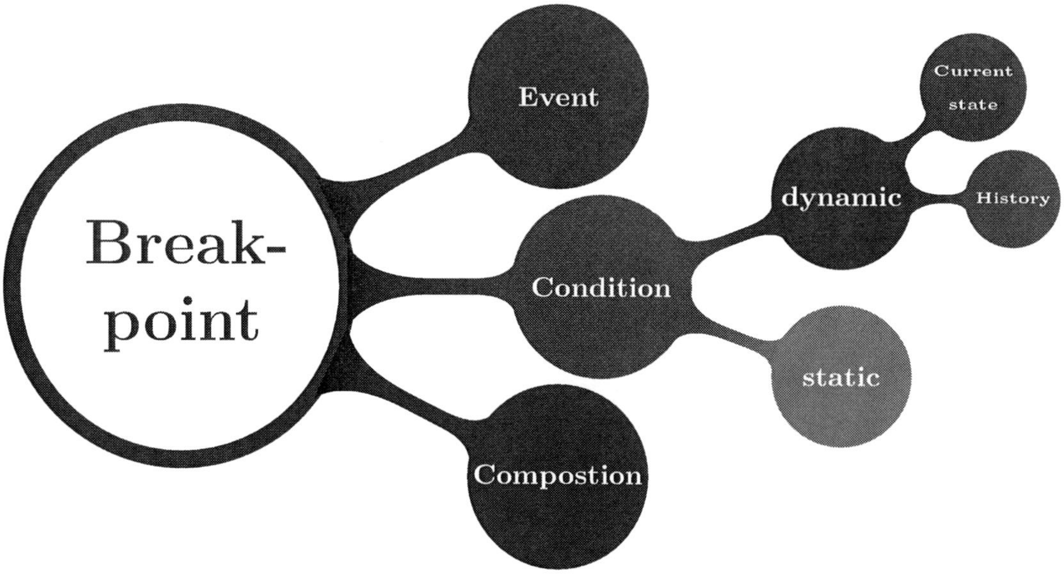

Fig. 1: Design space of breakpoint definitions.

Our breakpoint design space has three main concepts. The first one reflects the observation that a breakpoint always suspends the execution when a specified ***event*** occurs at run-time. Examples of such program elements are source-code lines or fields. This leads to a coarse distinction into what is often called breakpoint kinds, e.g., line-breakpoints or watch points. We have not found it necessary to further split this concept into sub-concepts.

The second concept is narrowing down the selection of events using ***conditions***, for example to avoid program suspension every time a line is reached or a field is accessed. Thereby, conditions can refer to either the **static** context in which an event occurs (like only selecting field accesses performed in certain methods) or the **dynamic** context (like predicates over local variables).

In the sub-concept of dynamic conditions, we found another relevant distinction, namely whether the condition supports access only to values in the

[1] According to `https://www.baeldung.com/java-ides-2016`.

current program state (such as values of variables or fields) or values in the past **history** of the execution (such as how many times a breakpoint was hit).

The third concept refers to the ability to ***compose*** a new breakpoint by referring to one or more other breakpoints. An example would be to specify an order, e.g., one breakpoint must be reached first in order to activate another.

We continue to further discuss the breakpoint design space. In particular, we will match all breakpoint mechanisms that we found in our study to the concepts and sub-concepts of the design space. We explain those mechanisms and group them in cases where different approaches provide very similar or equivalent ones.

2.1 Events

Ultimately, a breakpoint selects an event at which the execution is suspended. Thus, a breakpoint definition at least includes an event kind and an according parameter. An event can often be associated with certain locations in the program, which we call *breakpoint shadows*. For a line breakpoint, this association is obvious; for a watchpoint, the events can, e.g., be associated with the expressions or statements that read or assign the corresponding field.

kind	**parameters**	**shadow**
line	filename, line number	statement
change	field, variable, object(s)	assignment
read	field, variable, object(s)	reading statement
method call	method, object(s)	method call statement
method enter	method	first method statement
method exit	method	return statement
object creation	class	first constructor statement
class load	class	N/A (first statem. in initializer, if present)
exception	class	N/A (**throw** statement, if explicitly thrown)

Table 1: Summary of breakpoint base events.

Static unconditional *line breakpoints* are the most basic form, where the kind of event is "reaching a line during program execution" and the parameter would be the concrete line number and the name of the file containing the line.

In most IDEs you can also set a *watch point* on fields. As a result the execution is halted every time the field's value *changes* or is *accessed*, independent of the line it happens in. NetBeans additionally offers these *watch points for local variables.*

Another option is to set a *method breakpoint*. This causes the suspension of the program at every *entry* or *exit* of the method. Further, *class load breakpoints* halt execution when a specified class is loaded. *Exception breakpoints* suspend execution every time an exception of a specified type is thrown.

Object-centric breakpoints [15] suspend the execution, whenever objects are interacted with, either through field accesses, method invocations or instance creations. Such breakpoints are composed of an event in our design space and a dynamic condition to constrain the interacting objects (cf. Section 2.2).

Table 1 summarizes the concept "breakpoint base events" and the way these events can be parameterized in breakpoint definitions. The "shadow" column indicates the source code location at which the execution should be suspended. Class loading and the occurrence of an exception may be triggered implicitly; in this case, the execution is suspended at the statement that triggered the event, which, however, is not predictable. It should be noted that shadows for object creation are always present in the compiled `.class`-file: If constructors are absent in the source code, the compiler automatically adds a default constructor. As a class may have multiple constructors, in general an object creation breakpoint has multiple shadows.

In the approach of Yin et al. [18], breakpoints are defined by AspectJ pointcuts [9] with a few extensions. The same kinds of base events as discussed above are supported. Nevertheless, AspectJ allows the usage of wildcards in the class, method and field names, which facilitates a more compact definition of breakpoints on multiple program elements with similar names.

2.2 Conditions

If it is not desired that the execution is suspended each time an event occurs, a condition can be specified. Conditions may refer to the static context in which the breakpoint shadow appears, for example a method or class, or the dynamic context, i.e. the program state. The dynamic conditions are further split up into those that only access the current state at the time of the base event of the breakpoint, and those that access information in the execution history. Table 2 presents a summary of the conditions detailed in the remainder of this subsection.

kind	**parameters**	**context**
filter	class or method name	static
predicate	Java expression	current program state
instance filter	instance ID or field expression	current state
exception handling	caught/uncaught	current state
hit count	positive integer	execution history
control flow	call-stack layout	execution history
stateful breakpoints	regex over primitive breakpoints	execution history

Table 2: Summary of breakpoint conditions.

Static Static conditions are based on the structure of the program itself. This includes conditions based on types, the type hierarchy or call sites. IntelliJ allows developers to specify *class filters* and *caller filters* for breakpoints. Class filters define the classes in which the breakpoint triggers. Caller filters ensure that it only triggers on calls from particular methods.

Dynamic—Current program state There is also the possibility to define dynamic conditions which must hold to pause the program when a base event selected by a breakpoint occurs. The most general dynamic condition is a *predicate* that can access all variables and fields in the scope of the shadow of the base event.

Furthermore, IntelliJ supports the definition of *instance filters* to specify which objects may currently be active in order for a breakpoint to trigger. However, this requires determining the instance ID of relevant objects manually during the debugging session. Yin et al.[18] support a similar concept, however, in terms of a field expression. The mechanism of object-centric debugging [15] also imposes restrictions on the currently active objects. It assumes that the program is already running and the desired objects can be selected from the actual objects.

For exception breakpoints, it is possible to distinguish between thrown exceptions that are *caught* or *uncaught*, respectively.

Dynamic—Execution history The most basic example of a dynamic constraint over the execution history is the *hit count* for a breakpoint. Here, the program is only suspended when the base event has occurred as often as specified.

Chern et al. [5] present an approach for debugging with *control-flow* breakpoints. They are defined as "dynamic breakpoints, which are conditional on the control-flow through which they were reached". They can be beneficial if a bug only occurs inside a method if it is called from one or more particular methods.

Bodden introduced *stateful breakpoints* [4], a debugging approach based on parameterized runtime monitors. For a stateful breakpoint, the underlying events are labeled as "ordinary breakpoints". Using these labels, a desired event order can be specified as a regular expression over them. The execution is suspended, when the specified order is encountered. While implementations of parameterized runtime monitors do exist, to our knowledge, support for stateful breakpoints has not been implemented yet. "Trigger points" in Eclipse or the "Disable until breakpoint is hit" feature in IntelliJ are variants of stateful breakpoints.

2.3 Breakpoint composition

Yin et al. also offer the possibility to define new breakpoints based on existing ones. For this purpose, a breakpoint can be named, and new breakpoints can extend them by *strengthening* or *weakening* its condition.

Stateful breakpoints can also be seen as a composition mechanism, where primitive breakpoints are composed to form a complex one. In the approach proposed by Bodden, however, such complex breakpoints cannot be further composed, while the approach of Yin et al. facilitates unlimited levels of composition. Table 3 summarizes the identified properties of breakpoint composition.

property	**extent**
composition operator	weakening, strengthening, temporal order
composition levels	one, unlimited

Table 3: Summary of breakpoint composition options.

3 A Unified Approach to Breakpoint Specification

Our goal is to deliver a unified debugging approach which covers a broad range of different kinds of breakpoints. The workflow of our debugging approach starts with instrumenting bytecode so that an XML stream of the execution trace is created during program execution. Breakpoints are represented by XQuery expressions that describe elements in the XML stream. We split our implementation into a back-end, i.e., the bytecode instrumentation, and a front-end, i.e., a processor for the XQuery expressions, which can operate on the XML stream. The XML elements, which correspond to execution events, are emitted simultaneously with the occurrence of the events; similarly, the XQuery evaluation is performed simultaneously: When an XML element is selected by the expression, we are still at the corresponding execution event and can suspend the execution accordingly.

XQuery [16] (XML Query Language) is an extension of XPath [2], its expressions consist of axes and a path towards a node. The axes provide options to select a specific group of elements from a path expression. They select a range of elements with a defined relation towards the element given from the expression. The existing axes are: **self, ancestor, ancestor-or-self, child, descendant, descendant-or-self, following, following-sibling, namespace, parent, preceding, preceding-sibling**.

The main addition of XQuery over XPath are the FLWOR expressions (**for**, **let**, **where**, **order**, **return**). With these commands XQuery expressions define functions, which take an XML document as input. For the purposes of this paper, we only consider functions that can return a list of selected nodes from this document.

The addition of new elements to the document corresponds to the execution of a breakpoint shadow in the program. When evaluating the XQuery expressions while simultaneously generating the stream, i.e. during program runs, this raises the problem of trying to evaluate them over an incomplete document. Thus, we have to restrict the use of axes such that path expressions can only refer to elements already present in the document. Otherwise the breakpoint would depend on future execution events and thus could not be evaluated at run-time.

3.1 Program Trace as XML Stream

Our prototype is implemented as an agent for the Java virtual machine. This used the bytecode instrumentation library ASM to insert instructions into the bytecode of each loaded class to emit the XML tags corresponding to the program trace. Table 4 gives an overview of the XML elements that are used in the trace, examples of the attributes they may have and the elements they may have as children. Note that in the bytecode, constructors are represented as methods with special names. Therefore, they are covered by our method-related XML elements. In addition to the attributes listed in the table, all elements of the category "Shadows" have as attributes the location of the statement or method in terms of the filename and linenumber. Values are represented as text in the XML document, whereby the representation of primitive values is straight-forward. For object values, we produce a unique identifier. For illustration, consider Listing 1, which shows a simple Java program. Listing 2 shows a simplified version of the program trace as XML document produced by our prototype.

Meaning	Element	Attributes	Children
		Shadows	
method invocation	CALL	type, name, modifiers	ARGS, Shadows
method return	RETURN		VAL
local variable read	GET		VAR
local variable write	SET		FIELD
field read	GET		VAR
field write	SET		FIELD
exception	THROW		VAL
loading a class	LOAD	type	
try block	TRY	type	Shadows
exception handler	HANDLER	type	
		Other	
field info	FIELD	type, name, modifiers	VAL
local variable info	VAR	name, index, type	VAL
value	VAL		value as PCDATA
arguments	ARGS		VAL

Table 4: Overview of XML elements used in a program trace.

```
class Example {
  public static void main(String[] args) {
    isEven(3);
  }
  private static boolean isEven(int i) {
    boolean b = i % 2 == 0;
    return b;
  }
}
```

Listing 1: Simple Java program to demonstrate translation into XML.

The following XQuery expression illustrates our approach for defining breakpoints: It corresponds to a conditional method breakpoint, which suspends the execution at calls to the method isEven when the argument has the value 3.

```
//CALL[@name='isEven' and @declaringType='Example']/args[@name='i']
    /var/val[text()='3']
```

3.2 Mapping breakpoints to XQuery expressions

In this section we will explain our approach to mapping breakpoints to XQuery expressions. We start by describing the breakpoints for simple base events (cf.

```
<CALL declaringType="Example" name="main" parameterTypes="[Ljava/lang/
    String;" resultType="V" public="true" static="true">
  <ARGS>
    <VAR name="args" index="0" type="[Ljava/lang/String;">
      <VAL>1313922862</VAL>
    </VAR>
  </ARGS>
  <CALL declaringType="Example" name="isEven" parameterTypes="I"
      resultType="Z" private="true" static="true">
    <ARGS>
      <VAR name="i" index="0" type="I"> <VAL>3</VAL> </VAR>
    </ARGS>
    <GET> <VAR name="i" index="0" type="I"/> </GET>
    <SET>
      <VAR name="b" index="1" type="Z"> <VAL>false</VAL> </VAR>
    </SET>
    <GET> <VAR name="b" index="1" type="Z"/> </GET>
    <RETURN> <VAL>false</VAL> </RETURN>
  </CALL>
</CALL>
```

Listing 2: Simplified XML stream for example program.

Table 1), proceed with the advanced breakpoint conditions (cf. Table 2) and discuss how they can be combined with the base events. Because of the limited space, we only highlight selected breakpoint templates[2]. Finally, we will discuss how breakpoint specifications can be combined (cf. Table 3) in our approach.

Base Events The simplest and most prevalent kind of breakpoint is a *line* breakpoint. Since all elements corresponding to a base event have the attributes linenumber and filename, a line breakpoint can be straight-forward mapped to a plain path expression: Select element of any type (the * in the listing), which is a descendant of the document's root (as represented by //) and which has the proper attribute values for the line number and file name. The following query is equivalent to a breakpoint in line 10 of file Program.java:

```
//*[@linennumber=10 and @filename='Program.java']
```

The remaining basic breakpoint types including the event component of object-centric breakpoints can be expressed by similar plain path expressions. The name of the element type is provided and the selection condition (provided between square brackets) refers to different attributes. For example, the listing below defines a watchpoint (i.e., reading or writing) on the field T.f.

[2] For a full list, see: `https://www.uni-marburg.de/en/fb12/research-groups/psw/files/xml-breakpoints.pdf`

```
//set/field[@name='f' and @declaringType='T']
//get/field[@name='f' and @declaringType='T']
```

Conditions Filter conditions restrict breakpoints to those base events that are triggered within a specific class or method. In our XML stream statement executions (which are ultimately selected for suspending execution) are always the children of a CALL element whose attributes declaringType (and name for method filters) store the lexical context. Thus, a breakpoint with a filter consists of the filter location, followed by the specification of the base breakpoint—which can be a complex breakpoint on its own—added as the child axis:

```
//CALL[@declaringType='T' and @name='m']/child::/base-breakpoint
```

In contrast to breakpoints in traditional IDEs, our approach makes it possible for watchpoints to refer to the value to be assigned to a field or variable:

```
base-breakpoint/child::val[position()=2 and text()='v']
```

According to the design space of breakpoint definitions, this is a *predicate* on the current program state. Other predicates can be mapped similarly, since XQuery fully supports arithmetic and logic expressions.

When using *instance filters*, the execution of a specified statement only triggers a breakpoint if its context refers to a certain object. For this kind of conditional breakpoint we use an XQuery **let** expressions where we first assign the base-breakpoint expression to a variable, say x. (Thereby this base breakpoint may already be compound.) In a where clause, we specify a path (relative to the selected element) to the context value and require that it is equal to the expected value. In the example below, assume that the base breakpoint is a method call, then it defines an instance filter for the receiver object (the first argument for non-static methods). To restrict breakpoints in object-centric debugging, XQuery expressions can be defined similarly, whereby we directly fill in the identifier of the expected context object. This requires that the corresponding expression is defined while the program is already running.

```
let $x :=base-breakpoint
where $x/args/val[1]/text()=$x/preceding::path-to-value/text()
return $x
```

We can define breakpoints for particular execution paths, called *stateful breakpoints* in [4], which connect contexts of events in the execution history. For instance, to select the event when the read() method is invoked on an InputStream after the stream has been closed, the following expression can be used:

```
for $x in //CALL[@name='close' and @declaringType='InputStream']
for $y in $x/following::CALL[@name='read' and @declaringType='InputStream']
where $x/args/var[0]/val/text()=$y/args/var[0]/val/text()
return $y
```

This expression selects a CALL element for read() following a CALL element for close() where the identifiers of the receiver object (the first argument) are equal.

Composition XQuery is a functional language, thus it allows abstracting expressions into custom functions and to provide named breakpoint specifications. Since the XQuery 3.0 standard, it also supports higher-order functions, i.e., functions can be passed as arguments to other functions. Together, these features provide us with compositionality of breakpoint specifications.

The XQuery expressions presented in this paper ultimately represent sequences of XML elements from the stream. XQuery offers features to combine such sequences. Consider the variables `$seq1` and `$seq2` stand for two breakpoint specifications, then we can generally map the *composition operator* weakening from our design space to *unions* in XQuery: `($seq1,$seq2)`. Strengthening can be achieved by appending a condition or another axis to a breakpoint specification.

With XQuery's ability for higher-order functions, composition can be modular. We do not have to copy the definition of breakpoint specifications in order to compose them, but we can use the name of the function in which they are defined. Because we have higher-order functions, and because function applications can be unlimitedly deep, in terms of *composition levels*, our approach is also unlimited.

3.3 Performance

Currently, we only provide a proof-of-concept reference implementation, which directly implements the semantics presented in the previous section. This consists of a Java bytecode instrumentation to provide the XML stream and an XQuery processor to evaluate the breakpoint specifications on the fly. The instrumented bytecode creates the XML document as a character stream. For the XQuery processor, we use the community edition of the Saxon library. While existing XQuery processors, including Saxon, can process XML streams, they can only provide the result set when the document is fully processed. Therefore our reference implementation completes the XML document at each evaluation step by adding closing tags for all currently open tages, such as CALL. Naturally, this is very slow, but guarantees a correct implementation of our approach.

In preliminary experiments, this approach has slowed down the program execution by a factor of ~300x. Furthermore, the memory requirement increases with the execution time as the growing document must be kept in memory. However, we are exploring three paths to optimizing the performance, which are promising and which we outline in the following.

First, we allow to restrict the instrumentation sites by providing a configuration at program start. In practice, breakpoints are typically defined prior to the execution. We can determine which subset of the possible instrumentation sites potentially influence the result set of the corresponding XQuery expressions via static analysis. Preliminary experiments have shown that the slow-down linearly depends on the number of the executed instrumentation sites and reductions down to the order of 1% are realistic for typical breakpoints.

Second, as an alternative to completing the XML document at each evaluation point, we have started to implement an XQuery processor that can handle incomplete XML documents and constructs the result sets incrementally. This is feasible in our case because we only use a restricted subset of XQuery that determines the selection of an XML element purely on the elements present in the document at the time of the evaluation.

Third, with our own XQuery processor, the need for a specification-conform textual representation of the XML document is avoided. Instead we can use an in-memory representation which is more compact and can be processed faster. In addition, this rids us from the necessity of keeping the full trace in the history.

4 Related Work

We have examined other work on the topic of supporting debugging and program understanding by using information about the execution trace.

Czyz et al. [6] present an approach for declarative and visual debugging in Eclipse called JIVE. Their idea is to visualize both the current state and the execution history. The current state is depicted in an object diagram showing objects with their structural connections as well as important method activations. The execution history is visualized by a sequence diagram presenting object interactions. Both visualizations are interconnected and can be used for forward and reverse stepping. Furthermore, the tool allows formulating queries over both current and past states. In contrast to our implementation this approach uses the Java Development Tools (JDT) and the Java Platform Debugging Architecture (JDA) instead of bytecode instrumentation to collect information about program execution. Using JDA's Debug Interface (JDI) their tool receives notification of certain runtime events. In addition in some cases JIVE retrieves information from the call stack. Similar to our concept this approach uses information about the execution trace to support developers in understanding and debugging programs.

Anslow et al. [1] describe an idea for storing program traces in a native XML database. Additionally, XQuery is used for extracting subsets of the information. The results are then visualized whereby the developer's understanding of the component is enhanced.

Both approaches above do not, however, allow to define breakpoints in an advanced way. Queries over the traces are not evaluated simultaneously with the program execution but either when the program is already suspended [6] or after the execution stopped [1].

Oracle's HotSpot VM contains a commercial feature for execution tracing, called Flight Recorder[3]. Similar to the approaches to trace-based debugging discussed in Section 1, the motivation behind this tool is to provide detailed information about the execution of a program. It offers tracing for three different kinds of events. *Duration events* take some time to execute and are logged when they complete. In terms of our approach these relate to `CALL` tags. However, in our approach we do not wait for a method to return, but start logging right away in a more granular fashion, in order to be able to stream the execution events. *Instant events* occur instantly and are logged right away. This relates to basically all bytecode instructions that cause an XML tag to be created. Examples for

[3] See `https://docs.oracle.com/javacomponents/jmc-5-4/jfr-runtime-guide`.

this are GET, SET, and RETURN. Finally, *sample events* are logged at a regular interval. Similar to our BITE debugger [17], the trace data is logged in a circular buffer, and may be stored to disk.

We have previously explored XML as format for program traces but in the context of offline debugging [3]. There, XQuery was proposed to navigate in the trace. However, this trace format is less complete than the one presented here and mapping existing breakpoint mechanisms was not a concern.

5 Conclusion

In this paper, we have presented a comprehensive overview of current mechanisms for defining breakpoints during debugging. For this purpose, we have investigated the three most popular Java IDEs as well as academic literature on advanced breakpoint mechanisms. This has led to a design space with the concepts *events*, *conditions* and *composition* that allowed us to categorize all breakpoint mechanisms and to identify differences as well as overlap. In our study, we identified nine kinds of base events and seven concepts of conditions. The concept of composition is divided into composition operators and the levels of composition. Inspired by this design space, we have developed a unifying approach to defining breakpoints. This is based on providing a trace of the program execution as an XML stream and breakpoints as XQuery expressions.

Due to the high expressiveness of XQuery, our proof-of-concept implementation is very suitable as a testbed for new breakpoint mechanisms and their interaction with existing ones. The XQuery language has been shown to be Turing-complete [8]. Although we restrict the XQuery language to facilitate immediate evaluation when a new element of the trace is appended to the XML stream, we believe that our restrictions do not limit the expressiveness as such. This has yet to be shown properly, but we consider the fact that we could express all known breakpoint mechanisms from the design space in the restricted XQuery language as a very strong evidence. In this way we have also shown that the information provided in our structured execution trace is sufficient for existing breakpoint mechanisms. If additional information is required for future breakpoint mechanisms, the trace can be extended with any new event that has a shadow and any new context data that is computationally accessible.

A preliminary performance evaluation has shown that the direct implementation of this approach is very slow, probably prohibitively so. But we have already identified three possible approaches for drastically optimizing the performance. Partial implementations are already available and we intend to work them out further in the future.

References

1. Anslow, C., Marshall, S., Biddle, R., Noble, J., Jackson, K.: Xml database support for program trace visualisation. In: Proceedings of the Australasian Symposium on Information Visualisation. pp. 25–34. Australian Computer Society, Inc. (2004)

2. Berglund, A., Boag, S., Chamberlin, D., Fernández, M.F., Kay, M., Robie, J., Siméon, J.: Xml path language (xpath). World Wide Web Consortium (2003)
3. Bockisch, C., van't Riet, M., Yin, H., Aksit, M., Lin, Z., Chen, Y., Zhao, J.: Trace-based debugging for advanced-dispatching programming languages. In: Proceedings of the 10th Workshop on Implementation, Compilation, Optimization of Object-Oriented Languages, Programs and Systems. p. 3. ACM (2015). https://doi.org/10.1145/2843915.2843922
4. Bodden, E.: Stateful breakpoints: A practical approach to defining parameterized runtime monitors. In: Proceedings of the 19th ACM SIGSOFT Symposium and the 13th European Conference on Foundations of Software Engineering. pp. 492–495. ESEC/FSE '11, ACM (2011). https://doi.org/10.1145/2025113.2025201
5. Chern, R., De Volder, K.: Debugging with control-flow breakpoints. In: Proceedings of the 6th International Conference on Aspect-oriented Software Development. pp. 96–106. AOSD '07, ACM (2007). https://doi.org/10.1145/1218563.1218575
6. Czyz, J.K., Jayaraman, B.: Declarative and visual debugging in eclipse. In: Proceedings of the 2007 OOPSLA Workshop on Eclipse Technology eXchange. pp. 31–35. eclipse '07, ACM (2007). https://doi.org/10.1145/1328279.1328286
7. Eisenstadt, M.: My hairiest bug war stories. Commun. ACM **40**(4), 30–37 (Apr 1997). https://doi.org/10.1145/248448.248456
8. Kepser, S.: A simple proof for the turing-completeness of XSLT and xquery. In: Proceedings of the Extreme Markup Languages Conference (2004)
9. Kiczales, G., Hilsdale, E., Hugunin, J., Kersten, M., Palm, J., Griswold, W.G.: An overview of aspectj. In: European Conference on Object-Oriented Programming. pp. 327–354. Springer (2001)
10. Lewis, B.: Debugging backwards in time. arXiv preprint cs/0310016 (2003)
11. Masuhara, H., Kiczales, G.: Modeling crosscutting in aspect-oriented mechanisms. In: Proceedings of European Conference on Object-Oriented Programming. pp. 2–28. Springer-Verlag (2003)
12. Nagy, I.: On the Design of Aspect-Oriented Composition Models for Software Evolution. Ph.D. thesis, University of Twente, Enschede, Netherlands (2006)
13. Perscheid, M., Siegmund, B., Taeumel, M., Hirschfeld, R.: Studying the advancement in debugging practice of professional software developers. Software Quality Journal **25**(1), 83–110 (Mar 2017). https://doi.org/10.1007/s11219-015-9294-2
14. Pothier, G., Tanter, É.: Summarized trace indexing and querying for scalable back-in-time debugging. In: European Conference on Object-Oriented Programming. pp. 558–582. Springer (2011)
15. Ressia, J., Bergel, A., Nierstrasz, O.: Object-centric debugging. In: International Conference on Software Engineering. pp. 485–495. IEEE (2012)
16. Robie, J., Chamberlin, D., Dyck, M., Snelson, J.: Xquery 3.0: An xml query language. Recommendation, W3C (2014)
17. Schulz, S., Bockisch, C.: A blast from the past: Online time-travel debugging with bite. In: Proceedings of the 15th International Conference on Managed Languages & Runtimes. pp. 13:1–13:13. ManLang '18, ACM (2018). https://doi.org/10.1145/3237009.3237012
18. Yin, H., Bockisch, C., Aksit, M.: A pointcut language for setting advanced breakpoints. In: Proceedings of the 12th Annual International Conference on Aspect-oriented Software Development. pp. 145–156. AOSD '13, ACM (2013). https://doi.org/10.1145/2451436.2451454

Uma arquitetura de sistema de informação multiagente orientada a processos

Gedir Fabiano de Moraes Gonçalves[1 [0000-0002-5366-3989]], Claudio Henrique Medaber Jambo[1 [0000-0003-1242-7944]], Vera Maria Benjamim Werneck[1 [0000-0002-6537-2441]], and Flávia Maria Santoro[1 [0000-0003-3421-1984]]

Universidade do Estado do Rio de Janeiro - Centro de Tecnologia e Ciências - Instituto de Matemática e Estatística, Rio de Janeiro - RJ - Brasil

Abstract. *In this work, we present* `AAdapt`*, an intelligent multi-agent system architecture that proposes a mechanism to work together with Process-Aware Information Systems (PAIS) systems. The* `AAdapt` *allows the monitoring of context elements of the process, identifying situations that may be unwanted, and execute plans to work around these situations. The agents in* `AAdapt` *were modeled using the methodology O-MaSE (Organization-based Multiagent Software Engineering) and reasoning based on Belief, Desire, and Intentions (BDI) to allow flexibility to adapt business processes and make decisions according to available background information. In the modeling of the Adapt agents, the goals model, the role/function model, and the agent class model were created, which guided the implementation of the Java / Jadex code. Adapt makes decisions according to context information obtained from the process engine (PAIS), external sensors, and the ontology of the process domain. The implementation of* `AAdapt` *was held to a process vessel to dock and had the Protégé software for the process domain ontology creation, the software Camunda (PAIS), and development codes in Java / Jadex.*

Keywords: O-Mase · Agent · Modeling · Multi-agent · Belief · Desire · Intention · BDI · PAIS · Business Process Management · BPM.

1 Introdução

Os processos de negócios estão presentes em toda a vida de uma empresa, sejam eles para a prestação de um serviço ou para a fabricação de um bem, e possuem potencial para aumentar a produtividade e reduzir custos. A Gestão de Processos de Negócios ou *Business Process Management* (BPM) é uma área que recebe cada vez mais a atenção de gestores em face de os negócios serem cada vez mais competitivos.

Na era digital, as organizações vivenciam uma evolução cada mais rápida que requerem respostas mais ágeis e precisam tratar eventos exógenos ao processo (tais como uma mudança na cotação do dólar, uma mudança na corrente marítima, o aquecimento de *data center*, uma mudança na velocidade do vento, etc). Neste contexto, é fundamental que os processos sejam mais flexíveis. Porém, os sistemas de suporte a processos tradicionais - *Business Process Management Systems* (BPMS) - estão implementados com base em uma arquitetura que implementa fundamentalmente processos bem estruturados [1]. Desta forma, não atendem aos requisitos necessários para prover flexibilidade e adaptação às diversas circunstancias e mudanças de contexto.

Beverungen et al. [2] discute diversos desafios em BPM, e particularmente alguns relacionados a requisitos de BPMS para atender novos tipos de processos digitalizados. Algumas outras pesquisas têm se dedicado a propor soluções para flexibilização de processos, seja em tempo real ou não, tais como Marin et al. [3], Nunes et al. [4] e Kir e Erdogan [5]. No entanto, nenhuma destas abordagens resolve o problema de forma automática e integrada a BPMS existentes.

Nesse contexto abordagens que incluam processos decisórios flexíveis são fundamentais, sendo uma solução proposta nesse artigo por meio do desenho de uma nova arquitetura para os sistemas *Process-Aware Information Systems* (PAIS). [6] "[...] PAIS é um sistema de software que gerencia e executa processos operacionais envolvendo pessoas, aplicativos e / ou fontes de informação com base em modelos de processo".

O objetivo deste artigo é apresentar o `AAdapt` (Adaptação por agentes) que é uma arquitetura multiagentes que utiliza as informações de contexto oriundas de ontologia do domínio do processos, dos sensores externos e do PAIS para compará-las com as suas crenças e desejos, permitindo assim aos agentes acionarem os planos estabelecidos para tratar eventos exógenos que podem gerar situações de exceção ao processo.

A arquitetura de sistema multiagente do `AAdapt` permite a tomada de decisões quando situações de exceção ao processo são identificadas. Esses agentes inteligentes utilizam as informações de contexto para chegar a conclusões, responder perguntas ou elaborar um plano de ação.

A arquitetura proposta do `AAdapt` contribui para a modelagem e para a integração de agentes com o processo de gerenciamento de processos. Apresentando um mecanismo integrado com motores de processos (PAIS) que permite a tomadas de decisões baseadas no contexto da execução do processo, permitindo mais flexibilidade para os fluxos de trabalho.

O restante do artigo está organizado da seguinte forma: na Seção 2 são apresentados trabalhos relacionados com a proposta deste artigo, na Seção 3 é descrita a abordagem proposta com sua arquitetura e a metodologia de modelagem dos agentes. As informações sobre a implementação estão contidas na Seção 4, e, por fim, na Seção 5 são apresentadas as observações finais e trabalhos futuros.

2 Trabalhos relacionados

Beverungen et al. [2] apontam duas questões atuais em BPM: os desenvolvimentos recentes em pesquisa e prática na interseção de BPM e Transformação Digital e a proposição de caminhos para pesquisas futuras para avançar na compreensão de BPM em um mundo hiperconectado. Os pesquisadores se concentram em quatro capacidades tecnológicas: Computação Social, Dispositivos Inteligentes,

Real-Time Computing e *Big Data Analytics*, e apresentam onze desafios estratégicos para uma corporação. Entre eles, está a capacidade de usar dados disponíveis durante a execução de um processo para permitir às organizações análise e adaptação de seus processos de negócios em tempo real. Para Marin et al. [3], as soluções de gestão de fluxo de trabalho tradicionais são muito rígidas e não fornecem meios para lidar com situações imprevisíveis. Para os autores, processos intensivos em conhecimento integram dados na execução de processos e requerem quantidade substancial de flexibilidade em tempo de execução.

Kir e Erdogan [5] propõem o *framework* AgilBPM que aborda dimensões de colaboração (objetivos corporativos, colaborações dinâmicas, qualidade de serviço) e de contexto (adoção de regras e conformidade, ações orientadas a dados, raciocínio). Os autores propõem a busca por processo compatível num repositório do processo ou, caso não encontrado, a utilização de um planejador externo para compor um novo fluxo de processo. Apesar da proposta tratar do tema da flexibilidade, não aponta uma solução para a adaptação em tempo real.

A proposta de Buhler [7] apresenta um fluxo de trabalho adaptativo no qual ferramentas de design são usadas para especificar um sistema multiagente, que pode então se adaptar de forma inteligente às mudanças nas condições ambientais. Os autores também afirmam que tradicionalmente os sistemas de gerenciamento de fluxo de trabalho não foram projetados para ambientes dinâmicos exigindo resposta adaptativa.

Hsieh [8] aponta que a capacidade de se adaptar dinamicamente a mudanças é um fator chave de sucesso para sistemas de gerenciamento de fluxo de trabalho. Os processos de negócios, o ambiente operacional, a variabilidade de recursos e as necessidades do usuário podem mudar com o tempo. O autor propõe um esquema de auto-adaptação para reconfigurar os agentes e os serviços de forma a acomodar as mudanças no fluxo de trabalho e capacidades dos atores.

No trabalho de Seiger [9] é apresentado um sistema multiagente cujos fluxos de trabalho são auto-adaptativos e baseados no *loop* de controle MAPE-K (Monitorar, Analisar, Planejar e Executar em uma Base de conhecimento). Esta base de conhecimento contém dados sobre o contexto físico e virtual do sistema. Ela é atualizada a cada alteração nesses dados e acessada pelos agentes.

Apesar dos trabalhos realacionados lidarem com a dificuldade de se adaptar os fluxos de trabalho às demandas cada vez mais sofisticadas e às constantes mudanças de escopo e avanços tecnológicos, nenhum deles apresenta uma solução para adaptação em tempo real que considere mudanças no contexto de forma dinâmica. Nunes [10] apresentou um trabalho de adaptação de processos por contexto, *GCAdapt*, utilizando quatro módulos para lidar com elementos de contexto e propiciar caminhos alternativos no processo. O trabalho utilizou *Planning Domain Definition Language* (PDDL) para replanejar os processos e foi a base para a proposta do AAdapt. O AAdapt propõe a utilização de uma arquitetura baseada em multiagentes inteligentes que permite flexibilidade para adaptar processos de negócios e dispensa a utilização de um planejador externo de processos.

3 Abordagem proposta: AAdapt

O `AAdapt` é uma arquitetura de sistema multiagente inteligente que propõe um mecanismo para trabalhar em conjunto com sistemas PAIS permitindo monitorar elementos de contexto do processo, identificar situações que possam ser indesejadas e executar planos para contornar essas situações.

Numa definição simples, um agente é um componente de software que opera um ambiente e é autorizado a executar ações como coleta de informação, comunicação, ou manipular o ambiente. O agente percebe e interage com o ambiente que conhece.

O agente pode captar informações de diversas fontes heterogêneas de dados como informações provenientes de sensores externos, de sistemas e de ontologias.

Para [11] um agente é "tudo o que pode ser considerado capaz de perceber seu ambiente por meio de sensores e de agir sobre esse ambiente por meio de atuadores.".

Um agente é um componente que interage com um ambiente, podendo identificar situações a partir da coleta de informações e por fim realizar uma ação. São códigos escritos numa linguagem de programação como `Java`, Python ou C++ que tomam decisões baseadas nas restrições e regras que foram informadas durante a sua programação

Há os agentes que se comunicam com outros agentes e formam um ambiente multiagente *multi-agent systems* (MAS), que são várias entidades autônomas interagindo. Um ambiente multiagentes consiste de recursos compartilhados ou serviços que muitas vezes é implementado como um componente de software externo, conforme [12].

3.1 Arquitetura do `AAdapt`

O `AAdapt` é composto por dois agentes, Figura 1, o `Communicator` e o `Executor`, que possuem uma base de crenças e metas e tomam suas decisões de acordo com informações de contexto disponíveis.

O `AAdapt` recebe informações de contexto (elementos de contexto) do motor de processos PAIS e analisa essas informações com base em suas crenças e metas atuais. Caso o agente seja confrontado com uma situação que viole seu sistema de crenças, ele deverá avaliar este contexto e, dependendo do resultado, devolver ao PAIS uma solução de contorno para a situação identificada. Caso o `AAdapt` não identifique uma situação que viole suas crenças o PAIS é informado para seguir com o fluxo padrão da tarefa do processo. A Figura 1 apresenta a arquitetura `AAdapt`.

O agente `Communicator` é responsável por interagir diretamente com o sistema PAIS procurando por situações de exceções a cada informação de contexto obtida dos sensores externos ou das informações enviadas pelo próprio PAIS.

Uma situação de exceção é identificada pelo agente `Communicator` e o agente `Executor` é acionado para identificar uma solução de contorno. O `Executor` analisa as crenças e metas e aciona os planos necessários para identificar a solução

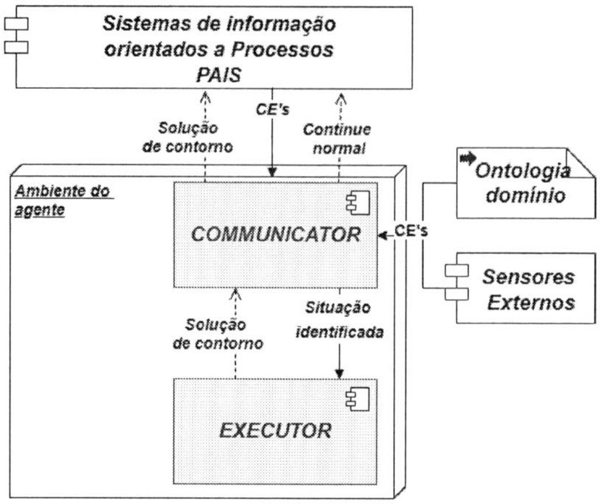

Fig. 1. Arquitetura do `AAdapt` interagindo com a arquitetura do PAIS, permitindo monitorar elementos e contexto a aplicar soluções de contorno.

de contorno. Por fim o `Executor` devolve ao `Communicator` qual caminho deve ser seguido que devolve ao sistema PAIS.

A arquitetura do `AAdapt` interage com a *engine* do PAIS permitindo a obtenção de informações de contexto e propondo caminhos alternativos para situações indesejadas no processos.

As informações ou elementos de contexto para as tomadas de decisões do `AAdapt` são obtidas do PAIS, dos sensores externos e da ontologia do domínio do processo. A Figura 2 apresenta a captura dos elementos de contexto pelos agentes.

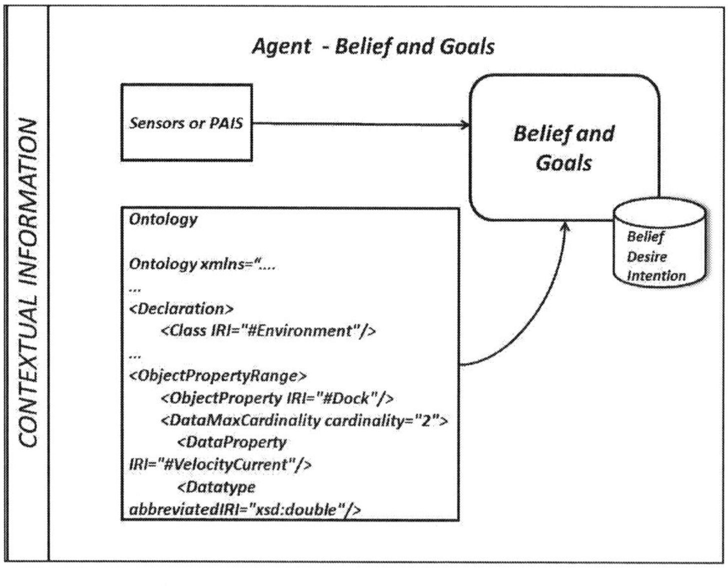

Fig. 2. Captura de elementos de contexto de sensores externo, do PAIS e da ontologia.

Esses elementos de contexto são analisados pelos agentes do `AAdapt` para comparar com suas crenças e desejos que, se violados, acionam os planos do agente para propor um novo caminho ao PAIS no processo. Na Figura 3 um exemplo do fluxo do PAIS enviando informações de contexto para o agente que verifica se ocorreu alguma violação de sua base de crença e metas. Se ocorrer uma violação o agente verifica se há um plano com uma solução de contorno e devolve essa ao PAIS.

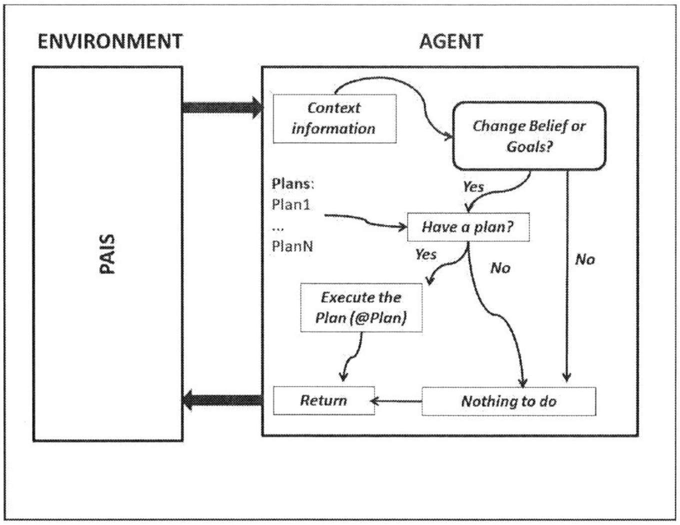

Fig. 3. Comportamento interno do `AAdapt` quando recebe informação de contexto do PAIS.

3.2 Modelagem

A metodologia escolhida para modelar o `AAdapt` foi a *Organization-based Multiagent Software Engineering* O-MaSE, é uma estrutura baseada na organização, que integra um conjunto de tecnologias concretas destinadas a facilitar a aceitação industrial [13].

A metodologia O-MaSE permite analisar e desenhar sistemas multiagentes baseados em organizações e tem como objetivo permitir facilidades e padrões no desenvolvimento de agentes. A metodologia O-MaSE possui um conjunto de tecnologias concretas para uma ampla aceitação da industria, sendo orientada a agente personalizável com conceitos bem definidos, suportados por *plug-ins*.

O O-MaSE possui um metamodelo, um conjunto de fragmentos de métodos e um conjunto de diretrizes que permitem aos usuários usar técnicas de engenharia para criar processos personalizados.

As principais vantagens encontradas da metodologia O-MaSE foram: (i) Utilização de um conjunto de fragmentos de métodos baseados em um meta-modelo comum; (ii) Permitir a definição explícita de atividades e tarefas;(iii)Permitir que as atividades sejam organizadas de maneiras diferentes com base na necessidade do projeto;(iv)Definição personalizada do conjunto de fases e iterações.

Os objetos da modelagem dos agentes do `AAdapt` utilizados foram o modelo de metas, o modelo de papéis/funções e o de modelo classes de agentes.

O modelo de metas (Figura 4), objetiva organizar as metas dos diferentes papéis/funções do sistema sinalizando as ações que podem ser realizadas pelo sistema. Este diagrama captura o propósito como uma árvore de metas, incluindo atributos e precedência.

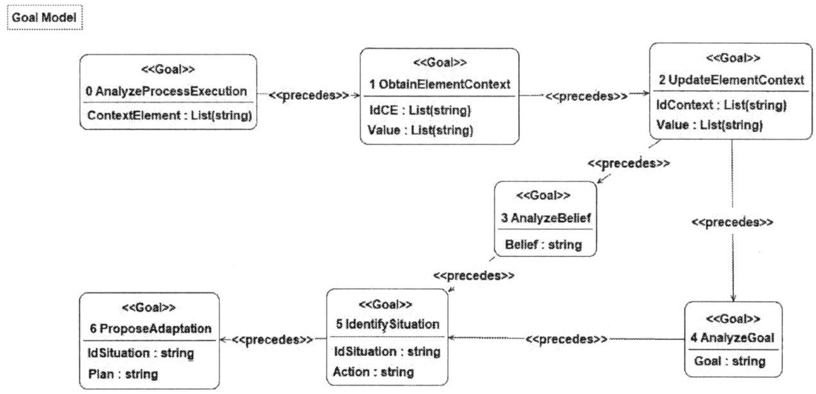

Fig. 4. Modelo de metas do `AAdapt`.

As metas *ObtainElementContext, UpdateElementContext, AnalyzeBelief, AnalyzeGoal* e *IdentifySituation* apresentadas na Figura 4 estão associadas a funções do agente `Communicator` e funcionam como um processo de monitoração do ambiente no qual o sistema multiagentes está inserido, obtendo e atualizando elementos de contexto e analisando as metas e crenças dos agentes para identificar situações em que o sistema precise tomar uma ação.

A meta *ProposeAdaptation* é o alvo das funções do agente `Executor`, é o momento que uma situação é identificada e o agente propõe uma adaptação ao processo. É a ação para a escolha e proposição de um caminho alternativo no processo quando uma situação indesejada é identificada.

Os papéis/funções (*Role*) são a base para que o objetivo de uma meta seja atingida. O modelo de papéis/funções (Figura 5) permite identificar e documentar as funções na organização que os agentes desempenham e assumem responsabilidade. Para garantir a consistência, cada meta folha (*(Goal)* deve ser suportada por pelo menos um papel/função (*(Role)*.

Cada meta identificada no modelo de metas é suportada por pelo menos um papel/função no modelo de papéis/funções, por exemplo, a *Goal ProposeAdaptation* é suportada pelas *Roles ProposeNewPlan IdentifyAdaptation*, conforme é apresentado na Figura 5. A cada papel/função estão associadas as tarefas que representam o comportamento esperado da função e cada papel/função está associada a pelo menos um agente.

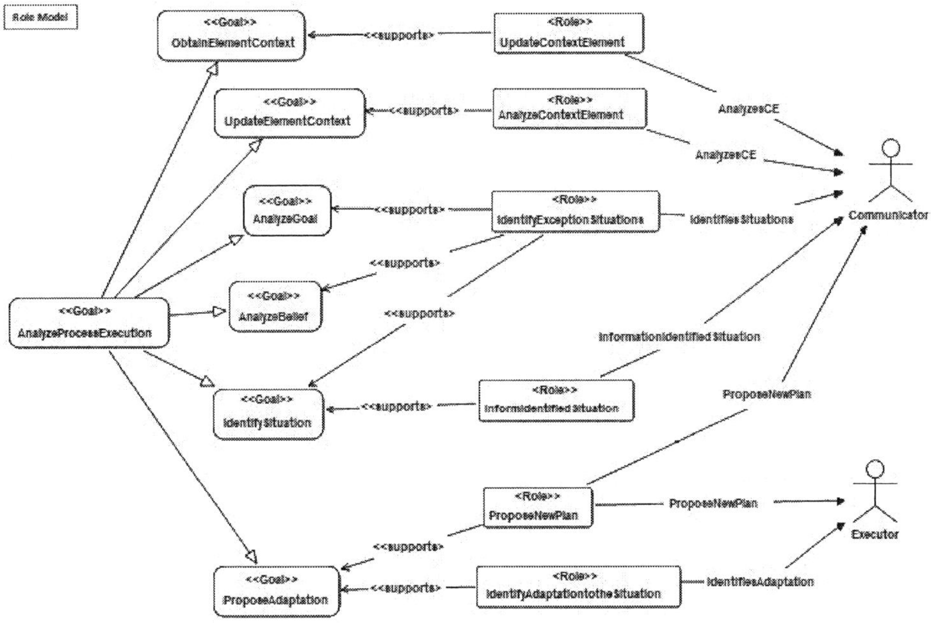

Fig. 5. Modelo de papéis e funções do `AAdapt`.

O modelo de classes de agentes (Figura 6) tem por objetivo identificar os tipos de agentes que participam da organização. No modelo de classes de agentes foram identificados o agente sistêmico (PAIS) e os agentes *Communicator* e *Executor*. O PAIS interage com os agentes para a consecução do objetivo de fornecer um processo alternativo na eventualidade de uma exceção no processo padrão.

Os agentes percebem e podem realizar ações no ambiente em que operam, assim eles desempenham funções e assumem as responsabilidades dessas funções, Tabela 1. Essas funções possuem a capacidade de atingir os objetivos da organização.

Table 1. Responsabilidades dos agentes do `AAdapt`.

Agente	**Atividade realizada**
Communicator	Recebe informações (elementos) de contexto do PAIS.
Communicator	Recebe informações (elementos) de contexto dos sensores externos.
Communicator	Carrega informações (elementos) da ontologia.
Communicator	Verifica se suas crenças e objetivos não foram violados.
Communicator	Identifica situações de exceção no processo.
Communicator	Encaminha situação de exceção identificada para o agente *Executor*.
Communicator	Encaminha para o PAIS a solução de contorno identificada pelo agente *Executor*.
Communicator	Informa ao PAIS continuar o processo normalmente.
Executor	Recebe do *Communicator* uma situação de exceção identificada.
Executor	Identifica um plano para a situação de exceção identificada.
Executor	Encaminha para o agente *Communicator* a solução de contorno.

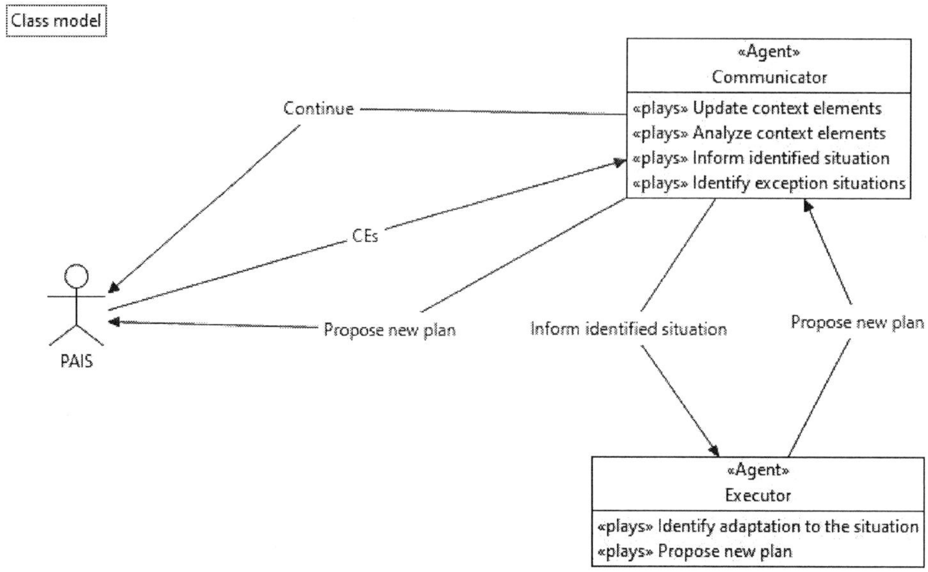

Fig. 6. Modelo de classes do `AAdapt`.

3.3 BDI - Crenças, desejos e intenções dos agentes

Os agentes com BDI são um tipo de agente inteligente com capacidade de tomada de decisão, possuem raciocínio baseado em crenças, desejos e intenções, BDI.

Os agentes do `AAdapt` possuem raciocínio baseado em crenças, desejos e intenções, *Belief, Desire and Intentions* (BDI), que é uma arquitetura para desenvolvimento de agentes inteligentes simples e robustos, fornecendo por padrão várias classes já pré-definidas para implementação. Um agente é caracterizado por suas crenças, objetivos (desejos) e intenções - ele terá a intenção de fazer o que acredita que alcançará seus objetivos, dado suas crenças sobre o mundo [14].

A arquitetura de agentes BDI descreve claramente o comportamento dos agentes e como alcançar suas metas. Dessa forma, facilita o projeto de comportamentos complexos tornando o comportamento do agente mais compreensível à medida que sua meta é alcançada e a execução do plano é realizada.

A Figura 1 apresenta a arquitetura do `AAdapt` e nela há dois agentes, o `Communicator` e o `Executor`, ambos agentes foram criados utilizando o *Java / Jadex* no *framework* Eclipse.

O agente `Communicator` é responsável por receber elementos de contexto (CE's) de sensores externos e do sistema PAIS e analisar esses elementos ante uma base de dados de crenças e objetivos para identificar uma situação de exceção no processo e informá-la ao agente `Executor`. O agente `Communicator` carrega parte de suas crenças da ontologia do domínio do processo.

O agente `Executor` recebe uma situação identificada pelo `Communicator`, procura uma proposição de adaptação para o processo e retorna para o agente `Communicator` a solução de contorno identificada.

Os *Beliefs* representam as crenças que o agente tem sobre o ambiente em que está operando, por exemplo a velocidade máxima da corrente marítima permitida num atracadouro. Com elas o agente pode raciocinar e assegurar desejos como atracar com segurança uma embarcação, as *Desire*, e executar ações como manobrar a embarcação, as *Intentions*. No exemplo abaixo uma crença de que o barco é menor ou igual ao espaço disponível no atracadouro.

```
@Belief(dynamic=true)
    protected boolean dockEnabled = boatSize <= sizeAvailable;
```

Para a identificação de situação são analisados as *@Belief and @Goal* do agente que são suas crenças e objetivos.

As metas (Goal) podem ser implementadas como uma classe separada ou como uma classe interna do Java e podem ser atendidas por diferentes planos. As metas podem ter submetas que podem, por suas vez, terem outras submetas e são representada pela anotação *@Goal*. Como exemplos:

```
@GoalMaintainCondition(beliefs="distanciaEmbarcacoes")
@GoalTargetCondition(beliefs="atracarEmbarcacao")
```

Por fim o *Plan* que é o mecanismo que permite executar códigos dentro do agente.

```
@Plan(trigger=@Trigger(factchangeds="dockType"))
    public void updateModePlan()
```

4 Implementação da solução proposta

Nesta seção, apresentamos uma implementação da arquitetura proposta para um caso específico. O objetivo é demonstrar a viabilidade da proposta em um cenário de aplicação. O cenário escolhido é um processo de atracar uma embarcação num cais, pier ou trapiche.

4.1 Tecnologias utilizadas

O sistema `AAdapt` foi criado usando um arcabouços de ferramentas, linguagens e metodologias: `O-MaSE`, `agentTool3`, `Java 8 J2SE`, ide `Eclipse`, `Camunda`, `Protégé` e *plug-in* `Jadex`.

A ferramenta utilizada para a modelagem O-MaSE foi a agentTool3 (aT3) [1] que possui integração com o *framework* de programação Eclipse `Java` fornecendo ferramentas para a criação de modelos de classe, funções / papéis, metas, entre outros, que permite a análise, projeto e implementação de sistemas multiagentes seguindo a metodologia *Organization-based Multiagent Software Engineering* (O-MaSE).

[1] Pode ser obtido gratuitamente em http://agenttool.cs.ksu.edu/

O modelo de metas, modelo de funções/papéis e modelo de classes de agentes, Figura 4, Figura 5 e Figura 6 respectivamente, foram criados dentro do *plug-in* `agentTool3`.

`Camunda` [2] é um software de automação de processos que permite orquestração e automatização de processos, possuindo uma plataforma na forma de código aberto. Baseado nas linguagens existentes de *workflow* e nos sistemas de gerenciamento de *wokflow*, Camunda é um sistema PAIS - *process-aware information systems*. O `Camunda` pode acessar o *Workflow Engine* através de REST para iniciar instâncias de processo e completar tarefas. Também pode adicionar o *Workflow Engine* como uma dependência simples do Maven e usar uma API `Java` em seu próprio aplicativo, chamando o código `Java` de dentro de um fluxo de trabalho BPMN. As duas tecnologias para acesso a *engine* do BPMN são REST e `Java` API.

O `Jadex` [3] é um mecanismo de raciocínio baseado em crenças, desejos e intenções, BDI do inglês *Belief Desire Intention*, que permite desenvolver agentes inteligentes distribuídos em `Java` e XML (*Extensible Markup Language*) por meio de uma técnica de Componentes Ativos (*Active Components*), combinando uma arquitetura de componente de serviço hierárquica com lógica de negócios baseada em agentes BDI, BPMN *(Business Process Modelling Notation) Workflows*, micro agentes, GPMN (*Goal Oriented Process Notation*) ou componentes XML.

Durante a fase de testes e tratamento de erros do sistema também foi utilizada a ferramenta Insomina [4] para fazer *Get* e *Post* no PAIS e um servidor Phyton para captar e analisar o tráfego das portas TCP.

4.2 Cenário de aplicação

O cenário de aplicação utilizado foi o processo de atracar uma embarcação num pier, cujo modelo é descrito na Figura 7.

Na aproximação da embarcação, a tarefa do PAIS **Obter dados da Embarcação** coleta elementos de contexto da embarcação. Os dados coletados são enviados para o agente `Communicator`. Em seguida, a tarefa **Obter dados do atracadouro** obtém informações do cais ou trapicho, espaço disponível e tipos possíveis de atracação. Nesse momento, se o agente `Communicator` identificar uma situação adversa, pode acionar o agente `Executor` para fornecer uma solução de contorno.

Caso a atracação não seja cancelada, na próxima tarefa do processo é definido o tipo de manobra a ser realizada na tarefa do processo **Definir tipo de manobra**, como manobrar de boreste ou bombordo.

Na próxima tarefa, dados meteorológicos são coletados, **Obter fatores Ambientais**, como velocidade do vento e corrente marítima. Esses elementos de contexto são enviados para o agente `Communicator` que pode identificar uma

[2] Pode ser obtido gratuitamente em https://camunda.com/

[3] Pode ser obtido gratuitamente em https://www.activecomponents.org/

[4] Pode ser obtido gratuitamente em https://insomnia.rest/

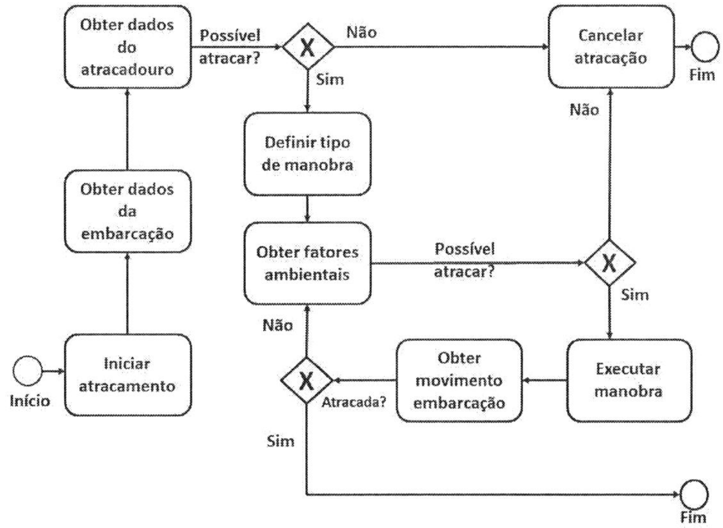

Fig. 7. Modelo do processo 'Atracar embarcação'.

situação adversa e identificar, por exemplo, risco de abalroamento. Nesses casos de identificar uma situação indesejada o agente `Executor` é acionado para localizar um plano para contornar a situação.

Esse processo de coleta de elementos de contexto continua constante durante as próximas tarefas **Executar manobra** e **Obter movimentação da embarcação**, obtendo valores de elementos do contexto, identificando situações e executando plano para contorná-las até que o processo de atracar seja concluído ou seja cancelado.

4.3 Ontologia do domínio do processo

A ontologia tem raízes na filosofia e representa o conhecimento de forma explícita por meio de conceitos e relações que representam o grupo específico de compreensão das pessoas naquele domínio [15].

Uma ontologia é uma linguagem que permite classificar objetos em categorias dentro de um domínio de conhecimento, uma forma de definir um catálogo sobre um objeto que irá permitir definir conceitos e mitigar dúvidas sobre o seu significado.

A ontologia para o domínio do processo utilizado neste artigo foi criada com a linguagem *Web Ontology Language* (OWL), que é uma linguagem lógica de semântica Web, com o software Protégé [5] e pode ser vista parcialmente abaixo.

$< DataMaxCardinalitycardinality = "2" >$

$< DataPropertyIRI = "\#VelocityCurrent" / >$

$< DatatypeabbreviatedIRI = "xsd : double" / >$

$< /DataMaxCardinality > ... < DataMaxCardinalitycardinality = "20" >$

[5] Pode ser obtido gratuitamente em https://protege.stanford.edu/

< *DataPropertyIRI* = "#*VelocityWind*" / >

< *DatatypeabbreviatedIRI* = "*xsd* : *double*" / >

Os agentes do `AAdapt` obtém parte das informações de contexto da ontologia do domínio do processo. Principalmente os aspectos restritivos que podem violar as crenças e metas dos agentes. No caso do processo de atracar uma embarcação os dois grandes impeditivos são a velocidade da corrente marítima acima de 2kn nós (3,704Km/h) e o vento forte acima dos 20kn nós (37,04Km/h), como pode ser visto na definição de valores máximos aceitáveis, *DataMaxCardinality cardinality*, dos atributos *VelocityCurrent* e *VelocityWind*.

Na Figura 8 é apresentada a hierarquia de classes da ontologia OWL do processo de atracar embarcação com as classes *Environment, Navy* e *Pier* no primeiro nível e suas respectivas classes filhas.

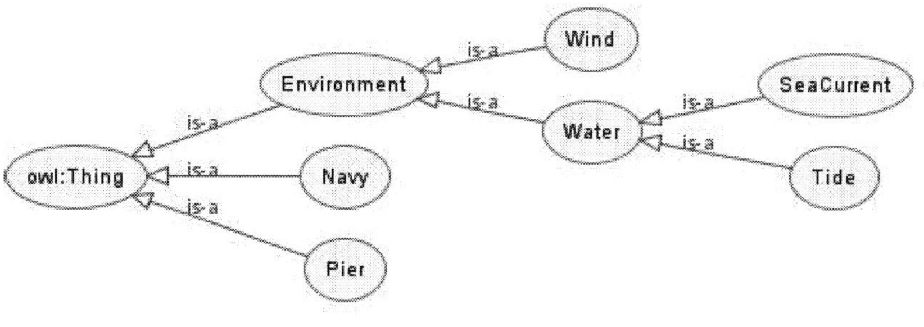

Fig. 8. Visão gráfica da ontologia do domínio do processo 'Atracar embarcação'

Na bateria de casos de testes realizado no sistema `AAdapt` os agentes conseguiram utilizar os elementos de contexto para conduzir o processo de atracação da embarcação do PAIS com segurança. Para os testes foram utilizadas informações de contexto dinâmicas obtidas com simuladores de sensores externos que produziam condições meteorológicas que impactam diretamente nas decisões dos agentes. Com esses testes vários caminhos do processo foram exercitados para ratificar que as tomadas de decisões estavam em conformidade com o esperado.

5 Conclusão

O `AAdapt` contribui para a área de modelagem de agentes e integração com gerenciamento de processos propondo tomadas de decisões baseadas no contexto da execução, permitindo que motores de processos PAIS possam receber orientações em tempo de execução de qual fluxo das tarefas deve ser seguido. Também implementa uma análise baseada em contexto utilizando vários mecanismos para obtenção de informações e restrições de contexto, seja pelo PAIS, pelos sensores externos ou por informações ou restrições provenientes de uma ontologia. O trabalho está em desenvolvimento e apresenta algumas limitações no tocante à generalização dos agentes para domínio de processo diferente. Foi criado um sistema com dois agentes em Java / Jadex e a utilização dos conceitos apresentados nesse artigo. Foi realizada a integração entre o sistema PAIS e os agentes inteligentes e aplicado com sucesso no processo de atracar embarcação.

Este artigo contribui com a discussão do uso de sistemas multiagentes inteligentes que permitem integrar elementos de contexto para a tomada de decisões.

Vislumbra-se como trabalho futuro a melhoria da arquitetura numa trilha de trabalho na generalização do AAdapt para que possa ampliar cenários de uso.

References

1. Dumas, M. and La Rosa, M. and Mendling, J. and Reijers, H. A.: Fundamentals of business process management. 2nd edn. Springer Publishing Company, Berlim, Germany (2018).
2. Beverungen, D., Buijs, J.C.A.M., Becker, J. et al: Seven Paradoxes of Business Process Management in a Hyper-Connected World.Bus Inf Syst Eng 63, 145–156 (2021).
3. Marin M.A., Hauder M., Matthes F.: Case Management: An Evaluation of Existing Approaches for Knowledge-Intensive Processes. In: Lecture Notes in Business Information Processing, vol 256 Springer, Cham. (2016).
4. Nunes, V. T., Santoro, F. M., Werner, C. M. L. and Ralha, C. G.: Real-Time Process Adaptation: A Context-Aware Replanning Approach. in IEEE Transactions on Systems, Man, and Cybernetics: Systems, vol. 48, no. 1, pp. 99-118, (2018).
5. Huseyin Kir and Nadia Erdogan: A knowledge-intensive adaptive business process management framework. Information Systems, 101639 (2021).
6. van der, A., Wil, M.P.: Transactions on Petri Nets and Other Models of Concurrency II: Special Issue on Concurrency in Process-Aware Information Systems. Springer Berlin Heidelberg, Berlin, Heidelberg(2009).
7. Buhler, Paul A., Vidal, José M.: Towards Adaptive Workflow Enactment Using Multiagent Systems. Information Technology and Management, 61-87 (2005).
8. Hsieh, Fu-Shiung, Lin, Jim-Bon.: A self-adaptation scheme for workflow management in multi-agent systems. Journal of Intelligent Manufacturing, 131-148 (2016).
9. Seiger, R., Huber, S., Aßmann, Uwe.: Toward a framework for self-adaptive workflows in cyber-physical systems. Software & Systems Modeling, 1117-1134 (2019).
10. Nunes, V. T.Dynamic Process Adaptation: Planning in a Context-Aware Approach. 211 p. Tese (Doutorado) — Universidade Federal do Rio de Janeiro, Engenharia de Sistemas e Computação - COPPE, Rio de Janeiro, 2014.
11. Russell, Stuart and Norvig, Peter.: Artificial Intelligence: A Modern Approach. Prentice Hall Press (2020).
12. Shehory, Onn and Sturm, Arnon.: Agent-Oriented Software Engineering: Reflections on Architectures, Methodologies, Languages, and Frameworks. Springer (2014).
13. García-Ojeda, J. and Deloach, S.: The O-MaSE Methodology. Handbook on Agent-Oriented Design Process, 253-285 (2014).
14. Norling, E.: Folk psychology for human modelling: extending the BDI paradigm. Conference: Autonomous Agents and Multiagent Systems, 202- 209 (2004).
15. Oliveira, A. B. F. de and Werneck, V. M. B.: Ontologias. Cadernos do IME / UERJ : Série Informática : Vol. 15 : Dezembro, (2003).

Label it be! A large-scale study of issue labeling in modern open-source repositories

Joselito Júnior, Gláucya Boechat, and Ivan Machado

[1] Federal University of Bahia - UFBA, Salvador - Bahia, Brazil
[2] {joselito.mota, glaucya.boechat, ivan.machado}@ufba.br

Abstract. In a wave of growth, open-source projects need to modernize and change how they deal with processes, methods, and communication with their contributors. We could observe that open-source projects are constantly evolving to improve their management of the entire community. Starting with community communication, software development, managing open-source projects faces crucial challenges. One of the enabling environments that open-source communities found to achieve community communications objectives was code repositories with integration with issue trackers. Using issue trackers in their projects should encompass an infrastructure capable of hosting the project source code and community participation. Some issue trackers use a structure in which the issue's title and description are the key information. However, we have observed a slight change in this strategy over the years, as more and more data are fundamental to solving the issue. For example, labeling the issues could enable users to provide the issue with more contextual information. By understanding how modern issue trackers handle issue labeling, this study analyzes the impact, engagement, and influence that labels have on the Github repositories, based on a database of 10,673,459 issues mined from 13,280 repositories in 180 Github featured topics. We found that 78.75% of the repositories label their issues, with more adherence from those repositories that contain big numbers of issues. The labeling practice is essential and prioritized as a first step in the issue resolution process in 65.91% of the first events. Issues with labels draw more attention and impact by collecting more subscribers, assigns, and comments, helping to engage contributors to the resolution.

Keywords: Github · Issue labeling · Issue trackers

1 Introduction

Over the years, software development has grown both in size and importance. To accommodate the urging and increasing demand for more robust, reliable, and efficient software solutions rapidly, it is often necessary to join efforts from people based in different locations to deliver their potential to contribute to the software project. Such a scenario is widespread in open-source software projects, where people could work as contributors regardless of their physical location, but rather for their motivations or interests [16].

In this wave of growth, open-source projects need to modernize and change how they deal with processes, methods, and communication with their contributors. That is why there is a constant evolution in software technology and the community and their interactions [22]. Open-source projects are constantly changing to improve their management of the community as a whole. Starting with community communication, software development, managing open-source projects stands crucial challenges. Communication within the community and an environment that favors continuous integration and maintenance of systems are first-class dimensions that characterize a representative, and well-structured repository [21] [24]. One of the enabling environments that open-source communities found to achieve these goals was code repositories with integration with issue trackers. Using issue trackers in their projects should encompass an infrastructure capable of hosting the project source code and enabling the community participation (e.g., developers, testers) to provide detailed information about their systems using the issue-reporting mechanism. The issues would be later on assigned to any community member capable of handling it [2].

The use of an issue tracker with the reporting of problems and establishing a problem-solving process brings an essential ally in the maintenance and evolution of the software [18]. However, an issue should be described in the most comprehensive way possible [19], so that it does not make it difficult for developers to understand the problem he should handle [4] [6] [7]. Incomplete information and unsuitable classifications can confuse developers about the causes of the problems, leading to correction and validation delays, harming all users who need changes in the software.

Most issue trackers use a structure encompassing the issues' fields of title and description, and these are the key elements an issue should contain. In addition, some trackers have enabled users to attach labels to incorporate more contextual information into the issue. This practice consists of a text field where the user could assign words or small definitions to associate with a given issue. Issue labeling consists of incorporating issues with meaningful text fragments, or simply labels (or tags), that could readily assist software developers in the rapid and objective perception of the reported problem [26] [28].

Issue labeling is present in Github-based repositories. Therefore, this study seeks to analyze the impact, engagement, and influence that labels have on the Github repositories, based on a database of 10,673,459 mined issues from 13,280 repositories in 180 Github featured topics.

In this study, we addressed the following Research Questions (RQ):

RQ1. How representative is the labeling activity practice in the repositories? This RQ aims to analyze and show how representative the labeling activity is in repositories by applying labeling issues in all the repositories from the database. We want to study the adherence and popularity of issue labeling by project contributors to discover any usability on the repository.

RQ2. What is the impact of labels on issue engagement that differs from non-labeled issues? Acknowledging that all issue "movements" are traceable, this RQ investigates the impacts of the labeling activity in issues by the contributors' engagement. We studied certain events as users' subscriptions to follow the discussion in the issue, the assignment event to a contributor in both labeled and unlabeled issues. We looked at the advantages and disadvantages of label issues from the perspective of repository improvement.

RQ3. What is the level of priority project contributors give the labeling activity when opening a new issue? In this RQ, we took the perspective of the priority given by the project for labeling when reporting an issue. We study when the labeling in the issue's event list occurs to understand if this is a first recurring practice and is prioritized in the first moments in the resolution process through repositories.

RQ4. What is the relevance of labeling issues for repositories with a different number of issues? This RQ aims to analyze the labeling activity in repositories with a different number of issues. The analyzed repositories were split into four groups to reach this goal, depending on the number of issues each has. It is possible to make inferences that could help understand and compare the labeling practice's recurrence in different repositories sizes by analyzing such a perspective.

2 Background

2.1 Repositories

Repositories have different ways to work, and as such, but the literature encompasses many practices and behaviors that characterize a repository. Munaiah et al. [21] described that a repository's representativeness involves seven dimensions: community, continuous integration, documentation, history, issues, license, and unit testing.

According to Rodriguez et al. [24], Software Engineering repositories have concepts as: source code, software configuration management (SCM), issue tracking, developers' messages, user messages, project metadata, and usage data. Those concepts involve elements that projects must have to frame in well-structured repositories.

It is worth mentioning that either the two definitions above address issue tracking (or bug repositories) and issues as essential factors to define a repository. Bug repositories or issue trackers are used to report and maintain problems or suggestions about the software [3]. The importance of a well-structured organization and adequate communication is also essential for solving these problems or even avoid introducing new defects [5] [20]. These reporting channels allow the community to help in the software maintenance process. The combination of user feedback, community work, and maintainability are critical factors for the success of repositories [25], including in Github repositories [11].

2.2 Issues

The issue as a defect follows a timeline that consists of insertion, detection, and removal. It is called the defect life-cycle [29]. Users commonly report the detection of a defect through issue reports. Based on the reports' detailed information, developers try to reproduce the defect as described in the issue to understand its likely causes and then proceed to the resolution phase.

The components present in Github issues are very similar to those of known issue trackers, but those components has some features that other platforms do not have. When it is necessary to write an issue, it is required to fill in some components such as title, description, and comments, encompassing all necessary details to enable reproducing the issue. In the description and comments fields, it is possible to add lists, mark code snippets, quotes, warnings, and other elements through the Markdown syntax [14].

Github also includes other fields that contributors could use in a Github issue besides the title, description, and comments. A Github issue has events that show all the activities performed in the issue. It also enables to configure sending notifications to users about updates in the discussion. Besides, it includes a feature to assign issues to contributors [12], the issue status informing whether the issue status, i.e., either *open* or *closed*, and also, the focus of this study, the labeling issues activity.

2.3 Labels

A label is one type of issue component and one more option that Github provides developers who wish to add extra information about the reported issue. The platform provides a standard list of nine labels with a short description for each. They are: *bug, documentation, duplicate, enhancement, good first issue, help wanted, invalid, question* and *wontfix*. Developers responsible for the repository could also create custom labels that better suit their needs.

The concept of tags in a social system is a free field for text insertion and personalization [26]. The Github labels follow a similar idea for those tags and can add accessible and quick information about the issue.

Labels have different characteristics, whether created by either humans or machines [23]. They could apply to any related function, including reuse, management, and re-finding information [26] in many software artifacts such as architecture, components, documentation, testing, and others [28]. For an issue, labeling refers to bugs and improvements [8].

3 Methodology

3.1 Searching for relevant repositories

In this study, we looked for repositories with many events or that are influential. Github hosts a page [14] with all featured topics on the platform, which means a classification of what types the repositories are. Altogether there are 180 topics from different subjects and domains, such as programming languages, browser plugins, compilers, and other topics. Each topic has thousands of repositories. Given that **number of stars** is one the most widely used popularity metrics of a Github repository [9] we used such a counting to select the most popular ones.

3.2 Mining repositories issues and preprocessing issues' components

We mined data about issues and pull-requests, which contains the following metadata: *id, author, title, body, description, status, creation date, events, repository labels, issue labels, reactions*, and *comments*. The mining process retrieved 10,673,459 issues from 13,280 repositories of Github featured topics from September 2019 to August 2020. All issues were saved and structured in the MongoDB database. The pre-processing phase carried out the process of filtering unnecessary data for our analysis. We used a Python script with regular expressions [27] to remove unnecessary items such as *code quote, tags, hyperlinks, tables and references, citations and comments repeated replies, warnings, exceptions, class names, paths, special characters, numbers, multiples blank spaces and stop words removal to title, body,* and *comments.* Github uses the Markdown markup language to format its text structures, including all the issue texts [13]. The usage of Markdown facilitates removing structures that would not add information in the process of analyzing issues. In addition, aspects of its syntax structure have been removed from the issue texts, opening up a corpus text only. An event list records all the issue movements. Understanding this, we examined the list of events to find new evidence of labeling activity through a built-in script.

3.3 Data analysis

To conduct the study and answer the **RQ1**, we perform a search to find labeled issues in the repository with a Python algorithm. If the repository labeled at least one issue with a valid label, the repository performed the labeling. All the activities performed in an issue, such as following a discussion, assignment, closing, labeling, and others, are recorded in a timeline called *events*. The **RQ2** involved studying the events in all issues of the repositories by searching occurrences of events, such as issue subscription, assignment, and comments of labeled and unlabeled issues. The answer to the **RQ3** goes through the algorithm analysis of the issue event list to count if the first activity performed on the issue is the labeling activity. The final amount of first labeled issues is analyzed. If the repository does not practice labeling first, then it is analyzed at which stage of the issue the labeling in the repository is mainly used.

We split the database into four groups by considering the median amount of issues: *The largest, Large, Small,* and *The smallest.* The **RQ4** results are reached after the correlation of labeling activities and the number of issues in those groups, and the algorithm rated the repository by the median of issues, as Figure 1 shows.

The first split used the median number of issues for the entire base and had two parts: repositories with a median greater than or equal and less than 142.

Repositories greater than or equal to 142 issues fall into the groups *The Largest* or *Large* repositories. Those with less than 142 issues fall into the groups *Smaller* or *The Smallest* repositories.

To define *The Largest* and *Large* repositories, we performed another median calculation in the new group. Repositories with a median greater than or equal to 546 issues fall into *The Largest* group, and repositories with less than 546 issues fall into the *Large* group. Similarly, to define either *Small* and *The Smallest* groups, if the median contains a median greater than or equal to 35 issues, it falls into the former, otherwise into the latter one. Figure 1 shows all the group's calculation process.

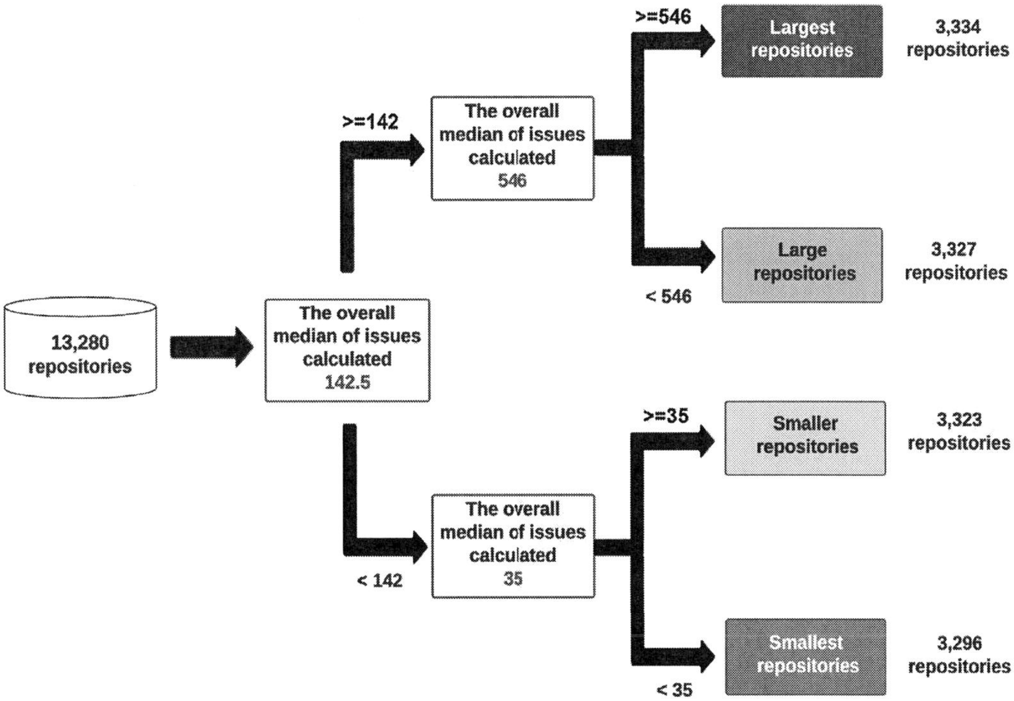

Fig. 1. Classification process of the size of the repositories by the number of issues

4 Results

This section shows all the data results after mining, pre-processing, counting, and analyzing 10,673,459 issues from 13,280 repositories from Github feature topics. The median number of issues in the database was 143, and the standard deviation of 2.889. It is worth mentioning that all the research package, including the database, the results tables, and the scripts implemented and used, are available at [17].

4.1 How representative is the labeling activity practice in the repositories? (RQ1)

From the set of analyzed 13,280 repositories, we observed that 10,458 (78,75%) labeled their issues, while 2,822 (21,25%) did not label any issues. Although the repository's adherence to labeling is representative, the number of labeled and unlabeled issues is very close. Out of the 10,673,459 issues in the database, 4,917,544 (46,07%) were labeled, leaving a margin of 5,755,915 (53,93%) without labeling. The median of issues labeled by the repository is 21, and the standard deviation found was 1,999. Figure 2 shows the number of issues in the database and the labeled issues.

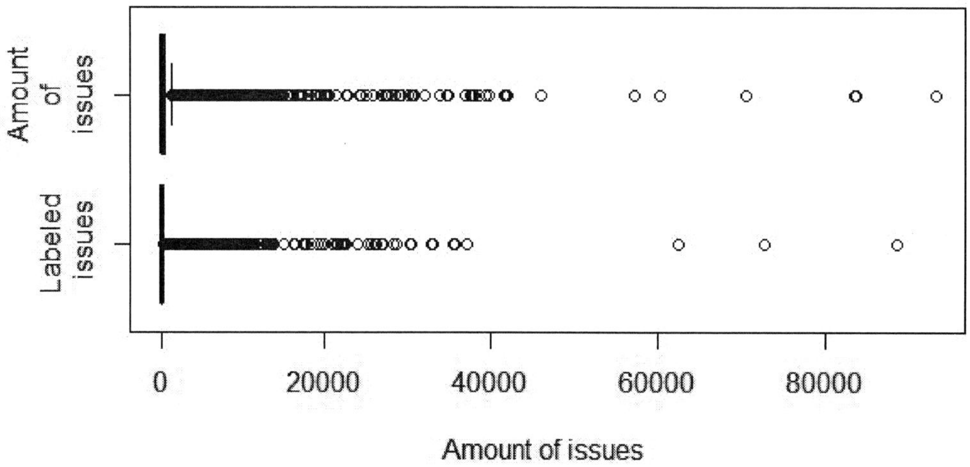

Fig. 2. Boxplot of the total number of issues with the issues labeled.

We found that labeling is somewhat representative, and most repositories frequently use this practice, and labeling occurs almost half the time an issue is reported. However, there is still a considerable number of issues that are not labeled. Each repository has variations in the number of issue labels, so one repository labels many issues, but others label just a few issues. This scenario reflects how each repository handles labeling priority.

4.2 What is the impact of labels on issue engagement that differs from non-labeled issues? (RQ2)

Performing a search in the events of all repositories retrieved interesting results about labeled and unlabeled issues. Unlabeled issues have 66.64% (107,574,958 events) of the events; the labeled issues only have 33.35% (53,830,132 events). We expected to reach such a number due to a slightly larger number of unlabeled issues. We could find some trends about issue subscribing more deeply by analyzing the events: there were 66,48% (10,127,463 subscribers) in labeled issues and 33.52% (5,106,845 subscribers) of unlabeled issues. Issues with labels have more assignments to contributors than unlabeled, 81.72% (1,736,294 assigns) in labeled issue and 18.27% (388,224 assigns) in unlabeled issues. We found 57.69% (20,553,963 comments) of the comments in labeled issues and 42.31% (15,075,414 comments) when the issue does not have a label.

Although issues without labels have a more significant number of associated events, labeled issues draw more attention and impact repositories issues by collecting more subscribers, assignments, and comments than unlabeled issues, presenting as a factor to consider when using repositories.

4.3 What is the level of priority project contributors give the labeling activity when opening a new issue? (RQ3)

In this RQ, we analyzed the number of labeled issues. Finding the time for labeling issues is the critical key to know the priority given to this activity. To discover the labeling moment, we accessed the list of events of all issues labeled from each repository in our database and counted all the labeling moments. The events of an issue present some activities carried out, such as assignments, closings, labeling time, and others. Then, we calculate when issues are labeled in first events, the number of issues labeled first when the labeling activity is more frequent, and the frequency it happens. Figure 3 shows when the labeling event occurs most when an issue is registered.

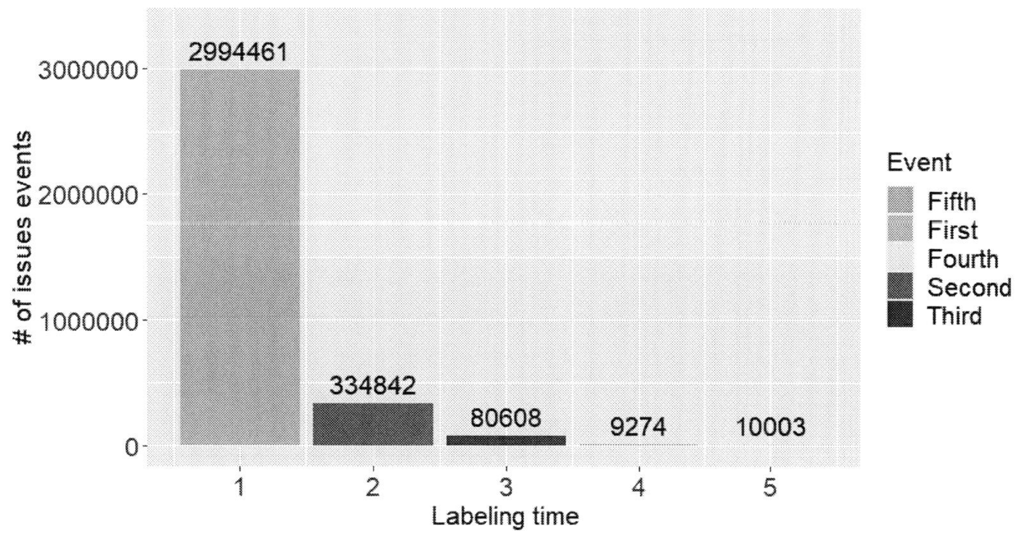

Fig. 3. When the labeling event often occurs in labeled issues.

As Figure 3 shows, the labeling activity happens massively in the first issue event. 2,994,461 issues were firstly labeled; this represents 60.89% of the total issues labeled amount. Labeling as the first activity is also dominant in 8,754 (65.91%) of the repositories.

From these results, we could infer that the labeling activity, when performed, is prioritized as one of the first events when reporting an issue among several event actions. As a first event prioritized by project contributors many times in labeled issues, we can infer an essential role in the issue resolution process.

4.4 What is the relevance of labeling issues for repositories with a different number of issues? (RQ4)

We first analyzed whether the issue tracker size correlates with the labeling activity by performing the Spearman's rank correlation in each repository issue and the ratio of labeled issues. The Spearman's rho value is 0.42, indicating a moderate correlation between repository issue size and labeling activity.

After performing the correlation, we analyzed each case in particular. By splitting the repositories into groups, we could identify outliers in our study and evaluate how repositories with a similar number of issues behave when labeling. As a result, we found that The Largest group had a labeling ratio of 48,68%, representing 4,570,266 labeled issues. The Larger group labeled 28,45% of their issues or 277,957 ones. In the Smaller group, 16.82%, or 7,634 issues, were labeled out of its total. Last, in The Smallest group, 23.44% or 61,687 issues were labeled. Figure 4 shows such results.

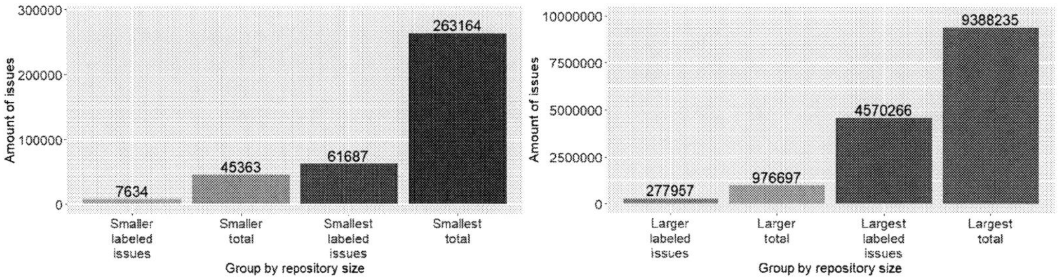

Fig. 4. Smaller, Smallest, Larger and Lagest labeled issues and total amount of issues.

Even with more significant adherence from the repositories to the labeling activity, we could observe that only part of the issues is labeled. As Figures 4 and 4 show, we found out that repositories belonging to the upper median groups (Largest and Larger) are more used to label their issues. We can conclude that the more issues the repository has, the more issues need to be labeled by the contributors. On the other hand, smaller repositories tend to leave the labeling activity aside and focus on resolving issues without this practice.

5 Discussion

The analysis of the repositories allowed us to find critical information about the issue labeling activity in the Github repositories. Firstly, we found that the labeling activity is very characteristic in the Github repositories we analyzed, as most of them label at least one issue. We observed that 10,458 (78.75%) repositories label their issues, while 2,822 (21.25%) did not label any issues.

Larger repositories prioritize and label many issues. This is likely due to an organizational structure that encourages this type of practice to resolve issues. On the other hand, we observed that small repositories, usually encompassing few issues, do not label their issues.

Another fact observed in repositories that employ labeling activity, is that not all issues are labeled. Considering the set of repositories that label their issue, we found a number of 4,917,544 (46.07%) labeled issues, while (53,93%) issue are unlabeled.

Despite having fewer labeled issues, the gain that labeling brings to community engagement and communication is enormous. Our study found that the labeled issues are indeed more striking in the eyes of contributors, with the most significant number of events happening around them and people interacting through the comments of the issues and subscriptions to follow up on the proposed question. If the contributors knew about the gain that an issue brings in numbers, they would label their issues more.

The contributors who see the labeling activity as a good practice started with the first event already labeling issues. We noticed that this practice often becomes the first or second action to be taken at the time of resolution for those who label. Therefore, there is an importance in this activity in the repositories that apply it.

Still, this study's central message is that the labeling activity brings more benefits than not using it. Even if they are large or smaller repositories, the gain in the engagement of personnel and organization when using these structures is significant in compensation for the non-use of the practice.

6 Threats to Validity

6.1 Internal Validity

Knowing that repositories that belong to different families and organizations bring particularity and different aspects to each other, we seek to find heterogeneity in the repositories using the Github listing, adhering only to the 100 most popular ones. Thus, repositories that did not have issues, or were less frequent, were removed from our study because they did not have enough data analysis input.

6.2 External Validity

We could not generalize the findings of the labeling activity for platforms other than Github and other repositories of different new topics. However, to encompass a more significant number of repositories, we use precisely the list with the repositories of various Github topics with different properties and sizes to seek a more excellent approximation when generalizing the data to others systems of the platform.

In addition, the time of data collection can also be a limiting factor in our study since the repositories used in this study were mined in a specific time frame, and the issues reported later on were not considered in this analysis. For this, we considered the most significant number of valid issues from our database for the study.

6.3 Construct Validity

We had an initial concern about the selection metrics of studied repositories. Therefore, we attempted to carefully employ and analyze correlation, labeling time, and the numbers related to the labels themselves. Besides, we were careful to present the data adequately and without interfering with the results.

6.4 Conclusion Validity

Considering our study is data-intensive, data analysis through metrics plays a central role in achieving the results. The way we presented it might influence how we analyzed the findings. To avoid misinterpretations or bias, we performed the search and selected different label and usage data representations in the repositories. We employed well-established methods from the literature to measure and present the study data.

7 Related Work

Bissyandé et al. [8] presented a study that aimed to understand issues and software project activities, including an overview of ten popular tags used in reported issues classified by issue type: bug report and feature request. Also, the study shows a shortlist of all labels and analyzes only the labels bug and enhancement. On the other hand, our study sought to analyze a set of mined repositories, regardless of specific label, the representativeness of the labeling activity in the repositories, including different sizes, the impact labels have on engagement, and issues resolution.

Social and technical aspects were the focus of Treude and Storey [28], who studied the creation and behavior of tags on the Jazz platform in an industrial environment, obtaining relevant data on the use of labels in the industrial development domain. Our study analyzes other aspects of a heterogeneous number of open-source repositories, such as the overall impact and engagement in different repositories of different sizes and domains, whose dynamics of use change significantly.

Cabot et al. [10] explored the use and influence of labels on Github repositories and issues using the GHTorrent [15] database. The study described the number of labels, the most used ones, and their influence on the project through a correlation between time to solve and issue age. The study also created clusters of types of labels, called label families, and classified them. Our study provides a more in-depth analysis of the representativeness of the labeling activity in different types of repositories. In addition, we considered other metrics to measure the engagement, such as the number of subscriptions to the issue, followers, and comments, and to analyze the level of importance of the labeling at the time of issue resolution getting the labeling moment as a priority method.

Alonso-Abad et al. [1] studied the prediction of issue labeling using data from seven Github repositories in the GHtorrent database. They presented a list of the leading labels used by these repositories. The study focused on labeling prediction and showed the performance of this practice with text mining techniques and the possibility of indicating closest labels. The focus of the work is on label prediction and performance as analyzing the best techniques for predicting those labels, similar to automatic labeling, unlike our study, which involves an exploratory analysis of the impacts that labels bring to the repository on engagement, repository size, and other aspects.

8 Conclusion

Maintenance and evolution in large-scale systems and communities are among the most significant challenges that open-source systems development could encounter. A platform that provides a good work and communication environment can be decisive for maintaining these communities. Indeed, project settings for more significant community integration have improved significantly. We could state that, in the past, the issues only encompassed their title and description. Modern issue trackers have employed more robust structures, comprising several options for issue data personalization. Among these, labeling has come to assist the developer in solving issues and keeping the gear running more strategically.

With this emerging new use of labels, our study sought to shed light on this activity performed in the latest versions of repositories, based on Github, and show that they are not mere functionalities present on the platform that they offer a rich feature to support developers. Therefore, our study mined 10,673,459 issues from 13,280 repositories of 180 Github featured topics and found that about 78.75% of the repositories label their issues, with more adherence from those repositories that contain big numbers of issues. The labeling practice is essential and deemed the first step in the issue resolution process in 65.91% of the first events. Issues with labels draw more attention and impact by collecting more subscribers, assigns, and comments, helping to engage contributors to the resolution.

As future work, we want to study more about the labeling activity and its different types of occurring labels in the repositories and the influence that certain domains have on creating specific labels. We also intend to do a joint analysis of contributors to investigate the creation and use of certain types of labels in the repositories.

Acknowledgments. This study was financed in part by the Coordenação de Aperfeiçoamento de Pessoal de Nível Superior - Brasil (CAPES) - Finance Code 001, and FAPESB grant JCB0060/2016.

References

1. Alonso-Abad, J.M., López-Nozal, C., Maudes-Raedo, J.M., Marticorena-Sánchez, R.: Label prediction on issue tracking systems using text mining. Progress in Artificial Intelligence **8**(3), 325–342 (2019)
2. Anvik, J., Hiew, L., Murphy, G.C.: Coping with an open bug repository. In: Proceedings of the 2005 OOPSLA Workshop on Eclipse Technology EXchange. p. 35–39. Association for Computing Machinery, New York, NY, USA (2005)
3. Anvik, J., Hiew, L., Murphy, G.C.: Who should fix this bug? In: Proceedings of the 28th International Conference on Software Engineering. p. 361–370. ICSE '06, Association for Computing Machinery, New York, NY, USA (2006)
4. Aranda, J., Venolia, G.: The secret life of bugs: Going past the errors and omissions in software repositories. In: 2009 IEEE 31st International Conference on Software Engineering. pp. 298–308 (2009)
5. Bernardi, M.L., Canfora, G., Di Lucca, G.A., Di Penta, M., Distante, D.: Do developers introduce bugs when they do not communicate? the case of eclipse and mozilla. In: 2012 16th European Conference on Software Maintenance and Reengineering. pp. 139–148 (2012)
6. Bettenburg, N., Just, S., Schröter, A., Weiß, C., Premraj, R., Zimmermann, T.: Quality of bug reports in eclipse. In: Proceedings of the 2007 OOPSLA Workshop on Eclipse Technology EXchange. p. 21–25. Association for Computing Machinery, New York, NY, USA (2007)
7. Bettenburg, N., Just, S., Schröter, A., Weiss, C., Premraj, R., Zimmermann, T.: What makes a good bug report? In: Proceedings of the 16th ACM SIGSOFT International Symposium on Foundations of Software Engineering. p. 308–318. SIGSOFT '08/FSE-16, Association for Computing Machinery, New York, NY, USA (2008)
8. Bissyandé, T.F., Lo, D., Jiang, L., Réveillère, L., Klein, J., Traon, Y.L.: Got issues? who cares about it? a large scale investigation of issue trackers from github. In: 2013 IEEE 24th International Symposium on Software Reliability Engineering (ISSRE). pp. 188–197 (2013)
9. Borges, H., Tulio Valente, M.: What's in a github star? understanding repository starring practices in a social coding platform. Journal of Systems and Software **146**, 112 – 129 (2018)
10. Cabot, J., Izquierdo, J.L.C., Cosentino, V., Rolandi, B.: Exploring the use of labels to categorize issues in open-source software projects. In: 2015 IEEE 22nd International Conference on Software Analysis, Evolution, and Reengineering (SANER). pp. 550–554. IEEE (2015)
11. Dabbish, L., Stuart, C., Tsay, J., Herbsleb, J.: Social coding in github: Transparency and collaboration in an open software repository. In: Proceedings of the ACM 2012 Conference on Computer Supported Cooperative Work. p. 1277–1286. CSCW '12, Association for Computing Machinery, New York, NY, USA (2012)
12. Github Inc. : Assigning issue article (2020), https://docs.github.com/en/free-pro-team@latest/github/managing-your-work-on-github/assigning-issues-and-pull-requests-to-other-github-user

13. Github Inc.: Mastering markdown (2020), https://guides.github.com/features/mastering-markdown
14. Github Inc.: Page of all features topics in github (2020), https://github.com/topics
15. Gousios, G.: The ghtorent dataset and tool suite. In: 2013 10th Working Conference on Mining Software Repositories (MSR). pp. 233–236. IEEE (2013)
16. Hertel, G., Niedner, S., Herrmann, S.: Motivation of software developers in open source projects: an internet-based survey of contributors to the linux kernel. Research policy **32**(7), 1159–1177 (2003)
17. Joselito Mota Júnior, Gláucya Boechat, I.M.: Label it be! a large-scale study of issue labeling in modern open source repositories (supplementary material). Zenodo (Jul 2021). https://doi.org/10.5281/zenodo.5090336, https://doi.org/10.5281/zenodo.5090336
18. Koponen, T.: Life cycle of defects in open source software projects. In: IFIP International Conference on Open Source Systems. pp. 195–200. Springer (2006)
19. Lientz, B.P., Swanson, E.B., Tompkins, G.E.: Characteristics of application software maintenance. Communications of the ACM **21**(6), 466–471 (Jun 1978)
20. Mockus, A.: Organizational volatility and its effects on software defects. In: Proceedings of the Eighteenth ACM SIGSOFT International Symposium on Foundations of Software Engineering. p. 117–126. FSE '10, Association for Computing Machinery, New York, NY, USA (2010)
21. Munaiah, N., Kroh, S., Cabrey, C., Nagappan, M.: Curating github for engineered software projects. Empirical Software Engineering **22**(6), 3219–3253 (2017)
22. Nakakoji, K., Yamamoto, Y., Nishinaka, Y., Kishida, K., Ye, Y.: Evolution patterns of open-source software systems and communities. In: Proceedings of the International Workshop on Principles of Software Evolution. p. 76–85. IWPSE '02, Association for Computing Machinery, New York, NY, USA (2002)
23. Nayebi, M., Kabeer, S.J., Ruhe, G., Carlson, C., Chew, F.: Hybrid labels are the new measure! IEEE Software **35**(1), 54–57 (2018)
24. Rodriguez, D., Herraiz, I., Harrison, R.: On software engineering repositories and their open problems. In: 2012 First International Workshop on Realizing AI Synergies in Software Engineering (RAISE). pp. 52–56 (2012)
25. Schneider, K., von Hunnius, J..: Effective experience repositories for software engineering. In: 25th International Conference on Software Engineering, 2003. Proceedings. pp. 534–539 (2003)
26. Storey, M., Ryall, J., Singer, J., Myers, D., Cheng, L., Muller, M.: How software developers use tagging to support reminding and refinding. IEEE Transactions on Software Engineering **35**(4), 470–483 (2009)
27. The Python Software Foundation: Regular expression in python (2020), https://docs.python.org/3/library/re.html
28. Treude, C., Storey, M.: Work item tagging: Communicating concerns in collaborative software development. IEEE Transactions on Software Engineering **38**(1), 19–34 (2012)
29. Zubrow, D.: Ieee standard classification for software anomalies. IEEE Computer Society (2009)

Towards Heuristics for Supporting the Validation of Code Smells

Luiz Felipi Junionello[1] and Rafael de Mello[1][0000-0002-9877-3946]

CEFET/RJ, Rio de Janeiro, Brazil
luiz.junionello@aluno.cefet-rj.br, rafael.mello@cefet-rj.br

Abstract. The identification of code smells is largely recognized as a subjective task. Consequently, the automated detection tools available are insufficient to deal with the whole subjectivity involved in the task, requiring human validation. However, developers may follow different but complementary perspectives for manually validating the same code smell. Based on this scenario, our research aims at characterizing a comprehensive and optimized set of heuristics for guiding developers to validate the incidence of code smells reported by automated detection tools. For this purpose, we conducted an empirical study with 12 experienced software developers. In this study, we invited developers to individually validate the incidence of code smells in 24 code snippets from open-source Java projects. For each validation, developers should provide arguments for supporting their decisions. The study findings revealed that developers tend to look from different perspectives even when they agree about the incidence of a code smell. After coding the 303 arguments given into heuristics and refining them, we composed an optimized set of validation items for guiding developers on manually validating the incidence of eight types of code smells: data class, god class, speculative generality, middle man, refused bequest, primitive obsession, long parameter list, and feature envy. We are currently planning a survey with specialists for identifying opportunities for evolving the set of validation items proposed.

Keywords: code smells · code review · heuristics · validation.

1 Introduction

The variety of maintenance requests over different source code elements frequently challenge software developers [1]. This challenge typically results from the structural complexity of the source code, requiring considerable reading and comprehension efforts from these professionals for performing even simple tasks. For mitigating these efforts, one key practice addresses continuously identifying and combating the incidence of code smells. Code smells are known as indicators of deeper problems within a source code, commonly introduced due to the negligence of good programming practices. The incidence of code smells harms maintenance activities[18] [10] once it hampers the source code readability and comprehension. Besides, different works associate the incidence of code smells with the acceleration of the software degradation in the long term[19] [9].

Due to its granularity, manually identifying and fixing smelly code in entire software systems or modules is definitively not a trivial task. In this sense, several detection tools have been proposed in the last decade to automate the detection of code smells [2]. Even though these tools may save effort on identification activities, they cannot be considered the final word [17] [2]. After a tool reports candidates to code smell, developers should manually validate these issues, distinguishing false positives from the actual ones. Among others, neglecting such validation may lead developers to unnecessarily modifying several code elements associated with false positives. Consequently, a lack of validating candidates to code smells may result in a considerable waste of maintenance effort. Besides, it may lead developers to accidentally introduce new and even worse issues in the source code, including bugs and design problems [6].

However, one can see that manually validating the incidence of code smells is a considerably subjective task. Distant from the generic definitions available at catalogues and raw thresholds, the decision about the incidence of code smells may be highly influenced by contextual factors, including technological, organizational, and human ones [4] [5] [6]. Indeed, even colleagues reviewing the same system module may have different interpretations about the incidence of smelly code due to their background [4] [3]. Consequently, the subjectivity involved in the identification of code smells frequently leads developers to disagree on their final decisions[3]. On the other hand, the diversity of perspectives from two or more reviewers working together- when possible -contributes to increasing the performance of smell identification tasks [4] [14] [15]. However, allocating developers for conducting group reviews may be unfeasible due to several reasons, including schedule and budget restrictions.

Besides, our recent studies on the developers' social representations [6] [8] reveal the need for guiding these professionals on reflecting about several technical and non-technical aspects surrounding the manual validation of code smells. In this way, we argue that coding and reusing heuristics followed by different developers is a promising strategy towards reaching this guidance. By heuristics, we understand a set of particular attention points for enabling the developers' analysis and, consequently, supporting their decision-making. The set of heuristics to be applied in each issue will depend on the type of code smell reported by the detection tool. For instance, let's suppose that a certain tool had detected a possible incidence of the speculative generality smell. This code smell is characterized by a code element written just for accommodating future features, which suggests that it would be discarded. While one reviewer would opt by analysing whether the class can perform some relevant task, a second reviewer would opt by checking whether this class actually needs to be used by other code elements. Once both strategies may be considered valid, a third reviewer may use them as a starting point to reflect before accepting or discarding the reported smell.

In this paper, we report our first study towards a comprehensive and optimized set of heuristics for guiding developers on validating the incidence of code smells. This research proposes combining the power of detection of already existing automated tools with the empowered rationale of experienced software developers for improving the effectiveness of smell identification tasks. For composing the first version of this set of heuristics, we conducted a controlled study in which we invited 12 developers to validate 24 suspected code smells reported by a detection tool. These issues address eight popular types of code smells, including *God Class*, *Long Method*, *Long Parameter list*, and *Refused Bequest*. We extracted the projects and code elements used in our study among the dataset used by Hozano et al. for assessing the developers' agreement about the incidence of code smells [3]. In the original study, these 24 cases were identified as examples of considerable disagreement among developers.

In our study, the participants provided arguments for accepting or rejecting the incidence of code smells in each case analysed. In total, 288 arguments were gathered and submitted to open coding, resulting in 40 distinct heuristics distributed among the eight types of code smells investigated. Most of these heuristics go beyond the classical definition of code smells investigated. Then, we used them for compiling a set of 22 validation items (questions) for supporting developers in reflecting on the incidence of the different types of code smells investigated.

Section 2 presents the related work. Section 3 describes the settings of our empirical study. Section 4 presents the results of our study, reporting its main findings. It also presents a discussion of the heuristics found for each type of code smell. Section 5 presents the validation items composed based on the heuristics found. Section 6 discuss the main threats to validity identified in our study. Finally, Section 7 concludes the paper and indicates future work.

2 Related Work

To the best of our knowledge, there was no previous study investigating heuristics to support the manual validation of code smells reported by automated tools. However, there is a set of relevant studies that addressing key motivations for our research.

Regarding the limitations of automated detection tools, Fernandes et al. [2] conducted a comprehensive review of automated code smell detection tools. After identifying 84 detection tools and comparing their capabilities and characteristics, the authors selected four tools to perform a in-depth comparison: *inFusion*, *JDeodorant*, *PMD* and *JSpIRIT*. In this comparison, they analyzed the precision and recall of these tools on detecting Long Methods and Large Classes. In general, the tools showed a low performance when detecting different code smells, such as Large Class and Long Method. For instance, although PMD reached 100% of precision for Large Class, the recall was 14%. The results for Long Method were better, with JSpIRIT reaching 67% of recall and 80% of precision while PMD reached 50% recall and 100% of precision.

While the previous study focused on comparing detection tools based on metrics and thresholds, Pecorelli[16] performed a comparative investigation between the performance of smell detection tools based on machine learning and tools based on metric-based heuristics. For this purpose, the authors used a large dataset composed of previously validated code smells. Different from their initial expectation, the authors found that machine learning detection tools are not yet at a stage in which they can be used without manual validation. Among others, the findings from the aforementioned studies indicate the risk involved in only relying on automated smell detection. Depending on the dataset and the smell type, certain tools may reach considerably low levels of precision and recall (coverage). In this way, our research focuses on guiding developers for optimizing their precision on smell identification tasks.

From a human-centered perspective, it is also important to note that the precision of identifying code smells may be influenced by different human aspects [5]. de Mello et al. [4] conducted a multi trial empirical study aiming at characterizing the influence of three distinct developers' characteristics over the precision of smell identification tasks: professional experience, familiarity with the module investigated, and the level of interaction among them during the identification tasks (pair x solo). The study findings revealed that developers working in pairs reached higher precision than developers working solo, especially between developers having some professional experience. Besides, the authors found evidence that developers having previous knowledge of the module to review tend to focus on different aspects when identifying code smells from those without this knowledge. Therefore, pairing developers with and without this knowledge represents a better choice once these individuals tend to provide complementary viewpoints of the code elements. More recently, the benefits of collaboratively identifying code smells were also observed over different experiments [15].

Among the findings of the aforementioned studies, we observed that developers tend to invest considerable effort in taking *ad-hoc* decisions, despite the automated assistance available. Besides, they frequently diverge on their decisions about the same code element, although sometimes showing some concerns in common beyond formal rules and metrics. To better understand this behaviour, we conducted a pioneer investigation on the social representations of the identification of code smells [6] [7] [8]. The theory of social representations considers that a task such as identifying code smells is collectively seen based on the set of beliefs, values, and behaviors unconsciously shared between its practitioners [13]. Consequently, social representations continuously work as an invisible force influencing how individuals deal with the task. The findings of our investigation on social representations revealed considerable gaps between the research on smell identification and its practice. These gaps suggest the need of building proper support for developers manually validating the incidence of code smells [8], reflecting about its semantics, change impact analysis, among others.

The dataset and part of the instrumentation of the study reported in this paper were obtained from an investigation on the agreement among developers on validating automatically detected code smells [3]. Hozano et al. conducted an empirical study in which 75 developers validated the incidence of different types of code smells reported by smell detection tools. The authors found that the level of agreement among developers was low in all types of code smells investigated, ranging from 0.24 to 0.32 (Fleiss Kappa). Also, the authors could not find any relevant difference in the agreement levels when analyzing specific categories of developer's backgrounds. After each round composed of ten evaluations, the developers were asked to summarise the heuristics adopted. As a result, the authors observed that several cases of agreement among developers involved similar heuristics.

Different from [3], our study focus on identifying and analyzing heuristics rather than measuring agreement, assuming that disagreement is intrinsic to the nature of an *ad hoc* identification task. For this purpose, we intentionally selected a subset of the tasks with higher disagreement levels from [3], asking developers to justify their decisions after each validation task. In this way, we intend to identify and code the first set of heuristics to lead developers extrapolating their particular insights when validating code smells.

3 Study Design

Different developers may adopt different heuristics for concluding that some code element is poorly structured or not. These heuristics typically emerge from an *ah hoc* and individual reasoning process. Consequently, the heuristics adopted by them may significantly vary but may also be limited to single perspectives. By having this in mind, our research aims at characterizing a comprehensive set of heuristics used by developers for validating the incidence of code smells. Based on these heuristics, we intend to compose an optimized set of hands-on validation items to support this task. For this purpose, we understand that extracting a diverse set of arguments from different developers represents one valid strategy.

3.1 Research Question

Based on our research goal, we defined the following research question:

Which heuristics do developers follow to validate the incidence of code smells?

By answering this research question, we want to characterize how different developers validate the possible incidence of code smells detected in the context of real software projects. From this, we want to discover more common criteria and possibly unexpected arguments that may help developers in future validation tasks. Based on this knowledge, we will develop more relevant and accurate sets of heuristics for supporting the validation of each type of code smell investigated.

For this purpose, we designed a controlled experiment partially inspired in the experimental settings of the Hozano et al. [3] empirical study. In that work, the authors' goal was to measure the level of agreement among developers about the possible incidence of code smells in 225 different code snippets. These code code snippets were extracted from five popular open-source projects developed using the Java programming language: *GanttProject*, *Apache Xerces*, *ArgoUML*, *jEdit*, and *Eclipse*. From this set, we extracted a subset composed of three code snippets for each type of code smell investigated in our study. All the code snippets selected resulted in considerably low levels of agreement in the original study. Thus, we expect that diverse sets of heuristics may emerge from different on evaluating them.

3.2 Population and Sample

The target population of our study is composed of software developers having knowledge about code smells and code reviews. Considering the findings of previous studies with developers (see Section 2) and our research objective, we established the settings of our study sample. First, we opted by investigating developers validating code smells individually once developers would feel free to provide more diverse and unique arguments in this scenario, which is more interesting for reaching our goal. Second, we assured that all study participants have solid professional experience with software development, leading to more reliable insights. Third, considering the nature of the projects involved in the study (large open-source projects), we checked that none of the study participants have previous knowledge of the modules analysed. It would lead developers to feel more comfortable providing less biased arguments, especially those favorable to the incidence of poorly structured code.

The study sample is composed of 12 Master/Doctorate students having solid experience with software development. Besides, most of these professionals are specialists in code smells. After executing the study tasks, we applied a characterization form. In this form, we asked about the experience of the study participants from three distinct perspectives: *self-assessment*, *years of experience*, and *number of projects*. From the self-assessment perspective, most participants declared high or very high experience levels in software development (9/12), as well in Java programming (7/12). Besides, no participant declared having no development experience in Java. From the 12 participants, eight declared experience in identifying code smells. From these, six also conducted researches on this topic. Table 1 summarizes the average experience of the participants in terms of years and number of projects on each skill.

Table 1. Average experience of the participants in the different skills measured.

Metric	Software Dev.	Java	Smell Ident.
years of experience	5.92	4.75	1.00
# of projects	9.42	7.17	3.08

The different perspectives used for characterizing the participants' experience led us to conclude that the sample investigated is experienced in building software for different Java projects. Besides, most of the participants are also skilled in the identification of code smells. In the characterization form, we also asked the participants to briefly summarize their experience in software development. Based on the answers provided, we also observed that most of the developers have experience working with different programming languages, building systems for different domains.

3.3 Instrumentation

Through a validation form, we asked the participants to individually validate the incidence of code smells over 24 different code snippets, three to each code smells investigated: *Primitive Obsession, Long Parameter List, God Class, Data Class, Speculative Generality, Feature Envy, Middle Man,* and *Refused Bequest.* All 12 participants evaluated the same code snippets. The code snippets used in the study were picked from the same database used in Hozano et al. study [3]. For each validation task, the validation form indicated the exact location of the candidate to code smell in the code snippet. If needed, the study participants also had the option to access the whole source code of each project involved in the study.

After performing each validation task, the subjects were asked to justify their decision, providing detailed arguments on why they concluded that a certain code snippet is smelly or not. For supporting a deeper and accurate analysis, the participants were previously prepared to allocate four hours of their time to perform all the tasks. Besides, each participant received the summarized definition of each type of code smell involved in the study.

3.4 Data Analysis

We summarize the data analysis procedures in Figure 1. We first performed open coding over the arguments given by each participant to each validation task. During the coding process, we tried to identify and categorize the heuristics behind each answer given. In this way, we considered mapping the different actions performed and eventual criteria adopted by the participants for decision making. In the second step, we classified the set of heuristics given on each individual validation as favourable to the acceptance of the code smell (accepting heuristics) or rejecting the code smell (rejecting heuristics). This classification was based on the final decision made by each participant to each task. Then, we grouped all the accepting/rejecting heuristics coded by code smell type. Finally, we performed a refinement of the results (fourth step). For this, we identified opportunities for grouping similar heuristics, eliminating redundancies. We also identified opportunities to splitting too high-level heuristics into two or more.

4 Results

The 12 participants performed all the 24 validation tasks, resulting in a set of 288 validations. In total, 301 arguments were coded, including repetitions.

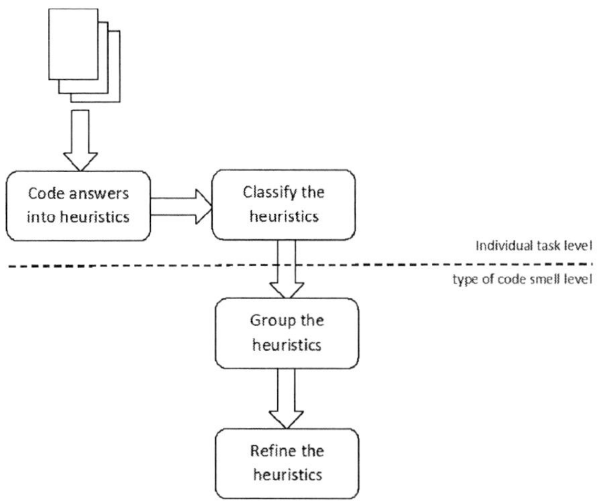

Fig. 1. The steps followed for coding the heuristics.

From these, 32 (11.80%) arguments were discarded since they do not address rationale or criteria followed by the participants to support their decisions. In most of these cases, the participants only reported evasive arguments, such as "It has/has not a smell". From the remaining 271 arguments, we found that 57.93% of them address accepting the code smell while 42.07% are favorable to rejection. After step 4, 84 distinct arguments were identified considering all the code smells evaluated, 41 for acceptance and 43 for rejection.

Tables 2 exemplifies the coding process by showing the heuristics coded based on the arguments given for the first validation task addressing the incidence of the Long Parameter List code smells. Table 3 present the final set of heuristics refined for Long Parameter List, considering the heuristics coded from the three validation tasks.

Table 2. Heuristics coded for the first validation task about the incidence of Long Parameter List and their frequency (f).

Accepting Heuristics	*f*	**Rejecting Heuristics**	*f*
Too many complex parameters	2	Needed parameters	2
Too many parameters	1	All parameters are used	2
Unused parameters	1	Acceptable number of parameters	2
Parameters should be encapsulated	1	It is a constructor	1
Total	5	Total	7

The following subsections summarize the final set of heuristics coded by type of code smell. Some of these heuristics directly address the general definitions of the code smells. However, we also found several other heuristics provided by the

Table 3. Refined set of heuristics addressing the incidence of Long Parameter List and their frequency (f).

Accepting Heuristics	**f**	**Rejecting Heuristics**	**f**
Too many parameters	6	Needed parameters	5
Too many complex parameters	5	All parameters are used	5
Parameters should be encapsulated	3	It is a builder	4
Unused parameters	2	Acceptable number of parameters	2
Unnecessary parameters	2	Easy to understand	2
Inappropriate use of builder	2		
Total	20	Total	18

participants extrapolating these definitions. These findings address our initial expectation that developers would apply *ad hoc*, implicit, and useful heuristics for evaluating the incidence of a code smell.

4.1 Data Class

Most of the arguments given to accept or reject the incidence of Data Classes surround the concern on whether the class was actually used just to store data or whether it has logical methods to process its own data. However, several heuristics were employed. For instance, while most of the arguments focus on the incidence/lack of getters and setters, other ones address the effective role of the class methods and their constructors. Besides, other arguments address to which extent data from the class is externally manipulated.

4.2 Feature Envy

The arguments favorable to the incidence of Feature Envy predominantly address the fact that the code element only accesses external data. Besides, the scope of the responsibilities involved was also taken into account. Different heuristics were employed for rejecting the incidence of this smell in the code snippets analysed. For instance, one heuristic employed was that just a single external object is manipulated. Another heuristic address the importance of the so-called "envy" behaviour as necessary for supporting external objects. Besides, a common heuristic adopted addresses observing the balancing between the manipulation of internal and external data.

4.3 God Class

The number of responsibilities and lines of code were the two more common arguments reported for accepting a God Class. While in some cases the number of lines of code was used as a single argument, in other cases the high amount of lines of code was interpreted as a side effect of assuming several responsibilities.

Besides, the participants argued in other cases that even large classes having too many responsibilities are not smelly once their responsibilities seems pertinent.

4.4 Long Parameter List

In this code smells, developers employed several heuristics. The more common heuristic address reflecting about the amount of the parameters listed. However, other ones address specific characteristics of the code snippets analysed, such as the complexity of the parameters, the possibility of encapsulating them, their relevance, and the role of the corresponding method in the context of eventual design patterns adopted.

4.5 Middle Man

Middle Man was revealed to be a confusing code smell for less experienced participants. Nonetheless, most of the arguments for accepting these smells directly address its basic definition: the class actually had delegated its responsibilities to another class. On the other hand, developers employed different heuristics for rejecting the code smell, including verifying the use of only local data, verifying the number of methods playing a middle man role, and even considering the incompleteness of the class evaluated.

4.6 Primitive Obsession

Primitive obsession has a relatively straightforward definition: several primitive variables are improperly used. In most cases, the reported code smell was accepted/rejected once the participants concluded that complex types could/could not replace the primitive variables found. However, in some cases, the participants opted by rejecting the incidence of the code smell once they concluded that some primitive elements are needed due to different reasons according to the code snippet evaluated.

4.7 Refused Bequest

Refused Bequest was another code smell in which developers frequently used heuristics based on its generic definition. Another heuristics adopted was checking whether inherited methods are unused or merely overridden. As Middle Man, this smell also showed to be confusing to some participants. From the 36 answers given, we discarded nine due to the lack of clear arguments.

4.8 Speculative Generality

Speculative Generality addresses code elements only designed for future purposes. Developers applied different heuristics for accepting the incidence of this smell. For classes, the heuristics include checking the lack of methods and the pertinence of inheritance relationships. For methods, the heuristics coded include analysing its external use and the lack of responsibilities.

5 Composing Validation Items

Based on the findings of our study, we compiled the first version of validation items for supporting the developers in reflecting on the incidence of code smells (see Table 4). These items are expressed through questions designed to stimulate developers' rationale during the validation tasks. Considering the typical large incidence of code smells, we intentionally condensed the heuristics coded to each code smell type into a smaller set of validation items.

Different from the metric/rule-based heuristics applied for automated detection, our validation items do not intend to be deterministic. We do not propose any conclusive thresholds nor any recommendation for accepting or rejecting code smells. However, we expect that the set of validation items proposed could help developers minding different and relevant perspectives before their final decision. Besides, it is important to note that we designed the validation items to validate candidates to code smells previously detected. Thus, we do not recommend using them as a surrogate of detection tools.

6 Threats to Validity

An important threat to the validity of our study addresses the influence of the code snippets' characteristics over the heuristics coded. In other words, if the participants evaluated another set of code snippets, probably different heuristics would be found. To mitigate this bias, we acted in two moments. In the study design, we selected code snippets from different projects having different structural characteristics to the eight types of code smell investigated. During the composing of the validation items, we tried to capture the general essence of the heuristics.

Another important threat address the researchers' bias in the coding activities. To mitigate them, the first author performed each coding step followed by a meeting with the second author for double-checking and solving disagreements. Then, both authors collaboratively worked on composing the validation items. Despite that, we are aware that some level of bias would persist. Thus, we plan to submit the validation items to the assessment of several specialists in code smells.

Finally, we are aware that the general definitions given to each code smells during the execution may have influenced their arguments. However, the results indicated that several participants frequently went beyond these definitions in their arguments. Besides, we understand that the definitions allowed the less experienced developers on smell identification to provide useful arguments.

7 Conclusion and Future Work

It is undeniable that developers should give the final word about the incidence of code smells. In this way, some settings on allocating developers in smells identification tasks may work better than others. However, the most common

Table 4. Validation items designed to support developers analysing the incidence of code smells.

Data Class
1-Does the class have other methods than getters and setters? 2-Does the class have other methods than its constructor? 3-Is the class data being externally manipulated?
Feature Envy
1-Does the method call external methods too frequently? 2-Can you visualize an alternative implementation of this method focused on manipulating its own data?
God Class
1-Does the class have clear responsibilities from other classes? 2-Does it make sense for you to split this class into one or more classes? 3-Does the class size hinder its readability/comprehensibility?
Long Parameter List
1-Does the method signature have too many parameters? 2-Are there too many parameters composed of complex types? 3-Do the parameters' names contribute to reaching a clear understanding of their purpose? 4-Does the method actually use all its parameters? 5-Are all parameters actually needed? 6-May the parameters be passed more simply?
Middle Man
1-Does the class perform any relevant logical task? 2-Does the class clearly delegate its responsibilities to other classes?
Primitive Obsession
1-Does replacing one or more primitive variables with objects sound to be the best choice? 2-May two or more variables be consolidated into a single complex type?
Refused Bequest
1-Does the inheritance conceptually make sense? 2-Does the class inherit methods never used? 3-Does the class inherit methods that are not adherent with its definition? 4-Are there too many methods being overridden?

setting involves developers performing this task individually. In this paper, we propose a set of validation items for supporting the manual validation of code smells. This set is composed of questions intentionally designed to lead developers to reflect on relevant aspects of the source code according to the code smell type. These questions were depicted after coding and grouping heuristics from the arguments given by experienced developers for accepting/rejecting the incidence of code smells in several code snippets.

We are currently planning the empirical evaluation of the validation items with specialists in code smell detection. For this purpose, we are designing an opinion survey involving researchers experienced in code smells from different institutions. Through this evaluation, we intend to observe the pertinence and perceived relevance of the validation items proposed. Besides, we also intend to improve the original set of validation items by adding new heuristics proposed by these specialists.

After evolving the validation items, we plan to integrate them into an automated detection tool. With this integration, developers would set the detection tool for asking about each validation item according to the type of code smell reported. Although the validation items may come to developers' minds along the time, developers may also use the answers given to the validation items for empowering their communication during the tasks. Besides, we plan to conduct a controlled study to assess the contribution of this integrated solution over the effectiveness of the smell validation tasks.

8 Acknowledgements

We thank to the students from PUC-Rio involved in this study. We also thank to Mario Hozano and Anderson Uchoa to the valuable contributions to this work. This research was supported by PIBIC-Cefet/RJ and by CNPq 152179/2020-8.

References

1. Bennett, K. and Rajlich, V.: Software maintenance and evolution: a roadmap. In: Proceedings of the Conference on the Future of Software Engineering (ICSE'00), pp. 73-87. ACM (2000)
2. Fernandes, E., Oliveira, J., Vale, G., Paiva, T., Figueiredo, E.: A review-based comparative study of bad smell detection tools. In: Proceedings of the 20th International Conference on Evaluation and Assessment in Software Engineering (EASE), pp. 1-12. (2016)
3. Hozano, M., Garcia, A., Fonseca, B. and Costa, E.: Are you smelling it? Investigating how similar developers detect code smells. Information and Software Technology, 93, pp.130-146 (2018)
4. de Mello, R., Oliveira, R., Garcia, A.: On the influence of human factors for identifying code smells: A multi-trial empirical study. In: 2017 ACM/IEEE International Symposium on Empirical Software Engineering and Measurement (ESEM), pp. 68-77. IEEE, Canada (2017)

5. de Mello, R., Oliveira, R., Sousa, L., and Garcia, A. Towards effective teams for the identification of code smells. In: 2017 IEEE/ACM 10th International Workshop on Cooperative and Human Aspects of Software Engineering (CHASE), pp. 62–65. IEEE, Argentina (2017)
6. de Mello, R., Uchôa, A., Oliveira, R., Oliveira, D., Fonseca, B., Garcia, A., de Mello, F.: Investigating the Social Representations of Code Smell Identification: A Preliminary Study. In: 12th International Workshop on Cooperative and Human Aspects of Software Engineering (CHASE), pp. 53–60. IEEE press, Canada (2019)
7. de Mello, R., Uchôa, A., Oliveira, R., Oliveira, D., Oizumi, W., Souza, J., Fonseca, B., Garcia, A.: Investigating the Social Representations of the Identification of Code Smells by Practitioners and Students from Brazil. In: XXXIII Brazilian Symposium on Software Engineering (SBES), pp. 457–466. ACM, Brazil (2019)
8. de Mello, R., Uchôa, A., Oliveira, R., Oizumi, W., Souza, J., Mendes, K., Oliveira, D., Fonseca, B., Garcia, A.: Do Research and Practice of Code Smell Identification Walk Together? A Social Representations Analysis. In: 2019 ACM/IEEE International Symposium on Empirical Software Engineering and Measurement (ESEM), pp. 1–6. IEEE, Brazil (2019)
9. Fowler, M.: Refactoring: improving the design of existing code.Addison-Wesley Professional (2002)
10. Lima, R., Souza, J., Fonseca, B., Teixeira, L., Gheyi, R., Ribeiro, M., Garcia, A., de Mello, Rafael: Understanding and Detecting Harmful Code. In: Proceedings of the 34th Brazilian Symposium on Software Engineering (SBES), pp. 223-232. ACM, Brazil (2020)
11. Liu, H., Ma, Z., Shao, W., Niu, Z.: Schedule of bad smell detection and resolution: A new way to save effort. IEEE Transactions on Software Engineering, 38(1), pp. 220-235, IEEE (2011)
12. Mäntylä, M., Lassenius, C.: Subjective evaluation of software evolvability using code smells: An empirical study. Empirical Software Engineering, 11(3), pp. 395-431, Springer (2006)
13. Moscovici, S.: Notes towards a description of social representations. European journal of social psychology, 18(3), pp. 211–250, Wiley (1988)
14. Oliveira, R., Sousa, L., de Mello, R., Valentim, N., Lopes, A., Conte, T., Garcia, A., Oliveira, E., Lucena, C.: In: 2019 2017 IEEE/ACM 39th International Conference on Software Engineering: Software Engineering in Practice Track (ICSE-SEIP), pp. 33–42. IEEE, Argentina (2017)
15. Oliveira, R., de Mello, R., Fernandes, E., Garcia, A., Lucena, C.: Collaborative or individual identification of code smells? On the effectiveness of novice and professional developers. Information and Software Technology, 120, 106242. Elselvier (2020)
16. Pecorelli, F., Palomba, F., Di Nucci, D., De Lucia, A.: Comparing heuristic and machine learning approaches for metric-based code smell detection. In: 2019 IEEE/ACM 27th International Conference on Program Comprehension (ICPC), pp. 93-104. IEEE (2019).
17. Paiva T, Damasceno A, Figueiredo E, Sant'Anna C.: On the evaluation of code smells and detection tools. Journal of Software Engineering Research and Development, 5(1), pp. 1-28 (2017)
18. Palomba F., Bavota G., Di Penta M., Fasano F., Oliveto R., De Lucia A.: On the diffuseness and the impact on maintainability of code smells: a large scale empirical investigation. Empirical Software Engineering, 23(3), pp. 1188-1221 (2018)
19. Van Gurp J, Bosch J.: Design erosion: problems and causes. Journal of systems and software. 61(2), pp. 105-19 (2002)

Towards the Consolidation of Cybersecurity Standardized Definitions: a Tool for Ontological Analysis

Beatriz Franco Martins[1 [0000-0001-9190-1047]], Lenin Javier Serrano Gil[1,2 [0000-0002-1631-7139]], José Fabián Reyes Román[1 [0000-0002-9598-1301]], José Ignacio Panach[3 [0000-0002-7043-6227]], and Oscar Pastor[1 [0000-0002-1320-8471]]

[1] PROS Research Center, Universitat Politècnica de València,
Camino de Vera s/n, 46022 Valencia, Spain,
{bmartins, lserrano, jreyes}@pros.upv.es, opastor@dsic.upv.es
[2] Ingeniería de Sistemas e Informática, Universidad Pontificia Bolivariana
Km 7 via Bucaramanga - Piedecuesta, Santander, Colombia
[3] Escola Tècnica Superior d'Enginyeria, Universitat de València,
Avinguda de l'Universitat, 46100 Burjassot, Valencia
joigpana@uv.es

Cybersecurity is defined as "information technology security" and today managing all the elements involved in this domain is usually quite complex and immense. It is for this reason that companies keep actively looking for efficient and solid solutions in this matter. One of the solutions used by organizations to explore security between assets and possible attacks is Knowledge Graphs (KG). In this context, large amounts of data are generated, which can yield misinterpretations of the results (information) if the data meaning not well characterized and conceptualized. To facilitate an innovative solution to this problem based on KG, this work seeks to facilitate a characterization of the domain supported by the best practices of Conceptual Modeling (specifically in the branch of Ontologies). This paper focuses on conducting studies that allow us to expand our terminological approach, thus generating a large amount of data that allows us to provide a software solution (REST-API) for managing domain data (using NoSQL technologies). Thanks to this ontological analysis platform, the correct use in the development and implementation of KGs by stakeholders will be guaranteed.

Keywords: Ontology, Ontological Analysis, Cybersecurity Ontologies, Knowledge Graphs, OntoUML

1 Introduction

Nowadays, organizations are focused on the active search for solutions that ensure efficient and safe management and protection of their assets. An application context, especially for big companies, is related to cybersecurity. This is a broad/extensive and quite complex domain that requires an interdisciplinary approach. One of the mechanisms by which organizations bet to explore security between assets and possible attacks is *Knowledge Graphs* (KG) [37]. Concerning the Conceptual Modeling (CM) standpoint, the grounding of concepts is fundamental to implement KG, and it is one of the most relevant ontology applications [14]. Indeed, "A knowledge graph acquires and integrates information into an ontology and applies a reasoner to derive new knowledge" [10]. That is why the application of ontologies in the cybersecurity domain emerges today as a research topic of great importance and interest.

However, before providing a proposal to achieve a pragmatic and iterative solution that meets the needs of organizations in terms of cybersecurity, we look for the solution proposals that exist in the state-of-the-art. Previously, we conducted a pilot study [29] looking for existing works that deal with cybersecurity requirements from an ontological perspective. In our search over the state-of-the-art, we looked for existing works presenting the use of ontologies to the cybersecurity domain. We found relevant ontologies that intent to provide semantics for the consensual terminology used by their community. These terms have definitions provided by a huge number of standards, however, each standard focuses on a particular viewpoint and practical application. Besides, in these conceptualizations, the same terms do not always translate into equal ontological concepts. In other words, the semantics provided by these ontologies depends on their ontological commitment [15,19] denoting the complexity of this domain.

Therefore, we defined a framework to classify ontologies capable of giving a homogeneous view of the proposals found in [29]. This framework is based on an orthogonal view of recognized classifications [11,12,14,19,41] of ontologies. Indeed, the results we took from the proposed ontology classification framework provided a huge amount of data about the ontologies as well as the domain itself. Therefore, we develop a Representational State Transfer Application Programming Interface (REST API) for data manipulation and a Not only SQL (NoSQL) database to store these data. Our goal is to provide data analytics and reasoning using these data and in future work provide a tool to facilitate the process of *Ontological Analysis* [14]. Through this document, we present the REST API we develop and some initial results these approaches provide.

Likewise any project within the scope of Ontology Engineering, this one requires the use of a methodology. Therefore, we resort to a methodology that follows the best practices in Ontology Engineering, we opt for the Systematic Approach for Building Ontologies (SABiO) [2]. This methodology advocate for the need to develop a Reference Ontology [19] before its implementation, and a set of well-defined steps to achieve the solution of the problem raised. Section 3 presents the backend solution that we developed following this methodology. Moreover, as the relational aspects are the most relevant regarding the data we are dealing with, the option to an implementation using a NoSQL database sounds natural. The choice to use a NoSQL database instead of triple stores in this project is also a design decision concerning the results we expect to have.

We have organized the rest of this paper in the following way: Section 2 presents issues related with the ontological analysis process regarding complex domains. Section 3 details the proposal of a REST API to support ontological analysis in complex fields, like cybersecurity which is our case-of-study. Section 4 presents the state-of-the-art. Section 5 depicts the actual state of the proposal with some further research directions.

2 Analysis of complex domains

Complex domains like cybersecurity, genome mapping, banking and finance, and others that are highly standardized, regulated, with a great amount of data, and that deals with heterogeneous data sources need a requirement process with special attention in semantics [29]. Thus, it is important to focus on ontological aspects such as competence issues, ontological commitment, representation language, and others to allow clear conceptualizations and interoperability among these ontologies [21]. However, this is not a simple task concerning the scenario we are dealing with, especially when the interoperability among –complex– domain ontologies is a central requirement. For instance, in state-of-the-art study we were able to find different definitions about same concepts, depending on the cybersecurity standard on which the definition is taken or the viewpoint adopted. Although concepts like *Risk* and *Risk Assessment* represent distinct "things" in the domain, we were able to find an ontology where the notion of *Risk*, in fact, has a semantic nearer the notion of *Risk Assessment*. Moreover, this ontology is supported by a very well-known and accepted cybersecurity standard. We found many similar issues in our study.

Ontological Analysis has been used to address problems like misinterpretations, misunderstanding, and disambiguation, including contextual and cognitive issues. Proposals like [1,9,25] are examples of Ontological Analysis application. The philosophical goal of an ontological analysis is to answer questions like "What is X?". Regarding the Conceptual Modeling community, an "ontological analysis can be defined as the process of eliciting and discovering relevant distinctions and relationships bound to the very nature of the entities involved in a certain domain, for the practical purpose of disambiguating terms having different interpretations in different contexts" [17].

The process of ontological analysis encompassing the cybersecurity domain is not trivial because of the aforementioned domain characteristics. This plus the dynamic interoperability requirements we are dealing with indicates that a tool to support ontological analysis seems to be a good option. The ontological analysis intends to avoid problems like the problem of two different terms (*Risk* and *Risk Assessment*) meaning similar things because this issue induces misunderstandings and models' misinterpretations. Besides, it is impossible to guarantee the validity of information provide these kind of models especially concerning in terms of the FAIR principles(*Findability*, *Accessibility*, *Interoperability*, and *Reuse*) of digital assets [24]. Moreover, having in mind that the high number of cybersecurity standards and regulations an ontological analysis tool can be an important resource for comparing the definition of the different terms provided by them.

3 An ontology for ontological analysis

The goal of this proposal is to provide data analytics and reasoning from state-of-the-art about some domain of knowledge (in this case the cybersecurity domain) providing a tool to facilitate the process of *Ontological Analysis* [14]. This problem involves two different perspectives which come from distinct stakeholder roles: the *Domain Specialists* and the *Ontology Engineers*. While Domain Specialists concerns to identify the relevant knowledge aspects that are part of an ontology, Ontology Engineers regard to verify if this ontology expresses this knowledge with the expected meaning by classifying and analyzing it. Therefore, the tool we propose has to cover the domain aspects as well as its ontological support taking closer these two perspectives. To achieve this we propose the following Competence Questions (CQs):

CQ1 What are the sources of definitions supporting the domain terminology used?
CQ2 Which definitions for a particular term provide the same meaning concerning its represented concept? And which do not?
CQ3 Which are the domain terms, definitions, and sources that support ontologies?
CQ4 Are the resulting conceptualizations well-grounded ontologies?
CQ5 Are the resulting conceptualizations well-defined ontologies?

Regarding the Ontology Engineering process, ontologies must provide answers to a set of CQs [13]. Besides, following the SABiO methodology the CQs define the ontology scope and provide to it evaluation capabilities [2].

3.1 The reference ontology

We propose a reference ontology, the Ontology for Ontological Analysis (O4OA), to answer these CQs. They were elicited as functional requirements [2] to the O4OA. We conducted the ontology elicitation through online meetings since the stakeholders could not participate in person [4]. A multidisciplinary group of stakeholders attended online meetings, providing different contributions. This is a group composed of Ontology Engineers, Cybersecurity Domain Specialists, Literature Review Specialists, the team of the organization that finances the project, among others when it is needed. We are receiving the cybersecurity domain advice of specialists of our research group and others who are members of the project consortium we participate in. This case-of-study has a strong and pragmatic focus as this research is part of a project to develop a Digital Knowledge Graph through an Adaptable Analytics API solution with the financial support of Accenture LTD. It is part of the requirements of this research that the approach is suitable for other domains as well, and the choice of a complex domain for the case-of-study reinforces this. It is also important to clarify that Ontology Engineers participated in taking on different roles, sometimes eliciting requirements and sometimes as clients of the project, depending on the context discussed and their roles in the group.

Given the requirements (CQs) and the results from the study [29], we start the ontology engineering process to the O4OA. We represent our proposal by using the OntoUML [5] language, also following the SABiO methodology orientations. Firstly we focus on the requirements about the any domain itself, in this case, we use the cybersecurity domain as case-of-study. We aim to define the concepts and relationships involving the domain terminology. Figure 1 shows a fragment of the O4OA describing the sources of the terminology definitions.

Figure 1 present the notion of *Source* thought the *OntoUML RoleMixin Alternative pattern* [5] in which a `Source` is the role played by many kinds of documents. In this situation, the `Document` is defined as a *<<category>>* [6] because it aggregates properties of individuals with different identity principles. Indeed, policies, standards and

[4] Strategy adopted due to the COVID-2019 pandemic.
[5] https://ontouml.readthedocs.io/en/latest/patterns/rolemixin_alt/index.html
[6] https://ontouml.readthedocs.io/en/latest/classes/nonsortals/category/index.html

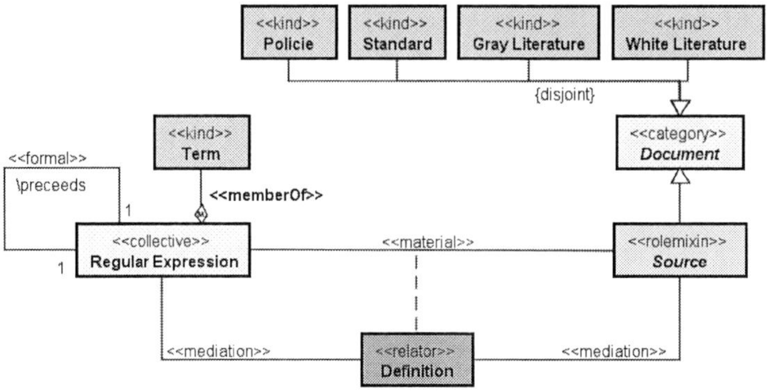

Fig. 1. Fragment of the O4OA describing the sources of the terminology definitions.

the types of literature documentations exists with no dependence and with their proper identity, they are *<<kind>>* [7]. As a source is the role may be documents (like standards, policies, among others), and any other sort of relevant information and its identity is fluid it is defined as a *<<rolemixin>>* [8]. As a matter of fact, the notion of *Source* as a role is relational dependent because it provides definitions for the set of regular expressions (`Regular Expression` as OntoUML *<<collective>>* [9]). Therefore, we deal with this relational aspect applying the *OntoUML Relator pattern* [10]. Meanwhile, we use the *OntoUML notion of Part-Whole* [11] through the relation `memberOf` [12] to represent the terms (`Term`) that compound each regular expression in the domain.

Besides the domain and its terminology, the O4OA must deal with the ontologies as artifacts made to describe this domain. Thus, it is important to point out that O4OA is an ontology to classify ontologies. This means that we will use the word `ONTOLOGY` (highlighted in this way) when we refer to an element that is represented in O4OA. Figure 2 shows how the `ONTOLOGY` as an artifact is an element represented in O4OA. At this rate, an `ONTOLOGY` can have other `ONTOLOGY` ("sub-ontologies") smaller parts, denoted by the relation `componentOf` [13] between a composite ontology and its parts (that are `ONTOLOGY`). This relation appears in the *Weak Supplementation Pattern*, which states that every whole must be composed by at least two parts [18,20]. The perception that `Atomic Ontologies` and `Composite Ontologies` are sub-types of `ONTOLOGY` is denoted by the OntoUML notion of *<<subkind>>* [14]. And finally, Figure 2 also presents the notion of `characterization` [15] thought the `Number of Axioms` as a *<<perceivableQuality>>* [16] of `ONTOLOGY`.

[7] https://ontouml.readthedocs.io/en/latest/classes/sortals/kind/index.html
[8] https://ontouml.readthedocs.io/en/latest/classes/nonsortals/rolemixin/index.html
[9] https://ontouml.readthedocs.io/en/latest/classes/sortals/collective/index.html
[10] https://ontouml.readthedocs.io/en/latest/patterns/relator/index.html
[11] https://ontouml.readthedocs.io/en/latest/relationships/aggregations/intro.html
[12] https://ontouml.readthedocs.io/en/latest/relationships/aggregations/memberOf/index.html
[13] https://ontouml.readthedocs.io/en/latest/relationships/aggregations/componentOf/index.html
[14] https://ontouml.readthedocs.io/en/latest/classes/sortals/subkind/index.html
[15] https://ontouml.readthedocs.io/en/latest/relationships/characterization/index.html
[16] https://ontouml.readthedocs.io/en/latest/classes/aspects/quality/index.html

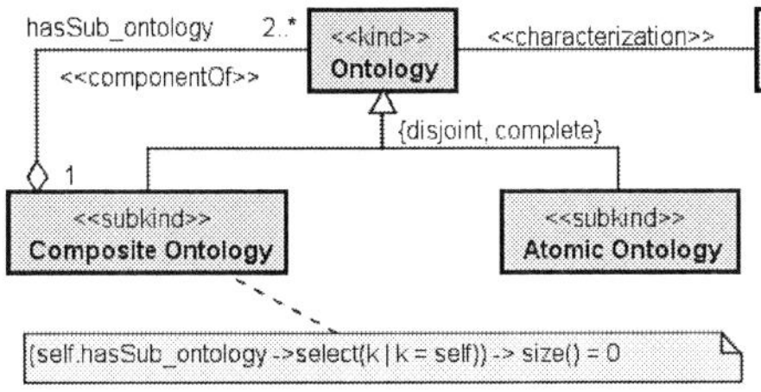

Fig. 2. Fragment of the O4OA describing the ontologies as artifacts.

Usually sub-ontologies deal with parts of a major domain (sub-domain) to facilitate their description and comprehension. Also, the relation `componentOF` is: *Shareable* (a ontology can be part of many ontologies), *Irreflexive* (there are no ontology that is part of itself), *Asymmetric* (if a ontology *B* is part of an ontology *A* then *A* can not be part of *B*), *Acyclic* (an ontology can not be in its part-hood transitive closure, i.e. part of its parts, or parts of parts of its parts, and so on), and *Transitive*. Moreover, this relation requires a constraint to guaranty the correct transitivity avoiding that sub-ontology as composed by itself or any of its parent ontologies, as depicted in the model through an OCL [17] rule in Figure 2 commentary box.

As the framework to classify ontologies we propose requires an orthogonal classification for their involved ontologies, we also describe in O4OA these classifications. Figure 3 shows the classification according of an `ONTOLOGY` according to its Application Level [19], Figure 4 according to its Generalization Level [14,41], and Figure 5 depict the bi-dimensional [11,12] classification (according to the Formalization and Axiomatization Levels).

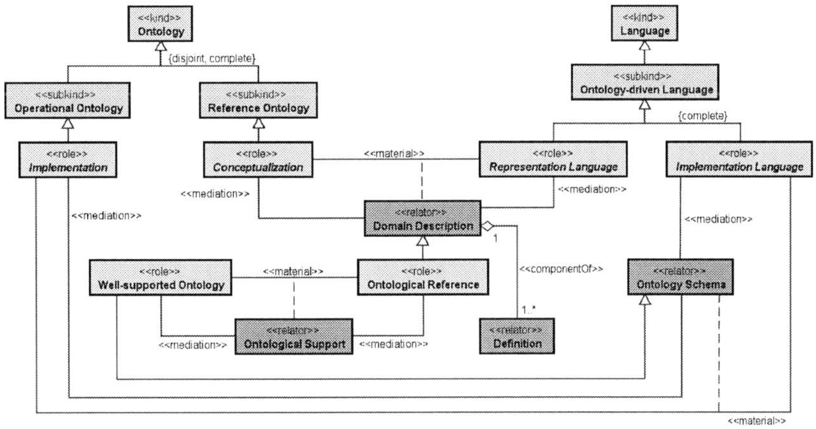

Fig. 3. Fragment of the O4OA describing the Application Level for classification of ontologies.

The Application Level divides ontologies in two types: Operational Ontologies and Reference Ontologies. The former should be a conceptualization constructed to make

[17] https://www.omg.org/spec/OCL/About-OCL/

the best possible description of the domain while the later is the actionable version of a Reference Ontology that uses the more appropriate language intending to guarantee desirable computational properties [19]. Figure 3 presents these definitions as the roles (*<<role>>* [18]) an ontology (`ONTOLOGY`) can play when it describes a domain (`Domain Description`) or when it is an schema (`Ontology Schema`) used as an implementation of this description thought a particular ontology-driven language. We use the *OntoUML Relator pattern* to represent the relational aspects of this classification.

Figure 3 also shows that definitions (`Definition`) are the discretionary part of the structures that make up a domain description. Therefore, it is possible to compare the sources that support a conceptualization with the general sources available about the domain. This helps Ontology Engineers to identify the concepts, the definitions that support these concepts, and what is the ontological commitment taken.

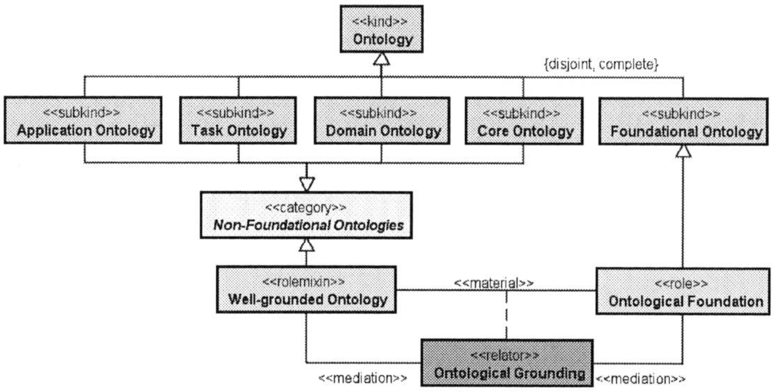

Fig. 4. Fragment of the O4OA describing the Generalization Level for classification of ontologies.

The most accepted classification of ontologies according to its generalization level is Guarino's proposal [14] which classifies ontologies in four types: Upper Ontologies (also known as High-level Ontologies or Foundational Ontologies), Domain Ontologies, Task Ontologies, or Application Ontologies. We also consider in this classification the Core Ontologies [41] as the ones between the Foundational and Domain Ontologies, not so general as the firsts either so specific as the latters. Figure 4 present that this classification differentiates the ontologies through some of its characteristics. Therefore, we describe them as *<<subkind>>* considering that they are types of ontologies (`ONTOLOGY`). We also use the *OntoUML Relator pattern* to describe how Foundational Ontologies grounds the non-foundational ontologies.

Figure 5 present the bi-dimensional classification perspective of [11] thought a categorization taxonomy also using the *<<subkind>>* and the *<<category>>* notions. This representation also is based on the ontology characteristics that made them formal or informal [40] at the same time as made them lightweight or heavyweight [12]. Together both classifications typify the ontologies as seven other subtypes.

[18] https://ontouml.readthedocs.io/en/latest/classes/sortals/role/index.html

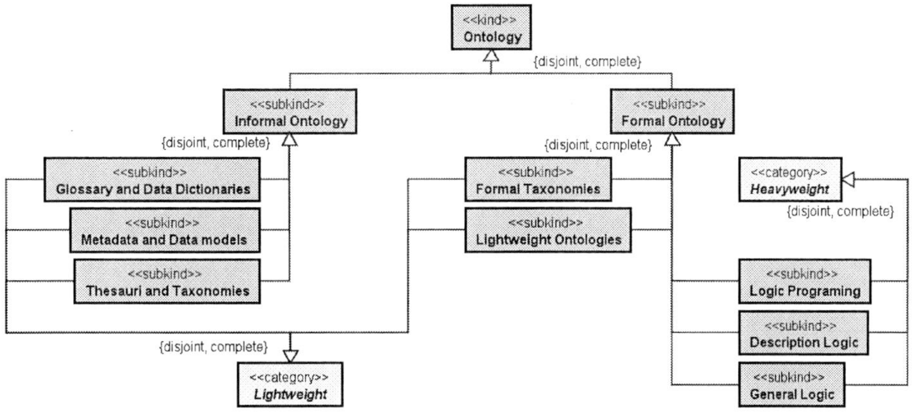

Fig. 5. Fragment of the O4OA describing the Bi-dimensional (Formalization and Axiomatization Levels) classification of ontologies.

3.2 Implementing a background solution

Given the O4OA models, we propose a NoSQL database schema it thought a MongoDB[19] persistence solution because it is a free and flexible tool. Over this persistence platform we develop a REST API [20] to store and manipulate the resulting survey data at the server-side (backend) following the *Model-View-Controller* (MVC) architecture. For instance, below we present the NodeJS code that implement the *model* of the `ONTOLOGY` persistence structure.

```
var mongoose = require('mongoose');
var Schema = mongoose.Schema;
var OntologySchema = Schema({
   name: String , briefing : String , domain: String , language: String , // Ontology informations
   cqs: [{ cq: String }], // Competence questions
   subOntologyOf: { type: Schema.ObjectId, ref :'Ontology' },      // Subontology (composition)
   groundedOver: { type: Schema.ObjectId, ref :'Ontology' },       // Grounding ( inheritance )
   grounding: String ,                                             // Grounding details
   implementationFor: { type: Schema.ObjectId, ref :'Ontology' },  // Implmentation
   implementaton: String ,                                         // Implementation details
    classification :
      { applicationLevel : { type: Schema.ObjectId, ref :' ApplicationLevel ' },
        granularityLevel : { type: Schema.ObjectId, ref :' FranularityLevel ' },
        formalizationLevel : { type: Schema.ObjectId, ref :' FormalizationLevel ' },
        axiomatizationLevel : { type: Schema.ObjectId, ref :'AxiomatizationLevel' }},
  axioms: Number,              // Number of axioms
   definitions : [{ type: mongoose.Schema.Types.ObjectId, ref: "Definition"}]}); // Definitions
module.exports = mongoose.model('Ontology', OntologySchema);
```

At the *controller* level we implement the required code to select and manipulate the NoSQL data. For instance, the selection for the ontologies we found. In this case, we intend to cross the ontology analysis results, including the definitions it uses, with the standards' definitions. To provide a classification for the ontologies, we use MongoDB's facility to store data in tree structures. Thus, we define four trees, each one to store the classifications we use. Besides, we make the necessary restrictions to ensure the integrity of the proposed framework. For example, we restrict the two-dimensional classification to guarantee the integrity between the criteria of formalization and axiomatization. Below we present an API code fragment that queries the ontologies' content.

[19] https://www.mongodb.com/

[20] Implemented with NodeJS (https://nodejs.org/en/)

```
function getOntology(req, res){ // Get ontology
    var ontology = new Ontology();
    ontology._id = req.params.id;
    Ontology.aggregate([
        { $match: { _id : ontology._id } },
        { $lookup : { from : " definitions ", localField : " definitions ", foreignField : "_id", as : " definitions " } },
        { $lookup: { from: "regexes", localField : " definitions .regex", foreignField : "_id", as: "regex" } },
        { $lookup : { from : "terms", localField : "regex.term", foreignField : "_id", as : "term" } },
        { $graphLookup : { from: "regexes", startWith : "$regex.next", connectFromField : "regex.next", connectToField : "_id", as : "next" } },
        { $lookup: { from: "ontologies", localField : "subOntologyOf", foreignField : "_id", as: "subOntologyOf" } },
        { $lookup: { from: "ontologies", localField : "groundedOver", foreignField : "_id", as: "groundedOver" } },
        { $lookup: { from: "ontologies", localField : "implementationFor", foreignField : "_id", as: "implementationFor" } }
    ]).exec((err,ontology) => {
        if(err) return res.status(500).send({message: 'Incorrect request.'});
        if(!ontology) return res.status(404).send({message: 'Unknow ontological analysis.'});
        return res.status(200).send({ontology});
    });
}
```

Another example of the use of the API refers to the domain structures. For instance, we consolidate sources of the terms, and definitions found in the study. With this approach it is possible to query definitions by regular expressions regarding the domain perspective.

3.3 The cybersecurity case-of-study

To validate our proposal we use the data resulting from our study [29]. We aim to consolidate the definitions of the terms previously found. Therefore, we propose a survey [28,36] because the amount of standards is vast as well as the number of terms. We invite 18 (eighteen) cybersecurity students to participate in this survey. It is important to note that the survey is part of a collaboration with the Department of Systems Engineering and Informatics of the Universidad Pontificia Bolivariana (UPB, Colombia) [21].

The students searched for each term one or more definitions in all these standards. We define a questionnaire with a spreadsheet template in which the students present their impressions about the meaning, context, and use of each definition depending on which source it is. We divided the terms among the students, so each student worked with only two different terms, covering a total of 36 single terms. However, the students were able to add additional terminology that composes a set of regular expressions with these terms. Therefore, we cover 43 of the terms found in the paper's pilot study search. The students had two weeks to present their results.

We present an example of the results produced querying definitions by regular expressions (RegEx) for the term *Confidentiality*. The code below shows a fragment of this term's querying result [22] took over the database.


```
{
    "definitions": [
        {
            "source": [{
                    "label": "CCMB-2017-04-002"
            }],
            "text": "Confidentiality is enforced by preventing unauthorised disclosure of user data in transit between the two end
                    points.\nThe end points may be a TSF or a user. Confidentiality of TSF Data during transmission is necessary to
                    protect such\ninformation from disclosure. Some possible implementations that could provide confidentiality
                    include the use of cryptographic algorithms as well as spread spectrum techniques."
        },
        {
```


[21] https://www.upb.edu.co/es/home

[22] The JSON file was edited suppressing, the surplus of data. The objective is to provide a better presentation and reduce size.

```
10          "source": [{
11                  "label": "CCMB-2017-04-004"
12          }],
13          "text": "An evaluator may have access to sponsor and developer commercially-sensitive information (e.g. TOE design
                    information, specialist tools), and may have access to nationally-sensitive information during the course of an
                    evaluation. Schemes may wish to impose requirements for the evaluator to maintain the confidentiality of the
                    evaluation evidence. The sponsor and evaluator may mutually agree to additional requirements as long as these
                    are consistent with the scheme.\nConfidentiality requirements affect many aspects of evaluation work, including
                    the receipt, handling, storage and disposal of evaluation evidence."
14      },
15      {
16          "source": [{
17                  "label": "CCv31-Release 5"
18          }],
19          "text": "An evaluator may have access to sponsor and developer commercially-sensitive information (e.g. TOE design
                    information, specialist tools), and may have access to nationally-sensitive information during the course of an
                    evaluation. Schemes may wish to impose requirements for the evaluator to maintain the confidentiality of the
                    evaluation evidence. The sponsor and evaluator may mutually agree to additional requirements as long as these
                    are consistent with the scheme.\nConfidentiality requirements affect many aspects of evaluation work, including
                    the receipt, handling, storage and disposal of evaluation evidence."
20      },
21      {
22          "source": [{
23                  "label": "ISOIEC270002018"
24          }],
25          "text": "confidentiality\nproperty that information is not made available or disclosed to unauthorized individuals,
                    entities, or processes (3.54)"
26      },
27      {
28          "source": [{
29                  "label": "RecX800"
30          }],
31          "text": "The property that information is not made available or disclosed to unauthorized individuals, entities,
                    or\nprocesses."
32      },
33      {
34          "source": [{
35                  "label": "RecITU-T-X1212"
36          }],
37          "text": "Three enabling concepts of information security\nConfidentiality\nMeasured data may include personal
                    information, which is essentially privacy sensitive. Thus, the use of such data needs to be handled carefully,
                    accompanied by agreement with end users. The extent of sharing such information must be under strict control."
38      },
39      {
40          "source": [{
41                  "label": "Nieles"
42          }],
43          "text": "Confidentiality - Preserving authorized restrictions on information access and disclosure, including means
                    for protecting personal privacy and proprietary information."
44      },
45      {
46          "source": [{
47                  "label": "NIST800-37Revision2"
48          }],
49          "text": "confidentiality\n[44 USC 3552]\nPreserving authorized restrictions on information access and disclosure,
                    including means for protecting personal privacy and proprietary information."
50      },
51      {
52          "source": [{
53                  "label": "NIST800-53Rev4"
54          }],
55          "text": "Confidentiality\n[44 U.S.C., Sec. 3542]\nPreserving authorized restrictions on information access and
                    disclosure, including means for protecting personal privacy and proprietary information."
56      },
57      {
58          "source": [{
59                  "label": "Stouffer"
60          }],
61          "text": "Confidentiality\nPreserving authorized restrictions on information access and disclosure, including means for
                    protecting personal privacy and proprietary information.\nSOURCE: NIST SP 800-53 [22]"
62      },
63      {
64          "source": [{
65                  "label": "SpecPubl800-26"
66          }],
67          "text": "Confidentiality - The information requires protection from unauthorized disclosure."
68      }
69   ]
70 }
```

Firstly, the very same definitions appear in different sources: line 17 [8] is the same as 11 [7], line 29 [6] is the same as 23 [23], and lines 47 [26], 53 [27] and 59 [38] are same as 41 [31]. However only one of those is the primary source while the others are references to it, in this case, the primary sources are at the lines, respectively the 17 [8] in the previous release, 29 [6], and 53 [27]. With this tool we intend to gather all the considering domain terminology definitions according to their sources, to facilitate our analysis.

In common, all definitions consider the term *Confidentiality* a **Property** that can be assigned to many different **Individuals**[23]. Some of the aforementioned refer to kinds of *Information* like *Proprietary*, *Sensitive* or *Personal*, others refers to *User Data*. Indeed it is important to see that the *Data* term's meaning is not the same as *Information* since not all data refers to information. Moreover, in a step forward we need to determine if the property of some individual being *Confidential* is quantified or not; and if it is, what is its quality structure the and how to measure if (it is possible) [22]. This kind of analysis is an example of how terminological validation is important, indeed this is part of an ontological analysis concerning the cybersecurity domain.

Taking care of the ontologies we found in the study we load all information we could catch about them in the state-of-the-art. For example, the code below shows a fragment of the information we collect about the SECCO ontology, which is a sub-ontology of CRATELO [4,32,33,34]. This code result presents the information we catch about the SECCO ontology, as below. We can see that the result also shows the definitions this ontology use and from which source these definitions came. The source can be any standard or document. Here we reduce file results showing only one definition since the file is large.

```
{  "ontology": [
      {  "definitions": [
         ...
            {  "source": "Schumacher2003",
               "text": "(Risk). The risk is the probability that a successful attack occurs.",
               "regex": {"term": {"syntax": "risk" }}},
         ...
         ],
         "name": "SECCO",
         "domain": "Security",
         "subOntologyOf": [
            {  "definitions": [...],
               "name": "CRATELO",
               "domain": "Cybersecurity",
               "language": "OWL-Lite" }
         ],
         "language": "OWL-Lite",
         "groundedOver": [
            {  "definitions": [...],
               "name": "DOLCE-Spray",
               "domain": "General",
               "language": "OWL-Lite",
               "implementationFor": "601ae1769bbf9122c8a732cf" }
         ]
      }
   ]
}
```

All of this denotes how huge and complex is to provide a conceptualization of the cybersecurity domain. Therefore, one of the goals of the survey we made and its resulting API is to get together domain terminology definitions according to their sources, to facilitate our analysis. Then, we are cross comparing the result of this analysis with the definitions used in the ontologies we found in the pilot study, as a next step.

[23] Property and Individuals in the ontological sense [15]

4 Related works

At the state-of-the-art we found some proposals presenting tools for ontological analysis, however, most of them are domain-dependent, like [3,35]. This happens because these tools mainly involve implementations (*Domain Operational Ontologies*), using languages like OWL, RDF, and SPARQL for instance. Their objective is to map data and provide human accessibility of this data concerning its ontologies, usually using annotations. These approaches are relevant in terms of implementation, some evolve to be a general solution. The Cytoscape [24] is one of those, however it still deals with *Operational Ontologies*. We found similar approaches that are general and that provide data treatment, verification, annotation, and visualization, like [30,39].

Instead of the proposed tools we found, our approach is agnostic regarding the domain plus targeting most fundamental ontological aspects that interfere with the domain understandability. Indeed, our goal is to provide a platform for ontological analysis concerning the validation of Domain Reference Ontologies.

5 Conclusions

In this work, we present our proposal for an API in which we can consolidate definitions of the terms used in the cybersecurity domain. We present an example showing how complex is the set of definitions for a single concept, indeed this complexity gets increased concerning the vast amount of concepts, their relations, and the context in which they are applied. Our intention is also to analyze the standard support that provides the grounding for the concepts over the cybersecurity domain.

The REST API using a NoSQL database sounds a relevant contribution to help Ontology Engineers on ontological analysis where complex domains are the scenario. The objective of this kind of approach is to identify the semantics of the concepts used, their similarities, and differences. From this initial step, we aim to provide a link between the domain terminology, its context with its representations in ontologies, following the approach of [16]. Besides, the control of this information allows us to do reasoning and present results from a friendly interface, both are future research works preceding a final solution proposal to provide interoperability among operational ontologies as KGs.

Acknowledgments. This work has been developed under the project Digital Knowledge Graph – Adaptable Analytics API with the financial support of Accenture LTD.

References

1. Almeida, J.P.A., Guizzardi, G.: An ontological analysis of the notion of community in the rm-odp enterprise language. Computer Standards & Interfaces **35**(3), 257–268 (2013)
2. de Almeida Falbo, R.: Sabio: Systematic approach for building ontologies. In: Guizzardi, G., Pastor, O., Wand, Y., de Cesare, S., Gailly, F., Lycett, M., Partridge, C. (eds.) Proceedings of the 1st Joint Workshop ONTO.COM/ODISE on Ontologies in Conceptual Modeling and Information Systems Engineering. CEUR Workshop Proceedings, vol. 1301 (2014)

[24] https://cytoscape.org/what_is_cytoscape.html

3. Alzaabi, M., Jones, A., Martin, T.A.: An ontology-based forensic analysis tool (2013)
4. Ben-Asher, N., Oltramari, A., Erbacher, R.F., Gonzalez, C.: Ontology-based adaptive systems of cyber defense. In: STIDS. pp. 34–41 (2015)
5. Benevides, A.B., Guizzardi, G.: A model-based tool for conceptual modeling and domain ontology engineering in ontouml. In: International Conference on Enterprise Information Systems. pp. 528–538. Springer (2009)
6. CCITT & ITU-T (ed.): DATA COMMUNICATION NETWORKS: OPEN SYSTEMS INTERCONNECTION (OSI); SECURITY, STRUCTURE AND APPLICATION - SECURITY ARCHITECTURE FOR OPEN SYSTEMS INTERCONNECTION FOR CCITT APPLICATIONS. CCITT & ITU-T, Geneva - Switzerland (1991)
7. CCMB (ed.): Common Methodology for Information Technology Security Evaluation Evaluation methodology, vol. Version3.1. CCDB, revision 5 edn. (2017)
8. CCRA: Common Criteria Portal. https://www.commoncriteriaportal.org/cc/ (2017), [Online; accessed 23-Jun-2020]
9. Duarte, B.B., Souza, V.E.S., de Castro Leal, A.L., de Almeida Falbo, R., Guizzardi, G., Guizzardi, R.S.: Towards an ontology of requirements at runtime. In: FOIS. pp. 255–268 (2016)
10. Ehrlinger, L., Wöß, W.: Towards a definition of knowledge graphs. SEMANTiCS (Posters, Demos, SuCCESS) **48**, 1–4 (2016)
11. Giunchiglia, F., Zaihrayeu, I.: Lightweight ontologies. Tech. rep., University of Trento (2007)
12. Gómez-Pérez, A., Corcho, O.: Ontology languages for the semantic web. IEEE Intelligent systems **17**(1), 54–60 (2002)
13. Grüninger, M., Fox, M.S.: Methodology for the design and evaluation of ontologies (1995)
14. Guarino, N.: Formal Ontology in Information Systems. In: Proceedings of the 1st International Conference. pp. 6–8. IOS Press, Trento, Italy (June 1998)
15. Guarino, N.: The ontological level. Philosophy and the Cognitive Sciences (1994)
16. Guarino, N.: The ontological level: Revisiting 30 years of knowledge representation. Conceptual modeling: Foundations and applications pp. 52–67 (2009)
17. Guarino, N.: Introduction to applied ontology and ontological analysis (2012), https://iaoa.org/isc2014/uploads/SlidesGuarino01.pdf, accessed in April, 2021
18. Guizzardi, G.: Modal aspects of object types and part-whole relations and the de re/de dicto distinction. In: International Conference on Advanced Information Systems Engineering. pp. 5–20. Springer (2007)
19. Guizzardi, G.: On ontology, ontologies, conceptualizations, modeling languages, and (meta) models. Frontiers in artificial intelligence and applications **155**, 18 (2007)
20. Guizzardi, G.: The problem of transitivity of part-whole relations in conceptual modeling revisited. In: International Conference on Advanced Information Systems Engineering. pp. 94–109. Springer (2009)
21. Guizzardi, G.: Ontology, ontologies and the "i" of fair. Data Intelligence **2**(1-2), 181–191 (2020)
22. Guizzardi, G., Zamborlini, V.: Using a trope-based foundational ontology for bridging different areas of concern in ontology-driven conceptual modeling. Science of Computer Programming **96**, 417–443 (2014)
23. ISO Central Secretary: Information technology — security techniques — information security management systems — overview and vocabulary. Standard ISO/IEC 27000:2018-02, International Organization for Standardization, Geneva (2018)
24. Jacobsen, A., de Miranda Azevedo, R., Juty, N.S., Batista, D., Coles, S.J., Cornet, R., Courtot, M., Crosas, M., Dumontier, M., Evelo, C.T.A., Goble, C.A., Guizzardi, G., Hansen, K.K., Hasnain, A., Hettne, K.M., Heringa, J., Hooft, R.W.W., Imming, M., Jeffery, K.G.,

Kaliyaperumal, R., Kersloot, M.G., Kirkpatrick, C.R., Kuhn, T., Labastida, I., Magagna, B., McQuilton, P., Meyers, N., Montesanti, A., van Reisen, M., Rocca-Serra, P., Pergl, R., Sansone, S., da Silva Santos, L.O.B., Schneider, J., Strawn, G.O., Thompson, M., Waagmeester, A., Weigel, T., Wilkinson, M.D., Willighagen, E.L., Wittenburg, P., Roos, M., Mons, B., Schultes, E.: FAIR principles: Interpretations and implementation considerations. Data Intell **2**(1-2), 10–29 (2020). https://doi.org/10.1162/dint_r_00024
25. Jaramillo, C.M.Z., López, O.P., Guizzardi, G., Guizzardi, R.S.S.: Concept categorization in pre-conceptual schemas. In: Proceedings of the 14th Iberoamerican Conference on Software Engineering, CIbSE 2011, Rio de Janeiro, Brasil, April 27-29, 2011. pp. 11–24 (2011)
26. JOINT TASK FORCE: Risk Management Framework for Information Systems and Organizations - A System Life Cycle Approach for Security and Privacy. Tech. rep., NIST (2018)
27. JOINT TASK FORCE TRANSFORMATION INITIATIVE: Security and Privacy Controls for Federal Information Systems and Organizations Security and Privacy Controls for Federal Information Systems and Organizations. Tech. rep., NIST (2013)
28. Martins, B.F., Serrano, L., Reyes, J.F., Panach, J.I., Pastor, O.: Towards the Consolidation of Cybersecurity Standardized Definitions. Tech. Rep. Version 2, Universidad Politecnica de Valencia (2021), http://hdl.handle.net/10251/163895
29. Martins, B.F., Serrano, L., Reyes, J.F., Panach, J.I., Pastor, O., Rochwerger, B.: Conceptual characterization of cybersecurity ontologies. In: 13th IFIP WG 8.1 working conference on the Practice of Enterprise Modelling (PoEM 2020). pp. 323–338. Springer (2020)
30. Nguyen, T.H., Grundy, J., Almorsy, M.: Guitar: An ontology-based automated requirements analysis tool. In: 2014 IEEE 22nd International Requirements Engineering Conference (RE). pp. 315–316. IEEE (2014)
31. Nieles, M., Dempsey, K., Pillitteri, V.Y.: An Introduction to Information Security An Introduction to Information Security. Tech. rep., NIST (2017)
32. Oltramari, A., Cranor, L.F., Walls, R.J., McDaniel, P.: Computational ontology of network operations. In: MILCOM 2015-2015 IEEE Military Communications Conference. pp. 318–323. IEEE (2015)
33. Oltramari, A., Cranor, L.F., Walls, R.J., McDaniel, P.D.: Building an ontology of cyber security. In: STIDS. pp. 54–61. Citeseer (2014)
34. Oltramari, A., Henshel, D.S., Cains, M., Hoffman, B.: Towards a human factors ontology for cyber security. In: STIDS. pp. 26–33 (2015)
35. Pomaznoy, M., Ha, B., Peters, B.: Gonet: a tool for interactive gene ontology analysis. Bmc Bioinformatics **19**(1), 1–8 (2018)
36. Serrano, L., Martins, B.F., Serrano, J.F., Panach, J.I., Pastor, O.: Una encuesta acerca de la Definición de Conceptos de Ciberseguridad. Tech. rep., Universidad Politecnica de Valencia (2021)
37. Singhal, A., Ou, X.: Security Risk Analysis of Enterprise Networks Using Probabilistic Attack Graphs, pp. 53–73. Springer International Publishing (2017)
38. Stouffer, K., Pillitteri, V., Lightman, S., Abrams, M., Hahn, A.: Guide to Industrial Control Systems (ICS) Security NIST Special Publication 800-82 Guide to Industrial Control Systems (ICS) Security - Supervisory Control and Data Acquisition (SCADA) Systems, Distributed Control Systems (DCS), and Other Control Syst. Tech. rep., NIST (2015)
39. Usadel, B., Nagel, A., Steinhauser, D., Gibon, Y., Bläsing, O.E., Redestig, H., Sreenivasulu, N., Krall, L., Hannah, M.A., Poree, F., et al.: Pageman: an interactive ontology tool to generate, display, and annotate overview graphs for profiling experiments. BMC bioinformatics **7**(1), 1–8 (2006)
40. Uschold, M., Gruninger, M.: Ontologies and semantics for seamless connectivity. ACM SIGMod Record **33**(4), 58–64 (2004)
41. Van Heijst, G., Schreiber, A.T., Wielinga, B.J.: Using explicit ontologies in kbs development. International journal of human-computer studies pp. 183–292 (1997)

A Survey on Software Engineering Practices in Brazilian Startups

Renata Souza[1,2], Orges Cico[3], and Ivan Machado[1]

[1] Institute of Computing, Federal University of Bahia (UFBA), Salvador, Brazil
{renatamss, ivan.machado}@ufba.br
[2] Federal Institute of Bahia (IFBA), Santo Antônio de Jesus, Brazil
{renata.souza}@ifba.edu.br
[3] Norwegian University of Science and Technology (NTNU), Trondheim, Norway
{orges.cico}@ntnu.no

Abstract. Today's significant technological advancement allows early-stage software startups to build and launch innovative products quickly on the market. However, many of them die in the early years of their path due to market conditions, ignorance of customer needs, lack of resources, or focus, such as the misuse of well-established practices. The study's motivation is to analyze software engineering practices in startups from a practitioner's perspective. Our objective was to identify practices and tools the startups employ in their daily routines. We carried out an expert survey study with 140 software developers involved in software startups from different domains. The results show that startups in the initial and validation phases select practices and tools on an ad-hoc basis and based on the development team's prior knowledge. When they move into the growth phase, they recognize that they could have adopted better practices beforehand to support product scaling with a more mature team. The results also indicated that support tools are selected based on their integration with other tools and their ability to automate operational activities.

Keywords: Software Startups · Empirical software engineering · Survey Study

1 Introduction

An impressive number of entrepreneurs create novel startups around the world every day. Later, they might become famous and profitable, such as *Facebook, Instagram, Spotify, Linked-in, and Dropbox.* According to Sutton [30], a startup shares many features with small and medium-sized young companies. For example, they are usually immature, have limited resources, undergo multiple influences, use dynamic technology, and hunt at the market. A startup can be defined as an organization established to search for a repeatable and scalable business model [2]. Also, a startup is an organization dedicated to creating something new under conditions of extreme uncertainty [26].

As they have limited financial and human resources, they face various challenges, and barriers [14, 19]. Most of them die in earlier years [26]. Several critical challenges in every startup phase affect the strength and company stability [23]. It is crucial to prepare for what is to come so that an obstacle does not become unbeatable. Learning from others startups' experiences helps them find a way to succeed or fail faster [5, 8]. Therefore, it is necessary to leverage startup practices to understand the reason for these choices and their consequences.

This paper aims to shed light on the developers' perceptions of software engineering practices and tools employed by software startups in a Brazilian cohort. We carried out an expert survey study with 140 software developers involved in software startups from different domains. We sent an online questionnaire to professionals working in startups via email and social networks (*Facebook, Twitter, and LinkedIn*). The results show that the software startups are guided by the customer, who participates from creating the initial prototype up to product deployment, and the adopted practices and tools that speed up development activities.

The remainder of this paper is structured as follows. Section 2 covers the research-related background. Section 3 introduces the survey study methodology. The results and the discussion are located in Sections 4 and 5, respectively. Section 6 presents the implications for research and practice. The threats to this study's validity are discussed in Section 7. Finally, Section 8 outlines overall conclusions and directions for future work.

2 Background

2.1 Startups

Startups are companies that start from an early stage with very few assets, and low investment [3, 13, 15]. Some of them have the potential to achieve high scalability [31]. Many of these companies took advantage from the popularization of technologies for personal use, such as *Google, Netflix, and Spotify.* They start almost from scratch [16, 27, 28] and could reach a wide range of customers ignored by major competitors offering solutions (almost always services) based on technology and the Internet [6].

The startup concept definition, although simple, encompasses many variables. The primary way to recognize a startup refers to its business model characterized by an innovative idea that generates value and turns work into money [10]. Additionally, it could be considered a policy aimed at developing competent, self-managed teams that could quickly react to scenario changes. The promotion of creativity, collaboration, focus on agility, continuous training, rewards for solving complex problems, and all actions must always link to a long-term vision.

2.2 Startup lifecycle

Blank [3] defined the startup lifecycle as having four stages from a customer's perspective: (1) defining or observing a problem; (2) evaluating the problem; (3)

defining a solution; and (4) evaluating the solution. Crowne [8] identified the startup lifecycle from the perspective of product development as having three stages, as follows:

1. The *startup* phase is the period between product conception and the first scale.
2. *Stabilization* begins when the first customer receives the product.
3. *Growth* is when the Startup delivers the product to new customers without creating any overhead in the development team.
4. *Maturity* is when the company evolves into a mature organization.

Similarly, Wang [32] defines a lifecycle for software startups taking into account the product stages: concept, underdevelopment, functional prototype, functional product with limited users, functional product with high growth potential, and mature product.

2.3 Software Startups

Software startups share some characteristics with other types of startups, such as lack of resources, operating history, high-technology challenges, cutting-edge tools, and innovation-driven development [31]. Carmel [4] was the first one to refer to the term *software package startup* and the shorten term *software startup* in 1994. Sutton [30] argues that software startups are challenged by limited resources, immaturity, multiple influences, high-technology, and turbulent markets. Hilmola [17] states that most of the software startups are product-oriented and develop cutting-edge software products. Coleman [7] characterize software startups as product-driven, with a small development team, often developer-led, that develops software through various processes and without a methodology. Giardino [13], and Unterkalmsteiner [31] use the term software startups to refer to those organizations focused on the creation of high-tech and innovative products, with little or no operating history, aiming to grow their business in highly-scalable markets aggressively.

Large software companies relied for years on traditional software development. Nowadays, they realize they need to innovate to maintain their position in a highly competitive market. Also, they look to gain a significant advantage to adapt to market and technologies by focusing on cost efficiency, lead time reduction, and quality improvement. They find in startups this new way to keep their leading positions in a fast-moving and innovative market [12]. Software startups have become one of the critical drivers of economy and innovation, even though they are mostly inexperienced [30].

Coleman and O'Connor [7] investigated how software product startups establish their software development process. The study employed a grounded theory approach with the aim to characterized the experiences of small software organizations in developing processes to support their software development activities and the significant factors that might influence building processes: background of software, development manager background of founder, management style, process tailoring, market requirements. Hence, software startups depend mainly on the person's experience acting as software development manager who holds both expertise and know-how to meet company goals. Coleman and O'Connor [7] also claimed that startups are product-driven and developer-led. In this context, agile methods may have a lot to offer.

2.4 Related Work

Giardino et al. [14] and Wang et al. [32] performed a large-scale survey of 5389 responses and an in-depth multiple-case study to investigate the critical challenges of software startups. Giardino et al. [14] observed the challenges in an early-stage startup, while Wang et al. [32] observed challenges faced by software startups across lifecycle stages. Pantiuchina et al. [24] also conducted an extensive survey of 1526 software startups where they examined the use of five agile and lean startup practices. In this work, we observed the software engineering practices adopted by startups through the divergent lifecycle stages. The startup's life cycle classification was based on the responses provided by the developers. This classification was made through characterization made concerning the information of the team size, the number of customers, and product maturity, shown in the following sections.

3 Research Methodology

The study's motivation is to analyze software engineering practices in startups from a software practitioner's perspective. We chose a survey as our research instrument to reach a more significant number of opinions. Our goal in designing the study was to keep it as brief as possible while still gathering all relevant information. The survey received 140 responses. We did not ask for the identification of respondents or companies. We decided to preserve this information for reasons of confidentiality and attract more participants to our research. These participants were from all over the Brazilian territory. We applied the methodology recommended by Linåker et al. [21] and the research survey principles defined by Kitchenham and Pfleeger [25]. This section encompasses the planning details, execution procedures, and reporting of the desired and achieved results.

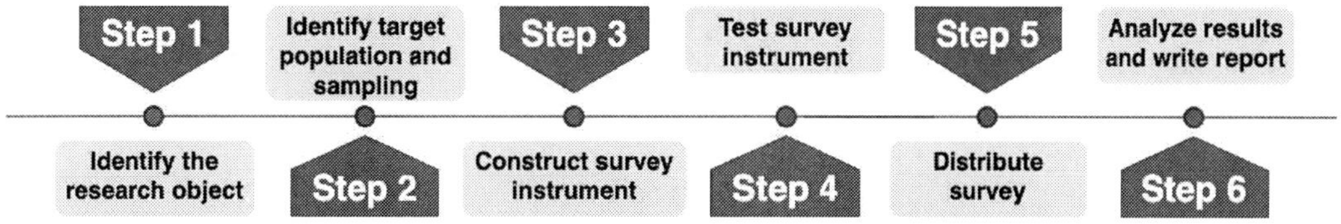

Fig. 1. Overview of the Research Methodology

We first identified the research object (Step 1), then the target population and sampling (Step 2). Next, we constructed the survey instrument (Step 3), tested it (Step 4), and distributed it to the participants (Step 5). The last action was to analyze the collected data (Step 6) and report the results. Figure 1 shows the research steps of this study. We utilized a web-based questionnaire to reach practitioners from Brazilian startup ecosystems due to Brazil's geographical dimensions.

3.1 Identifying the Research Object

Our objective was to identify software engineering practices and tools the startups employ in their daily routines. We also aimed to investigate whether there is any difference in practices and tools that depend on the startup's lifecycle. We formulated the following research questions:

RQ1: Do software startup use the same software engineering practices across different lifecycle stages? *We aim to leverage the practices software startups adopt through the different stages of their lifecycle and at what stage it differs.*

RQ2: What tools do software startups use to support software engineering practices across different lifecycle stages? *We aim to observe whether there is a change in the tool's adoption through the different stages of their lifecycle and at what stage it differs.*

Startups need to either follow or adapt existing software engineering practices. Otherwise, they would risk losing their market capitalization. In this effect, further studies are needed to investigate both practices and tool support to establish a common understanding of how software startups make their choices.

3.2 Identifying Target Population and Sampling

The StartupBase[4] is an official database of the Brazilian startup ecosystem supported by the Brazilian Startup Association[5]. Our target audience was software developers from software startups, while the population selected was Brazilian software startups. We chose software developers because they are the most representative group considering the respondents work for startups at different lifecycle stages and observe the same perspective. The survey included questions to reveal the participants' jobs, software development experience, and information on the organizations they worked for, such as size (ecosystem location) and project domain, to characterize the survey participants. We defined the following criteria to include participants in this survey study: (1) the respondent must work for a Brazilian software startup, and (2) the respondent must work as a software developer.

[4] https://startupbase.com.br
[5] https://abstartups.com.br/

3.3 Survey Instrument

The questionnaire comprises closed questions with a small number of open questions to obtain further information. We specified twelve topics divided into two groups. The first was to gather the participation consent, respondents' characterization, startups' characterization, and product characterization. The second group covered the practices considering each software engineering discipline: software requirements, software architecture, software design, software construction, software testing, software maintenance, management, and processes. We next specify the goals defined for each category:

- **Research participation consent:** free, prior and informed consent;
- **Respondents' characterization:** gather information about the respondents' profiles;
- **Startups' characterization:** gather information about when the startup was established, the number of customers, the revenue, the number of employees, and the business domain;
- **Product characterization:** characterize the product by type, public, lifecycle, revenue, need to pivot, and time that the team works on it;
- **Software requirements:** reveal the employed requirements engineering practices;
- **Software architecture:** identify decisions regarding system architecture;
- **Software design:** identify the decisions regarding user interface design;
- **Software construction:** leverage the main programming languages and development platforms the startup use;
- **Software testing:** leverage the startups' software testing practices;
- **Software maintenance:** leverage the employed maintenance techniques;
- **Project management:** leverage the project management practices;
- **Software process:** leverage the software process practices.

We used Survey Monkey[6] to prepare and disseminate the questionnaire. Supplementary material is available at [29].

3.4 Pilot Testing

We asked professionals and researchers with experience in software engineering and survey design to review the survey. The goal was to remove any misunderstanding and hence improve the instrument. The changes we made included: adding more answer choices to several questions, exchanging words to improve understanding, and changing some questions. We applied the questionnaire in September 2020. The questionnaire used at the end of the test contained the following questions:

1. Does the questionnaire contain anything expected to reach our goals?
2. Does the questionnaire contain any undesirable or unnecessary information to the context and purpose of the research?
3. Were you able to understand the questions properly?
4. Is there an error or inconsistency in the questionnaire?

[6] https://pt.surveymonkey.com/r/32FK9RP

3.5 Data Collection

On September 2020, we sent the survey invitation by email, *Facebook*, *Twitter*, and *Linked-in*. The invitation text contains the main instructions and the questionnaire link. We also sent reminders. We closed the survey in November 2020. We made a brief introduction with necessary information about the purpose of the study, justification of choice, and the importance of the respondent's participation. Participants were also informed about the privacy policies of the study in a clear and detailed manner.

3.6 Data Analysis

After assembling the data collection from the online survey, we took the following steps: *(1) data validation* - this is the phase in which we analyzed the results to verify if the answers met the criteria of consistency and integrity; *(2) participants' characterization* - data assembling and synthesis, including data they provided about the startups they work for as well as the software products or services their companies deliver; *(3) data partitioning* - this is the phase in which the researchers analyze the responses and group them into subgroups (data partitioning counts on data obtained in the demographic questions, such as the number of customers, number of employees, the startups' diversification of software products or services, and the financial collection); and *(4) data interpretation* - in this phase the quantitative analyses takes place [18].

4 Results

In this section, we report the results of our survey study. Some facts are worth mentioning from this survey application: all questions were mandatory, and we only analyzed responses whose respondents answered 100% of the questions. One hundred fifty-eight people answered the questionnaire. However, 140 responses met our quality criteria.

4.1 Characterization

Respondents. This section describes demographic data. We investigated the developers' education levels, expertise, roles, and working time to draw the observed sample profile. In terms of their professional experience in software development, 12% had up to 1 year of experience, 31% had between 2 and 3 years, 19% had between 4 and 5 years, 15% had between 6 and 10 years, and 23% had more than 10 years of experience. Software developers classify themselves as related to their expertise; 27% junior, 31% mid-level, and 42% were senior. Finally, the respondents played many different roles while working in startups: 58% played more than one role against 42%, who played only one role.

Product. We highlight startups' products or services. 65% startups characterized their products as Software-as-a-Service (SaaS), 31% as a software product, and 4% as a software and hardware product. 50% of the startups developed only 1 product, and the other half had two or more products. 50% startups developed a *Business-to-Business* (B2B) product, 23% a *Business-to-Consumer* (B2C) product, and 19% a *Business-to-Business-to-Consumer* (B2B2C) product. 4% claimed their product was both B2B and B2C. Finally, 4% did not know or preferred not to answer.

Startups. We also asked the respondents to provide us with information about the startups, such as the founding date, age, number of customers, revenue, number of employees, and lifecycle phases. 39% of 26 startups have 1 to 5 employees; 17% have 6 to 10 employees; 30% have between 11 and 50 employees, and 13% has more than 100 employees. Startups are from 13 different business domains. 57% have between 1 and 10 customers; 22% have between 11 and 100 customers; 9% is between 101 to 100 customers, and 13% has more than 1,000 customers. Regarding the startup lifecycle, 52% of startups are in the early stage, 17% of them in Validation, and 30% in Growth.

One of the size classifications of companies by revenue that the Brazilian Institute of Geography and Statistics (IBGE)[7] uses organizes companies as follows: micro-entrepreneur, less than or equal to BRL 81K (USD 15.4K[8]); micro-enterprise, less than or equal to BRL 360K (USD 68.44K); small company, greater than BRL 360K and less than or equal to BRL 4.8M (USD 912.56K); medium-sized company, greater than BRL 4.8M and less than or equal to BRL 300M (USD 570M); large company, greater than BRL 300M.

4.2 Startup Software Engineering Practices (RQ1)

To answer the research question, *do software startup use the same software engineering practices across different lifecycle stages?*, we examined the occurrence of software engineering practices reported by software developers.

Software Processes. We asked the professionals if they used to employ any formalized software engineering process. Most of them stated they commonly followed software development processes (61.5%) and process management (50%).

Software Methodologies. Regarding the employed methodologies, we could observe that 96% of developers perceive the agile methods as the best characterized their practices, followed by the iterative approach (23%). Regarding the project planning activities they commonly used, the main reported ones were estimated at 70%, followed by delivery planning with 65%, scheduling with 54%, resource allocation with 46%, and process planning with 35%.

Requirements Engineering. In every startup, we gathered data from all professionals reported any requirements engineering phase in their software development process. Nevertheless, only 28% out of them stated their company had a formalized requirements engineering process. Requirements elicitation commonly employs prototyping in quick meetings with customers. In 80% of the

[7] IBGE is the Brazilian agency responsible for official collection of statistical, geographic, cartographic, geodetic and environmental information in Brazil. Further information available at https://www.ibge.gov.br/en/home-eng.html.

[8] Currency conversion on July 9th, 2021: BRL 1 = USD 0.19

reports, the participants stated they typically involve customers in such elicitation tasks. In addition, 73% said they used the brainstorming technique, 70% of the participants said they used prototyping, among others.

Design and Quality Attributes. We asked the participants about software architecture concerns. The responses indicate that the two most used architectural patterns are model-view-control (46%) and client-server (31%). The participants mentioned that they used the layered architecture (27%), ruled-based (15%), and event-based (11%) patterns. Other noted architectural patterns were piper and filter (8%), reflection (8%), peer-to-peer (4%), broker (4%), and batch (4%). In terms of quality attributes (QA), 73% of the participants identified usability as the most relevant QA. 65% indicated that performance is a relevant QA as well. Additionally, 61% pointed out that security/integrity and legal aspects are also relevant.

Implementation. Regarding approaches for developing/reusing source code, startups' software developers reported using frameworks (38%) to speed up product/service development and delivery. They also claimed to use architectural patterns (35%) and design patterns (35%) as reuse strategies. 27% claimed they built their products based on service-oriented systems (27%) and program libraries (23%). Next, configurable vertical applications (15%), ERP (Enterprise Resource Planning) systems (12%), program generators (12%), software product lines (8%), and packaging of legacy systems (8%). Model-driven engineering and third-party components were other options presented by the survey participants, but none reported such practices.

Software testing. Regarding software testing practices, 69% answered that they performed automated tests. Furthermore, 62% said they use manual testing. Only 8% responded that they did not perform any testing practices. When asked who runs the tests, in 69% of the cases, the developers run the tests themselves. Conversely, only in 15% of the cases was the developer who performed the test a person who did not implement the source code. Furthermore, 23% claimed that customers ran tests. We also asked the developers about the test level they commonly performed. 77% stated that their startups performed unit testing, 42% performed component testing, 58% performed integration testing, and 27% performed acceptance testing. 8% did not use to perform testing activities.

Deploy. When considering the time to deliver software, 19% released it between 1 to 2 days, 12% stated they released a software version between 3 to 7 days, 15% between 1 and 2 weeks, 19% between 3 and 4 weeks, and 16% at two months or more. When it comes to delivering the software to the customer, most participants affirmed that 15% spend between 1 to 2 days; 12% between 3 to 4 weeks, (38%) within 1 to 2 weeks; and 19% percent reported that they released between 2 to 3 months.

Maintenance. Regarding the code maintenance techniques adopted in the startups, 38% stated that they did not use any software maintenance techniques. Among the startups that used these techniques, 38% said they only used code understanding to maintain products or services, 27% said they used migration,

15% applied to re-engineer, 4% used reverse engineering, and 4% discontinued the application.

4.3 Tool Support (RQ2)

To answer the research question, *what tools do software startups use to support software engineering practices across different lifecycle stages??*, we examined the occurrence of tools reported by software developers. Table 1 shows the set of support tools pointed out by the participants. They are helpful to handle the following project lifecycle phases: software requirements, software architecture, software design, software development, software testing, software configuration management, and project management. The choice of tools that support software development seems to be adopted primarily according to the team's awareness of existing tools.

In addition, we could enlist a set of reasons why the participants decided to choose a particular support tool to use in their projects: the tool should allow (and improve) the communication between team members; allow rapid changes in the development and testing of the software product or service to meet customers' needs; allow prototyping of the product or service; automate development activities (such as automated versioning, code integration, continuous deployment, and automatic build generation); and allow the analysis of data generated by users to generate knowledge about their preferences.

Table 1. Support tools per software development lifecycle phase.

Software Requirements	**Software Architecture**	**UI Design**	**Software Development**	**Software Testing**	**Software Configuration Management**	**Project Management**
JIRA	UML Designer	Adobe XD	TypeScript	TestComplete	GitLab	JIRA
DOORS	Papyrus	Sketch	Android Studio	Selenium	Bitbucket	Trello
GitLab	Diagramo	Zepplin	Eclipse	JUnit	Subversion	GitLab
MS Office	Plant UML	Balsamiq	JetBrains	JIRA	GIT	
	draw.io	Pencil	NetBeans	TestFLO		
		Axure	PyCharm			
		Fluid	Unity			
		In Vision	RStudio			
			Visual Studio			
			XCode			

5 Discussion

The survey results revealed that software professionals focus their efforts on speeding up the construction of the software product based on customer guidelines and concentrate mainly on usability, performance, and security. Project planning is primarily based on deliveries and validations with their customers, who become involved in software development activities, from eliciting requirements through prototypes to testing and delivering the product or service. Although architectural styles and design patterns are prevalent, software architecture decisions are based on the software development team's knowledge in an *ad-hoc* manner. Software development is based on agile practices, regardless of other well-established software development processes. Also, the development process is mainly schedule-driven and focused on planning for delivery to the customer. When it comes to productivity, we found a general interest in employing frameworks and third-party API projects.

We investigate the differences between software practices adopted by software startups to their lifecycle stage. We observe that startups adopt a similar set of practices and tools in the three stages: startup, validation, and growth. However, looking at the frequency of responses, we notice that they value more practices and tools that support seamless integration, automated testing, automated security verification, and faster delivery to the user as they enter the growth stage. Startups realize that choices made in earlier stages have affected software quality and software development speed. And now, a new challenge is to solve the accumulated problems while adopting good software development practices, minimal documentation, and automated testing to provide security and meet the growing needs or demands of the increasing customer base.

6 Implications for Research and Practice

In this section, we present the relevant implications that emerge from the analysis of this study:

- **Research Implications.** The discoveries made by the academic and scientific community must be transferred to software startups. Software startups work in an innovative and complex environment and need recommendations on which best practices and tools to adopt at each stage of their lifecycle and recommendations on avoiding pitfalls that affect the short and long run in a direct, clear and precise way.
- **Practice Implications.** By observing how they choose and use software engineering, we identified a startup culture. The culture is how they see and act in which they permit themselves not to have the correct answers for every question and difficulty. They incessantly focus on the customer's pain and how to solve it but focus on finding the right question to be resolved. In this way, they have the opportunity to construct an answer or a solution that fits better that can be validated and refined with the customer's presence. There is the possibility of making mistakes on this path, starting over and trying again more assertively to build an answer or a solution with relevance.

7 Threats to Validity

Construct Validity: During the pilot test, some respondents reported that the instrument's filling time was extensive. As such, our survey respondents may not have adequately answered questions, preferring short answers to more detailed descriptions. We grouped the questions into specific sections to better target questions and answers to reduce threats to validity. Another threat was the respondents' understanding of the questions. To help ensure the survey's understandability, we asked professionals and researchers with experience in software engineering and experience in survey design to review the study to ensure the questions were clear and complete.

Internal Validity: Another observed threat may be selecting practitioners to the sample. We understand that the number of responses obtained may not adequately represent the entire population of startup software professionals, characterizing a threat to internal validity. However, as we decided to include only professionals from startups that work in different domains (and mostly have offices in several Brazilian cities), we believe this set might represent.

External Validity: The respondents of our survey may not adequately represent all startup software practitioners. Thus, our results could not be statistically relevant. Nevertheless, we believe that the 140 responses we analyzed provide a rich qualitative data source to reveal valuable insights.

Reliability: This threat indicates that the interpretation might influence the research results. Two authors of this paper carried out the analysis process by working together to mitigate such a threat. We discussed any disagreements in the assignment until we reach a consensus.

8 Conclusion

Software startups are born with disruptive ideas and business models. Some of them have to pivot until they find a valuable and scalable business model. They need to find a strategy to scale and enter a growth phase decreeing its continuity or closure. However, there are significant challenges software startups commonly to reach higher levels on the growth scale. Among the challenges, improving software engineering practices is a demanding task for software startups.

This study analyzes how Brazilian software startups have dealt with software engineering practices from a software practitioner's perspective. We surveyed 140 responses from software developers working in Brazilian software startups. Our study shows that startups in the initial and validation phases choose software engineering practices on an *ad-hoc* basis and primarily based on the development team's knowledge. When they move into the growth phase, they recognize that they could have adopted better software development practices to support the product scale with a more mature team. The developers decide to use support tools that integrate with others and automate operational activities. Future work directions should consider extending this study to reach professionals from other global regions to perform a cross-validation analysis to verify whether the results are still valid when considering different scenarios.

Acknowledgments. This research was partially funded by INES 2.0; CNPq grants 465614/2014-0 and 408356/2018-9 and FAPESB grant JCB0060/2016.

References

1. Bajwa, S. S. (2020). Pivoting in Software Startups. In Fundamentals of Software Startups (pp. 27-43). Springer, Cham.
2. Blank, S. (2010). What's A Startup? First Principles. Steve Blank.
3. Blank, S. (2020). The four steps to the epiphany: successful strategies for products that win. John Wiley and Sons.
4. Carmel, E. (1994, January). Time-to-completion in software package startups. In 1994 Proceedings of The XXVII Hawaii International Conf. on System Sciences.
5. Cavalcante, B. H., Leal, G. C. L., Balancieri, R., de Farias Junior, I. (2018). Technical Aspects of Software Development in Startups: A Systematic Mapping. 2018 XLIV Latin American Computer Conference (CLEI) (pp. 100-109).
6. Chanin, R., Pompermaier, L., Fraga, K., Sales, A., Prikladnicki, R. (2017, May). Applying customer development for software requirements in a startup development program. In 2017 IEEE/ACM 1st International Workshop on software engineering for Startups (SoftStart) (pp. 2-5).
7. Coleman, G., O'Connor, R. V. (2008). An investigation into software development process formation in software start-ups. Journal of Ent. Inf. Manag.
8. Crowne, M. (2002, August). Why software product startups fail and what to do about it. Evolution of software product development in startup companies. In IEEE International Engineering Management Conference (Vol. 1, pp. 338-343).
9. Cukier, D. (2017). Software startup ecosystems evolution: a maturity model. Doctoral dissertation, Universidade de São Paulo.
10. Dash, A. (2019). Scaling the Innovativeness of Start-ups in India. SEDME (Small Enterprises Development, Management and Extension Journal), 46(3), 196-204.
11. Edison, H., Wang, X., Abrahamsson, P. (2015). Lean startup: why large software companies should care. In Proceedings of the XP2015 (pp.1-7).
12. Edison, H., Smørsgård, N. M., Wang, X., Abrahamsson, P. (2018). Lean internal startups for software product innovation in large companies: enablers and inhibitors. Journal of Systems and Software, 135, 69-87.
13. Giardino, C., Paternoster, N., Unterkalmsteiner, M., Gorschek, T., Abrahamsson, P. (2015). Software development in startup companies: the greenfield startup model. IEEE Transactions on software engineering, 42(6), 585-604.
14. Giardino, C., Bajwa, S. S., Wang, X., Abrahamsson, P. (2015). Key challenges in early-stage software startups. In International Conference on Agile Software Development. Springer (pp. 52-63), Cham.
15. Giardino, C., Unterkalmsteiner, M., Paternoster, N., Gorschek, T., Abrahamsson, P. (2014). What do we know about software development in startups?. IEEE software, 31(5), 28-32.
16. Giardino, C., Wang, X., Abrahamsson, P. (2014, June). Why early-stage software startups fail: a behavioral framework. In International conference of software business (ICSOB). Springer (pp. 27-41), Cham.
17. Hilmola, O. P., Helo, P., Ojala, L. (2003). The value of product development lead time in software startup. System Dynamics Review, 19(1), 75-82.
18. Kitchenham, B., Pfleeger, S. L. (2002). Principles of survey research: Part 5: populations and samples. ACM SIGSOFT Soft. engineering Notes, 27(5), 17-20.

19. Klotins, E., Unterkalmsteiner, M., Gorschek, T. (2015, June). software engineering knowledge areas in startup companies: a mapping study. In International Conference of Software Business (pp. 245-257). Springer, Cham.
20. Klotins, E. (2017). Using the case survey method to explore engineering practices in software start-ups. In 2017 IEEE/ACM 1st International Workshop on software engineering for Startups (SoftStart) (pp. 24-26).
21. Linåker, J., Sulaman, S. M., Maiani de Mello, R., Höst, M. (2015). Guidelines for conducting surveys in software engineering.
22. Melegati, J., Goldman, A., Kon, F., Wang, X. (2019). A model of requirements engineering in software startups. J. Inf. and software technology, 109, 92-107.
23. Nguyen-Duc, A., Weng, X., Abrahamsson, P. (2018). A preliminary study of agility in business and production: cases of early-stage hardware startups. In Proceedings of the 12th ACM/IEEE International Symposium on Empirical software engineering and Measurement (pp. 1-4).
24. Pantiuchina, J., Mondini, M., Khanna, D., Wang, X., Abrahamsson, P. (2017, May). Are software startups applying agile practices? The state of the practice from a large survey. In International Conference on Agile Software Development (pp. 167-183). Springer, Cham.
25. Pfleeger, S. L., Kitchenham, B. A. (2001). Principles of survey research: part 1: turning lemons into lemonade. ACM SIGSOFT Soft. Eng. Notes, 26(6), 16-18.
26. Reis, E. (2011). The lean startup. New York: Crown Business, 27.
27. Souza, R., Malta, K., De Almeida, E. S. (2017). software engineering in startups: a single embedded case study. In 2017 IEEE/ACM 1st SoftStart (pp. 17-23). IEEE.
28. Souza, R., Malta, K., Silva, R., Masiero, P., Almeida, E., Machado, I. (2019). A Case Study about Startups' software engineering practices: A Preliminary Result. In Proceedings of the XVIII SBQS (pp. 198-203).
29. Souza, R., Cico, O., Machado, I. (2021). Supplementary Material to "A survey on the software engineering practices in Brazilian Software Startups". [Online] Available: https://doi.org/10.5281/zenodo.5082313 In Proceedings of the XXIV Ibero-American Conference on Software Engineering.
30. Sutton, S. M. (2000). The role of process in software start-up. IEEE software, 17(4), 33-39.
31. Unterkalmsteiner, M., Abrahamsson, P., Wang, X., Nguyen-Duc, A., Shah, S., Bajwa, S. S., and Baltes, Guido H., Conboy, K., Cullina, E., Dennehy, D., others (2016). Software startups–a research agenda. e-Informatica Soft. Eng. J, 10(1).
32. Wang, X., Edison, H., Bajwa, S. S., Giardino, C., Abrahamsson, P. (2016, May). Key challenges in software startups across life cycle stages. In International Conference on Agile Software Development (pp. 169-182). Springer, Cham.
33. Winkel, D., Wilcox, J., Teckchandani, A. (2019). The 60-Minute MVP. Entrepreneurship Education and Pedagogy, .

AUTHOR INDEX